Prat[illegible]

Islam, South As

Islam, South Asia, and the West

Francis Robinson

OXFORD
UNIVERSITY PRESS

OXFORD
UNIVERSITY PRESS

Oxford University Press is a department of the University of Oxford. It furthers the University's objective of excellence in research, scholarship, and education by publishing worldwide. Oxford is a registered trademark of Oxford University Press in the UK and in certain other countries

Published in India by
Oxford University Press
YMCA Library Building, 1 Jai Singh Road, New Delhi 110001, India

First Edition published in 2007
Oxford India Paperbacks 2008

ISBN-13: 978-0-19-569835-0
ISBN-10: 0-19-569835-5

Typeset in Nalandagaramond 10/12.5
by Le Studio Graphique, Gurgaon
Printed in India by Replika Press Pvt. Ltd., Haryana 131 028

Contents

Acknowledgements

Chapter 1, first published in Francis Robinson (ed.), *The Cambridge Illustrated History of the Islamic World* (Cambridge, 1996), pp. 208–49.

Chapter 3, first published in Judith M. Brown and Wm. Roger Louis (eds), *The Oxford History of the British Empire: Volume IV, The Twentieth Century* (Oxford, Oxford University Press, 1999), pp. 398–420.

Chapter 4, first published in *Transactions of the Royal Historical Society*, Sixth Series, vol. 8 (1998), pp. 271–89.

Chapter 5, first published in Mushirul Hasan and Asim Roy (eds), *Living Together Separately: Cultural India in History and Politics* (New Delhi, Oxford University Press, 2005), pp. 354–65.

Chapter 7, first published in *Journal of the Royal Asiatic Society*, Third Series, vol. 14, Part 1 (April 2004), pp. 49–58.

Chapter 8, first published in *Asian Affairs*, vol. 33, Part 3 (October 2002), pp. 307–20.

The following chapters were all first published in the *Times Literary Supplement*: Chapter 9, 21 January 1994; Chapter 10, 3 February 1995; Chapter 11, 8 December 1995; Chapter 12, 30 June 1999; Chapter 13, 22 October 1999; Chapter 14, 31 March 2000; Chapter 15, 26 January 2001; Chapter 16, 28 December 2001; Chapter 17, 10 May 2002; Chapter 18, 11 October 2002; Chapter 19, 3 February 2003; Chapter 20, 11 April 2003; Chapter 21, 19 September 2003; Chapter 22, 24 October 2003; Chapter 23, 1 April 2005.

Chapter 24, first published in the *Economic and Political Weekly* (30 October 2004), pp. 4782–4.

NB. In their original form these articles adopted different systems of transliteration. In the interests of giving this collection a unified presentation, the system adopted by the *Encyclopaedia of Islam*, second edition, has been used with the usual changes of 'j' for 'dj' and 'q' for ḳ.

Introduction

'Every piece of work', I declared in the introduction to *Islam and Muslim History in South Asia*, 'has a context both intellectual and personal.'[1] The essays in this volume were all written in the decade 1994–2004. For most of the period I was engaged in what is currently termed 'senior management' at Royal Holloway, University of London. In these circumstances a personal and intellectual context came to be represented by the graduate students who worked with me over the period, providing continuing access to the thrill of research—if only vicariously—and much-needed scholarly companionship. I refer to Claudia Liebeskind and her work on both Awadhi Sufis and Unani Tibb in the nineteenth and twentieth centuries, Sa'id Kazembeyki and his pioneering research on the Iranian province of Mazandaran in the nineteenth century, Azra Asghar Ali's work on the emergence of Muslim feminism in British India, Yoginder Sikand's on the workings of the Tablighi Jama'at in India, Britain, and Bangladesh, Amit Dey's on changing representations of the Prophet in Bengal, Paolo Durisotto's on the rulers of Bikanir and the Raj, and Markus Daechsel's on society and politics in interwar Lahore.[2] As you read these essays you will note the contributions—for which I am profoundly grateful—that these students have made to my own understandings.

A further aspect of the intellectual context of this decade was less that of the great historians—who helped shape my historical understanding as set out in *Islam and Muslim History*—although they still worked their magic. It was more that of the major issues of the contemporary world which have come to press with increasing weight upon scholars in the field. These are—Hindu revivalism, Muslim revivalism, and the impact of the West—themes which are echoed, to some degree, in the three elements in the title of this book, that is, 'South Asia', 'Islam', and 'the West'.

For the past one hundred and fifty years and more, Hindu revivalism has been a fact of Indian religious and political life developing in counterpoint to British rule and the Christian and

Enlightenment ideas that came with it, to past Muslim domination and present Muslim revivalism, and to the inclusive secularism that became a powerful theme in the movement for independence. Over the past two decades the emergence of a political Hinduism out of Hindu revivalism to dominate, for a period, national politics has been a matter of great concern to historians of India, in particular, and to intellectuals, in general. It has meant—the demonization of Muslims and other minority groups; the destruction or appropriation of Muslim buildings; and attempts to rewrite history from a Hindutva perspective in contexts ranging from school textbooks and the work of professional historians through to archaeology. Iconic events in the process have been the demolition of the Babri Masjid in 1992 and the pogrom against the Muslims in Gujarat in 2002.

Historians became powerfully aware that, along with the struggle for power in India, there was also a struggle to control the past. It was, moreover, a struggle in which, in relation to Indian society at large, the partisans of political Hinduism seemed to have the upper hand. In consequence, historians became highly sensitized to their responsibilities as public intellectuals. Thus, senior scholars such as Shahid Amin or Asghar Ali Engineer might write for the press on such matters, a junior scholar such as Yoginder Sikand has striven through a website and prolific print production to build interfaith understanding by making available knowledge of past and present practice, and senior scholars such as Mushirul Hasan and Asim Roy might hold an international conference to discuss the nature and, therefore, by implication, the potential of India's 'composite culture'. This sharpened sensitivity was felt no less by historians of India from abroad. It is there in Barbara Metcalf's presidential address to the American Association of Asian Studies in 1995,[3] in which she sets out the new approaches to history that are required in the context of its politicization in South Asia and elsewhere (see Chapter 24). It is the thrust behind the collection of essays put together by Bruce Lawrence and David Gilmartin which, under the suggestive title, *Beyond Turk and Hindu*, aimed to undermine the stereotypes of medieval Indian history that fed the discourse of political Hinduism.[4] It is clearly the intent behind Richard Eaton's important essay in this volume, 'Temple Desecration and Indo-Muslim States', which demonstrates that Muslim destruction of temples from the twelfth century onwards had less to do with iconoclasm than with a rational process of state building and state maintenance (see also Chapter 16).[5] It is, of course, one thing for historians to become more sensitized to the fact that what they do has a bearing on matters of great public import to the peoples of South Asia at large, it is quite another for them to match the skills and resources of the politicians in reaching out to these people. Perhaps the balance of power will begin to shift as the liberalization of India's economy and its growing wealth enable the media market to be filled with a much wider range of products. But for all this to work professional historians will have to accommodate themselves to the sometimes irksome requirements of the mass media, in the same way that they have met those of the highbrow press.

Through the nineteenth and twentieth centuries Muslim revivalism has been a growing fact of global life. In South Asia it became entangled with British rule, Hindu revivalism, and the politics of nationalism to help shape the political landscape we know today. In the world at large it interacted with Western imperial expansion to give shape to some Muslim states; it subsequently proved itself more than a match for the secular nationalism of many independent Muslim states; and, by the late twentieth century, came to have such a presence in the Muslim world, and beyond, that some Western commentators have begun to talk of its political form—which has often embraced a powerful anti-Western rhetoric—in terms of a 'clash of civilizations'.[6] Such talk, as Chapter 8, 'Islam and the West: Clash of Civilizations?', endeavours to demonstrate, is ill-advised and dangerous. Nevertheless, along with global warming, and the economic rise of India and China, the widespread presence of Muslim revivalism, in both its non-political and political forms, is, arguably, one of the great dynamic facts of the global scene today.

Many of the articles in this volume have been written, one way or another, under the shadow of Muslim revivalism. Like many scholars of the Muslim world over the past decade I have felt the need to explain both how matters have come to be as they are, and how they are not as some might wish to represent them to be. So, for instance, in Chapter 7, 'Other-Worldly and This-Worldly Islam and the Islamic Revival', I demonstrate how the ideas behind Muslim revival and reform emerged from a long-standing discourse amongst Muslims over other-worldly and this-worldly piety, which came to have a new urgency as Muslim powers declined and the West came to a position of dominance in the Muslim world. In this context there was a shift in piety towards a this-worldly faith of social action. This shift has taken many different forms according to different social, economic, and political contexts. Some Muslim reformers have been compared with Martin Luther of the Christian Protestant Reformation,[7] others have compared the whole reforming movement with that 'Reformation'.[8] But, whatever comparisons have been made, it should be clear that these ideas have emerged from a debate amongst Muslims and exist in a continuing debate amongst them. They are not directed at the West *per se*, but can be profoundly opposed to the impact of the West upon their societies. As Chapter 8 suggests, there is no clash of civilizations, but the West can go a long way towards creating one if it wishes.

The lazy use of the term 'fundamentalism' to describe the political development of 'protestant' Islam—or what most scholars term today as 'Islamism'—has tended to conceal, from many Western eyes at least, the fact that Islamism is a profoundly modern movement. Classically, it has been supported by those in transition from one social location to another, often from the countryside to the city. It is fashioned by 'modern' experience, supported for the most part by those with 'modern'/western-style educations, and has helped people survive in the contexts of the 'modern' economy, the 'modern' state, and the broad psychological demands of 'modern' life. These facts must draw our attention back to the significance of the shift amongst Muslims to a this-worldly faith of social action, which found parallels in religious change amongst all the main South Asian religions.[9] To what extent was this shift a forerunner of an Islamically-supported modernity? To what extent might it be the breeding ground for a modernity shaped, in part, by Islam itself? I have explored aspects of this question in two articles, 'Islam and the Impact of Print in South Asia' and 'Religious Change and the Self in Muslim South Asia since 1800'.[10] The last part of Chapter 7, which draws on recent anthropological research in Egypt and Iran, takes the possible relationship between Islamic reform and forms of 'modernity' further. This is an area in which I intend to do further research. It is clear to me that deeper understanding of this relationship, particularly if it can produce a modified, even respectful, Western approach towards Islamism, is a matter of the first importance.

Since the Crusades, Western power has been a fact in at least some part of the Asian and Muslim world. But, whereas the West's impact in the twelfth and thirteenth centuries was little more than the bloodsucking activities of a flea, by the nineteenth century the industrialization of Europe enabled it to have an impact of great transformative power. Nevertheless, it was a power which, as it worked in different Muslim and South Asian societies, was also substantially shaped by local forces. The outcome has been legacies of great influence in these societies themselves, but also on the former imperial powers. Most of the essays and reviews in this volume deal with aspects of the West's engagement—in particular, that of Britain's—with the Muslim and South Asian worlds, as well as the responses of Muslims and South Asians to this experience. Coverage ranges from the conquest of almost all the Muslim world between 1800 and 1920, with Britain in the vanguard in shaping the system of Muslim states which was to emerge from European empire, to the great sense of loss and humiliation which Muslims felt at the end of the one thousand years in which the fortunes of Islam had run hand in hand with power—a sense which laid a distinctive mark on Muslim literary cultures in the nineteenth and twentieth centuries. We are constantly reminded of the tragic legacies, the waste of human life and potential, which resulted from the Western imperial presence, whether it be in the policies which led to the partition of India, the Palestinian disaster, or the Iranian revolution. Arguably, the last-mentioned might never have occurred but for the Anglo-American intervention in 1953 which enabled the overthrow of the constitutional and nationalist government of Muhammad Musaddiq. Masoud Banisadr's story, which figures in Chapter 23, speaks of the miseries this meant for just one family.

One aspect of Western power in relation to Muslim and South Asian societies was 'Orientalism', that is, the way in which the West—as Edward Said taught us to understand—in ruling the 'Orient', produced a vast body of knowledge and discourse about it which formed a reality in which the 'Oriental' was forced to exist, even though it was often at some distance from the facts.[11] Many of the essays in this volume reflect the influence of 'Oriental' knowledge on events, whether it be its past impact on imperial policy—the tendency of the British, for instance, to see India in terms of its religious communities and their belief in Muslim 'fanaticism'—or its continuing influence on current US policies—the essentializing nature of Huntington's 'clash of civilizations' thesis or a US policy in Iraq, which has led Americans to show little respect for Iraqi lives and not to bother to count their dead. Tragically, amongst those influencing US policy towards the Muslim world has been Bernard Lewis, a fierce critic of Said's argument,[12] a White House favourite during the George W. Bush years,[13] and a prominent expert on the Muslim world for the viewers of US television. No one doubts his learning and his academic achievement, as demonstrated, for instance, by *The Emergence of Modern Turkey* (London, 1961), but over the past thirty years there has been growing concern over the uses to which his learning has been put, in particular, a tendency to interpret the Arab and the Muslim worlds in essentializing terms, giving the impression that they are undifferentiated and unchanging.[14] Chapters 11 and 20 review two recent works by Lewis. 'Through the Minefield' addresses Lewis's *The Middle East: 2000 Years of History from the Rise of Christianity to the Present* (London, 1995) and finds that whereas on this occasion it is difficult to pin charges of essentialism upon him, there are problems of selectivity, tone, and judgement. Could one really ignore the impact of British policies on the Palestinians while producing a favourable assessment of these policies overall on the peoples of West Asia? 'Thoroughly Modern Muslims' addresses Lewis's *What Went Wrong: The Clash between Islam and Modernity in the Middle East* (London, 2002). This is a piece of 'Orientalist' essentialism, unworthy of the author, which concludes that, in the twentieth century, 'it became abundantly clear in the Middle East and, indeed, all over the lands of Islam that things had indeed gone badly wrong', and Islam was the reason. This is a judgement which ignores the impact of Western imperialism on the Muslim world as well as the outcomes of recent scholarship. As the review states, this can be read as a historian's manifesto for regime change, a source of justification for the neo-conservative and openly pro-Israeli clique in the White House that wished to impose democracy on West Asia by force. It is a case in point which reminds us of the dangers of misdirected scholarship and of the massive responsibilities of scholars, in confronting the present as well as the past.

We now turn to consider the specific contexts of each essay. Chapter 1, 'Knowledge, its Transmission and the Making of Muslim Societies', was first published as an essay in my *Cambridge Illustrated History of the Islamic World* (Cambridge, 1996). It was designed, of course, to be enhanced by illustrations, but the text would appear to sustain itself without them. The approach was one profoundly influenced by my work on the *'ulama* of Farangi Mahall[15] and first exemplified in my *Atlas of the Islamic World since 1500* (Oxford, 1982), which was to see the transmission of formal Islamic knowledge and spiritual knowledge and the making relevant of this knowledge to different societies in different places at different times, as playing a central role in the making and remaking of Muslim societies. Considering the transmission of Islamic knowledge over 1,400 years it makes clear how revolutionary the last two hundred years of Western hegemony in the Muslim world have been, whether it be the impetus it has given to forms of Islamic reform and the downgrading of spiritual knowledge, or the repositioning of Islamic knowledge itself as it has had to make way for the new learning from the West. As has been the case with all revealed religions, there has been a major and ongoing struggle to make revelation relevant to the present, and to do so with authority. This chapter reveals some of the creativity Muslims have shown in doing so, and the vigorous debate it has inspired.

Arguably, in no region of the Muslim world have Muslims been as creative as in South Asia. Demonstrating this creativity is one of the features of Chapter 2, 'The 'Ulama of South Asia from 1800 to the mid-Twentieth century', which was written for a conference held in honour of the late K.A. Nizami, the distinguished Aligarh historian, and convened by Bruce Lawrence at Duke University in the late 1990s. This essay, however, goes further. It shows how, in the nineteenth and twentieth centuries, the 'ulama—in particular the reforming 'ulama—in the absence of effective Muslim political power, came to acquire a leading role in Muslim society such as they had not had before. This happened because the loss of the patronage of Muslim rulers meant that they could only survive if Muslim society supported them, and this meant they had to provide services that Muslims valued. Thus, in the last decades of British rule, 'ulama were able to put pressure on the government, particularly in the matter of Islamic law, as few would have thought possible. It has also meant that, over the past half century, in the rather special circumstances of Pakistan, they have come to have unprecedented influence over the nation's affairs.

During the mid-1990s the British went through a period of soul searching about their identity. It was in part a function of the devolution of power within the United Kingdom to separate Scottish and Welsh assemblies (in Northern Ireland effective devolution was dependent on the state of play between London, the Unionists, and the IRA/Sinn

Fein). It was in part a function of the ending of formal empire as the last significant territory, Hong Kong, returned to China. But, in a much larger part, it was a function of the angst generated amongst many by the prospect of surrendering sovereignty to the European Union. As the British moved away from a present which had been profoundly shaped by empire, scholars took the opportunity to take stock of that empire and its impact. Chapters 3 and 4 are products of that process. 'The British Empire and the Muslim World' was written for Volume 4 of *The Oxford History of the British Empire* (Oxford, 1998), whose editor-in-chief was the US scholar, Wm. Roger Louis. It sets out how, by 1920, the British came to rule more than half the Muslim peoples of the world and how, for much of the twentieth century, they were the greatest influence on their development, providing the context in which many Muslims experienced the transition to 'modernity'. The article makes clear the extent of British responsibility for the shape of the modern Muslim world, in terms of states, as well as illustrating how it provided the framework in which Indian Muslims, and Indian Muslim movements, were able to globalize.

'The British Empire and Muslim Identity in South Asia' was written for a workshop on the British Empire held at the Institute of Historical Research, London, in September 1997. The title, as far as I recall, was not one I chose, but one under which I was asked to write. The result demonstrated in relation to Indo-Muslim identity that British rule and religious and social change amongst Muslims interacted in producing outcomes, whether it was the sharpening of the distinction between Muslim and non-Muslim or the adding of a pan-Islamic dimension to Muslim identity, or the gendering of Muslim identity, or its acquisition of a new strand of individualism. There is the concluding suggestion, which has yet to be tested, that India's Muslims may have been unique in the Muslim world in the intensity of their self-conscious identity as Muslims.

'Living Together Separately: The 'Ulama of Farangi Mahall c. 1700–c. 1950' was written for Mushirul Hasan and Asim Roy's conference on 'composite culture' in India, which was held in December 2002 under the auspices of the Academy of Third World Studies at Delhi's Jamia Millia Islamia. The memory of the pogrom against Muslims in Gujarat earlier in the year lay heavily on the occasion. It was in this context, I suspect, that Jamia's genial vice-chancellor of the day told me that he did not find my contribution 'helpful'. This is a difficult area, and not least in the light of what has been said above about the responsibilities of scholars. In the long run, however, there is little to be gained from avoiding the facts. These, moreover, in the case of the Farangi Mahall family, did have a positive outcome, *pace* the vice-chancellor, for those concerned in promoting a liberal and secular agenda. Yes, according to their own records, from the late seventeenth to the early twentieth century the family did seem to live in India in a way which made little contact with their Hindu environment. Doubtless, much the same could be said of the contact of Hindu families with Muslims at the time. But, from the 1930s, some members of this family of ʻulama broke with the tradition to work with Hindus in politics and in literature, and to marry them. They went from ʻliving together separately' to ʻliving together', which was surely a step in the best possible direction.

ʻWomen as Patrons of Art and Culture: The Begums of Bhopal' was written for a special issue of *Marg* devoted to female patronage of the arts in India, which was never published. Since this was written our knowledge of the remarkable lives of Bhopal's women rulers has been greatly expanded, first, by Shaharyar Khan's *The Begums of Bhopal: A Dynasty of Women Rulers in Raj India* (London, 2000), which rises well above mere family piety, and, second, by the work of Siobhan Lambert-Hurley on Begum Sultan Jahan, which is about to be published in book form in *A Muslim Women's Movement in India: The Begum of Bhopal* (Routledge/Royal Asiatic Society Books). What strikes one immediately about these women is how readily we can make contact with them through their own autobiographical writings. Indeed, I doubt if there are any nineteenth-century Indo-Muslim women's voices to match theirs. Their range of patronage is broad—from architecture and scholarship through to specialized forms of needlework. Their determination to support the advancement of women across a broad front is clear. It is, moreover, a particular blessing that we can still enjoy Begum Sultan Jahan's gardens through her paintings of them, some of which can be found in the Ranken collection in the India Office Library.

The last two essays, Chapters 7 and 8, are both in their different ways responses to the concern Westerners felt in the early twenty-first century about the Muslim revival in its political and terrorist dimensions. ʻOther-Worldly and This-Worldly Islam and the Islamic Revival' was a lecture given at the Royal Asiatic Society in 2003 in memory of Wilfred Cantwell Smith, the great scholar of comparative religion, who founded departments in the subject at the universities of Harvard, McGill, and Halifax (Nova Scotia). Smith was always amongst the most acute observers of religious change in the Muslim world; early works such as *Islam in Modern India* (1946) and *Islam in Modern History* (1957) still repay careful reading. The essay starts from an observation in the latter work about the growing dynamism demonstrated in the Muslim world in the nineteenth and twentieth centuries and, as we have set out above, places it in the context of a long-term shift in the emphasis in Muslim piety from other-worldliness to a this-worldly faith of social action. It suggests that it might be part of a religiously-inspired path to forms of 'modernity'.

'Islam and the West: Clash of Civilizations?' began life as a plenary lecture given at a conference on 9/11 hosted by the Yale History Department; my task was to look at the Islamic background. The conference took place less than six weeks after the event. The atmosphere amongst US citizens was suffused with patriotism. Almost every bridge on the road up from Newark seemed to be adorned with the star-spangled banner; Lynne Cheney, the vice-president's wife, had been in contact with the conference organizers just before I arrived to assure herself that they were not engaged in treachery. The lecture was given several times in the subsequent weeks until it found its final form in June 2002 at the Anniversary General Meeting Lecture of the Royal Society of Asian Affairs.

My concern was to give my audiences a historical framework in which to place the Muslim world. I, therefore, reminded them that for a thousand years Muslims had inhabited the dominant world system; that over the past two hundred years they had been subjects first, of European empire and then to American hegemony; that the mourning of lost power was a feature of some Muslim literary cultures,[16] and so was protest against the bullying and hypocrisy of the West. At the moment this did not amount to a clash of civilizations. There was much that Muslims and Westerners shared and, however much Islamist organizations might huff and puff, the Muslim world was much divided and most Muslims would follow the self-interest of their particular group. This said, the West now stood before the bar of Muslim public opinion. Muslims were watching intently and feeling deeply. As the wife of an '*alim* reminded me in February 2005, as we took breakfast in Lucknow's Farangi Mahall: 'We feel humiliated by what is taking place in Iraq'. The conclusion made in 2002 is yet more strongly made today. If the West fails to show more respect, if it fails to stand up for justice and fair dealing in relation to the Muslim world, it might just begin to create a real clash of civilizations.

The second part of the volume consists of reviews of important books on India and the Muslim world. Chapters 9 to 23 appeared in the *Times Literary Supplement*, and Chapter 24 in the *Economic and Political Weekly*. This is work I particularly enjoy—taking relatively obscure learning to a wider public and, doing so with a licence, within reason, to entertain. In the case of all contributions to the *Times Literary Supplement*, it should be noted that the titles were supplied by the editorial staff; my suggestions with the exception of one were rejected! Chapters 9, 11, 17, 20, and 24 deal in part with aspects of 'Orientalism'. 'Through the Minefield' (Chapter 11) and 'Thoroughly Modern Muslims' (Chapter 20) address the work of Bernard Lewis, of which enough has been said. 'Modern Islam and the Green Menace' (Chapter 9) expounds the essence of the important work by Aziz al-Azmeh which demonstrates, amongst other things, how much Islamist thinkers owe to the work of Western 'Orientalists'. 'When India Ruled the Waves' (Chapter 17) takes on four books about India, three of which involve revisions of 'Orientalist' understandings, in particular, that which regarded India as 'medieval' and 'unchanging' before the arrival of the West. Thus Sanjay Subramanyam illustrates the vigour and resilience of South Indian polities in the eighteenth century, Ashin Das Gupta notes that Vasco da Gama might have arrived with a bang in 1498 but Indian Ocean trade remained dominated by Indian shipping until the end of the eighteenth century, and Cynthia Talbot in a scintillating work demonstrates that the Telegu country from the twelfth to the fourteenth century was dynamic, with expanding commerce, growing numbers of religious institutions, and an evolving political system. The important point which all make is that, if the dead hand of 'Orientalist' scholarship could be thrown off, and the real nature of South India in particular be understood, it would be realized that India had an early modern history which invites fruitful comparison with that of Europe. 'Islamic Contestations' (Chapter 24) echoes the title of Barbara Metcalf's important collection of essays. It is also her way of referring to a significant theme of her life's work which has been to remind us that Muslim beliefs have not been captured in some essentialized aspic, as 'Orientalists' and some

Islamists might have us believe, but that Muslims, like their Hindu counterparts, have been engaged in recent times in renewing and rethinking the historical traditions of their faiths.[17]

One of the major events of the past millennium was the establishment of Muslim rule in India. It prepared the way for one third of the subcontinent's peoples to become Muslim and for one third of the world's Muslims to come from the subcontinent. It created the environment in which in the sixteenth and seventeenth centuries, the Mughal Empire, the greatest of the early modern Muslim empires, was to flourish. It established the platform on which, from the eighteenth to the twentieth century, India was to generate leading ideas and important organizations for the Muslim world. In the process the centre of gravity of the Muslim world was shifted substantially to the east. Chapters 12, 13, 14, 15, and 21 deal with books covering the rise, the magnificence, and the decline of Muslim power in India. 'A Greater Raj' (Chapter 13) reviews an outstanding book in which Peter Jackson examines the rise and fall of the Delhi Sultanate. With painstaking scholarship devoted to evidence from manuscripts, inscriptions, and coins, but not from architecture, and reviewing most judiciously the secondary literature, he has established the standard work in the field which should endure for a generation or more. What is particularly important in the light of the contested nature of India's past is the way in which he demonstrates that the rule of the Delhi sultans, like that of the Mughals and the British, was dependent on Hindu support. 'Heroes in the Harem' (Chapter 21)—a title which I dislike, not least for its resonance of 'Orientalizing' prurience—reviews Abraham Eraly's *Mughal Throne*, a work on the great Mughals and the peak of Muslim power in India. Several points stand out: the way in which Eraly brings to life the Mughals and their families—although Ruby Lal's recent work represents a substantial advance on his understandings;[18] his judicious discussion of Aurangzeb—a hate figure for political Hinduism—whom he shows to be as harsh on Muslims as he is on Hindus; but most important is the serious attempt this book makes to take history to a wider public. Many more books of this kind are needed to blunt the propaganda weapons of political Hinduism. 'A Pit Full of Honey' (Chapter 15) addresses Ralph Russell's anthology of literature in Urdu, the wonderful language which was generated out of the interactions between the Turkish and Persian-speaking rulers of India and the local population. This book performs the all-important task of explaining literature in Urdu to the British, who are discovering that it is the second most widely spoken language in their land. There is no little magic in the thought that the language which was generated in the camps of the great Muslim courts as they traversed India should now come to be one of the many streams which enriches contemporary British culture.

Chapters 12 and 14 deal with aspects of the decline of Muslim power. 'Glimpses of a Lost World' (Chapter 14) addresses C.M. Naim's translation into English of the autobiography of the poet, Mir Taqi Mir. At one level this is a marvellous introduction to the world of humanity, affection, and love in eighteenth-century India. At another, it reminds us of the turbulence and uncertainties which beset people as Mughal power drained away into the soil of India. There is the poet's misery after the Afghan sack of Delhi; there is his constant search for patrons as power and resources become widely dispersed; there is, towards the end of his life, the arrival of the British in Upper India, who were finally to destroy the environment in which his courtly poetry flourished. The 'House of Mirrors' (Chapter 12) takes us forward by one hundred years. The British were firmly in the saddle and had only recently displayed the extent of their power in their brutal suppression of the Mutiny uprising and in their savage and destructive revenge on the cities of Delhi and Lucknow. This review of Shackle and Majeed's translation of Hali's *Musaddas* reminds us of the importance of this epic poem in helping to create the mood in which Muslim separatism might flourish: the glorious achievements of the past, the abject condition of Muslims in the present both in India and abroad, and the need to adopt an Islamicized version of 'Victorian values' in order to succeed in the future. It also reminds us of how many Muslims feel today: their anger at their powerlessness in the face of the West, the rage and self-hate that flows from their weakness, and the feeling of the need to act to gain salvation, or at least salve their pride.

Sufis—Muslim mystics—were an important part of the Muslim presence in South Asia, mediating between the people and the powerful, providing spiritual and material comfort for those in need, and playing a key role in the 'conversion' of millions to Islam. 'Between Two Worlds' (Chapter 19) reviews Riazul Islam's major work on Sufis in fourteenth-century South Asia. His central theme is the tension Sufis experienced between the other-worldly and this-worldly demands of their faith. It was a tension made acute by the growing influence of the ideas of Ibn 'Arabi and one which became more acute as, from the early nineteenth century, Islamic reform shifted the emphasis in piety towards this-worldly action. This said, there is much that is attractive that Riazul Islam reveals to us about fourteenth-century Sufi attitudes to this-worldly responsibilities. These are neatly summarized in Shaykh Sa'di's tag: 'Worship of God is nothing but service of the people'. 'The Music of the Sufis' (Chapter 16), which reviews Simon Digby's *Sufis and Soldiers in Awrangzeb's Deccan*, his translation of the *malfuzat* of two Sufis who had come from Bukhara to establish themselves in the seventeenth-century Deccan. One, Baba Musafir, was a contemplative whose life focussed on a cycle of study, meditation, and prayer. We learn much about his work of spiritual care, but also about the daily working of his *khanqah*—fascinating stuff. The second was Baba Palangposh, a military Sufi who guarded the army of Ghazi al-Din Khan, the Mughal general who founded Hyderabad state. His task was to boost morale in battle through the force of his *tawajjuh* (attention); he was thought to go ahead of the troops firing arrows. Digby's translation of the malfuzat is to be followed by a volume of commentary, which should considerably advance our knowledge not just of Sufism in the seventeenth-century Deccan but also of Mughal life in general. Indeed, study of Sufi sources—because Sufi *pir*s wrote guidance for their followers, and because their followers recorded the lives and sayings of their pirs—have been one of the more productive ways in which our understanding of social, cultural and religious change amongst Indian Muslims have been advanced over the past generation. The contributions of K.A. Nizami and Annemarie Schimmel should come quickly to mind, although they reach way back beyond the current generation, but so should those of Richard Eaton, Carl Ernst, Bruce Lawrence, Claudia Liebeskind, P.M. Currie, Arthur Buehler, Thomas Dahnhardt, and Nile Green.[19]

Chapters 10, 22, and 23 all address major processes in the history of West Asia. 'Never Argue with the Camel-driver' (Chapter 10) reviews an excellent study of the Hajj by F.E. Peters. He ranges from its origins in seventh-century Arabia to its current form in which over two million Muslims make the pilgrimage and represent the greatest annual gathering of humankind. We are left in no doubt of the extraordinary demonstration of faith which the Hajj has demonstrated down the ages and of the impact which it has had on those performing it. Barbara Metcalf has studied some of the *safarnamahs*—the journals kept by some pilgrims. I look forward to more such work being done on the journals of pilgrims and from a wider range of societies than those of South Asia.[20] Not only do they provide the window onto a central act of Muslim piety, through which changes in concepts of the self and interpretations of religious symbols can be viewed, they also provide the material to help build understanding and respect amongst non-Muslims. 'Stories from the Cradle' (Chapter 22) reviews thirty-six childhood reminiscences collected by the US anthropologist, Elizabeth Fernea, from West Asia and North Africa. What stands out from these twentieth-century stories is the power of women and family in making life bearable and the way in which few lives seem not to have been touched by the exercise of Western power or its consequences. For the thoughtful, it is sobering stuff. 'No Fun, No Bread, No Chance' (Chapter 23) reviews the memoirs of Masoud Banisadr, cousin of Abol Hasan Banisadr, the first president of the Islamic Republic of Iran and prominent member of the Mujahideen, who, from the moment they were edged out of the revolutionary alliance down to the present, have been active opponents of the Islamic regime from abroad. Masoud tells an amazing story of an ideologically-driven opposition which is as deranged and inhumane as the ideological regime which it opposes. It is a tale of tragedy, loss, displacement, and the triumph of the human spirit. In the twentieth century the peoples of Iran and West Asia have had more than their fair share of such experiences. We can only be grateful that the lesson Banisadr draws from them is that the first criterion of human action should be humanity.

'Mixed Fortunes' (Chapter 18) reviews William Dalrymple's deservedly popular *White Mughals: Love and Betrayal in Eighteenth-century India.* At the same time a love story, a tragedy, and a metaphor for the transition of British power from partnership to dominance in relation to India, it is also a celebration of a time when Westerners and Asians lived together as equals, and in full enjoyment of their shared humanity. It is no coincidence that Dalrymple should have written such a celebration now. Like Masoud Banisadr he knows that humanity is the best measure of human action, whether it be in the relations between persons or between nations.

Casting an eye over the contents of the volume it is hard not to reflect on one's good fortune to be engaged with history which combines the personal and the human with themes of such excitement and such grandeur. We have already addressed those of Hindu and Muslim revivalism and the withering and distorting power of the West in relation to the non-Western world. To these should be added, first, the great project on which Muslims have been engaged over the past fourteen centuries in building bridges between revelation and human circumstance, a project which has faced especial challenges over the past two centuries, and second, the tension between other-worldly and this-worldly piety which has existed throughout Islamic history and which has made, over the past two centuries, a decisive shift in a this-worldly direction. The impact of this shift is beginning to offer the tantalizing prospect of Islamically-derived ideas helping to drive the train of 'modernity'. This book will have done its work if, on the one hand, it enables the reader to have some empathy with what it has meant to be human in another place at another time and if, on the other hand, it enables the reader to have a stronger sense of perspective over and a greater understanding of some of the great issues of the Muslim and South Asian past, many of which bear upon the present.

December 2006
London

NOTES

1 Francis Robinson, *Islam and Muslim History in South Asia* (Delhi, 2000), p. 1.

2 All the theses of these students have either been published or are about to be published as books: see Claudia Liebeskind, *Piety on Its Knees: Three Sufi Traditions in South Asia in Modern Times* (Delhi, 1998); Mohammad Ali Kazembeyki, *Society, Politics and Economics in Mazandaran, Iran, 1848–1918* (London, 2003); Azra Asghar Ali, *The Emergence of Feminism Among Indian Muslim Women, 1920–47* (Karachi, 2000); Yoginder Sikand, *The Origins and Development of the Tablighi Jama'at: A Cross-country and Comparative Study (1920–2000)* (Hyderabad, 2002); Amit Dey, *The Image of the Prophet in Bengali Muslim Piety* (Kolkata, 2005); Markus Daechsel, *The Politics of Self-Expression* (Routledge/Royal Asiatic Society Books, 2006 forthcoming); Paolo Durisotto, *Traditional Rule and Modern Conventions* (Routledge/Royal Asiatic Society Books, forthcoming).

3 'To Little and Too Much: Reflections on Muslims in the History of India' in Barbara D. Metcalf, *Islamic Contestations: Essays on Muslims in India and Pakistan* (Delhi, 2004), pp. 193–216.

4 David Gilmartin and Bruce B. Lawrence (eds), *Beyond Turk and Hindu: Rethinking Religious Identities in Islamicate South Asia* (Gainesville, Fl., 2000).
5 Ibid., pp. 246–81 and Richard M. Eaton, *Essays on Islam and Indian History* (Delhi, 2000), pp. 94–132.
6 S.P. Huntington, *The Clash of Civilizations and the Remaking of World Order* (New York, 1996).
7 This has been the lot of a host of Islamic reformers from Jamal al-Din al-Afghani (1838–97) to Tariq Ramadan, the grandson of Hasan al-Banna, founder of the Muslim Brotherhood (1962–), see 'Introduction' in Michaelle Browers and Charles Kurzman (eds), *An Islamic Reformation?* (Oxford, 2004), pp. 4–6.
8 Ibid., pp. 6–12 and M. Iqbal, *The Reconstruction of Religious Thought in Islam* (Lahore, 1975). p. 163.
9 Francis Robinson, 'Fundamentalism, Tolerance and India's Heritage', *Journal of the Asiatic Society*, vol. XLV, no. 3, (2003), pp. 5–13.
10 See Francis Robinson, *Islam and Muslim History in South Asia* (Delhi, 2000), pp. 66–104, 105–21.
11 Edward W. Said, *Orientalism* (London, 1978).
12 Bernard Lewis, 'The Question of Orientalism', *The New York Review of Books*, 24 June 1982, pp. 49–56.
13 David Frum, *The Right Man: The Surprise Presidency of George W. Bush* (New York, 2003), pp. 158, 170–1, 175, and 225.
14 Sulayman S. Nyang and Samir Abed-Rabo, 'Bernard Lewis and Islamic Studies: An Assessment' in Asaf Hussain, Robert Olson and Jamil Qureshi (eds), *Orientalism, Islam, and Islamists* (Battleborough, Vermont, 1984), pp. 259–86.
15 See, for instance, Francis Robinson, *The 'Ulama of Farangi Mahall and Islamic Culture in South Asia* (Delhi, 2001).
16 The Indian poetic genre of *shahr ashob* has a parallel in the Turkish concept of *huzun,* 'melancholy', which is brilliantly discussed in relation to the city by Orhan Pamuk in his memoir of Istanbul and exemplified by Resat Ekrem Kocu's unfinished *Istanbul Ansiklopedisi,* which had a powerful influence upon him. See Orhan Pamuk, *Istanbul: Memories of a City* (London, 2005), pp. 79–96 and 137–54.
17 Barbara D. Metcalf, *Islamic Contestations: Essays on Muslims in India and Pakistan* (New Delhi, 2004), p. 3.
18 Ruby Lal, *Domesticity and Power in the Early Mughal World* (Cambridge, 2005).
19 Among the works we think of are: Richard M. Eaton, *Sufis of Bijapur 1300–1700; Social Role of Sufis in Medieval India* (New Jersey, 1978), and *the Rise of Islam and the Bengal Frontier 1204–1760* (Berkeley, 1993); Carl W. Ernst and Bruce B. Lawrence, *Sufi Martyrs of Love: The Chishti Order in South Asia and Beyond* (New York, 2002); Carl W. Ernst, *The Eternal Garden*, second edition (Delhi, 2004);

Bruce B. Lawrence, *Notes from a Distant Flute: The Extant Literature of Pre-Mughal Indian Sufism* (Tehran, 1978); Sarah F.D. Ansari, *Sufi Saints and State Power: The Pirs of Sind, 1843–1947* (Cambridge, 1992); Claudia Liebeskind, *Piety on Its Knees: Three Sufi Traditions in South Asia in Modern Times* (Delhi, 1998); P.M. Currie, *The Shrine and Cult of Mu'in al-din Chishti of Ajmer* (Delhi, 1989): Arthur F. Buehler, *Sufi Heirs of the Prophet: the Indian Naqshbandiyya and the Rise of the Mediating Sufi Shaykh* (Columbia, S.C., 1998); Thomas Dahnhardt, *Change and Continuity in Indian Sufism* (New Delhi, 2002); Nile Green, *Indian Sufism since the Seventeenth Century: Saints, Books and Empires in the Muslim Deccan* (Abingdon, 2006).

20 'The Pilgrimage Remembered: South Asian Accounts of the Hajj' and 'What Happened in Mecca: Mumtaz Mufti's Labbaik' in Barbara D. Metcalf, *Islamic Contestations: Essays on Muslims in India and Pakistan* (New Delhi, 2004), pp. 295–316, 317–39.

Knowledge, its Transmission, and the Making of Muslim Societies

One day, goes a story concerning al-Shafi'i (d. 820), the founder of one of the four Sunni schools of law, his pupils brought him a slave-girl. Frustrated, after waiting in vain throughout the night for the eminent jurist she complained to the slave-dealer that he had sold her to a 'crazy man'. Hearing this al-Shafi'i declared, 'Crazy is he who knows the value of knowledge, and who then squanders it, or hesitates so that it passes him by.'[1] This story, and many like it, emphasize the centrality of the search for knowledge in good Muslim lives.

At the heart of this search was the Muslim concern to command all that could be known of the Quran, the life of the Prophet, and the skills to make the guidance they represented socially useful. This was knowledge man needed to gain salvation. Nevertheless, the high value placed on learning also came to include knowledge which might give men power in the world—such as the rational sciences, medicine, technology—always providing that it did not run counter to Islamic purposes.

Thus, learning for Muslims was an act of worship. It was, moreover, a supremely important one. 'An hour of learning', went the saying, 'is worth more than a year of prayer.' This emphasis had two outcomes of major significance in Islamic history. First, wherever Muslims went in the world there was a central core of knowledge in which all could share, although they might interpret it differently, and a central core of religious duties, which all should perform, although there might be minor differences of emphasis. Second, Muslims themselves, whether the state was concerned to play a role or not, took responsibility for preserving knowledge in their generation and transmitting it to the next.

THE FORMATION OF ISLAMIC KNOWLEDGE

The core of Islamic knowledge was shaped in the first five Muslim centuries. In the era that followed this core was to be further elaborated, but not significantly changed. To this day traditional Muslim scholars use many of the texts written by the great scholars of the Islamic Middle Ages, and often do so in ways that do not differ greatly from those of their medieval forebears. The elements that went to make this most influential body of knowledge came together as a consequence of the Arab conquests of the seventh century. Just as the material wealth of the early Islamic world derived from the Arab achievement in uniting the great economic regions of the Mediterranean basin and Asia so its wealth in knowledge derived from the opportunities it created for the mingling of a new complex of Semitic, Hellenistic, Iranian, and Indian strands of culture.

Revelation, Tradition, and the Law

At the heart of Islamic knowledge lay the Quran, which Muslims believed to be the word of God revealed to man through the Prophet Muhammad. From its opening chapter, which the faithful use as Christians might the Lord's Prayer, the Quran reminded Muslims of the central reality of God in human life:

Praise be to Allah, the Lord of the worlds,
The Beneficient, the Merciful,
Master of the day of Requital.
Thee do we serve and Thee do we beseech for help.
Guide us on the right path,
The path of those upon whom Thou has bestowed favours,
Not those upon whom wrath is brought down, nor those who go astray.[2]

Humans had a fundamental choice. They could submit to God and follow the commandments, or they could turn away from Him, follow human desire, and take the consequences. Man is left in no doubt as to the awesome nature of the Last Day, the pleasures of paradise and the horrors of hell. Much guidance is given about what men should believe in religion and how they should behave in worship, about what rules they should follow with regard to their fellow men and the gratitude to God which should infuse their daily lives.

Muslims refer to the Quran as the 'noble' or the 'glorious'; its Arabic is regarded as being without compare. Copying the Quran has been an act of piety performed by rich and poor alike. Learning the

Quran has been the normal starting point of Muslim education, whether or not the young children concerned could understand its Arabic. Although the revealed word was first written down in full under the third caliph, 'Uthman, and copies were sent to the major cities, the classical way in which it was transmitted was orally. Early Arabic script left possibilities for variant readings; in time seven traditions of recitation, distinguished by only minor differences, came to be regarded as canonical. As the written text of the Quran became available so the work of interpretation and exegesis began. Inevitably the commentaries which appeared as the outcome were subject to the sectarian controversies of the time. The first attempt at an overarching critical study was produced in thirty volumes by the historian and theologian, al-Tabari (d. 923). Over three centuries later the task was accomplished once again by al-Baydawi (d. 1286). To the present day his work has remained the standard for Muslims and non-Muslims alike.

The second source of knowledge was the record of the sayings and doings of the Prophet. Given that the Prophet was the model of the perfect Muslim life, it was only natural that believers should wish to know all he had said and done. The collective memory of these sayings and doings came to be known as the *Sunna*, the 'beaten path' or 'custom' of the Prophet. Individual statements of the sunna were known as *Hadith* (Tradition) which might go thus:

Ibn Umar reported that the Messenger of Allah said:
Whoever imitates a people, he belongs to them.

As time went on the Hadith multiplied till they numbered hundreds of thousands; they came to be invented to support legal, political, and theological positions of the day. In the ninth and tenth centuries, therefore, men travelled throughout the Muslim world to collect Hadith. After analysing them to see, on the one hand, whether their chain of narration from the time of the Prophet was sound and, on the other, whether their content was in harmony with the Quran, already authenticated Hadith, and reason, they were classified as sound (*sahih*), acceptable (*hasan*), or weak (*daif*). Six collections of Hadith came to have canonical status, of which those of Bukhari (d. 870) and of Muslim (d. 875) were the most esteemed. Bukhari winnowed the multiplicity of Hadiths down to 2,762. Subsequently, different movements built different collections of Hadiths. The Shias, for instance, accepted only those traditions transmitted through Ali and his followers.

Western scholars and some Muslim modernists have tended to cast doubt on the authenticity of some long-accepted traditions. Nevertheless, the traditions have played a major role in forming the character of Muslim communities and in developing like behaviour through much of the Sunni world. Moreover, when Muslim communities have felt particularly under threat, it is to the traditions that they have, more often than not, turned for renewed direction.

The guidance of the Quran and Hadith was encapsulated in practical form for Muslims in the law. This is usually referred to as the *shari'a* which meant originally in Arabic 'the path leading to the water', that is, the path to the source of life. The shari'a grew from the attempts of early Muslims, as they confronted immediate social and political problems, to derive systematic codes of behaviour from the word of God and the example of the Prophet. Four main schools of legal interpretation developed; the Hanafi, which grew up in the Abbasid capital of Baghdad and was founded by Abu Hanifa (d. 769); the Maliki, which grew out of the practice of the Medinan judge, Malik bin Anas (d. 795); the Shafi'i, which developed under the leadership of a disciple of Malik, al-Shafi'i (d. 820); and the Hanbali, founded by Ahmad ibn Hanbal (d. 855) in Baghdad. The first three schools all had formal differences of emphasis and technique. Hanafis, for instance, allowed more room for ijtihad, personal reasoning, than the others, while the Shafi'is were concerned to distinguish their use of Hadith from the more limited practice of the Malakis. All agreed, however, on important matters; all recognized each other's systems as equally orthodox. The Hanbali school, on the other hand, developed as a traditionalist reaction against what it regarded as the speculative innovations of the earlier established schools. Until the fifteenth century the influence of the Hanbalis tended to be limited to Iraq and Syria. The Hanafis, on the other hand, were strong throughout mainland Asia, the Shafi'is in lower Egypt, the Hijaz, Southeast Asia and East Africa, and the Malikis in the rest of Muslim Africa.

'Ulama, that is, scholars, those with *'ilm* or knowledge, developed these systems roughly thus. They treated the Quran as containing the general principles by which all matters should be regulated, and when the Quran was unclear they sought clarification in the Hadith. The foundations of the shari'a, then, were the unambiguous commands and prohibitions to be found in these sources. When points of law arose, on which the Quran and Hadith offered no firm guidance, most 'Ulama turned to *qiyas*, which meant arguing by analogy and applying to the problem the principles underlying a decision which had already been reached on a comparable issue. As the years passed, 'ulama increasingly came to agree on points of law, and the principle of *ijma*, or consensus of the community, came into play. 'My community,' went a very important Hadith, 'will never agree upon an error.' So, if the community as embodied in its legal experts came to agree on a point, that agreement gained the authority of revelation itself and the development of new ideas on the subject was forbidden. Steadily, more and more of the law was underpinned by ijma, and the area in which personal reasoning might be deployed was increasingly diminished. By the mid-tenth century most scholars had declared the 'gate of ijtihad' shut. Henceforth, if a man questioned the meaning of a text in such a way as to challenge the interpretation supported by ijma he committed *bida*, an act of innovation, which was as near as Islam came to the Christian concept of heresy.

The shari'a was comprehensive. It embraced all human activities, defining both man's relations with God and with his fellow men. In the first role it prescribed what man should believe and how by ritual acts he should express his belief; in the second it covered those areas which in European codes might come under the heading of civil, commercial, penal, personal law, and so on. No formal legal code was created at this time, nor subsequently, the shari'a being more a discussion of how Muslims ought to behave. In the process human actions were classified on a five-point scale: obligatory, meritorious, indifferent, reprehensible, forbidden. The shari'a told man all he needed to know about how to live righteously in this world and how to be prepared for the next.

The shari'a defined the constitution of the Muslim community. However, it was never to be applied in full. For one thing, it was impossible to enforce a system which included moral obligations as well as hard-and-fast rules. For another, it would always be subject to the realities of political power. Rulers could not afford to permit the interpreters of the law a completely free hand in the legal arena. They were unlikely to think it wise, even if they had the power, to impose the shari'a over local *'urf* or *'adat* customary law. Nevertheless, the shari'a was to be a potent ideal. All who accepted Islam accepted in principle the idea that the knowledge it represented should be spread as widely as possible so that it might fashion the lives of men.

Greek and Other Knowledge

A second strand was the great heritage of the ancient world in science, technology, the humanities, and the arts of government, which was drawn into the new Islamic civilization. One element was from the former Sasanian lands and found in large part in the Pahlavi language. There was the store of Iranian expertise contained in the *adab* literature—guides on the arts of government, the duties of various offices, and etiquette in the presence of rulers. There was the technical literature in fields ranging from arms and horsemanship through to agriculture and irrigation. There was scientific literature, notably in the fields of medicine, astronomy, and maths; not least amongst the last mentioned was the Indian system of numerical notation which in Arab hands was to begin its transformation to those in widespread use today. Of course, there were works of Iranian literature such as the fables of the *Kalila wa Dimna* and stories which were to be included in the Arabian Nights. The impact of this literature was such that under the Abbasids some, the Shu'ubiyya, tried to assert the superiority of Iranian culture over Arab, and Iranian ideas of kingship over Islamic ideas of caliphate. By the end of the ninth century the specific religious threats had been met by theologians and the more general challenges of Iranian culture had been countered by men such as al-Jahiz (d. 869) and Ibn Qutayba (d. 889) who succeeded in synthesizing Arab and Iranian traditions by producing a literature which bore an Iranian impress in style and subject but was firmly held within a frame of Arab and Islamic ideas.

More important was the impact of Greek culture which came to the Islamic world not in its classical form but as it had come to be elaborated in the late antique world. The Hellenistic traditions of Athens were sustained by Nestorian Christians working under Sasanian patronage at their educational centre of Jundishapur in southern Iran. The Hellenistic traditions of Alexandria were sustained successively in Antioch in Syria, Merv in Khurasan, and Harran in Mesopotamia. Theological debate in the eighth and ninth centuries led to curiosity about Greek thought and both traditions were transferred to Baghdad. A great programme of translation of works from Greek, and also from Syriac into which many Greek works had been translated, was established under Hunayn Ibn Ishaq (d. 873) and notably high standards were maintained in the publication of accurate and reliable editions. By the eleventh century at least eighty Greek authors had been translated, many major figures such as Aristotle, Plato, Galen, and Euclid being represented by several works. Among the subjects covered were philosophy, medicine, maths, physics, optics, astronomy, geography, and the occult sciences of astrology, alchemy and magic. Like the later Hellenes the Muslims were not interested in the Greek traditions of literature and history.

The most important area of knowledge transferred from the Hellenistic tradition was philosophy with its emphasis on reason, logic, and the laws of nature. This knowledge was used for theological purposes by the Mutazilites, 'those who keep themselves apart'. Confronted by Christian Trinitarian, Manichaean dualistic and anthropomorphic conceptions of God they were determined to assert His absolute unity and transcendence. Thus God had no attributes which belonged to his essence; the attributes mentioned in the Quran had only a metaphorical force. It followed from this that the Quran was not part of the essence of God, but created, a message inspired by God in Muhammad. It followed, too, that God did not predetermine men's lives; men were morally free and responsible for their own actions. Such views became the politically dominant views under the Caliph Mamun (813–33), and those dissenting, who included the founder of the Hanbali school of law, were persecuted.

Many Muslims were unhappy that the truth of Islam should depend on reason. The Quran and the example of the Prophet were the only firm basis of the faith. Men must submit to God, not claim to know better than Him. So the attributes of God had to exist because they were stated in the Quran. So the Quran was uncreated because it had been revealed by God and not inspired in His Prophet. So man's actions were predestined because God was Lord of all His creation.

Thus, in the eighth and ninth centuries two contrary theological positions developed: one in which God's presence in the universe came to be understood through reason and one in which it was to be understood only in so far as He had revealed Himself to man. An all-important bridge was built between these conflicting positions by al-Ashari (d. 935). A pupil of the leading Mutazilite theologian of Basra, al-Ashari was converted to the scripturalist position as a result of dreams he experienced during the fast of Ramadan. He now asserted

the literal truth of the Quran but, in his bridge-building mode, justified his position with reason. Reason, however, could operate only up to a certain point beyond which faith had to take over. So God was One: He had eternal attributes, but these were not Him, nor were they apart from Him. So the Quran was 'uncreated' but might become created when transmitted to men. So God willed all things, good and evil, but man acquired responsibility as the instrument of these actions. Differences remained amongst the followers of al-Ashari, for instance, about the precise nature of the uncreatedness of the Quran. But through history al-Ashari's synthesis of reason and revelation remained the classic Sunni theological position.

Al-Ashari's achievement set limits to the rationalist enterprise in the mainstream of Islamic thought, but it in no way put an end to philosophical speculation. Indeed, Islamic civilization, as it responded to Greek thought in the early centuries, produced a majestic series of philosophers: al-Kindi (d. 870), who was known as the 'philosopher of the Arabs'; al-Farabi (d. 950), who came from Turkistan; Ibn Sina (d. 1184), who worked as both physician and official; Ibn Tufayl (d. 1195), who worked as physician and vizier at the Almohad court; and Ibn Rushd (d. 1195), who succeeded Ibn Tufayl at the Almohad court. Amongst the ideas that men such as these asserted were that philosophical truth was universally valid, that religious symbolism was an inferior way of conveying truth, that reason was the surest path to truth and that God was the first cause in which essence and existence were one. Such ideas were bound to be unacceptable to the vast majority of the faithful. Philosophical knowledge was doomed to subsist on the margins of Muslim civilization and to have a greater influence on medieval Europe than on the Muslim world from which it came.[3]

Mystic Knowledge

The third strand of knowledge was mysticism or Sufism as it is generally called. Whereas the shari'a dictated the formal relations of a Muslim towards God and his fellow men, Sufism taught the Muslim how to know God in his heart. Sufis lived their lives and ordered their thoughts in ways designed to make possible a direct and personal experience of God.

Sufism grew as a distinct strand of Muslim devotion, which was inspired by the Quran, the religious practices of the Prophet, and the early Muslim community. It did so in part as the Arab Muslims came into contact with the Christian and the other mystic traditions of the lands they conquered, and in part in reaction to the moral laxness and worldliness of the Umayyad court at Damascus. The term 'Sufi' is probably derived from the Arabic *suf*, meaning wool, which referred to the simple woollen clothes worn by mystics in contrast to the rich apparel of the worldly.

In the beginning the basis of Sufi feeling was fear of God and of judgement. 'The believer wakens grieving and goes to bed grieving,' declared Hasan al-Basri (d. 725), the famous early mystic, 'and this is all that encompasses him, because he is between two fearful things: the sin which has passed, and he does not know what God will do with him, and the allotted term which remains, and he does not know what disasters will befall him....' But, by the second Islamic century, the doctrine of love had become prominent. 'I love Thee with two loves,' the woman saint, Rabiâ (d. 801), declared to God, 'love of my happiness, and perfect love, to love Thee as is Thy due.'[4] Sufis, however, did not remain satisfied with this intense gospel of love. By the third Islamic century they had begun to develop the doctrine of the 'inner way' or the spiritual journey towards God. There were different stages of the way corresponding to the different levels of Sufi experience. The mystic was first a seeker, then a traveller, and then an initiate. He progressed along the way through processes of self-abnegation and enhanced awareness of God. The nearer he came to God, the more God spoke with his lips, controlled his limbs, and moved the desires of his heart until he reached the final stage when self was annihilated and totally absorbed in God.

By this time two broad tendencies had developed—one ecstatic, the other sober. Both tendencies resigned themselves to God's will by embracing poverty. The ecstatic tendency ignored the Quran and the Law in moving to the final stages when the self was annihilated and totally absorbed in God. Typical of this tendency was al-Hallaj (d. 920) who carried his Sufi message through northern India and Central Asia. In manifesting his union with God he declared, 'I am the Truth' and was brutally executed in Baghdad for his pains. The sober tendency was typified by al-Junayd (d. 911) who was known as the 'peacock of the poor'. He insisted that mere self-annihilation was not enough. The self still had to persevere in the real world and that could only be done by living in conformity with the Quran and the Law.

Side by side with these varying ways of approaching God there were attempts to develop a metaphysical and philosophical understanding of God and his relationship to man. The metaphysical theories posited a transcendent God whose spiritual radiance was implanted in man. To discover the divine essence that lay within them men had to overcome their worldly nature. Again, with the translation of Greek and Syriac works into Arabic, Sufis adopted the intellectual mysticism of Plotinus (d. 270). For these men the universe emanated from God in stages of spiritual and then material manifestation. Man was able, by developing inner knowledge to ascend through the stages of material and then spiritual manifestation to the ultimate vision of God.

By the tenth and eleventh centuries social and political rivalries mingled with different strands of knowledge in Islam to express a series of tensions. The decline of the Abbasid caliphate had led to the rise of Shia regimes throughout the Middle East. While the Twelver Shias were largely unconcerned with proselytization, the Isma'ilis were great missionaries: the Isma'ili Fatimid rulers of Egypt sponsored missions from North Africa through to Central Asia and Afghanistan. Shia power, moreover, was not just a challenge to Sunni dominion and understandings of authority in Islam, it also created circumstances in which Hellenistic knowledge could flourish. The defence of Sunni Islam was taken up most vigorously in Baghdad and by followers of the Hanbali school of law, who permitted no place for the rational sciences in developing their understandings of Islam. The Hanbalis were at the heart of the second tension; they were no less concerned about the influence of rational schools of theology, such as the Ashari, amongst the Sunni community. For them Hellenistic learning was unnecessary as a support to revelation and the example of the Prophet. This tension, however, grew greater as the Asharite theologians, in their struggle to check the influence of philosophy, increasingly came to use philosophical methods in displaying their theology. Then, the claims of some Sufis—in particular, those of the ecstatic variety—to achieve knowledge of God through direct personal experience were a further source of tension; they challenged the upholders of the shari'a, lawyers, and theologians alike. Such claims devalued the role of law in Muslim society. They were, moreover, justified by a Hellenistic theosophical metaphysics; they were often associated with a belief in the miraculous prowess of saints as instruments of God's will or both; they had growing support amongst the Muslim population at large.

That these tensions did not open up an unbridgeable gulf between those immersed in the different strands of knowledge has much to do with the achievement of one man, the greatest figure in medieval Islam, indeed, the most influential figure after Muhammad, Abu Hamid al-Ghazzali (d. 1111). As a relatively young man al-Ghazzali had been appointed to the senior professorship at the Nizamiyya College in Baghdad. He was brilliant but, as he tells us in his moving autobiography, *The Deliverance from Error*, 'My teaching was concerned with branches of knowledge which were unimportant and worthless, ... my motive in teaching ... was not sincere desire to serve God but that I wanted an influential position and widespread recognition.'[5] He had a physical and mental breakdown, left his post, and lived the life of a Sufi. During his scholarly life al-Ghazzali examined the main strands in the thought of his time and produced a synthesis that has lain at the centre of Sunni Islam to this day. He explored the arguments of the Isma'ili Shias and refuted them one by one. He explored the potential of the rational sciences for enhancing religious understanding, most particularly in his attack on Ibn Sina in *The Incoherence of the Philosophers*, and demonstrated that while they were of great value in mathematics and logic, they could never enable men to know a transcendent God. Thus, al-Ghazzali reaffirmed the rational theology of al-Ashari in which reason was firmly subject to revelation. Finally, and very much as a result of his own personal crisis, he explored the possibilities of building a bridge between Sufism and shari'a Islam. In building that bridge he demonstrated that God was not to be discovered by intellect alone, but by personal experience. The Muslim must expect to know not just that knowledge which God had revealed to him but also to know God in his heart. al-Ghazzali's religious vision was published in his most important work, *Revival of the Religious Sciences*. He was given the title, 'Renewer of Islam'.

By the time of al-Ghazzali's death at the beginning of the twelfth century the basic shape of normative Islamic knowledge had been fashioned from the interaction between the knowledge revealed to man by God and the actions of His Prophet and the great heritage of knowledge in the Middle East derived from pre-Islamic sources. At the apex of Islamic knowledge stood the Quran and Hadith, whose guidance was embodied in the shari'a. These were serviced by the twin strands of rational and mystical knowledge, whose insights helped to make the shari'a of value both to individuals and to society, but were not permitted to trespass beyond the bounds set by revelation. This is what has been termed the 'Sunni–Shari'a–Sufi' consensus. Around this consensus, however, which was in itself a very broad 'church', there were other Islamic possibilities. There was the gnostic vision, which was present in Sufism, Isma'ili Shi'ism, and philosophy, and which saw the purpose of life not in fulfilling God's word on earth but in purification of the soul and detachment from earthly things. There was popular Islam which was most frequently represented in the worship of saints who, it was believed, could intercede for man with God and whose cults often mingled with pre-Islamic beliefs and customs. There were the Shias, whose practices differed from those of the Sunnis in few respects, but for whom the vital issue was loyalty to the family of Ali. These various traditions of Islamic knowledge and understanding represent, in the words of Ira Lapidus, 'a repertoire of cultural and religious ideas which remain operative in Islamic lands to the present day'.[6]

THE TRANSMISSION OF KNOWLEDGE TO C. 1800

Islamic knowledge was made available to society and transmitted to the generations to come by 'ulama and Sufis. It is important for those from a non-Muslim background to realize that these transmitters were not priests and performed no sacerdotal functions; in theory at least normative Islam tolerated no intermediaries between man and God. It is also important to realize that in most Muslim societies 'ulama existed less because a state willed their existence than because society valued the functions they performed. We now consider 'ulama and Sufis as transmitters of the knowledge which shaped both the outward form and the inner nature of Muslim societies down to the European irruption in the nineteenth and twentieth centuries.

The 'ulama and the Transmission of Formal Knowledge

The 'ulama were to be found in almost every corner of the Islamic world. They bore different titles in different regions: Mulla in the Persian-speaking lands of Iran, Central Asia, and northern India; Shaykh in the Arabic-speaking central Islamic lands; Kiyayi on the Indonesian islands; and Mallam or Karamoko in West Africa. They performed a wide range of functions. They might administer mosques, schools, hospitals, and orphanages; they might also be courtiers, diplomats, or leading bureaucrats. Their first task, however, remained the preservation and transmission of the shari'a. As scholars they defended their understandings of it, as qadis they administered it on behalf of the state, as muftis they expounded it on behalf of the community for whom they issued *fatawa* (sing. *fatwa*)—or legal decisions—free of charge. They reminded Muslims of their obligations under it in their sermons and instructed their children in it in their schools.

'Ulama might have a range of sources of support. Some lived off land grants or salaries from the state, but the majority were supported by the community—by the endowments of the pious, by the donations of the grateful, or by the proceeds of the crafts or trades in which they were engaged. In some areas where the state had periods of notable strength, as in the Ottoman Empire, numbers of 'ulama might come under state control, forming a kind of bureaucracy. In other areas, where the state was often weak, as in Indonesia or West Africa, they existed largely free from state control. Of course, during this long period there could be great shifts in the relationship between the 'ulama and a particular state. Nowhere was this more obvious than in Safavid Iran, to which Shia 'ulama were transplanted in order to bolster Safavid rule only to achieve such power in Iranian society that they came to challenge the authority of the state. This said, the 'ulama embraced a wide range of distinction and function—from those of the patrician families of Cairo, Damascus, and Baghdad, or those of the great clerical families of West Africa, such as the Jakhanke of Senegambia who can be traced back to the thirteenth century or the Saghananughu who can be traced back to the fourteenth century, to the leader of prayers in a small-town mosque or to the village school teacher.

Such men, who were both important and often prominent in their communities, were inevitably a focus of criticism. In fourteenth-century Cairo their pretensions were satirized by street players wearing outsize turbans and sleeves.[7] Under the Ottomans, we are told of 'ulama who loved the world, were constantly going to Istanbul to lobby for appointments, and had become rich, being made the subject of satire, and stoning by the mob.[8] Shaykh Sa'di of Shiraz (d. 1292) made the fall of a qadi into illicit sex and drink the theme of one of the stories in his *Gulistan*, which was famously depicted in a Mughal miniature of c. 1630.[9] That such comments should take place at all is an indication of the esteem in which 'ulama were generally held. 'Verily', declared the Prophet, 'the men of knowledge are the inheritors of the prophets.'

'Ulama taught in the reception rooms of their houses, in the courtyards of mosques and shrines, and also in madrasas or specially constructed colleges. Indeed, through much of the medieval Muslim world the madrasa, a term directly derived from a verb meaning 'to study', was the focus of education. The madrasa seems first to have developed as a specific institution in Khurasan. During the eleventh and twelfth centuries it came to be established in Iraq and Syria as part of an assertion of Sunni tradition in a region long threatened by Shia power. At the end of the twelfth century there were at least thirty madrasas in Damascus and a similar number in Cairo.

By this time the madrasa had become a major Islamic institution. Some foundations from this medieval period exist to the present day such as al-Azhar in Cairo, which was established in 972, or the Bu Inaniya in Fez, which was established in the mid-fourteenth century. So too in its arrangement of student and teacher rooms around a courtyard had the madrasa come to represent a classic form of Islamic architecture to set alongside the mosque and shrine. Magnificent relics of this form can be seen in the monumental madrasas, which fill three sides of the Registan Square in Samarqand, or in the semaniye madrasas, the apex of the Ottoman education system, which form part of the Sulaymaniye complex in Istanbul. Nevertheless, the number, and sometimes the magnificence of madrasas in many parts of the Muslim world should not lead one to believe that teaching and learning were highly formal or institutionalized processes. There were no examinations at entrance, no degrees on leaving. Moreover, salaries for teachers and stipends for students—as recent research on medieval Cairo reveals—were often low priorities for those making endowments. The madrasas were primarily a location in which teaching took place. The arrangements were normally informal; they were a person-to-person affair.

At the heart of the person-to-person nature of teaching was the fact that it was essentially oral. This was the way in which the Prophet had first transmitted the messages he received from God to his followers. Learning the Quran by heart and then reciting it out aloud was the first task of Muslim boys and girls. The methods of learning and of transmitting the Quran laid their impress on the transmission of all other knowledge. 'The Quran,' declared the great fourteenth-century historian, Ibn Khaldun, in a fine chapter on the art of teaching in his *Muqadimmah*, 'has become the basis of instruction, the foundation of all habits that might be acquired later on.'[10] Thus, when a teacher taught a text in the madrasa curriculum, he would dictate it to his pupils, who might write it down, and frequently commit it to memory. Many pedagogical texts were written in rhyme to assist this process. Subsequently, there might be an explanation of the text depending on its nature. The pupil completed the study of the book by reading back the text with the explanation. If this was done to the teacher's satisfaction, the pupil would be given an *ijaza* (meaning, to make lawful), which was a licence to teach that text. The personal and oral nature of the process of transmission is captured in the words of a tenth-century ijaza from the author of a text:

> I entrust my book to you with my writing from my hand to yours. I give you authorization for the poem and you may transmit it from me. It has been produced after being heard and read.[11]

The pupil would also see in his ijaza a list of all the names of those who had transmitted the text going back to the original author. He would know that he was but the most recent link in a continuing chain of oral transmission.

It might reasonably be asked why a culture which placed high value on the book, which saw great libraries amassed, which urged students to buy books, and which provided many opportunities for silent reading, should place such emphasis on oral transmission. The reason was that Muslims were fundamentally sceptical of the written word—particularly, the written word studied without supervision—as a reliable means of communication. 'When a student has to rely on the study of books and written material and must understand scientific problems from the forms of written letters in books,' declares Ibn Khaldun, 'he is confronted by ... [a] veil ... that separates handwriting and the form of the letter found in writing from the spoken words found in the imagination.'[12] To approach the true meaning of the text, which the author intended when he first published the text by reading it out loud, the student had himself to read it out aloud. To have authority over the transmission of the text the student had to read it out aloud to the satisfaction of a teacher who himself had authority over the text.

Two enduring features of Islamic culture illuminate the importance of person-to-person transmission. One is the literary form of the *tadhkirah* or collective biography. This might cover the scholars or a particular time, place, or family. It would record, after family details, who a man's teachers were, what he learned, and whom he taught. His own contributions to knowledge would be listed along with anecdotal evidence bearing on his reliability as a transmitter of knowledge. Such biographies, which record the person-to-person transmission of the central messages of Islam have been kept to the present day. The second feature is the enormous respect given to the teacher in the Islamic tradition. 'Know that ... one does not acquire learning nor profit from it,' declared a thirteenth-century educational manual, 'unless one holds in esteem knowledge and those who possess it. One [must also] glorify and venerate the teacher.'[13] The situation was little different at the beginning of the twentieth century. 'The pupil should walk several paces behind his teacher,' declared a leading north Indian scholar. 'He should strive to be the first to do his teacher's bidding ... and should they differ his teacher's word was final.'[14]

When a student began to sit at the feet of teachers in a madrasa, he would already have learned some Arabic, and, if fortunate, would have memorized the Quran. In the madrasa the student would study books of Arabic grammar and syntax, Hadith, Quran commentary, rhetoric, and the law and jurisprudence. Occasionally there was a little arithmetic, which 'Ulama needed if they were to give a fatwa on inheritance; there might also be some works in medicine or Sufism. Theology, and its supporting subjects of logic and philosophy, were not acceptable to all. Madrasas in the Hanbali, Maliki, and Shafi'i traditions either banned it altogether or offered it a fitful toleration; only madrasas in the Hanafi and Shia legal traditions found it generally acceptable.

By 1500 great classical texts had become established in most of the fields of madrasa knowledge. There was, for instance, the *Hidaya*, the basic work of Hanafi law written by Shaykh Burhan al-Din al-Marghinani (d. 1196). There was also the widely accepted Quran commentary of al-Baydawi. With time classical works such as these gained in authority; few new books were introduced. 'Ulama tended to confine themselves to writing commentaries and supercommentaries on the classical version until it was all but overwhelmed by layers of annotation. Sometimes, as in the case of the commentaries of those two great rivals at the court of Timur, Sa'ad al-Din Taftazani (d. 1389) and Mir Sayyid Sharif Jurjani (d. 1413), such works helped to make classical texts highly accessible to madrasa students. Indeed, they remained in use down to the twentieth century.

The tendency of this educational system was conservative. This is understandable. 'Ulama knew that they had received the most precious favour from God in the Quran and the life of Muhammad; they also knew that up to the day of judgement there would be no further guidance for man. It was their foremost duty to strive to pass on this gift in as pure a form as possible alongside the skills to interpret it for the benefit of the community. The further they got from the time of the Prophet, the greater was the chance that part of God's precious favour would be corrupted or lost. There was no likelihood of Muslims discovering more of the truth, only a danger that they might preserve less of it. Rote learning played an important part in the process of preservation and transmission, although at the higher levels scholars were concerned to emphasize the importance of understanding. Much of the knowledge, too, was normative. Men learned how things ought to be.

There was much in the educational system, too, which was elitist and had tendencies towards the 'closed shop'. There seems to have been an enduring fear amongst the 'ulama of late medieval Cairo that a democratization of education might lead to a lowering of standards. They inveighed against those colleagues who made much of their fine clothes and huge turbans for fear that emphasis on finery rather than learning might enable the ignorant to parade themselves as scholars. They inveighed against their colleagues who were so unprofessional as to repeat themselves, fall asleep in class, or be just plain wrong; such poor performance made it difficult to distinguish between the merely lazy and the fundamentally unqualified.[15] 'Nevertheless, there were also 'Ulama who believed that all Muslims should have access to madrasa learning. 'To lock the door of a madrasa,' declared Ibn al-Hajj (d. 1336–7), 'is to shut out the masses and prevent them from hearing the [recitation of] knowledge ... and being blessed by it and its people [that is, the 'ulama].'[16] This was not a good thing. If the 'ulama kept knowledge from the common people, they would not benefit from it themselves.

It is evident, despite the fear of some 'ulama for their elite professional standing, that knowledge and the special privilege of transmitting it, did seep into the wider community. Sixteenth-century Timbuktu, for instance, was not only a great centre of learning but also one in which there is reason to believe there may have been universal male literacy; well over one hundred and fifty Quran schools served a population of roughly 70,000.[17] In fourteenth- and fifteenth-century Cairo the many madrasas were well integrated into the local community. Besides the students, madrasa functionaries—for instance, Quran readers, muezzins, and porters—as well as the common townsfolk took lessons. At no point, however, were the people so involved in the transmission of knowledge as in the public recitations of Hadith. On these occasions, which were manifestations of piety as well as of learning, ordinary Muslims were able to acquire ijazas and become transmitters of precious knowledge which reached back through the Prophet's companions to Muhammad himself.[18] Even women were able to play their part. al-Sakhawi (d. 1497) offers 1,075 biographies of women amongst over 11,000 in his collective biography of the notables of his time. Of these 400 had some form of religious education. Amongst the various fields of knowledge women were most prominent in Hadith, where they were able to rival men. Remarkable in the field was Aysha, daughter of Muhammad ibn al-Hadi of Damascus. Such was her learning that the noted scholar of Hadith, ibn Hajr al-Asqalani (1372–1449), listed her amongst his teachers with pride, and such was her reputation that a seventeenth-century historian rated her the most reliable transmitter of her time.[19]'

The 'ulama were not only an elite within their own society. Many formed part of an international elite. This was so because learning was a truly international affair in which much was shared across the Islamic lands. As one might expect many books tended to be shared within regions dominated by a particular school of law. So, for instance, the Maliki 'ulama of Timbuktu used many of the same books as those of Morocco and Egypt.[20] So, too, did the Hanafi 'ulama of the Ottoman Empire, and Central and South Asia, where the helpful texts of Taftazani and Jurjani were especially popular. Moreover, because of the greater openness to the rational sciences of the Hanafis and the Shias, there was a considerable commonality of texts in this field between the Shia 'ulama of the Safavid Empire and the Sunni 'Ulama of the Mughal Empire.[21] Then, of course, there were works used through the Sunni world regardless of law school. This was naturally the case with the six canonical collections of Hadiths, but so it was too with great works of synthesis such as al-Ghazzali's *Revival of the Religious Sciences*, which was used from Spain through to South East Asia,[22] or Ibn Suyuti's (d. 1505) Quran commentary, *Jalalain*, which was as popular in West Africa as it was in North India.[23]

A shared world of books, of course, meant a shared world of debate and reference. When, in 1637 'ulama fell out in the Sumatran sultanate of Atjeh over the appropriate attitude to adopt to the works of Ibn 'Arabi (d. 1240) echoes of the dispute reached Medina where one of the leading scholars of the day, Ibrahim al-Kurani, wrote a magisterial work to resolve the points at issue.[24] Notable in the seventeenth and eighteenth centuries was the export of knowledge and understanding in the rational sciences from Iran into India, and then the subsequent export of outstanding Indian scholarship in the field to Egypt and West Asia where it helped to generate a revival of studies in the field.[25]

'Ulama had wide-ranging connections throughout this world of shared knowledge. There were the connections of family within a region—the descendants of Ghulam Allah who, from at least the fifteenth century, spread throughout the Upper Nile valley,[26] or the Farangi Mahall family of Lucknow who, from the late seventeenth century spread throughout India.[27] There were the connections of families across regions, for instance, those of the Majlisi family which, from the seventeenth century, came to spread from the cities of Iraq and Iran through to Murshidabad in Bengal,[28] or those of the Aydarus family which expanded from south Arabia in the sixteenth century to the point in the eighteenth century when it had important branches throughout the Indian Ocean rim from the islands of South East Asia through India to East Africa.[29] No less important were the travels of the 'ulama and the connections between teachers and pupils which thus resulted. Indeed, 'ulama took very seriously the exhortation in Hadith that they should travel in pursuit of knowledge. Al-Ghazzali, for instance, studied in Tus, Jurjan, and Nishapur and travelled as a scholar to Baghdad, Mecca, Damascus, Egypt, and back to his native Tus. 'Ulama, as we might expect, travelled from Timbuktu to the great centres of learning in Egypt and West Asia but, equally, a noted scholar, al-Maghili of Tlemcen, thought it worth his while to travel to west Sudan. Great schools, such as Ibrahim al-Kurani's school of Hadith at

Medina, attracted pupils from all over Asia—from the Hijaz, the Fertile Crescent, Anatolia, India, and the Indonesian islands. No recorded life reveals more dramatically how much was shared through the Islamic world than that of the great traveller, Ibn Battuta (1304–69), who, between 1325 and 1354, journeyed its length and breadth—the equivalent of well over forty modern countries—worked as a qadi from time to time, lived well, and dangerously, and survived to dictate a humane and engaging account of his adventures.

The Sufis and the Transmission of Spiritual Knowledge

Sufis, or the 'friends of God' as they were known, were more ubiquitous than the 'ulama. The latter tended to flourish in cities and at those times when there was state power willing to support the law. Sufis, on the other hand, reached out to all levels of society and to all parts of the world where Muslims lived. The style and methods of the Sufis, moreover, were particularly well adapted to those areas, often on the frontiers of Islam, where kin and tribal organization were paramount.

From the tenth century groups of disciples had begun to gather round particular Sufi shaykhs in order to learn how to follow his (or, occasionally, her) particular *tariqa* or way of travelling towards direct experiential knowledge of God. Sometimes they came together in khanqahs, or Sufi hospices, in which they might live an ordered devotional life and which were often dedicated to charitable and missionary work. Whether part of a khanqah community or not all disciples performed the central ritual of their tariqa, which was their shaykh's *dhikr* or special way of remembering God. This might involve repeating the name of Allah to focus the mind away from earthly things, or using breath control techniques to intensify the concentration. Often there was a collective ritual in which adepts by means of chant, music, or dance sought ecstatic religious experience. Once a disciple had placed himself in the hands of a shaykh he had to obey him at all costs, even if it meant going against the shari'a; he was to be, as the saying went, 'like a corpse in the hands of the washer of the dead'.

Central to the transmission of mystical knowledge across time and space were the connections of shaykhs and disciples. Particularly important in this regard were the shaykh's *khalifa*s, or successors, gifted disciples, who were designated to pass on the shaykh's teaching and to make disciples of their own. They became part of their shaykh's *silsila*, or chain of transmission, which went back through him and his predecessors to the saint who had founded their mystical way. Often khalifas became saints themselves.

On being initiated into a mystical way the disciple would swear an oath of allegiance to his shaykh, receive from him a *khirqa* or cloak, and be told the special protective prayer—*hizb al-bahr*—of the founder of the way. The disciple would also receive a certificate which would show the chain of transmission of spiritual knowledge, starting with the Prophet, and moving down through a companion, usually 'Ali, and then through one or two of the great mystics of the early Abbasid period, down to the saint who founded his way, and then down to his shaykh. The newly initiated mystic would know, in the same way as a pupil who received an ijaza to transmit Hadith, that he had become a repository of precious knowledge that went back to the foundation of the Muslim community.

The focal point for the followers of a particular Sufi way was the shrine of the founding saint. More often than not this was managed by the saint's physical descendants whose functions may well have come to be more ceremonial than spiritual. Such men administered the fabric of the shrine, its Sufi community, its endowments and its charitable works. The shrine of the founder of a major Sufi order—say that of 'Abd al-Qadir al-Jilani (d. 1166) in Baghdad, whose chains of succession spread throughout much of the Islamic world—was a focus of international pilgrimage. Lesser shrines were the focus of regional and local cults. As in the case of the madrasa, the rectangular shrine, often surmounted by a dome and surrounded by a compound with a khanqah and cells in which disciples might stay, became a feature of Islamic architecture. The custom of visiting the shrines of saints, moreover, became a feature of Islamic devotional life. Some Muslims did so because they felt that the resting places of those who were close to God were propitious for prayer, others because they wished to beg the saint to intercede for them with God. Each year the shrine would hold a major rite, known as the *'urs*, or wedding; it celebrated the moment when the saint's soul became united with God. A major feature of the rituals on this day would often be the recollection of the stages, in some traditions in devotional songs, by which spiritual knowledge passed down from the Prophet to the saint.

From the thirteenth and fourteenth centuries Sufis began to be organized in orders which came to number in their hundreds. The differences between them stemmed in part from variations in their rituals and their ways of remembering God and in part from the extent to which they followed the shari'a or permitted deviations from it. Overall, they represented relatively loose affiliations, indeed, loose enough for Naqshbandi Sufis in one part of the world to follow practices which might be deeply disapproved of by Naqshbandis in another. Nevertheless, the connections of spiritual brotherhood across the world, which these loose affiliations offered, were key channels along which Islamic knowledge travelled and by means of which it might, when the need arose, be reshaped and revitalized.

Some orders achieved influence across the Islamic world. The Suhrawardiyya, for instance, who were notably careful in observing the shari'a and who looked back to the Baghdadi Sufis, Abu Najib al-Suhrawardi (d. 1168) and his nephew Shihab al-Din (d. 1234), spread their influence from West Asia to the east Indian province of Bengal. The Shadhiliyya, who found the roots of their tradition in the Spanish Sufi, Abu Madyan Shuayb (d. 1197), not only broadcast their message from Morocco through North Africa to West Asia but also inspired several modern revivalist movements, as well as becoming the favoured home of European and American recruits to Sufism. The Naqshbandiyya—who derive their name, although not their specific way, from Shaykh Baha al-Din Naqshband (d. 1389) whose mausoleum lies just outside Bukhara—expanded throughout most of Asia and from the eighteenth century were both the inspiration for the most vigorous movements of Islamic assertion and the channels along which they spread. The Qadiriyya, however, who were descended from the Baghdadi saint, 'Abd al-Qadir al-Jilani, came to be the most widespread order. In West Africa in recent centuries they too have been associated with movements of Islamic assertion.

The influence of many orders, while still of great importance, has been restricted to a particular region. In India, for instance, the most influential order was the Chishtiyya, who made a point of eschewing those with political power. India, however, was also host to many irregular orders, such as the Malamatis and the Qalandars, whose practices were influenced by indigenous customs and not bound by the shari'a. In West Asia the Rifaiyya were remarkable for their dhikr, which made a loud and harsh sound—hence, their sobriquet the 'Howling Dervishes', and their strange practices such as fire eating and biting the heads off live snakes. In Anatolia and the Ottoman

Empire, there were the Bektashiyya, the favoured order of the Janissaries, who made confessions to their shaykhs, observed a Christian-like ritual involving bread, wine, and cheese, and believed in a quasi-Trinity of God, Muhammad, and 'Ali. There were also the Mawlawiyya, who were inspired by the great mystical poet Jalal al-Din Rumi (d. 1273) and who, on account of their dhikr of a constantly turning dance, have come to be known in the West as the 'Whirling Dervishes'.

Alongside the consolidation of the Sufi orders there also developed a mystical understanding of enormous importance to the development of Islam. The author was Ibn 'Arabi, a Spanish Sufi educated in Seville. On a pilgrimage to Mecca he had a vision of the divine throne. In the vision he was told that he stood foremost amongst the saints. This inspired his masterwork, *The Meccan Revelations*, in which he developed his doctrine of the unity of being (*wahdat al-wujud*). God was transcendent. Yet, he argued, because all creation was a manifestation of God, it was identical with Him in essence. It followed that God was necessary for men to exist but, equally, man was necessary for God to be manifest. In expounding his doctrine Ibn 'Arabi turned frequently to the famous tradition which conveys a message from God but is not included in the Quran: 'I was a hidden treasure and wanted to be known, thus I created the world that I might be known.' Moreover, in expressing his vision of the relationship between the Divine Being and the material universe, he generated both a rich symbolic vocabulary and produced a masterly synthesis of Sufi, philosophic and neo-Platonic thought.

For centuries Ibn 'Arabi has been accused of pantheism by scholars, Muslims, and Christians alike. His works have been banned in parts of the Islamic world. Nevertheless, in recent years, Western scholars have come to accept that he always maintained God's transcendence and that his vision rested firmly on the Quran. What concerns us, however, is his impact on the subsequent development of Sufism and Muslim religious understanding.

It should be clear, first of all, that such was Ibn 'Arabi's achievement and authority that he set the agenda for Sufi discourse, which, from now on, focussed on his concept of the unity of being and on the problems of reconciling his vision of God's relationship to the material world with that of the Quran. Not least among the vehicles of his ideas was poetry. And this was as much the case for poetry in

Arabic or the African languages as it was for poetry in the high Persian tradition—that of a Rumi, a Hafiz, or a Jami—or for poetry in the regional languages of Asia—that of a Yunus Emre (d. 1321) in Anatolia, a Bullhe Shah (d. 1754) in the Indian Punjab, and a Shah 'Abd al-Latif (d. 1752) in Indian Sind. The outcome of such widespread absorption of the idea of the unity of being was to lessen the importance of observing the shari'a. If everything was God, it made it less important to strive to put into practice on earth His revelation. Ecstatic union with Him would be enough. But, if some might regard this as the downside of Ibn 'Arabi's impact on the development of Islamic history, they could not fail to see that it also had an upside. The greater tolerance and flexibility which Ibn 'Arabi's vision brought to Muslim approaches to non-Muslim traditions, whether he intended the outcome or not, helped Sufis throughout the world to build bridges between Islam and a myriad local religious traditions.

Sufis had a key role in transmitting the message of Islam into regions and into societies where 'ulama were unlikely to move with confidence or ease. Indeed, in areas of the wider Islamic world they were often the first bearers of the faith. We know relatively little of their role in the central Islamic lands. However, we know rather more of their achievement in North Africa, Anatolia, the Balkans, and Central and South Asia. Here they filtered into lands freshly conquered by Muslim armies or worked their way along international trade routes and prepared the ground for the consolidation of Islam. It is not possible to consider the firm establishment of Islam in Central Asia or in the Sind and Bengal regions of India without considering the role of Sufis. Further afield Sufis were also crucial. In some—although not all—parts of sub-Sarahan Africa the founding myths of Islam go back to the arrival of wandering holy men. In Java they refer to the work of nine saints; in Sumatra, to the arrival of a Sufi on a ship sent by the 'king of Mecca'.[30]

In transmitting their messages to non-Muslim societies, Sufis, bolstered by the apparently latitudinarian thought of Ibn 'Arabi, tended not to insist on a strict application of the shari'a. For one thing they did not have the power to do so; for another they were usually concerned to minimize conflict with local religious traditions. Their policies, in fact, were normally to seek points of contact and social roles in the host community. They shared their knowledge of religious experiences with men of other spiritual traditions. They operated as intermediaries and buffers between men and women and all the uncertainties of life beyond their control. By accommodating themselves to local needs and customs they gradually built a position from which they might draw their clients into an Islamic milieu and educate them in Islamic behaviour. In the process they insinuated their ideas into the very interstices of human lives, as indicated by the following verses created by a Sufi and intended for the women of India's Deccan to sing as they ground corn:

The *chakki's* [grindstone] handle resembles *alif*,
    which means Allah,
And the axle is Muhammad, and is fixed there.
In this way the truth-seeker sees the relationship
    Ya *bism Allah*, hu hu Allah.
We put grain in the chakki
To which our hands are witnesses.
The chakki of the body is in order
When you follow the *shari'at*.
    Ya bism *Allah*, hu hu Allah.

Trans. R. Eaton[31]

Sufis manned the frontline in the transmission of Islamic knowledge—both to the masses in long-conquered societies and to largely non-Muslim societies as a whole. On that frontline the shrines of the saints were the fortresses and outposts. Here Sufis tendered religious services to the 'natives' and in the process fostered manifold expressions of what has come to be known as 'popular Islam'. Thus, worship of trees, fish, or crocodiles might become associated with particular shrines and pre-Islamic cults relating to St George or Khwaja Khidr might be incorporated into local Muslim beliefs; shrines, and also mosques, were often built on former Christian or Hindu holy places. Thus, too, a range of superstitious practices might be tolerated, for instance, the lighting of candles, the sweeping of the tomb, or the tying of a piece of cloth to the shrine to remind the saint of a request. Relics there were aplenty. Most shrines had the relics of a saint, his cloak, rosary, or turban. One or two places, not necessarily the shrines of saints, might have relics of the Prophet, hairs from his beard, or casts of his footprint. At such points the practice of Islam tended to reflect more the beliefs and customs of the societies it embraced than the behaviour and attitude laid down in the shari'a.

That Sufis through much of the Islamic world should permit such practices could be a major source of tension with the 'ulama. The latter were bound to feel ill at ease when they witnessed the flouting of the shari'a. Some 'ulama of the Hanbali school of law refused to have anything to do with Sufis at all. Most notable amongst their number was Ahmad ibn Taymiyya of Damascus (d. 1328). When Ibn Battuta, who accepted most Sufi practices, heard him preach in 1326, he thought he had 'a kink in his brain'.[32] Soon afterwards, moreover, the Mamluk government seemed to agree and placed him in prison where he died of a broken heart. Nevertheless, from the seventeenth century onwards there was increasing sympathy for his uncompromising attitude to Sufism. And today he is regarded as embodying the spirit of the Muslim revival and his books are much reprinted. This said, the tension between the bearers of the two great shaping forces of Islam should not be overestimated. Many 'ulama were Sufis, many Sufis were deeply learned in the shari'a. It was widely felt that the best learned and holy men were those who had achieved a judicious balance of the two forms of knowledge.

No less a source of tension was that between the transmitters of the two great Islamic traditions of knowledge and the wielders of political power. The tension was expressed in part in the conflicting attitudes of different groups of Sufis and 'ulama towards princes. 'My room has two doors,' declared the great Chishti saint, Nizam al-Din Awliya, whose order laid especial emphasis on avoiding princes; 'If the sultan comes through one door, I will leave by the other.'[33] Yet there were Sufi orders, like the Suhrawardiyya and the Naqshbandiyya, which had a particular interest, for some of their history at least, in political power. Moreover, 'ulama have always tended to support political order, however much they may have disapproved of individual princes, because such order was necessary to administer the shari'a.

On occasion, the tension could be expressed in the actual breakdown of relationships between the transmitters and the princes. It was such a breakdown which led the Mughal emperor, Jahangir, to throw the Naqshbandi shaykh, Ahmad Sirhindi (1564–1624), into gaol after he had crowed over the death of the emperor's father, Akbar, whom he described as 'one of the tyrants of the age' who had 'tortured many 'ulama' because of their strict compliance with the shari'a and their unflinching obedience to the prophets'.[34] It was such a breakdown, too, that led the leading scholar of late-seventeenth century Iran, Muhammad Baqir Majlisi (1627–98), to have tens of thousands of wine bottles in the Shah's cellars publicly smashed.[35] But, ultimately, the two sides had a considerable degree of interdependence; Muslim princes often needed the legitimation of Sufi and 'ulama support no less than the transmitters needed the support of state power for their knowledge.

'Ulama, Sufis, their Islam-wide Connections and Revival

When in the seventeenth and eighteenth centuries Muslim power began to decline, tensions between the transmitters of knowledge and the wielders of political power came to be exacerbated. Scholars and mystics responded by re-assessing the knowledge appropriate to their societies. There was a return to first principles, the Quran, and Hadith, and increasing scepticism of the value of the rational sciences, which by the nineteenth century extended to much of the scholastic inheritance of the Middle Ages. There was also growing criticism of the activities at Sufi shrines—in particular, saint worship and anything that suggested that saints or the Prophet might intercede for men with God. Alongside this, as might be expected, Ibn 'Arabi's Sufi vision came increasingly to be questioned, although his vocabulary retained a powerful hold over all discourse; the arguments of Ahmad Sirhindi—who had countered Ibn 'Arabi's doctrine of the 'unity of being' with one of 'unity of witness', replacing the concept that 'all was God' with one that believed 'all was from God'—became more widely accepted. Associated with the process were scholars who had always restricted their sources of authority to the Quran and Hadith, not least among them the adherents of the Hanbali school of law, who had always resisted both Sufism and the rational sciences. Of particular influence were the works of Ibn Taymiyya. Among those influenced was the extreme example of this new position, Muhammad ibn 'Abd al-Wahhab, the Arabian reformer whose name became a metaphor for Islamic puritanism. These new emphases in the repertoire of Islamic knowledge were of great importance. They meant a shift from an Islam which was integrationist to one which tended to emphasize the increasingly exclusive. They also meant a shift from an Islam which was 'other worldly' to one which was increasingly concerned to put God's guidance into practice on earth.[36]

This new emphasis in knowledge and on action was conveyed through much of the Islamic world by Sufis. This might seem odd as the new emphasis attacked many Sufi practices and, in its extreme manifestation, Sufism itself. Sufis, however, responded creatively to the reforming challenge; they absorbed the emphasis on the Quran and Hadiths as authorities within their Sufi framework, reduced the significance of ecstatic practices in their rites, and reviewed the role of metaphysical tendencies in their beliefs. A notable feature of this reformed Sufism was a new attention to the life of the Prophet, manifest in growing numbers of ceremonies celebrating his birthday and of biographies of his life. Some, in emphasizing how they followed the path of the Prophet, gave themselves the title *Tariqa Muhammadiyya*.[37] Not all Sufis were swept into these new forms of thought and behaviour. Nevertheless, the overall outcome was a sufi revival in which old orders were revitalized and new ones founded.

This new Sufi spirit was carried through much of Asia by the Naqshbandiyya who inspired notable movements in Indonesia, China, Central Asia, and the Caucasus. Networks of Naqshbandi scholars, moreover, played important roles in much of India and the Middle East. The new Sufi spirit was carried through much of Africa by orders flowing directly or indirectly from the Khalwatiyya, who had much influence in Egypt, in particular, amongst the 'ulama of Cairo's al-Azhar. There were, for instance, the Tijaniyya, whose influence spread to the Maghrib, and the Nilotic and central Sudan; the Sammaniyya, whose influence also spread to the Nilotic Sudan, Eritrea, and Ethiopia; the Sanusiyya, who spread from their headquarters in the Libyan desert through much of the Sahara, and the Sahiliyya, who became the dominant force in Somalia. Not infrequently these and other Sufi movements raised calls for jihad. On occasion such jihads led to the successful founding of Islamic states as in the case of the Sultanate of Sokoto, which was established in the early-nineteenth century by 'Uthman dan Fodio in northern Nigeria, or as in the Mahdist state, which was established in the late-nineteenth century by Muhammad Ahmad in the Nilotic Sudan.[38]

Recent scholarship has revealed many of the connections of 'ulama and Sufis which helped to underpin this Islam-wide movement of revival and reform. The role of leading scholars of Hadith in Medina such as Ibrahim al-Kurani and Muhammad Hayya al-Sindhi, has been noted. Among their pupils were many who figured in the eighteenth-century revival: 'Abd al-Rauf al-Sinkili (1617–90) of Sumatra, Shah Wali Allah of Delhi, Mustafa al-Bakri (d. 1749) of Cairo, Muhammad ibn 'Abd al-Wahhab, Shaykh Muhammad Samman (1717–95) and at one remove 'Uthman dan Fodio. The way in which the pupil–teacher connections of the Mizjaji family of the Yemen might overlap with those of the Medinan teachers of Hadith has been explored; it reveals that they include several of the figures above as well as Muhammad Murtada al-Zabidi (d. 1791), an Indian pupil of Shah Wali Allah who became a great figure in late-eighteenth century Cairo. Many revivalist scholars were also members of the Naqshbandi order. It is possible, for instance, to demonstrate that Ma Ming Hsin (d. 1781), who spread the 'New Sect' teaching amongst the Chinese Naqshbandiyya from 1781, had studied under a member of the Mizjaji family no less than it is possible to show how Mawlana Khalid Baghdadi (1776–1827), after studying under the successors of Ahmad Sirhindi in Delhi, stimulated Naqshbandi activity throughout Syria, Iraq, Kurdistan, Anatolia, and the Balkans, some of which continues down to the present. Probably at no previous time in Islamic history were the connections of 'ulama and Sufis across the world so many or so vigorous as they were in the eighteenth century. Nevertheless, their interactions were complex. We are well advised to be cautious when ascribing meaning to these connections and to be aware of the importance of local circumstances in stimulating developments. This said, the movement of ideas, and also of mood, along the connections of 'ulama and Sufis does illustrate the very real way in which these connections were the arteries and veins of the Islamic world along which the lifeblood of knowledge and fresh vitality flowed.[39]

RESPONSES TO THE CHALLENGE OF THE WEST AND WESTERN LEARNING SINCE 1800

The success of the West and the expansion of its sway over much of the Muslim world in the modern era transformed the context in which Islamic knowledge existed. Now there was the questioning and subversive presence of Western knowledge which year by year became more accessible and competed for a place in Muslim minds. Thus, European scientific achievement and the secular philosophies of the Enlightenment came to challenge belief in God and the ideas that He created the world, that He revealed Himself to man, and that through following His revelation man might gain salvation. Such knowledge also came to challenge much of the vast store of learning which Muslims had cherished down the centuries for the support of revelation and for the service of the community.

However, not only did Western knowledge become steadily more widely available in the Muslim world, it also came to have the support of the state: Islamic knowledge came to be uncoupled from power. To a greater extent this happened as a consequence of colonial rule. The British, the French, the Dutch, and the Russians developed the structures of the modern state in their empires and made it the means both to provide Western systems of education and to replace much of the shari'a with Western law codes. To a lesser extent the growth of state support for Western knowledge also came as a consequence of resistance to the possibility of colonial rule. Thus, the *Tanzimat* reformers of the Ottoman Empire in the nineteenth century or the Pahlavis of Iran in the twentieth strove to make their states strong enough to keep the foreigner out. The independence of Muslim states from the mid-twentieth century, moreover, made little difference. The process of entrenching Western knowledge in Muslim societies continued, their states usually adopting an ethnic or secular identity rather than an Islamic one. Admittedly, some token state support might be available for Islamic learning, but if it existed in any force it did so because society wished it.

To this challenging environment for Islamic knowledge should be added economic, social, and technological changes sparked off by the West. The penetration of Western trade and capital into Muslim societies stimulated large commodity trades and, as Muslims learned to buy Western finished goods, the destruction of local industries. Associated social changes saw the emergence of new elites to manage the new economic and political structures—technocrats, bureaucrats, bankers, intellectuals, industrial workers—all people who belonged to an existence outside the old urban communitarian world of the artisan workshop, the bazaar trader, the caravanserai and the quarter, which had long supported the work of 'ulama and Sufis. Associated technological changes saw the introduction of steam and electrical power, the telegraph, telephone, wireless, and television communications.

In this rapidly changing context, Muslims found that they must review the body of Islamic knowledge inherited from the past and see how they might make it relevant to the present. They discovered that the application of technology to the transmission of Islamic knowledge transformed access to it. They came to note, moreover, the increasing marginalization of 'ulama and Sufis from the activities of Muslim societies as a whole. It should be understood that in each society responses to the new context differed both according to the nature of Western imperialism as well as to the particular balance of social, economic, and political forces within it.

Responses to Western Knowledge

There were three broad strands of response: reformism, which re-evaluated but did not change, in essence, Islamic knowledge inherited from the past; modernism, which aimed to reconstruct that knowledge in the light of Western knowledge and the new economic and political realities; and Islamism, which was no less respectful of the new economic and political realities but wished to make them, and Western knowledge, subordinate to their utopian understanding of revelation. Within and beyond these broad strands, it must always be remembered, there were many competing voices.

Reformism carried the spirit and the principles of the eighteenth-century movement of revival and reform into the period of European domination. In the process it developed a form of 'Protestant Islam'. Without worldly power to create an Islamic society, responsibility for doing so was transferred to the individual Muslim conscience. Reformists knew, and it was often a heavy burden of knowledge, that they must will God's purpose on earth. The dissemination of knowledge of God's word and of the life of His messenger were at the heart of the reformist effort. Typical vehicles were the Deoband movement, founded in north India in 1867, which, by its centenary, claimed to have established 8,934 schools; or the Muhammadiyya of Indonesia, founded in 1912, which, by 1938, had founded 1,700 schools; or the Nurcular, who learned their message of personal discipline and moral responsibility from the writings of the Turkish Naqshbandi shaykh, Said Bediuzzaman Nursi (1873–1960). Reformists attacked the presence of logic and philosophy in the madrasa curriculum; the historic victories of al-Ashari and al-Ghazzali were no longer seen to be enough. Only amongst the Shias, and particularly in Iran, did the flame of Islamized Hellenic learning continue to burn brightly. Reformists, too, in their concern to shape the human conscience, continued the assault on Ibn 'Arabi's doctrine of the unity of being, on Sufi practices which suggested intercession for man with God, and on the host of local customs which intermingled with Islamic practice. To compensate for the loss of the emotional and spiritual dimensions of the faith which went with successful attacks on Sufism, yet more attention was paid to the life of the Prophet. His biography came in the twentieth century to be a prolific genre of devotional literature. Thus the reformists allowed only a sanitized proportion of the inheritance of Islamic knowledge from the Middle Ages to continue into the present. At the same time, they paid varying attention to what the new learning from Europe had to offer; the Deobandis would have nothing to do with it while the Muhammadiya found a place for modern science. Reformism was typically the response of the 'ulama more often than not supported by traditional mercantile elites.[40] Modernism was concerned to face up to the reality of Western knowledge and Western dominance. At the least modernists wanted Muslims to command Western science and technology, which they perceived to be the source of Western strength. At the most they wished to review Islamic knowledge as a whole, including its founding pillars, the Quran and Hadith, in the light of Western learning. Leading figures amongst the modernists were Sayyid Ahmad Khan of India, Namik Kemal of Turkey (1840–88), Shaykh Muhammad 'Abduh of Egypt, and Jamal al-Din al-Afghani. Not all these men had the same approach to Western and Islamic knowledge, but they knew that the way of the 'Ulama was that of certain decline. In the nineteenth and early twentieth centuries many modernists were attracted to pan-Islamic responses to the West, but, after the First World War brought the final onset of Western domination, they came to focus their attention increasingly on the nation-state. For the Indian modernist, Muhammad Iqbal, this was a nation-state to be built on Islamic principles, a Pakistan, but for the vast majority modernism became secularism and the future was envisaged in secular states, the Turkey of Ataturk or the Iran of Reza Shah, in which religion was a private affair. Modernists, therefore, had little place for the medieval inheritance of Islamic knowledge. In the schools they established, and even more in the educational systems fostered by secular Muslim states, Western languages and some of the Western humanities came to be studied alongside Western science and technology. Modernism was typically the response of Muslim ruling elites. For many, these elites, in seeking Western material strength, ran the grave risk of throwing out the Islamic baby with the bathwater.[41]

It is not surprising that reformism and modernism attracted criticism. 'To make speeches through which hate may be inflamed, to compose writings through which hearts may be wounded', complained the modernist, Altaf Husayn Hali, of the ways of the reforming 'ulama, 'this is the way of our theologians.'[42] 'Give up your literature,' announced the Indian satirical poet, Akbar Allahabadi (1846–1921), to the products of secular education, 'forget your history, break all your ties with shaykh and mosque—it could not matter less. Life's short. Best not worry overmuch. Eat English bread, and push your pen, and swell with happiness.'[43]

It was partly because neither reformism nor modernism produced satisfactory answers to the problem of what was appropriate knowledge for a Muslim society that Islamist answers came to be proposed. Islamists started from the principle that all human life and, therefore, all knowledge, must be subordinated to the guidance sent by God to man. As one Islamist said of the essence of that guidance; the shari'a offers a complete scheme of life 'where nothing is superfluous and nothing wanting'.[44] Notable leaders of Islamism have been Sayyid Abul A'la Mawdudi of Pakistan, Hasan al-Banna and Sayyid Qutb (1906–66) of Egypt, 'Ali Shari'ati and Ayat Allah Khomeini of Iran; notable organizations are the Jama'ati Islami of South Asia and the Muslim Brotherhood of the Arab world. Islamists have little difficulty with most of Western knowledge, although Darwinian evolution which contradicts the Quranic story of the creation, literally understood, has been a sticking point. They are alarmed, however, by the failure of the reformists to face up to the meaning of Western knowledge and are horrified by the way in which the modernists and the secular nationalists seem to have capitulated to it in its entirety. The dominance of the views of the latter, whom they characterize as suffering from 'Westoxification' or 'Occidentosis', over the educational systems of most Muslim states, is the great object of their attention. They have striven to Islamize the scholarly disciplines of the West; thus has been born, for instance, Islamic economics and Islamic sociology. Islamists represent, by and large, new elites who are competing for power. They have no desire at all to bring back into service the Islamic learning of the Middle Ages but rather aim to place Western learning in an Islamic mould and direct it to Islamic ends.

Over the past two hundred years the proper relationship of revealed knowledge to all the knowledge available in Muslim societies has been hotly disputed. If the trend for much of the period has been for Western learning to increasingly command centre stage, recent years have seen this position challenged by new champions of Islam.

This said, there has been one clear loser in this age of revolution: it is the mystical understanding of the faith. Reformists have subjected much of Sufism to withering fire. Modernists and secularists have fostered the wintry climate of post-Enlightenment knowledge. For Islamists, Sufis are an irrelevance. The new Muslim understandings of the past two centuries, and the new Muslim mastery of self and the environment, have rendered the world a less enchanted place; the realm in which the spiritual knowledge of Islam could flourish has shrivelled.

The Revolution in the Availability of Knowledge and its Consequences

Side by side with the uncoupling of Islamic knowledge from power in many societies, there has been a revolution in its transmission. This change began with the adoption of print during the nineteenth century. In some societies—for instance, Egypt—the process was tentative; leading scholars saw printing as a danger to religion and social order. In others—particularly where, as in India, Muslims were acutely aware of the threat to their faith from colonial rule—it was more positive. Reformist 'ulama seized upon print technology as a key means to spread their understanding of Islamic knowledge widely through society so that it might be defended both against the corruptions of local cults and the seductions of Western learning. By the end of the nineteenth century in north India over seven hundred newspapers and magazines in Urdu, the main Muslim language, had been started; four to five hundred books were being published every year, many of them on religious matters.

The adoption of print was just the first stage in the democratization of Islamic knowledge. Further stages came with the translation of the Quran, Hadith and other major Islamic texts into many of the languages of the Muslim peoples of the world. For the first time many Muslims have come to be able to read these texts in languages they understand. This development has been accompanied by the adoption of other forms of media technology and mass communication, radio, television, film, tape cassettes; it is now, for instance, well known that the telephone and the tape cassette were crucial to bringing the voice of Ayat Allah Khomeini to the Iranian people in the months immediately preceding the Iranian revolution. These new technologies of communication have opened up new forums of interaction and made new forms of contact among Muslims possible: they are the arenas in which the great disputes over knowledge take place; they are the vehicles through which new Islamic understandings, and especially those of the 'ulama, have been taken to the margins of the Islamic world; they are the means through which official versions of Islam are broadcast to the peoples of those states where Islam has once more come to be aligned with power.[45]

The rapid spread of print culture was to bring about a decline in the oral transmission of Islamic texts and a weakening of that person to person transmission of the central messages of the faith which reached back to the time of the Prophet. The process of change was already far advanced in Mecca in the 1880s. 'All students now bring to lecture printed copies of the text which is being treated,' observed the Dutch orientalist, Snouck Hurgronje, on his visit there in 1884–5, 'which circumstance has entirely changed the mode of instruction.'[46] Arguably, changes of religious understanding accompanied the penetration of the printed text into the believer's world; processes, barely perceptible in the era of manuscripts, were greatly intensified. Always remembering that these processes were also influenced by other aspects of the modern transformation of Muslim societies, we should note: the emergence of a new historical consciousness—Muslims came less to see their faith as one in constant decline since the time of the Prophet and more as one which might achieve greater stages of perfection on earth; the growth of an understanding of Islam as a system of beliefs and practices to which a commitment might or might not be made rather than part of the natural warp and weft of life; the tendency to see the Quran less as a ritual object and more as the subject of contemplative study; and the change in the image of the Prophet from Perfect Man to perfect person on which different groups of Muslims might impose their ideal vision. This said, oral transmission of religious guidance continues to have greater meaning for the Muslim than it does for the Christian. In all Muslim societies the memorization and recitation of the Quran remains a highly prized feat. Moreover, it is unlikely that print will ever have quite the impact it has had on the West; already the electronic media, which help to sustain some forms of oral transmission, have made rapid headway. It is worth noting, too, the approach of the Tablighi Jama'at, or 'Preaching Society', which was founded in India in the 1920s and is the most widely followed organization in the Muslim world.

This society insists that its missionaries learn texts by heart and communicate them person to person.[47]

The coming of print, and the process of translation, brought much greater freedom of access to religious knowledge. Muslims could now study with relative ease the great religious texts outside the framework of the madrasa and the authoritative interpretations of the 'ulama. Moreover, they increasingly did so from a basic education in Western learning. Not surprisingly this new freedom of access led to the new freedom of interpretation represented by the modernist and Islamist strands, as well as a host of sectarian positions. But, if print and translation helped to liberate Muslims from the monopoly of the 'ulama, it also helped to dissipate religious authority. Now, there were many new voices claiming to speak for Islam, voices which drew force from their acceptance of the realities of Western strengths in knowledge and power. The authority embedded in interpretations of texts handed down over hundreds of years has come to be much reduced.

Inevitably, the changing position of Islamic knowledge in Muslim societies, as well as its changing nature, has led to shifts in the position of the classical transmitters of learning. The position of Sufis declined with that of Sufism. Increasingly they are to be seen less as the cherishers of the glories of spiritual understanding at the heart of the Islamic tradition than as so many confidence tricksters fleecing the ignorant and deluding the gullible. Their devotional practices, moreover, have come to be less for the service of God—as in the case of the whirling dance of the Mawlawiyya of Turkey or the mystical songs (*qawwali*) of the Sufis of South Asia—than for that of the television programme or the tourist office. Only where Sufis were able to provide some substantial function for modern Muslim societies have they remained overtly, or covertly, at the centre of affairs as, for instance, in the case of the Muridiyya who have maintained a leading position in Senegal through their dominance of the peanut business, or in those of the Naqshbandiyya and the Qadiriyya in the Caucasus who kept the flame of Islam alight under Soviet rule.

'Ulama, too, were pushed towards the margins of society as their functions as teachers and lawyers were supplanted by the secular systems of the modern state. Their decline, however, does not equal that of the Sufis. For many Muslims in the twentieth century the 'ulama have remained symbols of a Muslim backwardness from which they wished to escape. Nevertheless, they still command residual respect in many societies. They may be treated as state employees, as in Turkey, or given places of honour on state occasions—the rector of al-Azhar was sitting next to Egypt's president, Anwar Sadat, at the official parade where he was shot in 1981. Nevertheless, it would be pointless to deny that for much of the twentieth century the 'ulama have been moving steadily down the paths of marginalization trodden by the Christian clergy of the Western world since the Enlightenment. But, as for Sufis, there have been specific circumstances where the 'ulama have been able to remain at the centre of affairs. This is notably the case of the Shia 'ulama in the Lebanon, in Iraq, and in Iran, where they have been the most effective representatives of their communities against oppression.

As 'ulama have come to be pushed to one side, their role as transmitters and interpreters of Islam to their societies has come to be challenged, if not supplanted, by scholars from outside the madrasa world. Many Muslim thinkers whose writings are prime sources of Islamic understanding for their societies are of this ilk: Iqbal and Mawdudi of Pakistan and al-Banna and Sayyid Qutb of Egypt fit this category, as does Khurshid Ahmad, the economist from Pakistan; Hasan Turabi, the lawyer from the Sudan; Rashid Ghannoushi, the teacher from Tunisia; and Mehdi Bazargan, the engineer from Iran. The personnel who carry forward the missionary and educational programmes of the notable Islamic organizations of the latter part of the twentieth century, for instance, the worldwide Tablighi Jama'at, the populist Muslim Brotherhood, the elitist Jama'ati Islami, the Islamic Tendency movement of Tunisia, or the Islamic Salvation Front of Algeria, are almost entirely lay educated. They have, moreover, in common with many other Islamic organizations born in recent years, strong support amongst student organizations, which they often dominate.

Since 1800 Western learning has confronted the Islamic world with very much the same problem that Hellenistic learning presented it from the ninth to the eleventh centuries. There is, however, one substantial difference. Al-Ashari and al-Ghazzali met the rational and philosophical challenges of Hellenistic learning from a position of Muslim dominance; modern Muslims have confronted the challenges of Western science from a position of weakness. In spite of this they have shown considerable creativity in their responses. They have striven to move Islamic civilization forward in the world while keeping it rooted in revelation. As the 'ulama and Sufis have seemed to fail to meet the challenge, new types of scholars have emerged from the community to provide answers. All these scholars, whether old or new, have interacted with each other across the Islamic world, so Muhammad 'Abduh was influenced by Jamal al-Din al-Afghani and Sayyid Qutb by Mawdudi. As yet, however, there has been no widely accepted consensus which would enable Muslims once more to regard the pursuit of learning as an act of worship. The issue of the proper relationship of revealed and earthly knowledge remains acute. What is important is that it remains the subject of vigorous debate.

NOTES

1 Jonathan Berkey, *The Transmission of Knowledge in Medieval Cairo: A Social History of Islamic Education* (Princeton, New Jersey, 1992), p. 3.
2 Maulana Muhammad Ali, *The Holy Qur'an*, sixth edition, (Lahore, 1973), p. 3.
3 Ira Lapidus, *A History of Islamic Societies* (Cambridge, 1988), pp. 192–208.
4 H.A.R. Gibb, *Islam*, second impression, (London, 1975), p. 90.
5 W. Montgomery Watt, *The Faith and Practice of al-Ghazali* (Oxford, 2000), pp. 58–9.
6 Lapidus, *A History of Islamic Societies*, p. 237.
7 Berkey, *Transmission of Knowledge*, pp. 182–3.
8 H.A.R. Gibb and Harold Bowen, *Islamic Society and the West: A Study of the Impact of Western Civilization on Moslem Culture in the Near East*, vol. 1, Pt II, (London, 1957), p. 109.
9 Toby Falk (ed.), *Treasures of Islam* (Syracuse, N.J., 1985), p. 144.
10 Ibn Khaldun, *The Muqadimmah: An Introduction to History*, translated by Franz Rosenthal, edited by N.J. Dawood (Princeton, 1967), p. 421.
11 An ijaza given by al-Mutarriz to his pupil, Abu Ja'far al-Tabari, the great historian and commentator on the Quran. J. Pedersen, *The Arabic Book*, translated by G. French, edited by R. Hillenbrand (Princeton, 1984), p. 36.
12 Ibn Khaldun, *The Muqadimmah: An Introduction to History*, p. 431.
13 F.E. Von Grunebaum and T.M. Abel, translated and edited, *Az Zarnuji: Ta'lim al-Mutallim at-Taàlum: Instruction of the Student: the Method of Learning* (New York, 1947), p. 32.

14 Statement by Mawlana 'Abd al-Bari, the leading scholar in the early twentieth century of the Farangi Mahall family of Lucknow (India), Altaf al-Rahamn Qidwai, *Qiyam-i Nizam-i Ta'lim* (Lucknow, 1924), p. 86.
15 Berkey, *Transmission of Knowledge*, pp. 182–8.
16 Ibid., p. 202.
17 Elias N. Saad, *Social History of Timbuktu: the Role of Muslim Scholara and Notables 1400–1900* (Cambridge, 1983), p. 23.
18 Berkey, *Transmission of Knowledge*, pp. 200–1.
19 Ibid., pp. 175–9.
20 Saad, *Timbuktu*, pp. 74–81.
21 Francis Robinson, 'Ottomans–Safavids–Mughals: Shared Knowledge and Connective Systems', *Journal of Islamic Studies*, vol. 8, part 2, (1997), pp. 151–84.
22 Peter Riddell, *Islam and the Malay–Indonesian World: Transmission and Response* (London, 2001), p. 185; Ibn Khaldun, *Muqadimmah*, pp. 352, 358, and 360.
23 Saad, *Timbuktu*, p. 76; Robinson, 'Ottomans–Safavids–Mughals', p. 182.
24 A.H. Johns, 'Islam in the Malay World: An Explanatory Survey with some References to Quranic Exegesis', in R. Israeli and A.H. Johns (eds), *Islam in Asia: Volume II, South and Southeast Asia* (Jerusalem and Boulder, 1984), pp. 115–61, and Riddell, *Islam and the Malay–Indonesian World*, pp. 125–32.
25 Robinson, 'Ottomans–Safavids–Mughals', p. 163.
26 P.M. Holt and M.W. Daly, *A History of the Sudan from the Coming of Islam to the Present Day*, third edition, (London, 1979), p. 33.
27 Francis Robinson, *The 'Ulama of Farangi Mahall and Islamic Culture in South Asia* (London, 2001), pp. 103–20.
28 J.R.I. Cole, 'Imami Shi'ism from Iran to north India, 1722–1856: State, Society and Clerical Ideology in Awadh' (Ph.D. dissertation, University of California, Los Angeles, 1984), pp. 90–101.
29 John Voll, *Islam: Continuity and Change in the Modern World* (Jerusalem and Boulder, 1982), pp. 72–3.
30 Nehemia Levtzion (ed.), *Conversion to Islam* (New York, 1979); R.M. Eaton, *Sufis of Bijapur 1300–1700: Social Roles of Sufis in Medieval India* (Princeton, 1978); and R.M. Eaton, *The Rise of Islam and the Bengal Frontier 1204–1760* (Berkeley, 1993).
31 Eaton, *Sufis of Bijapur*, p. 163.
32 H.A.R. Gibb, *The Travels of Ibn Battuta A.D. 1325*, I, (New Delhi, 1993), pp. 135–7.
33 Khaliq Ahmad Nizami, *The Life and Times of Shaikh Nizamuddin Auliya* (Delhi, 1991), p. 105.
34 Yohanan Friedmann, *Shaykh Ahmad Sirhindi: An Outline of his Thought and a Study of his Image in the Eyes of History* (Montreal, 1971), p. 33.

35 Roger Savory, *Iran under the Safavids* (Cambridge, 1980), p. 241.
36 For an overview of this shift, see Francis Robinson, 'Other-Worldly and This-Worldly Islam and the Islamic Revival' in this volume.
37 Annemarie Schimmel, *And Muhammad is His Messenger: The Veneration of the Prophet in Islamic Piety* (Chapel Hill, 1985), p. 216–38.
38 Francis Robinson, *Atlas of the Islamic World since 1500* (Oxford, 1982), pp. 118–29.
39 Ibid., and Nehemia Levtzion and John O. Voll (eds), *Eighteenth-Century Renewal and Reform in Islam* (New York, 1987).
40 Barbara Metcalf, *Islamic Revival in British India: Deoband, 1860–1920* (Princeton, 1982); Serif Mardin, *Religion and Social Change in Modern Turkey: The Case of Bediuzzamn Said Nursi* (New York, 1989); M.C. Ricklefs, *A History of Modern Indonesia since c. 1200*, third edition (Houndmills, Basingstoke, 2001), pp. 215–16 ff., but note that what is referred to as 'modernism' in the Indonesian context would normally be regarded as 'reform' elsewhere; Mitsuo Nakamura, *The Crescent Arises over the Banyan Tree* (Gadjah Mada, 1983).
41 Lapidus, *A History of Islamic Societies*, pp. 557–71.
42 Christopher Shackel and Javed Majeed, *Hali's Musaddas: The Flow and Ebb of Islam* (Delhi, 1997), p. 169.
43 Ralph Russell and Khurshidul Islam, 'The Satirical Verse of Akbar Ilahabadi (1846–1921)', *Modern Asian Studies*, vol. 8, I, p. 29.
44 S.A.A. Maududi, *The Islamic Law and Constitution,* ninth edition (Lahore, 1986), p. 52.
45 For the impact of print and its wide ramifications see 'Islam and the Impact of Print in South Asia' in Francis Robinson, *Islam and Muslim History in South Asia* (Delhi, 2000), pp. 60–104.
46 C. Snouck Hurgronje and J.H. Monahan trans., *Mekka in the Latter Part of the 19th Century* (Leiden, 1970), p. 192.
47 Yoginder Sikand, *The Origins and Development of the Tablighi-Jama'at (1920–2000): A Cross-country Comparative Survey* (Hyderabad, 2002).

'Ulama of South Asia from 1800 to the mid-Twentieth Century

'Ulama, the Islamic intelligentsia, have always played the key role in sustaining the Islamic quality of Muslim societies. As scholars they have reflected upon the significance of the central messages of Islam for their time, as teachers they have transmitted these messages and the skills to make them socially useful to the coming generations, and as muftis, and in other ways, they have interpreted these messages, whether as law or as general moral guidance, to society at large. It is the argument of this article that their role in the colonial period in South Asia—which we shall interpret as being from 1803, when Shah 'Abd al-'Aziz of Delhi declared India *dar al-harb*, to the early 1950s, when they succeeded in incorporating the 'Islamic clauses' in the Pakistani constitution—was of great importance in the history of South Asia.

At first sight this may seem unlikely. British rule removed 'ulama from their privileged position in state and society: their revenue-free grants were resumed; their learning was phased out as a requirement for state service; their shari'a law was superseded by Anglo-Muhammadan law in whose workings they had no place; their Unani Tibb—their Galenic system of medicine—was largely displaced by biomedicine, as had happened in western Europe. Increasingly, in the nineteenth and early twentieth centuries, Indo-Muslim society reorientated itself so as to be able to take knowledge and inspiration from outside Islamic civilization, from outside the realm of the 'ulama. For much of the period the 'ulama themselves despaired of the situation in which they found themselves. Some, like the leading pir, Hajji Imdad Allah (1817–99) fled India to settle permanently in the Hijaz. Others, like the young 'ulama of Farangi Mahall in the early twentieth century, knew they should be taking the lead in Muslim affairs but were powerfully aware both of their limitations and of the obstacles they faced.[1] Muslim modernists had no doubt that the 'ulama had failed Islamic civilization; this was the message of Altaf Husayn Hali's elegy on the rise and fall of Islam, when he considered contemporary theologians:

To make speeches through which hate may be inflamed, to compose writings through which hearts may be wounded,
To despise God's sinful creatures, to brand their Muslim brothers infidels
This is the way of our theologians, this is the method of our guides.
...
The commands of the Holy Law were so agreeable that Jews and Christians were filled with love for them
The entire Quran is witness to their mildness. The Prophet himself proclaimed 'Religion is easy.'
But here they have made them so difficult that believers have come to consider them a burden.[2]

While for much of their rule the British treated them as an irrelevance, whose learning and attitudes belonged to the 'Middle Ages', in the early years they did figure amongst the leaders of resistance and reappear in the First World War with the emergence of pan-Islamist politics. For the most part, they were seen to be relicts from an earlier age, fit only to be overwhelmed by the tide of Western progress.

The real story, however, is very different, particularly when viewed from the longer perspective provided by the twenty-first century. It is our concern to demonstrate that in the period 1800–1950 Indian 'ulama, as they addressed the meaning both of the loss of power and of colonial rule, showed great creativity in developing new ideas and in fashioning new institutional frameworks. The reforming 'ulama—those of Deoband, the Ahl-i Hadith, and their associates—in large part through their assault on intercessionary Sufism, developed a major new strand in Islamic understanding which reduced the emphasis of believers on other-worldly concerns, replacing them with a stronger focus on this-worldly concerns. At the same time, bereft of state support, these reformers created the institutions and practices which enabled them to root themselves instead in society. In the colonial context, which exposed Indian Muslims to Western civilization supported by the greatest political and economic power of the day, the 'ulama, in general, emerged as the defenders of Islamic civilization. Not only were they the standard bearers of Islamic law and Islamic forms of behaviour, they were also the promoters of Arabic and, to a lesser extent, Persian and Urdu, as well as much of the Islamic culture which could only be reached through these languages. In the process, they became, for the first time, an identifiable group, an institution, in India. Most certainly, they came to organize themselves as a group—or at least those with a reforming bent did—and, thus, in the last decades of British rule, while not able seriously to influence the struggle for independence, they were able to be an increasingly effective pressure group in legal matters. Once independence came, in India, they continued the role they had performed under the British, which was as patrollers of community boundaries and promoters of community interests—as they saw them. In Pakistan, however, they were able to help drive forward an Islamization of state and society, which would have been beyond the wildest dreams of their nineteenth-century forebears, and to achieve a position which gave them not just weight within their own state but a geo-political significance in the region.

At the heart of the role played by 'ulama under colonial rule was the fact that in the absence of effective lay Muslim leadership they felt, as never before, responsible for Muslim society. This was evident from the dar al-harb fatwa of Shah 'Abd al-'Aziz, in which he admitted that the Muslims had no authority and that from Delhi to Calcutta the Christians were in complete control, as Barbara Metcalf has admirably deduced. The Shah's stance on dar al-harb 'had clear implications for 'ulama like himself':

> If the state no longer provided a hierarchy of courts and personnel to administer Muslim law, then only the 'ulama could fill what was evidently a troublesome legal void. They could not, to be sure, compel compliance to the Law, but they could offer direction to the faithful on such issues as civil behaviour, trade, inheritance, and family relations, as well as more narrowly religious matters. They could be the center for an ideology that gave meaning to the life of observant Muslims. [3]

It was not surprising, therefore, that nine decades later, on the foundation of the Nadwat al-'Ulama, Shibli Nu'mani should make large claims for its role in the Muslim community. 'A very large part of the national life,' he insisted in his address to the Nadwa in 1894, 'is in the 'ulama's right of ownership (*huqq-i-malkiyat*) ... and they alone have or can have absolute sway (*mutliq-ul-inan*) over it.' All 'ulama should join the Nadwa which 'would then be so powerful that the entire Muslim community will be governed by its injunctions.'[4] By this time, of course, Shibli was asserting the role of the 'ulama not just against the colonial rulers but also against those creatures of colonial rule, the western-educated Muslims, whom he had come to know so well during his teaching stint at Aligarh. His vision was echoed by the various organizations of ‘ulama which came to be formed in the subsequent decades, and not least in the aims and objectives of the Jami‘yat al-‘Ulama-yi Hind, founded in 1919, clause 5 of which, for instance, declared its aim ‘to organise the Muslim community and launch a programme for its moral and social reform.’[5] Colonial rule both greatly expanded the vision which ‘ulama had for their role in society, and made it urgent that for the very survival of Islam they should play it. It stimulated a period of great creativity.

THE NINETEENTH-CENTURY ERA OF CREATIVITY AMONGST THE ‘ULAMA

This period of great creativity began with the utopian movement of Sayyid Ahmad of Rai Bareli. The Sayyid was a doer who understood, as Islamic reformers and Islamists were to discover in the following decades, that the salvation of Islam required action on earth. He opposed all forms of *shirk,* threats to the unity of God and asserted *tawhid,* His oneness. In 1818 he launched his campaign with attacks on intecessionary Sufism and the influences of Shia and Hindu customs on Sunni Muslim practice. In taking this line, he was reflecting in part the ideas of Shaykh Ahmad Sirhindi as reflected through the Wali Allah family and the Naqshbandiyya–Mujaddidiyya; in part, perhaps, those of Muhammad ibn ‘Abd al-Wahhab which had been dominant in the Hijaz for some years; and in large part his feeling—and one which was becoming increasingly common as the power of the West spread through the Muslim world from the eighteenth century onwards—that if Muslims had lost power it was because they had failed as Muslims. Ultimately Barelwi's campaign led to him and his followers fleeing British-controlled territory for the tribal lands of the North West Frontier where, from 1826, he was able to establish his community and to wage jihad, according to the Sunna, from Muslim-controlled territory on the Sikhs, who were thought to be interfering with Muslim life. The jihad led to the death of Barelwi and many of his followers at the hands of the Sikhs in 1830, although elements of his community persisted on the Frontier down to the First World War. The *Mansab-i Imamat* of Muhammad Isma‘il, grandson of Shah Wali Allah who was martyred with Barelwi in 1830, indicates clearly where

Barelwi and his followers were coming from. The tyrannical and irresponsible government of kings, including the Mughals, had led to oppression, immorality, and the flouting of the shari'a; Muslim power had declined and the Muslim respectable classes had suffered. What was needed was to establish not *siyasat-i amirana* (government by the rulers for their own advantage) but *siyasat-i imami* (government by the imam for the benefit of the people).[6]

Barelwi's jihad was the great iconic event of the early nineteenth century movement of reform. He left many supporters in Delhi and in the qasbahs of northern India. During the Sayyid's lifetime and after his death these followers brought a frisson of excitement and sense of challenge as they engaged in debate on behalf of reform wherever they were, be it Karamat 'Ali of Jawnpur in Bengal or Muhammad 'Ali of Rampur in Madras. In the 1860s their network of connections remained substantial, as the Patna and Ambala trials revealed. Similar movements took place in Bengal and in Malabar where the message of Islamic reform mingled with the resistance of Muslim peasants to oppression; in both cases leaders brought reforming ideas from the Arabian peninsular. This said, the great importance of Barelwi's movement was the driving desire it represented to find a way of being good Muslims, of fashioning an unsullied Muslim community in a world dominated by British power. [7]

This remained the concern of the next source of new ideas, the Deobandis.[8] The founders of this enormously important movement were in direct descent from the Wali Allah tradition and strongly influenced by Barelwi and his legacy. The failure of the Mutiny uprising of 1857–8, in which jihad had been a strand, and the brutal assertion of British power which followed it, made it clear that resistance had to be of a different kind. The basic doctrinal position of the Deobandis was similar to that of Sayyid Ahmad Barelwi. In the reformist tradition they closely adhered to the shari'a and emphasized the study of the revealed as opposed to the rational sciences. They avoided all forms of behaviour which might suggest the influence of the Shia, the Hindu, or the British world, and tolerated only a restrained Sufi practice with not the slightest hint of intercession. Their important innovation was to institutionalize this position through education. Muhammad Qasim Nanawtwi, who with Rashid Ahmad Gangohi founded the madrasa at Deoband in 1867, envisaged a great network of madrasas which would revitalize Islamic society.[9] Their especial concern was to sustain the widespread development of scriptural religion. Knowledge of God's word and of God's law and, therefore, of how to behave as a Muslim, was the first step in preserving Muslim society under colonial rule. The second was, in the absence of state power, to support God's guidance, to bring the individual human conscience into play as the sanction of the law. Thus a 'protestant' or 'willed' form of Islam came to be developed. Arguably amongst its clearest expressions is the *Bihishti Zewar* of Ashraf 'Ali Thanawi (1864–1943), for much of his life an eminent scholar and spiritual leader amongst the Deobandis.[10] The very purpose of the book, which was to bring knowledge of reforming principles to Muslim women, underscores the role of scriptural knowledge in the movement as a whole. Its content—the fearsome depictions of the Day of Judgement, for instance, or the advice on how to train the reflective Muslim self on a daily basis—illustrates how the individual human conscience and worries about salvation were being brought into play to bolster the Muslim community. We know, moreover, from the lives of those involved how heavily the responsibility weighed on them: Rashid Ahmad Gangohi, when reading the Quran alone at night would weep and shake and appear terrified at those chapters dealing with God's wrath.[11] Husayn Ahmad Madani, Principal of Deoband in the mid-twentieth century, often wept at the thought of his shortcomings.[12] The achievement of the Deobandis was to drive the process of jihad inwards, and to make knowledge of God's word and the individual human conscience the twin pillars on which Muslim society would survive under colonial rule.

There were some for whom the Deobandi position on reform did not go nearly far enough. These were the Ahl-i Hadith. They came from the same background of revival and reform as the Deobandis but were more extreme in their religious ideas, more intense in their commitment to them, more elitest in their social background, and more consciously sectarian in their behaviour. Like the Deobandis they were committed to purifying Muslim behaviour of all practices that were not in accordance with the shari'a. But in doing so they went much further. Whereas the Deobandis, adopting a position of *taqlid*, accepted the achievement of Islamic scholarship as it had been handed down to them, the Ahl-i Hadith rejected this scholarship and made direct use of the Quran and Hadith. They argued that the best way to be a true Muslim was to go back to these textual sources and use the jurisprudential techniques sanctioned by Hadith, as the founders of the great law schools had done themselves (that is, qiyas, argument by analogy, and ijma, the consensus of the 'ulama on a point of law), but they did so with very small scope for interpretation. Their approach meant immense personal responsibility for the believer; they went much further than the Deobandis in condemning the practices of Sufism, indeed, they regarded Sufism itself as a threat to true religious understanding. They were puritanical, adopting a literal and narrowly conceived understanding of the faith, but resolute in pursuing its requirements. Not surprisingly, theirs was the Indo-Islamic understanding which found most in common with the Wahhabis of Arabia. They lived in dread of judgement: the writings of Nawab Siddiq Hasan Khan of Bhopal, a leading member of the group, were imbued, for instance, with what Barbara Metcalf terms 'a pervasive pessimism, a fear of the end of the world'. They were resolute in fulfilling the requirements of the faith. Feeling embattled, they dressed differently, prayed differently, and, frequently in the late nineteenth century, found themselves at loggerheads with other Muslims.

As is not unusual with such intense ideological sects, the Ahl-i Hadith split. Towards the end of the nineteenth century a group emerged under Mawlana 'Abd Allah Chakralawi in Lahore which accused them of placing excessive reliance on Hadith. Chakralawi asserted that only the Quran could be used as contemporary guidance, Hadith merely referring to the human condition of the Prophet. The group, of course, came to be called the Ahl-i Quran. They were even more exclusive than the Ahl-i Hadith, not bothering to raise the question whether they could pray with others, but establishing their own prayer ritual with a series of distinctive practices including kneeling only on one knee. They prayed only in their own mosques, eliminated funeral and 'Id prayers, and prayers and alms offered for the sake of the dead. Their dispute with the Ahl-i Hadith was so bitter that eventually the government had to intervene to protect Chakralawi's life.[13]

The Ahl-i Hadith and the Ahl-i Quran were puritanical sects whose positions, by and large, were extreme versions of those of Deoband. They opposed almost all Sufi practice, placed an enormous emphasis on personal responsibility in religion, and attacked all those who were not as they were. Particularly significant was the intellectual influence of the Ahl-i Hadith. 'Not only did they stimulate the movement of the Barelwi 'ulama,' declares Barbara Metcalf, 'but they positively influenced the Ahl-i Quran, the Ahmadiyyah, and the modernists, all of whose jurisprudential styles derived from theirs.'[14] Arguably, too, the Islamism of Mawdudi owed much to their role in undermining the authority of taqlid. Indeed, the Aligarh modernism of Sayyid Ahmad Khan and the Islamism of Sayyid Abul A'la Mawdudi, the two strands of Indo-Islamic thought which were to have the greatest influence, both on the first decades of Pakistan and on the Muslim world in general, were both made possible by the intellectual achievements of the Ahl-i Hadith. Without their crucial break with past scholarship, and their concomitant fresh examination of the sources of Islam, the creative responses their traditions brought to the challenges presented to Islam by modernity would not have been possible.

Not all creativity flowed from the reforming tradition of the Wali Allah and his followers; there were also new ideas and emphases rooted in pre-reformed Islamic understandings. Indeed, these ideas developed in the nineteenth century in the process of resisting the movement of revival and reform. They came to crystallize in the late nineteenth century around the scholar and polymath, Ahmad Rada Khan of Bareilly (1856–1921). He used his Hanafi legal scholarship to justify Islam as it had been handed down—a custom-laden Islam which was closely tied to the Sufi world of the shrines where believers sought the help of saints to intercede for them with God. If the Deobandis wanted to conserve Islam as they found it in the Hanafi law books, the Barelwis wished to conserve it as they found it in nineteenth-century India. In the manner of the time they proselytized their position, regarding themselves as the true Sunnis—*Ahl-i Sunnat wa Jama'at*. Their relations with the Deobandis and the Ahl-i Hadith were marked by continuous polemic and, on occasion, rioting.

The new emphasis Ahmad Rada Khan brought to Muslim piety was to elevate yet higher than before the position of the Prophet. He stressed the Sufi concept of the light of Muhammad (*Nur-i Muhammadi*), which was derived from God's own light and which had existed like the Word in Christian theology from the beginning of creation. It had played a part in the very process of creation; it was omnipresent; it meant that the Prophet though human was also more than human. He had, moreover, unique knowledge of the unknown (*'ilm al-ghayb*) and, therefore, could be called upon to intercede for man with God. Along similar lines Ahmad Rada Khan asserted that saints could see with the light of God (*Nur-i Khuda*) and, therefore, their intercession could be called upon, and not just at their shrines but anywhere.

In keeping with such teaching the Barelwi leader paid great respect to the Prophet in his religious practice, paying particular attention to *mawlud* ceremonies (celebrations of the Prophet's birth) and to the time of *qiyam* during mawlud when it was believed that the Prophet was actually present. He also observed the 'urs celebrations of many Sufi saints, noting in particular the eleventh day of each month in commemoration of 'Abd al-Qadir Gilani, the most revered of all saints. And, of course, he justified a wide range of customary practices from bestowing amulets to drawing blood on Sundays. In his comfortable endorsement of the Islam of the shrines, Ahmad Rada Khan had broad popular support, finding especial favour, at the beginning at least, from the illiterate and the villager as opposed to the educated of the qasbah and town. He offered an answer to providing guidance to a rural Muslim world at a time when Muslims did not control the state.[15]

The traditions of the 'ulama of Farangi Mahall of Lucknow represented another pre-reformist school of thought which was largely resistant to the tides of reformism. The Farangi Mahallis claimed: first, that they had consolidated the rationalist traditions of Persianate Islamic scholarship on Indian soil; second, that building on these, they had created the Dars-i Nizami curriculum, a mode of teaching which raised comprehension above rote learning and which they spread through much of India; and, third, that they were great defenders of Ibn 'Arabi's 'unity of being' in their Sufi understanding as against the 'unity of witness' favoured by the reformers.[16]

Substantially, the Farangi Mahallis failed to produce an answer to the broad challenges presented by Western civilization and the loss of power. Indeed, they were not able to spread much beyond their madrasa their relatively innovative combination of Western subjects—English, philosophy, history, and science—studied with traditional Islamic subjects which they adopted in the early twentieth century. There was, however, one area in which they were creative, in a way which was deeply rooted in the Islamic tradition and which enabled large numbers of 'ulama in India and beyond to make regular incremental adjustments to change. This was the achievement of the jurisprudential technique of the great mufti, 'Abd al-Hayy (d. 1886–7).

Concerned that his colleagues uncritically accepted the legal decisions of scholars of the past, he refused to accept the established principle in the art of fatwa writing that he must be guided by the decisions of those muftis who had gone before him, that is, if something had been forbidden in the past then it must also be forbidden in the present. Previous decisions for him were limited to the time and place in which they were given. 'Abd al-Hayy went back to first principles adopting the formula that 'everything in shari'a is permitted, which is not prohibited'. So if Mulla 'Ali Qari had said in the past that women should not be taught to read, those decisions did not necessarily apply to nineteenth-century India. So, too, if Muslims worried about adopting Christian inventions such as electric fans in mosques, they need not; such innovations were not expressly forbidden. 'Abd al-Hayy's jurisprudential approach was an important enabling force making it possible for devout Muslims to meet, in good conscience, the demands of change, which is doubtless one of the reasons why his collection of fatawa has remained in print in South and West Asia to the present day.[17]

Context was enormously important to the development of new ideas. Towards the end of the nineteenth century, 'ulama increasingly came to realize the full impact of British power in the world. They saw how the education, law, culture, and beliefs for which they stood were being marginalized by the British; they were witnessing the emergence of a new race of Muslims, fashioned inwardly as well as outwardly by Western civilization; they heard regularly how British power encroached upon Muslim lands in West Asia; they were presented almost daily with reminders of the small account in which they were held by the ruling power. Thus the Nadwat al-'Ulama, founded in 1894 at the annual convocation of the Fayz-i Am Madrasa at Kanpur, set out to assert the importance of the Islamic tradition, the respect it should be given by the colonial power, and the pride in it which Muslims should cherish. Being an organization of learned men, moreover, respect for the Islamic tradition also implied respect to the central transmitters and interpreters of that tradition—the 'ulama. The Nadwa aimed to shape a positive view of the history and beliefs of Muslims and in doing so took a pan-Islamic approach. Among some of its earliest champions there was the idea that English should acquire a position in the Islamic curriculum and that there might be some serious engagement with Western thought. It was, however, never a source of new religious understanding and practice. Indeed, in time, it became, for the most part, a vehicle for reformist views. It was important for its role as a champion of Islam, its history, languages, and leading figures, a role which it has played to the present day from its handsome building by the Gumti in Lucknow.[18]

Context was also crucial to the formation of a particular piece of creativity in the late nineteenth- and early twentieth-century Punjab, which came to form the Ahmadiyya. The province was a cauldron of change. Here Christian missionaries flourished as nowhere else in northern India. Here, too, there was powerful Hindu revivalist activity directed first against Christians and then against Muslims. All, moreover, took place against the background of rapid economic and social change stimulated by the development of the canal colonies. The founder was Mirza Ghulam Ahmad (1859–1908) from an old Mughal service family of Qadiyan in East Punjab, who developed a passionate vocation as champion of Islamic orthodoxy against Christian missionary polemic and Arya Samaj Hinduism. As he strove to better rival missionaries he came to see himself as 'at least' a symbolic representative of Krishna and Jesus, as well as an Islamic Mahdi. In 1889 he proclaimed himself a minor prophet, with a messianic vision to rejuvenate Islam—'the expected messenger of the latter days'. Of course, bitter opposition followed Ghulam Ahmad's denial of the finality of Muhammad's prophecy and eventually he and his followers seceded from Sunni Islam and prayed in their own mosques.

In fact, Ghulam Ahmad and his followers differed from Sunni Muslims on only three major points: in his insistence as the spiritual prophet of the age that the only appropriate jihad was not war but missionary work; in his claim to be the resurrected Jesus, in defiance of the New Testament and the Quran; and in his denial of the finality of Muhammad's prophethood, which he explained by making a distinction between primary and secondary, or Mahdistian, prophethood. He was in a similar relationship to Muhammad, so he put it, as Jesus was to Moses.

Ghulam Ahmad certainly had some creative inspiration in coping with the challenges of the Punjab under British rule. He stole the clothes of rival religions and arrogated to himself a prophetic authority, which brought him and his successors great respect from their followers, whilst making them amongst the most hated and persecuted of those claiming to be Muslims. The Ahmadiyya, who are amongst the most highly educated of Muslims and vigorous proselytizers of Islam in over one hundred and thirty countries, are an extraordinary witness to what passionate believers will do to defend under dire threat their deepest convictions.[19]

Many important developments were embraced by these movements, but by far the most important stems from the Wali Allah tradition from the movement of the Mujahidin through to the Ahl-i Quran. At its heart was the attack on all ideas of intercession at Sufi shrines, and on all those ideas supported by the *wujudi* thought of Ibn 'Arabi which undermined tawhid, the oneness of God. This process involved placing the responsibility for following the straight path, for fashioning an Islamic society, and ultimately achieving salvation on the individual human conscience. To consciences well primed by awesome descriptions of the Day of Judgement, this was a terrible responsibility, for some a cause for daily fear and stress. In these new circumstances there was a great responsibility to spread knowledge and understanding of scripture. Hence the remarkable involvement of reformers in the new world of print, in publishing religious texts and translating them into the vernacular. There was no less a responsibility on the individual to learn how to think and behave as a Muslim, a responsibility which came to be laid on women as much as on men. In sum it meant the transfer of the prime focus of Muslim piety from the next world to this. It was only through a life of pious endeavour on earth that man could hope to achieve salvation. This knowledge that men must act on earth as Muslims—knowledge made more urgent and acute by the vast decline of Muslim power and the great challenges and constraints placed upon Muslim societies by Western dominance—has released vast amounts of energy amongst Muslims in India, and throughout the Islamic world, from the nineteenth century to the present. It is at the very heart of the Islamic revival.

Construction of a Base in Indian Society by the 'Ulama

As well as being creative in developing new Islamic understandings, 'ulama were also creative in sending down roots into Indo-Muslim society as never before. A major catalyst for this was, of course, the removal of revenue-free grants which had supported them under the Mughals and their successors. This said, for many, particularly those of the reforming tendency, there was great merit in being free of any dependence on or even association with the colonial state. The outcome was that 'ulama either had to have a private income or pursue a trade, or they had to provide a service which society at large was to value enough to be willing to subsidize. Addressing the last requirement with success and, in consequence, gaining a major constituency in Indo-Muslim society, was the key to a major strengthening of the position of the 'ulama over the period.

'Ulama in the Wali Allah reforming tradition took the lead in this process. They sought to broaden their constituency, as well as sustain Islamic society under colonial rule, by making knowledge of how to behave as a Muslim as widely available as possible. One way of doing so was by cutting down their writing in Arabic and Persian, which automatically confined their readership to a small elite mainly of 'ulama, and writing instead in Urdu and other Indian languages. Significantly, the process was exemplified in the early period of reform by Muhammad Isma'il, son of Shah 'Abd al-'Aziz and follower of Sayyid Ahmad Barelwi, in the two key works he composed—the *Taqwiyat al-Iman* and the *Sirat al-Mustaqim.* In these works—as he declared in his introduction—he made the fundamentals of the reforming message and the supporting quotations from the Quran and Hadith, more 'comprehensible to all who read or heard' them by writing 'in simple and easy Urdu'.[20] This emphasis on writing in languages, and in a style, which all would understand, was a powerful feature of writing amongst the 'ulama as they set out to cultivate their new public. They began to write growing numbers of guides to faith and ritual. They embraced popular idiom, writing lives of the saints, but much more importantly writing lives of the Prophet, as the advance of the reforming message meant that the example of the Prophet, the perfect model, increasingly came to displace the examples of the saints who might be associated with dubious local custom.[21] And, of course, as the growth of the newspaper press created a new forum in which Islam could be advanced, they became journalists.

The natural concomitant of writing *ab initio* in Indian languages was to make the classical works of Islam available in them too. This had been an early feature of the Wali Allah tradition—Shah Wali Allah himself translating the Quran into Persian, while one son, Shah Rafi al-Din, produced a literal translation into Urdu and another son, Shah 'Abd al-Qadir, produced an idiomatic one. As the nineteenth century went on, more translations were produced, spurred by rivalry between

Muslim groups. At least a dozen different translations were published, a process which continues to the present day.[22] These were joined by translations of the great collections of Hadith, collections of fatawa, the writings of al-Ghazali and Ibn Khaldun, many of the texts taught in madrasas, and much of the supporting corpus of medieval Islamic scholarship.

A key aid in building a constituency for the ‘ulama was the printing press. Muslims had known about the printing press since the late fifteenth century but had resisted its introduction in large part, so it is assumed, because the widespread, and unsupervised, availability of books undermined oral person to person transmission of knowledge, which was regarded as crucial to achieving the transmission of true meaning. In the early nineteenth century ‘ulama took the lead in adopting print, in the form of the lithographic printing press, because they had come to see it less as a potential source of weakness than as a key means to strengthening their position, and that of their community, under colonial rule. Faced by the threats both of Western secular knowledge supported by colonial power and by Christian missionaries, who attacked Islam on the streets and in the press, ‘ulama quickly came to use print to broadcast knowledge of Islam as widely as possible.[23] Just as Muhammad Isma‘il's *Taqwiyat al-Iman* and *Sirat al-Mustaqim* were written in accessible Urdu so also were they amongst the earliest works to be printed. Throughout the ninteenth century ‘ulama took the lead in producing printed editions of original works and translations of the great works of the Islamic tradition into Urdu and other Indian languages. In the second half of the century the Director of Public Instruction of the North West Provinces and Oudh commented on the unusual vigour of Muslim publishing, seeing it as a sign of Muslim revival. Christian missionary rivals, too, had no doubt that Muslims had learned the power of the press.[24]

Central to the rooting of reformist ‘ulama in Indo-Muslim society was the foundation of madrasas which were to train young men in the precepts of reformist Islam. The Dar al-‘Ulum at Deoband, founded in 1867 by bearers of the Wali Allah tradition, was, and remains, the classical example of this development. It taught the *dars-i nizami* curriculum developed by Farangi Mahall but with a particular emphasis on *manqulat*, the transmitted subjects, Quran, and Hadith, rather than *ma‘qulat*, the rational subjects of logic and philosophy. Its pupils were to be beacons of reformed Islam rather than given the skills which might make them government servants. Some vocational subjects were taught to enable former students, if necessary, to live independently of government patronage. Unlike other madrasas of the time, it was bureaucratically organized on the model of government and mission schools, with classrooms, professional staff, examinations, prizes, and annual reports on performance; it had an institutional existence that was greater than any individual or family involved in it. Most important of all, it was totally dependent on popular subscriptions; it would only survive so long as Indian Muslims believed it performed a useful function.[25]

There is no doubt that the madrasa at Deoband had an extraordinary impact in spreading the influence of reformist 'ulama. For a start, by its centenary in 1967 it had taught 7,417 students. But, no less importantly, it had affiliated (or established and affiliated), a vast number of schools. By 1900 these numbered over thirty and reached from Peshawar to Chittagong and Madras. By 1967 they numbered an incredible 8,934. We should note how the reformists shifted the prime function of madrasa education from the training of government servants to teaching those who would spread knowledge of Islamic norms and beliefs. 'By shaping standards of piety and belief for substantial numbers of Muslims,' Barbara Metcalf concludes, 'these 'ulama wielded an influence significant and persistent.'[26]

The wielding of influence did not end with the affiliation of madrasas, it was also the outcome of specific attempts of Deobandi scholars to spread their message in Indo-Muslim society by all possible means. They issued fatawa in support of their reformist beliefs. By the 1890s the burden of issuing fatawa to questions from all over India, which they aimed to do on the day the questions were received, had become so great that they founded a fatwa office (*dar al-ifta*). Every fatwa came to be registered and by Deoband's centenary they numbered 2,69,215. The existence of these fatawa gave Muslims, sensitive to colonial involvement in God's law, an opportunity to avoid the Anglo-Muhammadan law as administered through the British courts. More generally, they offered guidance and comfort for those concerned to be in good conscience as Muslims under colonial rule. Barbara Metcalf describes them as the most important 'single means' for spreading reformist beliefs.[27]

Deoband also spread its influence in the world of women. Appropriately, for a movement in which the printed word played a central role in the dissemination of ideas, the means of reaching out to women was a book—Ashraf 'Ali Thanawi's *Bihishti Zewar* (Heavenly Ornaments),[28] which was published at the beginning of the twentieth century, first in sections, and then brought together as the book which would form part of the trousseau of many Muslim women of South Asia. The purpose of *Bihishti Zewar* was nothing less than revolutionary. Whereas, traditionally the home, the women's world, was the place where custom tended to reign, where there was practice and behaviour which might undermine belief. Now, and not least because the Islamic purity of the public space—the man's world, was compromised by the presence of a Christian colonial power, women were to be enabled to acquire a full knowledge of the *shari'a* so that they could drive custom from the home and ensure that the highest standards of Islamic conformity might reign. Women were to become key exemplars and key transmitters of the reforming message. Indeed, as Ashraf 'Ali said, they were to become a learned person, a mawlwi.[29] But, in doing so, as Ashraf 'Ali was also careful to say, they must rely on the advice of 'ulama who were more learned than they were.[30] No attempt has been made as yet to assess the achievement of *Bihishti Zewar* in extending reforming influence to the other half of Indo-Muslim society. Certainly, it reached beyond the circles of those who could read, being designed to be read out aloud and to be orally transmitted.[31] It has, moreover, been published in many Urdu editions as well as in translations in the regional languages of South Asia, and in English. It is said to be the most widely read book after the Quran in the major languages of South Asia.[32]

From the 1920s scholars in the Deoband tradition developed specific systems for reaching beyond the ranks of the educated to the illiterate. They were concerned to take the essence of their scriptural reforming message to the Muslim masses and to engage significant numbers not of 'ulama but of ordinary Muslims in the process. The creator of this missionary movement was Mawlana Muhammad Ilyas (1883–1944), a student of Deoband. He had noted and admired the work done by Ashraf 'Ali Thanawi in resisting the Shuddhi movement which strove to bring the Meos of Mewat, south of Delhi, within the Hindu fold.[33] In 1926, he began his missionary work among the Meos, experimenting with techniques which led to the launch of the Tablighi Jama'at or 'Preaching Society' in 1934. The objectives of the society were: *all* Muslims should be involved in its work; they should focus on preparing themselves to achieve its ends; learning, teaching, serving, and promoting religion should be a way of life; and they should as a religious obligation move temporarily from their native place in seeking these ends.[34] In pursuing these objectives Ilyas declared that God had provided a six-point programme in the method of the Prophet:

1. the profession of faith;
2. the ritually prescribed prayer;
3. knowledge and remembrance of God;
4. respect for all Muslims;
5. sincere intentions; and
6. the giving of time.[35]

Missionary work itself involved direct action. Muslims, irrespective of their educational or economic background, were to come together in groups, usually of about ten persons. They were to spend their days on the mission living collectively in Muslim brotherhood. Bearing themselves gravely, sporting beards, wearing a Muslim cap and kurta-pyjama, and carrying a blanket and travel bag, they were to go from town to town and village to village. Once in a place they were to go from house to house, bringing everyone to the local mosque where they were to be given the Tablighi Jama'at's simplified reforming message. In addition to the emphasis on mass participation, notable features of the Society's mode of work were that members were forbidden to mix politics with their preaching, they were forbidden to engage in religious controversy, and they were required to fund their mission from their own pockets.[36]

This mass participation reform movement has grown to become, according to some, the most widely followed Muslim movement in the world. Its annual meetings in India, Pakistan, Bangladesh, the UK, and the USA attract vast audiences and much media attention. The annual meeting at Raiwind in Pakistan is said to be the second largest Muslim congregation in the world after the Hajj. It is not unreasonable to suggest that the Tablighi Jama'at has achieved a major extension of the Deobandi tradition of reform into Indo-Muslim society. In achieving this it has, in principle, substantially extended the potential area of influence of reforming 'ulama.[37]

Groups of 'ulama outside the reforming tradition adopted some of the techniques developed by the reformers to reach into Indian society. The ‘ulama of Farangi Mahall published newspapers and issued fatawa.[38] The Barelwis founded madrasas funded by popular subscription, published newspapers and journals, made the fatawa of their leader, Ahmad Rada Khan, widely available, went on preaching tours, and engaged in public debate.[39] The Ahmadiyya were notably vigorous in their missionary work. But nothing which these other groups of ‘ulama did in any way matched the range of activity of the reforming ‘ulama, their breadth and depth of appeal, or their overall impact on Indo-Muslim society.

THE ‘ULAMA AS GUARDIANS OF COMMUNITY BEHAVIOUR AND AS COMMUNITY CHAMPIONS

As ‘ulama developed their constituencies in Indo-Muslim society, and increasingly tried to embrace it as a whole, they became more and more concerned to police the boundaries of behaviour. This is evident in the biographical and malfuzat literature in which particular sayings or actions on the part of a scholar might be underscored as representing forms of behaviour to follow. But it is also evident in the fatawa literature which, for the most part, was the outcome of a two-way process initiated by a Muslim asking a question of a mufti. Much of the fatawa literature deals with *‘aqaid* and *‘ibadat*, faith and ritual. Through it, it is possible to see the particular distinctions between Deobandi, Barelwi, Farangi Mahalli, Ahmadi, and so on being reinforced, but also the forms of behaviour which Muslims wanted to get absolutely right. Thus Deobandis gave decisions which aimed to remove local customs, for instance, the idea that a saint might be able to intercede for a man with God. Barelwis, on the other hand, strongly supported the intercessionary power of saints.[40] Equally, Deobandis strongly disapproved of mawlud ceremonies on the birthday of the Prophet and in particular the highly controversial practice of qiyam, that is, of standing during the point in the ceremony when it was believed that the Prophet was present.[41] Farangi Mahallis, on the other hand, were strong supporters of mawlud, which they treated as another opportunity to get key messages about correct Islamic behaviour over to their followers.[42] The Barelwis attacked the Nadwat al-‘Ulama on the grounds that it undermined the purity of the Sunni *mazhab* by including the followers of Sayyid Ahmad Khan, Ahl-i Hadith, and Shias among its number.[43] The Ahl-i Hadith insisted on raising their hands during prayer and saying ‘Amin’ out loud, actions which were guaranteed to infuriate those amongst the congregation who were not of their number.[44] Taking an overview of the sectarian spectrum in the 1920s, Mawlana 'Abd al-Bari of Farangi Mahall reckoned that most arguments took place with the Shia and the Ahmadiyya, and that amongst those who followed the central traditions of Islam, that is the Ahl-i Sunnat, the Wahhabiyya, the followers of Muhammad ibn 'Abd al-Wahhab of Najd (d. 1787), were 'the furthest from the truth'.[45] By emphasizing their differences through fatawa, pamphlet wars, debates, and even, on occasion, through resort to the decision of the British courts, different groups of 'ulama marked out their ground and reached out to their supporters.[46]

Just as the 'ulama were concerned about distinguishing themselves from other groups of Muslims, they were, at the same time, no less concerned about distinguishing themselves from other religions. For the Deobandis this was closely bound up with their campaign against custom. Custom was, after all, Hindu practice which was being sustained within a Muslim society. Especially symbolic of their war against custom was their insistence on widow remarriage; no single requirement marked them out more clearly from the Hindu world. Rashid Ahmad Gangohi, so Metcalf tells us, began from the 1880s to define the boundaries more sharply. He issued fatawa 'that discouraged social and business intercourse with Hindus, forbad attendance at Arya Samaj lectures (unless one were skilled in debate), and deemed illegitimate the appearance of being Hindu, whether in dress, hair style, or the use of brass instead of copper vessels.'[47] To judge by the fatawa literature for the Barelwis and the Farangi Mahallis drawing distinctions between them and Hindus was less of an issue than for the Deobandis. For instance, just a few issues crop up in the fatawa of 'Abd al-Hayy of Farangi Mahall. Whereas a Muslim most certainly could not accept a Hindu donation towards building a mosque, he could eat food prepared by a Hindu, wear clothes washed by a Hindu dhobi, and abstain from cow sacrifice, provided it was to avoid a riot and not because he thought the beast was holy.[48] If these Farangi Mahallis and Barelwis refer infrequently to boundaries with Hindus, it is not because these were areas that they were not interested in policing but because in their Islamic understanding, in which they were not concerned to wipe out custom, the boundaries were better understood and less contentious. More visible concern for policing community boundaries came from Farangi Mahallis and Barelwis in the early twentieth century when Muslims came to be challenged in the public sphere.

'Ulama were no less keen to police the boundaries between their community and the world of their Christian rulers. Rashid Ahmed Gangohi of Deoband made it clear that the British fell short of Islamic standards in matters of law. They had established laws contrary to the *shari'a*, their financial institutions flouted it, they produced medicines, biscuits, and dyes which contained alcohol. It was crucially important that Muslims, at least when in India, did not copy the British style of dress.[49] Mawlana 'Abd al-Razzaq of Farangi Mahall (d. 1889–90) would not eat ice or sugar or write on English-made paper. He refused to see a disciple who dressed in English style, and when another came to see him wearing English boots declared: 'Although his feet tread upon the ground, I feel that they are trampling on my heart.'[50] His grandson, Mawlana 'Abd al-Bari took a similar line. When, in 1910, he discovered that students at Aligarh College dressed and ate more like the English than the Prophet, he immediately engaged the authorities in a vigorous correspondence on the importance of trousers not falling below the ankle and of eating off a mat placed on the ground. The mawlana, moreover, was constantly alert to the need for Islam to be given due respect in the colonial environment. When at the opening of the Nadwat al-'Ulama in 1908 he discovered that the student reading the Quran was doing so at the feet of the lieutenant-governor, he created a dreadful scene. He insisted that a chair be brought and placed upon a table so that the word of God had clear precedence in the protocol of the occasion over the representative of earthly power.[51]

This said, it must be made clear that 'ulama had no difficulty with adopting useful things brought to India by the British provided they were held within an Islamic frame and served an Islamic purpose. On this basis most Deobandis were able to accept innovations such as the camera, telegraph, toothbrush, and phonograph.[52] On the same basis, 'Abd al-Hayy of Farangi Mahall felt able to endorse the use of electric fans in the mosque and telegrams to announce the sighting of the 'Id moon.[53] Moreover, 'Abd al-Bari used the railway, motor car, and telegram intensively, and made much of a globe brought from Oxford in his teaching.[54] Both Deobandis and Farangi Mahallis were willing to endorse the learning of English, 'If there is any advantage in learning a language, even if it be the language of heretics,' declared 'Abd al-Hayy, quoting Mulla 'Ali Qari, 'it is very desirable to learn it.'[55] Both groups of 'ulama were willing to give qualified support to taking service under the English. They were, however, adamant that they would not accept any subsidies from their rulers.[56]

It was but a short step from policing community boundaries to becoming active community champions. The nineteenth century saw notable cases of the 'ulama acting as specifically Islamic champions against the claims of other faiths. There were the famed Agra debates of 1854 in which Mawlana Rahmat Allah Kayranawi got the better of the German missionary, Dr Pfander, refuting amongst other things the doctrine of the Trinity and illustrating the corruption of the Christian scriptures, and in the process using the work of modern European biblical criticism, of which Pfander was unaware, to advance the Muslim argument. The works produced by Kayranawi have remained the basis of the Muslim critique of Christianity in India and the wider world.[57] In the 1920s 'Abd al-Bari recommended them to his students to help them deal with Christian missionaries.[58] There were also the festivals of the knowledge of God held in 1875 and 1876 in which Deobandis, Christians, and Hindu Arya Samajists debated at Shahjahanpur. On the second occasion, both the Muslims and the Arya Samajists thought they had beaten the Christians.[59] And there was, of course, the single-handed campaign of Ghulam Ahmad of Qadiyan to champion Islam by claiming not only that he was the messiah of the Christian and Muslim traditions but also that he had the likeness of an avatar of Krishna.[60]

In the twentieth century the role of champion was less that of religious debater than of advocate of Islamic causes in the public sphere. It was the 'ulama who took the lead in voicing Islamic interests to government whether it was over the proposed demolition of part of the Kanpur Mosque in 1913 or the safety of the holy places of Islam and the Turkish Khilafat as the Ottoman Empire went into terminal decline from the second decade of the twentieth century. Again the 'ulama, in this case both Deobandis and Farangi Mahallis, when they were asked to address Secretary of State Montagu on the proposed reforms to the Indian legislative councils in 1917, produced a response described by the government as 'a nakedly impracticable demand for the predomination of priestly influence'.[61] As 'Abd al-Bari was to say, the only home rule for Muslims was shari'a rule.[62]

'Ulama were no less explicit when it was necessary to champion community interests against Hindus. When in October 1917 large numbers of Muslims were killed in the Shahabad riots, one of the most severe outbreaks of communal rioting experienced under British rule, 'Abd al-Bari by his own account became 'beside himself' and at a Lucknow meeting proclaimed jihad against the Hindus.[63] Indeed, so great was his anger and that of his fellow 'ulama that the first draft of their address to Montagu, which was prepared in the following days, was more a plea for protection against Hindus than anything else.[64] In the same way 'ulama, on this occasion in spite of the attempts of Muslim politicians to stop them, when the Arya Samaj launched its Shuddhi campaign to convert Meos to Hinduism, leapt to their defence with money and counter-missionary organization. 'Abd al-Bari began urging Muslims to sacrifice cows without regard to Hindu feeling and declared: 'If the commandments of Shariat are to be trampled underfoot then it will be the same to us whether the decision is arrived on the plains of Delhi or on the hilltops of Simla. We are determined to non-cooperate with every enemy of Islam whether he be in Anatolia or Arabia or at Agra or Benares.'[65] Not surprisingly, this heralded an end to any form of alliance between 'ulama in 'Abd al-Bari's camp and Hindus. The Barelwis, however, had always regarded it as a matter of principle that they should not ally with Hindus.[66]

As from the late nineteenth century onwards a political arena began to open up in India, the role of champions of the Islamic dimensions of community came to be added to the 'ulama's role of policers of the bounds of the permissible under the shari'a. This was a function that experience showed only they could perform; their non-madrasa-educated Muslim colleagues did not have the skills or the sensibilities to do so. As the work of the 'ulama came to be broadcast by word of mouth and through the press, it helped to foster distinctive allegiances as, for instance, the Deobandis and Barelwis won support for their understandings, but also a sense of Muslim community *tout court.* It was a process which was bound to sharpen distinctions between Muslim and non-Muslim.

THE EMERGENCE OF THE 'ULAMA AS A PRESSURE GROUP

The foundation of the Nadwat al'Ulama in 1894, when Shibli asserted that the 'ulama alone 'have or can have absolute sway' over national life, was the point when 'ulama began to organize as a pressure group in Indian politics. 'ulama attended the meeting from across the sectarian spectrum, including the Shias; only the Barelwis were unrepresented. As we have noted, the Nadwa failed in the long term to develop as a forum in which 'ulama from several persuasions might develop a programme of modern Islamic learning and represent their interests to government. However, this was not before the Nadwa had played a significant role in pressing the case for reforming British law on *waqf.* The problem arose because in 1894 the Privy Council had upheld a decision of the Calcutta High Court that Muslims were not entitled according to the shari'a to make endowments in favour of their descendants and ultimately the poor. In 1908, after the Government of India refused to interfere with the Privy Council's decision, Shibli brought the issue to a meeting of the Nadwa. A case was developed against the Privy Council's decision and approved by the executive committee of the Nadwa in 1910. Support was won from Sunni and Shia 'ulama from throughout India. Support was also gained from the All-India Shia Conference and the All-India Muslim League. By 1911, Jinnah had moved the Musalman Wakf Validating Bill in the legislative assembly and by 1913 it had become law. The Nadwa had had a great success as a pressure group of 'ulama: it was, however, its only success.[67]

By this time, the Farangi Mahallis had also begun to organize as a pressure group. They had revived the Majlis Mu'id al-Islam, first founded in 1878 to raise funds to support the Ottoman Empire in its war against Russia. The Majlis, which was based entirely on Farangi Mahall and its connections was, according to its constitution, 'an Islamic association which seeks to promote the way of the shariat for the benefit of Muslims' and 'to work for the religious progress of the Islamic community within the laws of the current government....' Like the Nadwa it had one success, if that is what it can be called, which was its address to Secretary of State, Montagu, in 1917, which, as we have already noted, was dismissed as 'a nakedly impracticable demand for the predomination of priestly influence'.

The two years following the address to Montagu saw events which were to trigger the formation of the organization of Indian 'ulama, their effective pressure group. The catalyst was the growing concern of 'ulama over the decline of the Ottoman Empire and its consequences, which had been worrying them since before the First World War. This came to combine with their concern that the Nadwat al-'Ulama had failed either to unite 'ulama or to express their interests. 'Ulama, in particular 'Abd al-Bari of Farangi Mahall, began to play an increasing role in politics. In December 1918, he led the Farangi Mahallis to the Delhi session of the Muslim League, where they gave their support to the position the League was taking on the Turkish Khilafat and the holy places of Islam; it was the first time 'ulama had been present in numbers at the sessions of the organization of Western-educated Muslims. Throughout 1919, 'Abd al-Bari was active on Khilafat issues, leading to the foundation of the Central Khilafat Committee at a conference in Lucknow in September. But, being able seriously to put pressure on the government involved working with people who were not 'ulama—Muslim politicians, Muslim merchants, and Hindus, whom they hoped to win with the help of Mahatma Gandhi. Such political allies, of course, might have other agendas. At the Delhi Khilafat Conference of 23–24 November 1919 'Abd al-Bari discovered the constraints this put on Muslim action. Gandhi, while describing the decision of the 'ulama to demand non-cooperation with the British as a 'sublime decision', was unwilling to carry the matter forward: the timing was wrong. He would not support a boycott of foreign goods; it would wreck the fortunes of Bombay businessmen on whom he and the Khilafat organization depended. He would not do a deal. There was a proposal, for instance, that the Muslims would give up cow slaughter in exchange for Hindu support for the Khilafat; such action, he felt, should be taken by Muslims and Hindus only of their own free will. The only action agreed to was the boycott of the celebrations of peace at the end of the World War. Thus, 'ulama discovered the limits of their influence in politics.[68]

Two days after the Delhi Khilafat Conference the 'ulama met to discuss how to overcome their weakness. They were weak, they concluded, because they were divided. They should make another attempt to unite, and so they formed the Jami'yat al-'Ulama-yi Hind. It embraced all 'ulama except the Barelwis. Its first session was held at the Amritsar Congress sessions of 1919 with 'Abd al-Bari as president.[69] Through the Khilafat protest to the mid-1920s the Jami'yat embraced 'ulama from a range of Islamic perspectives, but from then on it became the political organization of Deobandi 'ulama.

During the last thirty years of British rule, the Jami'yat worked for legal and political change. In the legal area it was determined to extend the campaign, which the nineteenth-century reformers had waged against custom in ritual and belief, to the place which custom had acquired in the Anglo-Muhammadan law. The problem was that British administrators, through a misunderstanding of the role of custom or usage in Islamic law, had tended to protect Hindu practices which converts had brought into Islam. From the beginning of the twentieth century, 'ulama had begun to target Muslims, such as the Mapillas in south India, the Memons in western India and communities in the Punjab and its adjoining territories, where Hindu custom survived in Muslim legal practice. They wished for the government to impose the shari'a on all by statute. So in 1918 those Mapillas who had followed the Marumakattayam or Aliyasantan law of succession were made subject to the shari'a. So, too, from 1920 Memons could opt to follow Islamic as opposed to Hindu laws of succession.[70]

In the 1920s the Jami'yat passed numerous resolutions urging the supersession of customary law by the shari'a, and succeeded in winning popular support for its campaign. In 1935 it had its first notable success when the shari'a was made supreme in the North West Frontier Province. In 1937, it had its crowning success when a similar legislation, the Muslim Personal Law (Shariat) Application Act, was passed for the whole of British India. Important forces behind the legislation were women's organizations which saw in the imposition of the shari'a a scope for the improvement of the position of women. The only disappointment was an amendment, successfully moved by Jinnah, and with the interests of his landed Muslim League supporters in mind, which enabled Muslims still to opt for customary law in adoption, wills, and legacies.[71] These were remarkable successes for the Jami'yat and Muslim public opinion. Indeed, in the last few decades of British rule the 'ulama suffered only two specific checks in pressing forward the shari'a. The first was the Child Marriage Restraint (Sarda) Act of 1929, when the clear shari'a provision that people might marry at puberty, which was deemed to be twelve for boys and nine for girls, was set aside in favour of eighteen for boys and fourteen for girls. The government was unmoved by substantial protest from 'ulama and others against the legislation. The second was the Dissolution of Muslim Marriages Act 1939. Ironically, this legislation was introduced into the Central Assembly by 'ulama who were worried about the numbers of women renouncing Islam merely to be able to divorce their husbands. But their bill was so changed in committee, notably by extending the right to issue divorce decrees to non-Muslim judges, that they found the ultimate form of the legislation un-Islamic.[72] These Acts apart, the campaign of the Jami'yat, as the colonial era entered its terminal stage, enabled the personal law in its Anglo-Muhammadan form to be more widely imposed than ever before.

With the formation of the Jami'yat al-'Ulama-yi Hind a significant group of 'ulama became players in Indian politics; they had a voice and a political programme. The Khilafat movement, which gathered pace after the foundation of the Jami'yat, illustrated their capacity for mass mobilization. Indeed, from 1920 to 1923 the force which strove to drive protest ever more extreme was the 'ulama. In 1920, they were the prime supporters of the adoption of non-cooperation with the British as a policy and it was their large attendance at the Calcutta Congress in September, under the leadership of 'Abd al-Bari of Farangi Mahall, which persuaded the organization of Indian nationalism to adopt this policy. In November 1920 the Jami'yat organized the Muttafiqqa Fatwa, which was signed eventually by five hundred 'ulama, which made non-cooperation a duty and declared it lawful to ally with the Hindus and to follow Gandhi. In 1921, they began to establish their own court structure—their Amir-i Shari'at organization—which was their parallel government. Throughout the year, they also pressed for the full-scale adoption of mass civil disobedience which, in December, they helped Gandhi drive through the Ahmadabad Congress. But, by this time, mere civil disobedience was no longer enough; they wanted full independence. When Gandhi abandoned Civil Disobedience through the Bardoli Resolutions of February 1922, many demanded at a Jami'yat al-'Ulama conference to seek this end with violence. Throughout 1922 they kept up the pressure for the adoption of Civil Disobedience, and at the Gaya Congress of December 1922, which they dominated, they persuaded the nationalist politicians, many of whom hankered after seats in the new Montagu–Chelmsford councils, to boycott the council elections.[73] As Jawaharlal Nehru wrote, reflecting on the events of 1921 and 1922: 'The influence and prestige of the Maulvies, which had been gradually declining owing to new ideas and a progressive Westernisation, began to grow again and dominate the Muslim community.'[74] Indeed, it had grown to such an extent that for a moment they had been able to dictate the overall course of the nationalist movement.

In 1923, the power of the Jami'yat and the 'ulama quickly declined. The emergence of a strong and independent Turkey meant that the Khilafat issue subsided; the rise of the Hindu Shuddhi movement refocussed the energies of the Jami'yat on the need to defend their community against Hindu conversion campaigns; the imminence of council elections forced nationalist politicians to ask themselves if they really wanted a life of agitational politics and prison. The Jami'yat was never again to wield the leverage they had in the politics of British India from 1920 to 1923. They were not to have such influence again until they emerged as major players in the politics of Pakistan in the late twentieth century.

From the early 1920s the Jami'yat fought for independence and addressed its political vision for Islam in independent India. Leading members of the Jami'yat, as Peter Hardy puts it, 'saw free India essentially as a future confederation of two religious and political communities'.[75] This was articulated at a Jami'yat conference at Badaun in December 1921. Its 'ulama envisaged that Muslims in independent India would be headed by an Amir-i Hind, who would be appointed and could be dismissed by the Jami'yat. The Amir was to see that the shari'a was put into practice as fully as possible and would deal with the head of the Indian republic as the head of a separate jurisprudential entity. He ran a state within a state. This vision was developed in 1928 in their fourteen points rejecting the Nehru Report. It was repeated in their Saharanpur proposals for the constitution of an independent India of 1931, with changes accepting joint electorates and adult franchise for both sexes, and safeguards for individual units in the working of a federal constitution.[76] Of course, as we have noted, such a vision ran alongside their specific campaigns to raise the shari'a over custom in the workings of Anglo-Muhammadan law. In the politics of the time the Jami'yat came to have particular weight when mass mobilization was required amongst Muslims. Twenty thousand 'ulama were said to have been arrested for their involvement in anti-British activities in the early 1930s.[77] Their involvement was key to the relatively good results of the Muslim League in the 1937 elections in the Upper Provinces.[78]

In the last ten years of British rule the League and the Jami'yat parted company. The League's espousal of two-nation theory and its adoption of the demand for Pakistan drove the Jami'yat firmly into the Congress camp. In 1938, Husayn Ahmad Madani, principal of Deoband and leading Jami'yat thinker, had already in a notorious controversy with Sir Muhammad Iqbal expounded a view directly opposed to two-nation theory. He saw a future for Muslims only within India. He talked of territory and the common characteristics of those living in that territory, as Hindus and Indian Muslims did, as defining a nation.[79] The Indian Muslims were a *millat*, or religious community, within a greater Indian nation. It was a view in harmony with the traditions of Jami'yat thinking. It was a view, moreover, reiterated by the Jami'yat's response in April 1942 to the Pakistan resolution[80] and repeated many times subsequently. It was a view strengthened by the fact that few 'ulama believed that Jinnah, Liaquat, and the other Western-education Muslim leaders had the knowledge or the desire to realize the kind of Islamic society they sought. Jinnah's undermining of the Shariat Application Bill of 1937 and the Dissolution of Muslim Marriages Bill of 1939 had been a severe lesson.[81] Throughout the war years the Jami'yat looked to a federal solution with a weak centre and strong provinces as the way in which their millat might be achieved within an Indian *qawm* or nation. It was a solution in which they could believe right up to July 1946 when the Congress rejected the Cabinet Mission's proposals.

Independence and partition in 1947 placed the Jami'yat in a position little different from that before the British left. Their community was not going to be sustained by what Peter Hardy has termed a 'jurisprudential apartheid' of broad scope.[82] It would have to subsist on what it could preserve of the shari'a within the framework of Anglo-Muhammadan law as it had done under the British. For the rest it would have to rely on the institutions and attitudes which the Islamic revival of the nineteenth century had fashioned to sustain a Muslim community—its systems for making knowledge of Islam as widely known as possible and the power of the individual human conscience to put that into practice. In April 1948, in pursuit of this aim, the Jami'yat turned itself into a non-political body working for the religious and educational benefit of Muslims.[83] It appeared that its formal political career, which had lasted since 1919 and in which at times it had been most influential, was over.

Not all Deobandi 'ulama approved of close association with Hindus or with the Congress. Ashraf 'Ali Thanawi, widely recognized as the major spiritual force of his time in Deoband, was the leading opponent of Madani. From the Khilafat period he had objected to Hindu–Muslim political collaboration—indeed, to any political involvement at all; for him Hindus were as much kafirs, and therefore inappropriate allies, as the British. Such feelings were only strengthened by the torrid experiences of Muslims in the minority provinces after the Congress victories in the 1937 elections. Thanawi took the line that the Muslim League was the Muslim party, and that, if they were to be the rulers of a Muslim state, it was for the 'ulama to make sure that they were religious and honest. In pursing this aim, he sent three separate deputations to Jinnah.[84]

After Thanawi's death in 1943, his disciples Shabbir Ahmad 'Uthmani, Zafar Ahmad 'Uthmani and Muhammad Shafi took up his campaign. When in 1945 the League instigated the foundation of the Jami'yat al-'Ulama-yi Islam to assist in its mobilization of mass support in the 1945–6 elections and to counter the activities of the Jami'yat al-'Ulama-yi Hind, Shabbir Ahmad 'Uthmani, a noted scholar and fine speaker, became president.[85] The Jami'yat al-'Ulama-yi Islam endorsed the League as the only national organization for Muslims. Many 'ulama not associated with Deoband were attracted to it[86] and its members contributed to the League's great success in the 1945–6 elections.[87] In a presidential address to a League conference during the election campaign, he acknowledged that the ignorance of religious matters in the League leadership would present major problems for the Islamic credentials of the future government of Pakistan, but the way to deal with this was for the 'ulama to join the League and persuade 'hundreds and thousands of earnest-minded Muslims to become its members. Then the majority will be yours and with the help of the masses you can achieve [Islamic] reforms of all kinds'.[88] He foresaw, moreover, that an Islamic state would not be created immediately. 'Pakistan,' he told the founding convocation of the Jami'yat al-'Ulama-yi Islam, 'may be considered to denote the first step in the establishment of a government on the principals of the Quran. After all the supreme "Pakistan" ... of Madina itself reached its zenith gradually.'[89]

No sooner was Pakistan established that 'Uthmani moved to realize the mode of proceeding he had laid before his followers. He went to Karachi to set up the Jami'yat al-'Ulama-yi Islam there and asked his key Indian supporters to join him. He accepted a seat on the Pakistan Constituent Assembly and in 1949 demanded with success the appointment of a committee of 'ulama to advise the Assembly on the requirements of an Islamic constitution. The Islamic Teaching Board that resulted put forward proposals which 'Aziz Ahmad describes as belonging to a constitution of a 'traditional medieval pattern'. For instance, the head of state should be a Muslim, the government should be run by an elite of Muslims chosen for their piety by the electorate, 'ulama should decide what laws were repugnant to the Quran, and so on.[90] Most of their recommendations were turned down. Their cause, however, was carried forward by the Jama'at-i Islami under the redoubtable leadership of Mawlana Mawdudi, while politicians felt bound to acknowledge them as, in search of power, they sought alliances with 'ulama. Thus, the demands of the 'ulama did leave their mark on the first constitution of Pakistan in 1956. For instance, the state was named the Islamic Republic of Pakistan; its head was to be a Muslim; Muslims were to be enabled to live their lives according to the Quran and the sunna; and a commission was to be set up not only to ensure that no legislation was to be passed that was repugnant to the Quran but also to review all existing legislation in the light of it.[91] None of this could be called a great victory for the 'ulama. Nevertheless, the scene was set for the continuing retreat of the forces of liberalism in the face of the growing pressure of the 'ulama and their allies, boosted from time to time by advantageous political circumstances, which have marked the politics of Pakistan down to the twenty-first century.[92] 'Uthmani's vision of a long, slow haul to produce a Pakistan built on Quranic principles, of some kind, has been shown to be correct.

THE SIGNIFICANCE OF THE 'ULAMA

How should we weigh the significance of the 'ulama over this period of a century and a half? Evidently, there were severe challenges to their authority. In the workings of law and education under the British they were marginalized; in general, they were offered just token respect such as precedence in durbars and the award of shams al-'ulama medals. Rival sources of knowledge and authority, backed by great power, became established in their society; they had to contend not only with a vigorous Christian presence but, much more importantly, with Western scientific knowledge and post-Enlightenment understandings which attacked the very roots of religious belief. Muslim elites came to be imbued with these rival sources of knowledge and distanced from the mental world and understanding of the 'ulama. Then, their high-risk strategy of translating many of their key Islamic sources into Indian vernaculars and printing them, while it did much to expand their support in society, also meant that Islamic interpretation was permitted to develop outside their control. Finally, and worst of all, under the colonial state, control of their law—their shari'a, was taken completely from them, falling into the hands of the British and then into those of councils, increasingly elected, largely non-Muslim, and in which it was difficult to make their voice heard. At one level there is no doubt that British rule thrust the 'ulama to one side.

The response of the 'ulama was a burst of creativity which reflected their manifold intellectual traditions and socio-economic contexts. Among the important outcomes of this creativity were the jurisprudential technique of 'Abd al-Hayy of Farangi Mahall, which enabled the shari'a to accommodate change, and the interpretative method of the Ahl-i Hadith, which enabled Muslim modernist and Islamist thinkers to circumvent the dead weight of medieval scholarship and produce Islamic understandings which might go a long way to embrace the realities of the modern world. But the most important aspect of that creativity was the development by those in the Wali Allah tradition of a way of being Muslim outside the framework of the colonial state. 'Ulama in this tradition, in particular, set about making the knowledge of how to be a Muslim as widely available as possible; they asserted the crucial importance of removing custom, or Hindu influences, from Muslim practice, and elevated the individual human conscience to playing the key role in ensuring that the law was observed (and Islamic society sustained). The response of 'ulama in the Wali Allah tradition to the challenges to their authority was to spread roots in Muslim society beyond the reach of Western-educated Muslim elites and the colonial state.

The success of 'ulama in being able to reach out to and mobilize a constituency beyond the reach of Western-educated Muslim elite and colonial rule was demonstrated in the thirty years before independence. The Khilafat non-cooperation movement was the most dramatic evidence of what they could do when almost entirely united; between 1920 and 1923 they were the key element in the nationalist movement's boycott of the Montagu–Chelmsford councils and its general confrontation with the British. But equally, although in a quieter way, the steady assertion of shari'a law in its Anglo-Muhammadan form over custom was a tribute to their capacity to mobilize public opinion behind their cause. In the campaign for Pakistan their weight was felt on both sides.

One important outcome of the determination of 'ulama in the Wali Allah tradition to build a constituency in society at large was a sharpening of the separateness of these Muslims from the wider Indian society in which they lived. Muslims, who willed their Islam upon themselves, were self-consciously different. They knew that their very salvation depended on celebrating difference; this knowledge could not help but have a divisive impact on Indian culture, 'composite' or not. At one level Muslim politicians may have exploited the categories of Muslim, Hindu, and so on which existed in the British mind. But at another level there was a separate Muslim world defined by law which existed in the books, the minds, and hearts of 'ulama, and which they were determined to realize to its fullest possible extent. Even though different groups of 'ulama went different ways in seeking to realize their vision of separateness, the fact that it was separate was of no little influence in itself.

A second, and somewhat ironical outcome, of the drive of 'ulama in the Wali Allah tradition to build a constituency in society was the development of underpinning for the emergence of individualism. Their attack on all ideas of intercession and their concomitant emphasis on personal responsibility for one's actions, their aim to replace a Muslim community which could no longer be supported by Muslim power with one which was created by Muslim will, their creation in effect of a this-worldly Islam in which Muslims knew that they must act on earth in the light of God's guidance to achieve salvation, stimulated developments not dissimilar to those associated with the Protestant reformation in Christian Europe. They have been summarized thus:

> the shift towards this-worldly Islam has emphasised new strands in Muslim selves. There is a sense of empowerment that comes with the knowledge that it is humanity that fashions the world. There is the sense of personal autonomy and individual possibility that comes with the knowledge that the individual makes choices. There is the transfer of the symbolic centres of meaning in life from the signs of God and friends of God to the mundane things of ordinary life. And there is the development of that extra dimension to the self, the interior space. Arguably the individual has become more complex and the possibilities for human fulfilment have become greater.[93]

These developments were reflected in the writings of Muslim thinkers in the twentieth century. They are found in new versions of the life of the Prophet; they have been seen at work amongst the followers of the Tablighi Jama'at, the mass movement outcome of the Wali Allah tradition. Tensions, moreover, were bound to emerge as reformism, on the one hand, set out to create a self-willed Muslim community, but did so using methods which encouraged individualism and possible resistance to the requirements of or the authority of the community. It is a tension present in the literature of twentieth-century Muslim South Asia.[94]

Finally, in weighing the impact of the 'ulama we need, for a moment, to consider the meaning of their achievement for the years since the mid-twentieth century. In India, their direct influence on politics was substantially reduced. Indeed, in 1948, as we have noted, the Jami'yat al-'Ulama-yi Hind abandoned politics to concentrate on the spiritual, moral, and educational uplift of the Muslim community. In the 1970s, as the secular consensus began to break down, it moved back into politics, intervening on community issues. The record of its interventions, not least that over the Babri Masjid in 1992, demonstrated its capacity to make much noise but to little effect.[95] The major influence lay with organizations such as the Tablighi Jama'at which, although it had been founded by 'ulama of the reforming tradition, by this time, earned their disapproval as an organization undermining their authority. The Tablighi Jama'at, nevertheless, continues the work of the reforming 'ulama in Indian society. It has continued in its emphasis on Islamic dress and education to stress the separateness of Muslims from the rest of India. As Yoginder Sikand states:

> by playing a major role in hardening inter-community differences, by crusading against composite, syncretic religious and cultural traditions that bind Muslims with others among whom they live, and by stressing external markers of 'Muslim identity' that sharply divide Muslims from others the TJ helps bolster a strong sense of Muslim communal identity which, in turn, has had its own share of obvious political implications.[96]

Amongst these political implications is the rise of Hindu fundamentalists to power in India, in part as a response to the Tabligh's proselytizing activities amongst Muslims. But, equally, an Indian goverment dominated by high-caste politicians with a Hindutva programme creates precisely the conditions in which Muslim activists might find common cause with the Dalit sections of Indian society in challenging high-cast dominance.

In Pakistan the work of the reforming 'ulama was reflected in the rise of 'ulama organizations to the point where they seemed to be positioned to challenge state power itself. For much of the period no one would have thought such an outcome likely. In Pakistan, in 1947, the 'ulama had begun with a very weak base of just 137 madrasas.[97] An Islamic modernist-cum-secular consensus, controlled by the army from 1958 onwards, and represented by the 1961 Muslim Family Laws ordinance—a classic example of Muslim modernist thinking—held firm control of the upper reaches of the state. But, by the 1990s, there were over 8,000 madrasas, about half of which were of a reformist persuasion.[98] 'Ulama from reforming madrasas had taken power in Afghanistan, they were a presence in cross-border activities in Kashmir, and their organizations were a powerful presence in the politics of Pakistan. Muhammad Qasim Nanawtwi's vision of a great network of madrasas which would revitalize Islamic society, would seem to have been realized.

It was from the 1970s that events took place which transformed the situation of the 'ulama. Sa'udi Arabia and the Gulf states began to pour money into the development of madrasas with the aim of combatting the leftward tendencies of the Bhutto government. Once Bhutto had fallen, the funds continued to flow, stimulated by the need to resist the growing influence of post-revolutionary Iran in the region and by fears of Soviet influence after Russia's invasion of Afghanistan. They were augmented further by remittances from the large numbers of Pakistanis who went to work in the Gulf region after the great oil price rise of the early 1970s. General Zia ul-Huq's state-led Islamization further supported the growth of madrasas. Then, on condition madrasas reformed their curriculum, their students were promised government jobs. The madrasas, in fact, were central to Zia's Islamization, ensuring that 'ulama were in control of Islamic thinking at the very time when 'Islam was poised to define public policy and lay claim to modern sectors of the economy and society'.[99] Indeed, the 'ulama became Islamists themselves with a specific focus on power, and began to edge the traditional Islamist organizations—such as the Jama'at-i Islami—with their lay membership, to one side.[100]

The return to democracy in the late 1980s and during the 1990s created the context for the transformation of many madrasa graduates into armed Sunni militants. The new regime closed off the government jobs and new wealth to which its predecessor had encouraged madrasa graduates to aspire. Some became involved in criminal networks, others in militant sectarian organizations. The Sipah-i Sahabah, which had been formed as a semi-autonomous division of the Jami'yat al-'Ulama-yi Islam, supported by funds from Sa'udi Arabia and Iraq, conducted a violent and bloody campaign against Shia individuals and Shia organizations.[101] This Sunni militancy also benefited from a socio-economic dynamic which saw a Sunni urban middle class increasingly concerned to break the hold which a Shia and Sufi-oriented landed elite had in the countryside.[102] By 1996 the position of the Sipah-i Sahabah had been strengthened by the Taliban—also students of the Deoband madrasas—who had, over a two-year period, succeeded in conquering the greater part of Afghanistan, and the Harakat al-Ansar—again with Deoband connections—which focussed on militant action in Kashmir. One observer saw the reforming 'ulama of the Deoband tendency being at the heart of an arc of Sunni militancy which stretched from Central Asia through Afghanistan and Pakistan into India.[103] Another saw the Taliban regime in Afghanistan, with its roots deep in Pakistan's society and economy, bringing Pakistan close to an Islamic revolution.[104] At the beginning of the twenty-first century the defeat of the Taliban and strong US support for the regime of Pervez Musharraf has reduced this possibility, but the underlying economic, social, and regional dynamics which had led to the strengthening of the reforming 'Ulama and their organizations have not gone away. Indeed, the reforming 'ulama, by rooting themselves in society, by making themselves champions of that society's interests, and by seizing the political opportunities that came their way, had acquired a strength that no one in the early nineteenth century would have believed to be possible.

NOTES

1 Good examples of this are the discourses amongst the Farangi Mahalli 'Ulama of Lucknow at the beginning of the twentieth century. See, Francis Robinson, 'Problems in the History of the Farangi Mahall Family of Learned and Holy Men' and 'Al-Nizamiyya: A Group of Lucknow Intellectuals in the Early Twentieth Century', *The 'Ulama of Farangi Mahall and Islamic Culture in South Asia* (Delhi, 2001), pp. 102–29, and 130–44.

2 Christopher Shackle and Javed Majeed, *Hali's Musaddas: The Flow and Ebb of Islam* (Delhi, 1997), pp. 169–71.

3 Barbara Daly Metcalf, *Islamic Revival in British India: Deoband, 1860–1900* (Princeton, 1982), pp. 51–2.

4 S.M. Ikram, *Modern Muslim India and the Birth of Pakistan (1858–1951)*, second edition, (Lahore, 1965), p. 134.

5 Ziya-ul-Hasan Faruqi, *The Deoband School and the Demand for Pakistan* (Bombay, 1963), p. 68.

6 Farhan Ahmad Nizami, 'Madrasahs, Scholars and Saints: Muslims Response to the British Presence in Delhi and the Upper Doab 1803–1857' (Oxford D.Phil., 1983), pp. 228–9.

7 Ibid., pp. 221–64 and Qeyamuddin Ahmad, *The Wahabi Movement in India* (Calcutta, 1960).

8 The passage on Deoband draws in large part on Metcalf, *Islamic Revival*, pp. 87–263.

9 Faruqi, *Deoband School*, p. 27.

10 For a partial translation and excellent analysis of this book see, Barbara Daly Metcalf, *Perfecting Women: Maulana Ashraf 'Ali Thanawi's Bihishti Zewar: A Partial Translation with Commentary* (Berkeley and Los Angeles, 1990).

11 Metcalf, *Islamic Revival*, p. 163.

12 Ibid., p. 166.

13 Ibid., pp. 264–96.

14 Ibid., p. 295.

15 Ibid., pp. 296–314; Usha Sanyal, *Devotional Islam and Politics in British India: Ahmad Riza Khan Barelwi and his Movement, 1870–1920* (Delhi, 1996).

16 Robinson, *'Ulama of Farangi Mahall*, pp. 41–68.

17 Ibid., pp. 121–3.

18 Metcalf, *Islamic Revival*, pp. 335–47, and see too, Jamal Malik, 'The Making of a Council: The Nadwat al-'Ulama', *Zeitschrift Deutsche Morgenlandische Gesellschaft*, no. 144 (1994), pp. 60–91.

19 Yohanan Friedmann, *Prophecy Continuous: Aspects of Ahmadi Religious Thought and its Medieval Background* (Berkeley and Los Angeles, 1989), pp. 1–46, and 123; and Francis Robinson 'Prophets Without Honour: The Ahmadiyya', *History Today*, vol. 40 (June 1990), pp. 42–7.

20 Metcalf, *Islamic Revival*, p. 200.

21 Annemarie Schimmel, *And Muhammad is His Messenger: The Veneration of the Prophet in Islamic Piety* (Chapel Hill, 1985), pp. 218–38; and for the use of the Prophet in this fashion in Bengal see, Amit Dey, 'The Image of the Prophet in Bengali Muslim Piety, 1850–1947' (unpublished Ph.D. thesis, London, 1999).

22 Francis Robinson, 'Islam and the Impact of Print in South Asia', *Islam and Muslim History in South Asia* (Delhi, 2000), pp. 66–104; Metcalf, *Islamic Revival*, pp. 202–3.
23 'Ulama, however, remained uneasy about permitting access to books without their involvement. See, Metcalf, *Perfecting Women*, p. 376.
24 Metcalf, *Islamic Revival*, p. 203.
25 Ibid., pp. 87–137.
26 Ibid., p. 137.
27 Ibid., p. 147.
28 Metcalf, *Perfecting Women.*
29 Ibid., p. 375.
30 Ibid., p. 376.
31 Ibid., p. 5. An English translation of *Bihishti Zewar* is required reading for women members of the Tablighi Jama'at in Britain.
32 Ibid., pp. 3–4.
33 Muhammad Khalid Masud, (ed.), *Travellers in Faith: Studies of the Tablighi Jama'at as a Transnational Islamic Movement for Faith Renewal* (Leiden, 2000), pp. liv–vi.
34 Ibid., Introduction, p. 11.
35 Christian Troll, 'Five Letters of Maulana Ilyas (1885–1944), the Foundation of the Tablighi Jama'at; translated, annotated and introduced', in Troll (ed.), *Islam in India; Studies and Commentaries, Volume Two, Religion and Religious Education* (Delhi, 1985), pp. 138–76.
36 Ibid., pp. 147–8.
37 Masud, *Travellers in Faith*; Yoginder Singh Sikand, 'The Origins and Development of the Tablighi Jama'at (1920s–1990s): A Cross-Country Comparative Study' (Ph.D. thesis, London, 1997).
38 Robinson, *Ulama of Farangi Mahall*, pp. 121–3, and 130–44.
39 Sanyal, *Devotional Islam*, pp. 68–96.
40 Ibid., pp. 110 ff.
41 Metcalf, *Islamic Revival*, pp. 150–1, and 301–2.
42 Robinson, *'Ulama of Farangi Mahall*, p. 121.
43 Sanyal, *Devotional Islam*, p. 220.
44 Metcalf, *Islamic Revival*, pp. 275, 286.
45 Robinson, *'Ulama of Farangi Mahall*, p. 164.
46 Metcalf, *Islamic Revival*, pp. 197, 259–60, and 313–14.
47 Ibid., p. 153.
48 'Abd al-Hayy Farangi Mahalli, *Majmua-yi Fatawa Hadrat Mawlana 'Abd al-Hayy Marhoom, Farangi Mahalli*, vol. I, tenth edition, (Lucknow, 1985), pp. 57, 115, 149, and 170.
49 Metcalf, *Islamic Revival*, pp. 153–4.
50 Altaf al-Rahman Qidwa'i, *Anwar-yi Razzaqiyya*, (Lucknow, n.d.) p. 59.
51 Mawlana Mawlwi Muhammad 'Inayat Allah, *Risala-yi hadrat al-afaq ba wafat majmu al-akhlaq* (Lucknow, 1348/1929–30), p. 35.

52 Metcalf, *Islamic Revival*, p. 154.
53 Robinson, *'Ulama of Farangi Mahall*, p. 123.
54 Ibid., pp. 69–102, and 145–76.
55 Ibid., p. 123.
56 For the ambivalent approach of Deobandis and Farangi Mahallis towards the British see, Ibid., pp. 194–201.
57 Avril A. Powell, *Muslims and Missionaries in Pre-Mutiny India* (London, 1993), p. 286.
58 Robinson, *'Ulama of Farangi Mahall*, p. 164.
59 Metcalf, *Islamic Revival*, pp. 221–31.
60 Robinson, 'Prophets Without Honour', pp. 42–7.
61 Francis Robinson, *Separatism Among Indian Muslims: The Politics of the United Provinces' Muslims 1860–1923* (Cambridge, 1974), p. 286.
62 Ibid., p. 288.
63 Ibid., p. 254.
64 Reacting to the news of large-scale Muslim deaths in the Shahabad riots of 1917, the first draft of the address of the Majlis Mu'id al-Islam's address to Montagu and Chelmsford was a list of demands for protection primarily from Hindus. This was extremely damaging to the joint Hindu–Muslim/Congress–League demand for reformed councils. So alert 'Young Party' politicians, who had the trust of the Farangi Mahallis, moved in quickly to rewrite the document as 'an impracticable demand for predomination of priestly influence' but one which would in no way harm Hindu–Muslim unity. Ibid., pp. 284–6 and especially n. 3 p. 285 and n. 1 p. 286.
65 Ibid., p. 339.
66 Sanyal, *Devotional Islam*, p. 301.
67 Tahir Mahmood, *Muslim Personal Law: The Role of the State in the Subcontinent* (New Delhi, 1977), pp. 39–45.
68 Robinson, *Separatism*, pp. 289–303.
69 The aims and objects of the Jami'yat were laid down as follows:
    1. To guide the followers of Islam in their political and non-political matters from a religious point of view.
    2. To protect Islam, centres of Islam (Hijaz and the Jazirat-ul-Arab) and Islamic customs and practices and defend Islamic way of life against all odds injurious to it.
    3. To struggle for the complete independence of the country.
    4. To achieve and protect the religious and national rights of the Muslims.
    5. To promote and protect the rights and interests of other communities of the country.
    6. To organise the 'ulama on a common platform.
    7. To establish good and friendly relations with the non-Muslims of the country.

8. To establish *Mahakim-i-shariyah* (religious courts) to meet the religious needs of the community.
9. To propagate Islam, by way of missionary activities, in India and foreign lands.

Jamiat-ul-Ulema-i-Hind (A Brief History) (Meerut, 1963), p. 4.

70 Mahmood, *Muslim Personal Law*, pp. 22–6. In 1938 it became compulsory for Memons to follow Islamic laws of succession.

71 Ibid., pp. 28–33.

72 Ibid., pp. 51–61.

73 Robinson, *Separatism*, pp. 303–37.

74 Jawaharlal Nehru, *An Autobiography* (London, 1936), p. 72.

75 Peter Hardy, *Partners in Freedom—and True Muslims: The Political Thought of some Muslim Scholars in British India 1912–1947* (Westport, Connecticut, 1971), p. 32.

76 Ibid., pp. 32–6.

77 Mushirul Hasan, *Legacy of a Divided Nation: India's Muslims since Independence* (Delhi, 1997), p. 211.

78 Rizwan Malik, *Mawlana Husayn Ahmad Madani and Jami'yat 'Ulama-i Hind 1920–1957: Status of Islam and Muslims in India* (unpublished Ph.D. thesis, University of Toronto, 1995), p. 272.

79 Hardy, *Partners*, pp. 37–9.

80 Faruqi, *Deoband School*, pp. 96–9.

81 Hardy, *Partners*, pp. 38–9.

82 Ibid., p. 34.

83 Hasan, *Legacy*, pp. 211–13.

84 Malik, *Madani*, p. 171.

85 Leonard Binder, *Religion and Politics in Pakistan* (Berkeley and Los Angeles, 1961), p. 30.

86 Ishtiaq Husain Qureshi, *Ulema in Politics: A Study Relating to the Political Activities of the Ulema in the South-Asian Subcontinent from 1556 to 1947* (Karachi, 1972), pp. 359–60.

87 Binder, *Religion*, p. 30.

88 Malik, *Madani*, p. 193.

89 Ibid., p. 198.

90 Aziz Ahmad, *Islamic Modernism in India and Pakistan 1857–1964* (London, 1967), pp. 238–9, and Binder, *Religion*, pp. 155–82.

91 Ahmad, *Islamic Modernism*, p. 243.

92 Ibid., p. 251.

93 Francis Robinson, 'Religious Change and the Self', *South Asia*, XXII, Special Issue, 1999, p. 25.

94 Ibid., p. 26.

95 Hasan, *Legacy*, pp. 309–14.

96 Sikand, *Tablighi Jama'at*, p. 312.

97 S.V.R. Nasr, 'The Rise of Sunni Militancy in Pakistan: The Changing Role of Islamism and the 'Ulama in Society and Politics', *Modern Asian Studies*, vol. 34, no. 1, p. 142.

98 Ibid., p. 142.

99 Ibid., p. 149.

100 Ibid., pp. 147–50.

101 Ibid., pp. 151–65.

102 Ibid., pp. 165–9, and Muhammad Qasim Zaman 'Sectarianism in Pakistan: The Radicalization of Shi'i and Sunni Identities', *Modern Asian Studies*, vol. 32, no. 3, pp. 689–716.

103 Nasr, 'Sunni Militancy', pp. 169–79.

104 Ahmed Rashid, 'Pakistan and the Taliban' in William Maley (ed.), *Fundamentalism Reborn? Afghanistan and the Taliban* (London, 1998) pp. 72–89, and Ahmed Rashid, *Taliban: Islam Oil and the New Great Game in Central Asia* (London, 2000), p. 216.

The British Empire and the Muslim World

By the 1920s the British Empire embraced substantially more than half the Muslim peoples of the world. For much of the twentieth century Britain was the greatest influence over their development. Imperial security in large part dictated which territories of former Muslim empires or petty Muslim states the British came to rule. Imperial interests in combination with those of rival empires and local forces dictated precisely, and sometimes not so precisely, where the boundaries of new states were to fall. By the same token they dictated which peoples would have to learn to live together, or not as the case may be, in the increasingly demanding environments of the modern economy and modern state. Imperial techniques of government shaped the developing politics of these dependencies, often leaving major legacies to the years when the British had gone. The British Empire was the context in which many Muslims experienced the transition to modernity.

The Islamic world system, as it has been termed, was almost at an end by the eighteenth century when British power began to assert itself. Long-distance trade, a shared body of knowledge, a common legal system, and a common language of learning had linked peoples from Africa's Atlantic coast through to Central and South Asia. As time went on their influence had reached to the China Sea and the islands of Southeast Asia. According to the pattern of commerce and the play of power great entrepot cities flourished from time to time in West Asia and the eastern Mediterranean region—Baghdad, Cairo, Istanbul, Isfahan. Ibn Battuta, the fourteenth-century Moroccan traveller, who spent twenty-four years journeying through this world visiting the territories of over forty modern Muslim states and finding employment as a judge, attests to the reality of this system. So, too, do those eighteenth-century scholars whose pilgrimages to Mecca were made from places as far afield as Timbuktu, Sinkiang, and Sumatra.

By the late eighteenth century the great empires which had dominated the Muslim world since the early sixteenth century were either dead or dying. The Safavid was long gone, having crumbled in an afternoon before a whiff of Afghan tribal power; the Mughal was reduced to a few villages around Delhi; the Ottoman was on the retreat but still held authority over much of the Balkans, West Asia, and North Africa. The Muslim world, however, was not in decline. Recent research has been at pains to emphasize the significant economic and political changes that were taking place in some areas: the growth of revenue farming, the spread of commercial agriculture, the rise of provincial elites, and the regionalization of power.[1] Side by side with these changes there was also a religious renewal of quite extraordinary vitality. It was expressed in jihad movements which touched almost every Muslim land. This spirit continued with vigour into the period of British Empire. Some of its manifestations revealed state-making capacity—as in the Wahhabi movement which underpinned Sa'udi power in Arabia, the jihad which led to the caliphate of Sokoto in West Africa, and that which led to the Mahdist state in the Sudan. Other manifestations came in response to the fact of British rule, such as the Islamic reformist movement of Deoband in nineteenth-century India or the Islamic 'fundamentalist' movement of the Muslim Brotherhood in twentieth-century Egypt.

The first major step towards the establishment of the British Empire in the Muslim world came in 1765 when the East India Company received from the Mughal emperor the right to raise revenue and administer justice in the rich province of Bengal. Subsequent major steps were the final defeat of Tipu Sultan—the last signficant Muslim power in India—at Seringapatam in 1799, and the defeat of the French at Acre in the same year, which secured British command of the eastern Mediterranean. From these first steps British power expanded through the Muslim world, the process gaining great pace between the 1880s and the end of the First World War, when it reached from West Africa through the central Islamic lands to Southeast Asia. In every area the strategic and, sometimes, the economic needs of empire combined with local forces to carve the shapes of modern Muslim states, and modern states in which Muslims live, out of former Muslim empires, caliphates, sultanates, and sheikhdoms.

In West Africa, British rule, along with that of the French, transformed the situation of Muslim peoples. Up to the end of the nineteenth century the savannah region to the south of the Sahara had been host to a series of Muslim empires and states which were expanding to the south and the west. They had participated in the long-distance trade across the desert in slaves, salt, and gold and some had been noted both for their wealth and their learning. British rule transferred the focus of economic effort towards the coast where Africans became involved in the production of cash crops—palm oil, cocoa, rubber—for export. Muslim peoples occupied the backlands of the new British colonies of Sierra Leone (1891), Gold Coast (1896), and Nigeria (1900). In Nigeria, which was by far the largest and most important, the Hausa Muslims of the north, who had peopled the Fulani caliphate of Sokoto, were thrust together from 1914 in one colony with people from the central and southern regions whose religions and traditions were different.

In the Nile valley British economic interests, stemming from the development of Egypt's cotton production under the Khedival regime, and her strategic interests, stemming from Egypt's control of the Suez canal, led to the occupation of the country in 1882. Officially declared a protectorate soon after the outbreak of war in 1914 mass opposition to British rule from 1919 had led to a qualified independence in 1922 in which Egyptians regained control of their internal affairs but Britain retained control of foreign policy, the army, and the canal. The security of Egypt, however, was closely bound up with the control of the Upper Nile valley, the Sudan, where, in 1881, the Sufi shaykh, Muhammad Ahmad, had led a rising against Egyptian rule and established the Mahdist state. This had been conquered by an Anglo-Egyptian army in 1898 leading to the formation of an Anglo-Egyptian condominion in 1899. From the early 1920s the condominion became no more than fiction as the British, with Sudanese support, took the administration entirely into their hands. In the nineteenth century, both the Egyptians and the Mahdists had had difficulty in imposing their authority over the non-Muslims who lived south of the tenth parallel. British power now held the southern peoples firmly within a Sudanese framework.

In East Africa security had led to the British presence in Somalia which was divided up with the Italians and the French in the late nineteenth century. Little had been done for the tribes of the region apart from resisting Muhammad ʻAbd Allah who, from 1899 to 1920, waged a jihad against the British. Muslim communities were established in all the British colonies of the region. Notable was the Sultanate of Zanzibar which became a protectorate in 1870, while in Uganda, Kenya, and Tanganyika there were Muslim communities, formed initially from the Swahili-speaking peoples who had been pressing inland from the coast during the nineteenth century. Through East Africa from Uganda to the Dominion of South Africa there were also Muslims of Indian origin, not least among them the Nizari Ismaʻili followers of the Aga Khan, whose migration the British had encouraged to assist in developing the resources of the region.

In West Asia, protecting British routes to the East, managing the former Arab provinces of the Ottoman Empire, and trying to honour the conflicting understandings reached with Arabs, Zionists, and the French during the First World War led to the formation of three new states, all of which were held in trust for the League of Nations. There was Iraq whose boundaries to the west and south had no rationale in nature. To the north the British had insisted in adding the province Mosul from the French sphere of influence—a mixed blessing bringing on the one hand a mountainous barrier and eventually oil, but on the other hand a large population of discontented Kurds. Indeed, Iraq was a patchwork of possible identities with Kurds and Turks as well as Arabs, with Jews and Christians as well as Shia and Sunni Muslims, plus a host of tribal groupings. In 1921, the Hashemite prince, Faysal, was established as king to compensate for the loss of his Arab state based in Damascus to the French. There was Palestine, which was carved out of three separate Ottoman districts and which for nearly two thousand years had been little more than a geographical expression. Here the British had agreed to provide the framework within which Zionists could establish for themselves a 'national home', an ambition which was likely to mean some cost to the 80 per cent of the population which was Muslim and the 10 per cent which was Christian. The third new state was Transjordan which had even less basis than the other two, as it embraced no administrative region, specific people, or historical memory. Originally intended as part of Palestine, it became a separate state when, in 1921, the British permitted ʻAbd Allah, the brother of Faysal, to establish a government there, partly to satisfy his ambition and, partly to settle the region.

In the Arabian peninsula Britain's interests were primarily strategic involving control of the coastline and the routes to India. In the Aden protectorates the British policed the region from Aden itself while curbing the ambitions of the Zaydi Imams who wished to reimpose the authority of North Yemen over the sultanates to the south. Further along the southern Arabian shore the Bu Sa'idi sultans of Muscat and Oman ruled with the help of British advisers. In the Gulf the sheikhdoms of Kuwait, Bahrain, Qatar, and Trucial Oman had all concluded treaties with the British in the nineteenth century and existed underneath the umbrella of British power. In each city state government was a family business, their revenues were slight, and the British intervened only when necessary. Moreover, in this desert world—where man exercised authority over man and not land—their boundaries remained ill-defined.

In India, British relationships with Muslims did not seem to involve state-making. Nearly half of all the Muslims ruled by the British were to be found in the subcontinent—some eighty million—yet Indian Muslims were less than 30 per cent of the population of the region. Equally, Muslims as a whole, as far as they considered such matters, did not seem interested in a separate political existence, which was hardly surprising as they were greatly divided by language, background, and economic condition. However, there were aspects of Muslim politics and British policies which could point in this direction. Muslims in northern India with British encouragement had been concerned to focus their energies on the educational initiatives centred around Aligarh College. This had provided the platform for the formation of an All-India Muslim League whose demands—for separate electorates for Muslims and extra representation where they were politically important—the British had been willing to include in both the Morley–Minto constitutional reforms of 1909 and those of Montagu–Chelmsford in 1919. By the 1920s, however, Muslim separatism was a weak force in Indian politics, giving little hint of state-making potential. Nevertheless, a Muslim platform existed for those who wished to make use of it.

In Malaya, between 1874 and 1914, the British had brought nine Malay sultanates and three Straits settlements under their government. The aim was to create the optimum conditions for the rapid economic and commercial development of the land in commodities such as sugar, coffee, rubber, and tin. At the same time they aimed to foster the advancement of the Malay people within the traditional framework of Malay Muslim society. It was a policy which gave the Malay Muslims the political realm, or at least its outward forms; the only area in which the sultans exercised effective power was in that of Islam where they took the opportunity to develop the centralized administration of religious affairs. On the other hand, immigrants, mostly Chinese, held the dynamic economic realm. There was a rapid change in the ethnic balance of the population which, by the late 1920s, stood at thirty-nine per cent Chinese and just under forty-five per cent Malay.

In addition to the many areas in which British power was to be directly involved in nurturing modern states which were to be wholly or in part Muslim, there were others whose modern shape was the result either of British influence or of attempts to resist it. Arguably, the existence of Iran owed much to the determination of Britain throughout the nineteenth century to preserve the country's independence and to hold back the advance of Russian power towards India. It was ironical that Britain's refusal to protect the Caspian province of Gilan from Bolshevik invasion in May 1920 led to the repudiation of the Anglo-Iranian agreement of 1919, which had been her attempt to assert hegemony over the land. By the early 1920s a new model army under Riza Khan was crushing regional revolts and making sure that the oil-rich province of Arabistan (Khuzistan) acknowledged the authority of Teheran rather than that of Britain.

In the case of Turkey it was primarily British power which had driven the Ottoman armies back through Syria to the Taurus mountains where the 1918 armistice line formed the boundary of the new state. Elsewhere, British attempts, with French and American support, to fight Turkish nationalism by supporting Greek ambitions in western Anatolia, had come to grief when Ataturk's armies drove the Greeks into the sea. The Treaty of Lausanne recognized Turkey's frontiers as they were at the 1918 armistice.

In central Arabia the British had initially thought of using the father of the Hashemite princes, 'Abd Allah and Faysal, Sharif Husayn of Mecca, as their agent of control. But then they stepped back and wisely allowed the local leaders to fight for supremacy. The victor was 'Abd al-'Aziz ibn Sa'ud, the founder of the twentieth-century incarnation of the Sa'udi state. British power settled the ultimate boundaries of this state, as it established the frontiers of Transjordan, Iraq, and Kuwait in the 1920s; resisted Sa‘udi attempts to incorporate the Yemen in the 1930s; and their ambitions in the Buraimi Oasis in the 1950s.

By the 1920s, expansion of British power had come to establish, or play a part in establishing, many states of the modern Muslim world, as well as states in which Muslim political interests might have a significant role to play. Even in the 1920s it is possible to discern potential areas of stress: in Nigeria and the Sudan there was potential for conflict between the Muslim north and the Christian or animist south; on the east coast of Africa and in the Malay states there was potential for conflict between indigenous peoples and economic immigrants; in Iraq the Kurds were already refusing to acknowledge the authority of Baghdad; in Palestine Arabs had already rioted against the Zionist presence; in India Muslim separatism, it is true, was weak, but the Muslim political platform was there to be used and Muslims themselves offered meagre support for Indian nationalism. There were many faultlines. Whether these became open cracks or sulphurous craters would depend both on factors outside Britain's control and on how Britain ruled her Muslim peoples.

British policies in the Muslim dependencies shaped their political development. These were, in part, dependent on cost and, given the limited resources of many territories, this had to be low; in part, dependent on those nostrums which found favour with officialdom; and, in part, dependent on British attitudes to the Muslim world. To these attitudes we now turn.

The British came to the Muslim world with attitudes formed by the rhetoric of Europe's long encounter with Islam. There was the Christian polemic against Islam with its accusations that Muhammad was an impostor, that his faith was spread by violence, that it endorsed sexual freedom on earth, and promised sensual bliss in heaven. These accusations were sustained by nineteenth-century missionaries who added to them issues such as the position of women and the existence of slavery. There was the memory of the crusades which influenced many a British speech regarding the Ottoman Empire down to 1920 and doubtless the odd decision such as Lloyd George's determination in that year to join France and the USA in letting the Greeks loose in Asia Minor. There was a religious romanticism which gave a special meaning, for some at least, to events such as the capture of Jerusalem in 1917 and the creation of a Jewish national home in Palestine.

On the other hand, there was the Enlightenment response to the Muslim world in which it became a marvellous store of opportunities not just to test Christian certainties but also to let the imagination roam. Galland's translation of the Arabian Nights in 1704, alongside growing numbers of travellers' tales, whetted the appetite for caliphs, genies, lamps, and fabulous happenings. The taste was developed by writers and musicians, poets and painters, reaching one of its apogees in the early decades of the twentieth century in the poetry of that unsuccessful member of the Levant consular service, James Elroy Flecker, and the films of Rudolf Valentino. Great were the possibilities of flowing robes and Muslim headgear whether it was Cambridge undergraduates hoaxing the civic authorities that they were the uncle of the Sultan of Zanzibar and his entourage in 1905[2] or T.E. Lawrence playing out his fantasies in the Arabian desert in the First World War. Amongst the problems of this exotic essence with which things Muslims were bestowed was the fact that it made Muslims seem more different, and perhaps less able to accept change, than was in fact the case.

British understandings of the Muslims they ruled were developed against this background. One perception which was widespread in India and Africa in the late nineteenth century was that Muslims were fanatics, prone to holy war against non-Muslims, and, therefore, difficult to reconcile to British rule. This view had its origins in the various jihad movements which the British encountered in early nineteenth century India. It was kept alive by the Mutiny uprising, which was considered, wrongly, to be a Muslim conspiracy, and it was not laid to rest by W.W. Hunter's famous tract, *The Indian Musalmans*, written in answer to the Viceroy's question whether the Indian Muslims were bound by their religion to rebel against the Queen. In the late nineteenth century Indian administrators continued to regard Muslim fanaticism—for some, the word 'Muslim' was usually accompanied by the term 'fanatic'—as the greatest danger to British rule. This understanding of Muslims was translated into Africa in the 1880s in discussions of 'Arabi Pasha's revolt in Egypt and the Mahdist rising in the Sudan. It was nourished by the jihads which spluttered into existence from time to time in the early decades of the twentieth century in French and Italian as well as British African territories. The use of the blanket term 'fanaticism' often concealed an unwillingness and, perhaps, an inability, to analyse what was really taking place in Muslim societies. It also meant that Muslims, as Muslims, tended to be seen as a problem and, frequently, as a force to be propitiated.

Closely connected to the fear of Muslim 'fanaticism' was the fear of pan-Islamism, of united Muslim action against the British Empire. The British were right not to dismiss the threat. In principle—though to no great extent in fact—Muslims could regard themselves as one community and the Ottoman caliph as the successor of Muhammad as leader of that community. There had always been networks of scholars and mystics across the Islamic world. Such connections were reinforced in the nineteenth century by the increasing numbers of Muslims performing the pilgrimage to Mecca and travelling in general. From the late nineteenth century knowledge of other Muslim societies was greatly increased by the growth of the press, notably in India and Egypt. Moreover, there was an influential Islamic thinker, Jamal al-Din al-Afghani (d.1897), who was arguing for a pan-Islamic response to the incursion of the West into the Muslim world. On top of this there was the policy of the Ottoman Empire under 'Abd al-Hamid II to foster connections with Muslims in British territories, whether they be in Cape Town, Zanzibar, or Bombay. The Government of India, furthermore, was left in no doubt about the pan-Islamic feelings of its Muslims as they protested with increasing vigour at the Western takeover of the central Islamic lands. Their protests reached a peak in the Khilafat movement of 1919–24, which was the greatest movement of protest against British rule since the Mutiny uprising. From 1920 the Government of India urged London to take into account Indian opinion in negotiating Turkish peace terms. Curzon and Lloyd George refused to be influenced; in 1922 the Secretary of State for India, Montagu, was forced to resign on the issue. The eventual decline of the Khilafat movement proved Curzon and Lloyd George right. Pan-Islamism, as Harcourt Butler often told his Indian colleagues, was 'more a feeling than a force'.[3]

Respect for Muslims as a former ruling people was another, somewhat different, aspect of British attitudes. It mingled with the sense that Muslims such as these were not unlike the British—upright and independent peoples, believers who worshipped one God, experienced in the work of government, and courageous in that of war. Indeed, there was a tendency for British officers—so often successful examinees who aspired to gentry status—to be over-impressed by the company they kept, whether it was the rulers of vast acres or those with summary power of life or death over many men. Aspects of such attitudes were explicitly expressed in two of the more fateful policies adopted in the early twentieth century. Thus, Lord Lugard spoke admiringly of the Fulani in fostering indirect rule in northern Nigeria, referring to 'their wonderful intelligence, for they are born rulers'.[4] In not dissimilar vein, Lord Minto, in replying to the famous deputation of Muslim nobles, landowners, and ministers of native states in 1906, whose initiative was to lead to the establishment of a separate Muslim political identity in British India, referred to the deputees as 'descendants of a conquering and ruling race'.[5]

Such evidence suggests clear links between British attitudes to Muslims and policy. Of course, all attitudes were bound to be modified by context whether rhetorical or real. Gladstone, for instance, thought Turks totally unqualified to rule the Christians of the Balkans but perfectly qualified to rule the peoples of Egypt, a good number of whom were Christian. British Indian administrators adopted a totally different attitude to the so-called 'aristocratic' Muslims of upper India as compared with the peasant cultivators of east Bengal. Nevertheless, the all-pervasive impact of British attitudes is striking, whether deployed through forms of indirect rule or the great example of direct rule, namely India.

In much of the Muslim British Empire in the 1920s and 1930s forms of indirect rule were in place. In northern Nigeria the British ruled through the sultan of Sokoto, his emirs, and the structure of Islamic government that existed under their authority. In Egypt the situation was rather more complex. British influence depended on the endemic rivalry between the king and the wafd, the support of the large landlords of the Delta and the mercantile interests which benefited from the British connection, and the presence of British troops. In the northern Sudan the British made a concerted attempt from the 1920s to rule through tribal and rural chiefs, but discovered by the mid-1930s that these men had less authority amongst their people than they had expected; they were then forced to deal directly with the urban elites. In the Gulf and along the south Arabian shore, influence was exercised through sultans, emirs, and shaykhs with the use of the odd adviser, the dispatch of gunboats, and a touch of airpower. In Transjordan British will was exercised through the Hashemite emir, 'Abd Allah, and British subsidies as well as the

British-officered Arab Legion on which he depended. In Iraq that will was also felt through the Hashemite monarch, the core of ex-Ottoman officials who had supported the Arab nationalist cause, the tribal shaykhs, and the large landowners whom the land and water legislation of the 1930s made into rich and even larger landowners. In Malaya the British maintained the fiction of ruling through sultans while taking into their hands anything needed to enable rapid economic growth. Palestine, however, offers an exception. Here a form of indirect rule was developed through the Jewish Agency set up by Article 4 of the Mandate. When the British offered the Arabs a similar agency in 1923, unwisely they turned it down. They were ruled directly.

The general outcome of British policies of indirect rule or influence was to privilege conservative elements in the modern state systems of these societies as they developed. Islamic law, for instance, in its more conservative forms, continued to be applied. In northern Nigeria it continued down to 1960 with the exception that inhumane punishments were banned. Even slavery was permitted to exist. In Malaya it achieved greater application as the sultans centralized Islamic religious organization and extended its control over village religious life. Forms of rule were supported which had difficulty in incorporating new elements into the political system. In Transjordan, Iraq, and Egypt the monarchies, even though the latter two had Parliaments of a kind, had difficulty in expanding their base of support to embrace the new social groups which were being mobilized by economic change. As always the nature of government helps to fashion the quality and style of opposition. In Malaya it was in part the Islamic reform of the Kaum Muda; in Egypt it was in part the nascent Islamism of the Muslim Brotherhood. The main opposition, however, came from the new Western-educated classes—government servants, army officers, lawyers—who wanted to break into the charmed circles which wielded state power. Their success depended in large part on the pressures generated by economic change, the management skills of those in power, and the impact of the Second World War.

There are, however, some specific outcomes of policies of indirect rule, or influence, which command attention. In states where Muslims formed only part of the population they led to uneven development which stored up major problems for these societies at or soon after independence. Take Nigeria, for example—the home, in a technical sense, of indirect rule. The special policies directed towards the north meant that by the time of independence in 1960 only a small fraction of the population had been exposed to Western and secular values as compared with the peoples of the east and south. The overall impact of the British presence, not least the rapid growth of commercial agriculture, had led to the consolidation of Islam at the centre of popular identity; northern leaders conducted their own relations with Muslim states such as Egypt and Sa'udi Arabia. Ahmadu Bello's attempt to 'northernize' government and commerce, which also meant to 'Islamize' them, was to be expected once British restraints had been lifted. It led to fear amongst the Christian peoples of the south, his assassination in 1966, and the subsequent Biafra civil war. The advance of Islam remains a continuing threat to Nigeria's secular and pluralist constitution.

The Sudan offers similarities to but also differences from the Nigerian situation. The imposition of indirect rule led to the total isolation of the southern non-Muslim province from Arab–Islamic influences of the north. It was the only way the British felt they could build up the self-contained tribal units which the system of rule required. At the same time Christian missionaries were given relatively free rein in the area. The outcome was that the two halves of the country grew apart. The Muslim north kept pace with the social and political advance of the wider Muslim world; the increasingly Christian south remained isolated and immobile. At independence in 1956 the peoples of the south were placed in the hands of the northerners. This was followed by continuing friction between the Christian south and the Muslim north leading to the outbreak of civil war in 1967, which has continued on and off into the 1990s.

In Malaya the British had themselves to deal with the early consequences of their policies towards the Malay sultanates. After the Second World War they found that the only way they could devolve power with Malay agreement was to ensure Malay supremacy in the political and administrative sphere. An enduring tension came to be established in the modern Malay state between the privileged position of the Malays and the recognition of Islam in the national identity, on the one hand, and the position of the non-Muslim Chinese and Indians, on the other. It was a tension which was on occasion to break into open strife.

In other areas it is possible to see how specific policies of indirect rule gave a distinctive shape or quality to the modern state which emerged. In the Gulf, British policies of recognizing the Gulf sheikhdoms as separate entities enabled the emergence of the larger ones as individual states at independence. The British also protected them from the claims of their overmighty neighbours, for instance, those of Iraq over Kuwait and Iran over Bahrain. Indeed, they created the environment in which these family-run small businesses could, as the wealth from oil began to flow in the 1950s and the 1960s, develop as family-run modern state corporations. In Jordan, where the British-officered Arab Legion had played such a distinctive role in establishing the state and where the dismissal of these officers in 1956 signalled the rapid diminution of British influence, the army continued to play the role of chief pillar of the Hashemite monarchy. It saved the regime in the great Arab nationalist crisis of 1955–8; it did the same in the Palestinian crisis of 1967–70.

No form of indirect rule had such a momentous outcome for the peoples of the region as that conducted in Palestine. Arguably, the transformation of the Jewish Agency of 1920 into the Israeli state by May 1948 was, from the beginning, a possible outcome of the terms of the Palestine mandate. Britain had undertaken, although against the grave reservations of the Foreign Office and her military administration in Palestine, to create 'such political, administrative and economic conditions as will secure the establishment of the Jewish national home',[6] and this is what emerged, albeit in nation-state form. But Britain's declared policy to the bitter end, with the one deviation of the Peel Commission recommendations, was to establish a bi-national state. The administration of the mandate, however, and the outcome, were disasters. Admittedly, when the first High Commissioner, Herbert Samuel, took up his post in 1920, few could have predicted the events which so complicated Britain's rule: the levels of Jewish immigration resulting from persecution in Europe, the levels of Arab intransigence resulting from justifiable anger and poor leadership, the impact of the Second World War, the holocaust, the rise of American influence, and the decline of British influence. By the mid-1930s the Palestinian Arabs were radical, politicized, organized and using strikes and violence. From 1937–9 there was open rebellion, in particular, against the recommendation of the Peel Commission that Palestine be partitioned and, in general, against the

British presence. The Palestinian plight attracted popular concern as well as that of intellectuals and students in Egypt, Iraq, and other Arab countries. The cause was also adopted by Islamic movements; Arab governments discovered they could win support by taking up the Palestinian issue. Nor was concern restricted to Arab lands. Palestine remained a continuing issue for Indian Muslims and featured regularly, for instance, in emotional speeches and resolutions of the All-India Muslim League. By 1947 Palestine was an economic and strategic liability for the British. There seemed, moreover, to be no solution agreeable to Zionists and Americans on the one hand and the Arabs on the other. In February 1947 the British referred the problem to the United Nations, refused to implement a UN partition plan of November 1947, and surrendered the mandate on 1 May 1948. The consequence of this imbroglio was a serious loss of goodwill from the Arab world towards Britain at a time when her position in that world depended on that very commodity. There was also the establishment of the Palestinian grievance which was to be a focus of relations between regional powers and super powers in the region for decades. At the same time, Israel, which was seen as a stake of Western provenance thrust into the heartland of Islam, was throughout the Islamic world a focus of resentment against the West.

If the outcome of British policy failures in Palestine was to help shape the political landscape of West Asia for years after independence, the same can be said for their impact on South Asia. Here, the princely states apart, the British were involved in direct rule. The classic Indian nationalist analysis of their ruling style was that the British divided Muslims from Hindus and ruled. Matters, however, were rather more complex. Certainly, British attitudes and British policies helped the development of Muslim organizations in northern India, but other crucial factors were the impact of both Muslim and Hindu revivalism. This said, Muslim separatism was a weak growth in the 1920s and 1930s and its political party, the Muslim League, did very badly in the 1937 general elections, winning rather less than a quarter of the Muslim seats available. That this party was able to be a serious player in the end-game of British India was because it won over four-fifths of the Muslim seats in the 1945–6 elections. Its fortunes had been transformed by the Second World War, the British need for Muslim support in that war (half the Indian army, for instance, was Muslim), the mistakes of the nationalist movement, and the leadership of Jinnah, the Muslim League's president. Ultimately, as Ayesha Jalal has revealed, India was divided because the Indian nationalists wished it.[7]

The dynamics of the process were instinct in the federal system set up by the 1935 Government of India Act. The nationalists wanted to inherit the strong central power wielded by the British. The Muslim League wanted a weak centre—indeed, Nationalist–Muslim parity there—to protect the Muslim provinces from an over-mighty centre. Ultimately, the nationalists insisted on partition. The emergence of Pakistan was the outcome of a combination of forces. With regard to the specifically British contribution, certainly British attitudes and policies had their part to play in establishing a Muslim political platform. But in the final act weight must be given to the dynamics of a federal system set up to enable the British to wield all the powers they needed in India from the centre while allowing Indians to get on with the business of government in the provinces. The consequences of partition have loomed over the subcontinent since 1947, bringing three wars and threatening more.

Muslim attitudes to the British varied according to their particular Islamic understandings and to their particular experience of British rule. They were subject, too, to change through time; the kind of person who was a cultural collaborator in the late nineteenth century was more than likely to be a dedicated nationalist opponent well before the mid-twentieth century. There were, nevertheless, some distinctive aspects to Muslim attitudes. The British were often seen primarily as Christians. Certainly they were people of the book, people who shared the same prophetic tradition, but by the same token they were people whose scriptures had been corrupted and whose beliefs were misguided. Early contacts could involve set-piece debates with Christian missionaries like those which were held at Agra (India) in 1854, one of whose Muslim protagonists became a pensioner of the Ottoman sultan and the formulator of the most influential modern Muslim critique of Christianity.[8]

At their most extreme, religious strategies for dealing with the Christian presence might involve attacking Christian revelation at its heart, as did the Punjabi Muslim, Ghulam Ahmad (d.1908), who founded the Ahmadiyya missionary sect. He claimed that he was the messiah of the Jewish and Muslim traditions; the figure known as Jesus of Nazareth had not died on the cross but survived to die in Kashmir.[9] But, equally, the problem of Christian power could be confronted with humour, as did the Indian satirist, Akbar Allahabadi (d. 1921):

The Englishman can slander whom he will
And fill your head with anything he pleases
He wields sharp weapons, Akbar. Best stand clear!
He cuts God himself into three pieces.[10]

A second set of attitudes focussed on the extent to which the manners and customs of the British could be followed and their material culture adopted. Thus, the Sultan of Pahang, 'Abd al-Samad (d.1898) declared that he never 'fired an English gun in his life nor wished to fire one, that he preferred walking to driving and eating with his fingers according to Malay custom rather than using forks; that wine was forbidden by the Koran and that he did not know how to play the piano.'[11]

For most of British rule Muslims debated what they could and could not accept from the culture of their ruler. For believing Muslims wine and pork were distinctive cultural markers; the freedom of women was a greatly contested issue. Tables and chairs, knives and forks, trousers and ties, however, came widely to be adopted, although ties went out of fashion in the late twentieth century when it came to be thought that they represented the sign of the cross.

A third set of attitudes embraces responses to British power. The context is crucial. Muhammad 'Abd Allah of Somaliland waged jihad for twenty-one years against the British. He celebrated the death of a British officer who had tried to cut off his defeat in 1913 thus:

O Corfield, you are a traveller who
Will not stay long here below
You will follow the path where there is no rest
You are among the Denizens of Hell
You will journey to the Next World.[12]

In different circumstances, where the fact of Britain's dominance was indisputable, there could be resigned acceptance. 'They hold the throne in the hand,' declared Akbar Allahabadi, 'the whole realm is in their hand. The country, the apportioning of man's livelihood is in their hand ... The springs of hope and fear are in their hand. ... In their hand is the power to decide who shall be humbled and who exalted.'[13] But then there were Muslims who genuinely gloried in the destiny they shared with their foreign ruler. Take Sayyid Husayn Bilgrami (d.1926), the distinguished Hyderabadi civil servant who had the major hand in drafting the Indian Muslim memorial to the viceroy in 1906. In verse of impeccable loyalty, but questionable merit, entitled 'England and India' he trumpeted:

England!' tis meet that for weal and woe
In calm or storm, our chosen place should be
Where honour calls us by the side of thee
Thy friend be friend to us, our bitt' rest foe
The trait' rous knave who schemes thy overthrow.[14]

There are, however, some lines of Muslim response which require more detailed examination. The first is that of jihad. For all the fear of Muslim fanaticism displayed by the British, once they had conquered a territory and consolidated their rule, jihad, although often a worry, was rarely a serious issue. One reason was that in British territories which experienced forms of indirect rule Islamic law continued to operate. Even in directly-ruled British India Muslim personal law, the most cherished element of the shari'a, continued to be imposed in its bastard Anglo-Muhammadan form. It had long been the position of Sunni 'ulama that, if the law was upheld, rebellion could not be justified. A second reason was that, legitimately, to conduct a jihad there had to be a reasonable chance of success. After Muslims had tasted the fruits of the Gatling gun and had come to appreciate the full weight of British power, they knew that they had little chance. Once this was understood, the alternative was *hijra* or flight from the 'land of war', as practised by the Caliph of Sokoto after the annexation of his territories, or the 30,000 Indian Muslims who, in 1920, fled to the North West Frontier, many to their deaths, as part of the Khilafat protest. Considerations such as these help to explain the failure of Muslims in Africa and elsewhere to respond to the Ottoman call for jihad against the British Empire on the outbreak of the First World War.[15]

The spirit of Islamic renewal which was no longer channelled into holy war now came to energize other responses to the British presence. The broad 'church' known as reformism was one. Amongst its more striking manifestations was the Deoband Madrasa of northern India, from which stemmed the Deoband movement. In this 'ulama created a way of being Muslim without the support of the state.

Spreading knowledge of how to be a good Muslim was central to its objectives, so it made good use of the printing press, of translation of texts into local languages, and of schools—by its centenary in 1967 it claimed to have founded over 8,000. Also central to its objectives was personal responsibility in putting Islamic knowledge into practice; the movement, therefore, was profoundly opposed to any idea of saintly intercession for man with God. To ensure its independence of the colonial state, it relied on popular subscription for support. Bureaucratic in organization, one of the ways it served its constituency was by offering a mail-order fatwa service. Most followers of Deoband supported the Indian nationalist movement and opposed the idea of Pakistan; they felt they did not need a Muslim homeland to be the kind of Muslim they were.[16]

Elsewhere no one went as far as Deoband in developing organizational structures to support what has been called a form of 'Islamic Protestantism'. In West Africa, however, ignoring the foreigner was a not uncommon response to the British presence.

For the most part Muslims could not ignore the British presence. They had to address the meaning of the new forces which were having such an impact on their lives: Western learning, the colonial state, and major economic change. This process led to the development of what is termed Islamic modernism. An important figure in this response to the West was the Egyptian, Muhammad 'Abduh (d. 1905), who, after participating in 'Arabi Pasha's revolt, was exiled in the years 1882–8 and returned to be chief mufti of Egypt from 1889 to 1905. He accepted the Quran and Hadith as God's guidance for man but made other areas subject to man's personal reasoning. He wished to put an end to blind acceptance of past authority; Islam had to be reinterpreted in each new generation. Thus, he threw open the door to new ideas. These led, through his intellectual successor, Rashid Rida, who talked in terms of the compatibility of Islam and an Arab national state, towards a purely secular nationalism.[17] 'Abduh's ideas were particularly influential in North Africa and Southeast Asia. In Malaya they informed those of the Kaum Muda or 'Young Faction' whose leaders had extensive contacts with West Asia, several studying in Cairo. In the second and third decade of the twentieth century they attacked the traditional Islam of the rural 'ulama and Sufis which was now administered by the sultans. After the fashion of Islamic reform they criticized all practice which hinted at intercession but, equally, they looked to a positive approach to issues such as the wearing of European clothes or whether it was possible to take interest from a post office or a rural cooperative. Such assaults on the religious fiefdoms of the Malay sultans were at one remove assaults on the British. By the 1930s Kaum Muda formed a nationalist opposition.[18]

The most clearly defined example of Islamic modernism was that created by Sayyid Ahmad Khan (d. 1898), the founder of Aligarh College (1875), and his followers in the Aligarh movement. The Sayyid, who was knighted by the British in 1877, was determined that Indian Muslims should come to terms with British rule. They needed to be able to command Western learning so he provided them with a Muslim-controlled environment for learning, which was modelled after a Cambridge college and in which they were taught by men from Cambridge. They needed to be able to play a role in the affairs of the colonial state, so he made sure that they knew how to debate Cambridge Union style, how to play cricket, and how to behave at tea parties.[19] Again, they needed to have as few religious obstacles to the process as possible so he used his personal reasoning, rejected the authority of the past, and strove to produce an Islamic theology for his time. The Quran and Hadith were reviewed in the light of modern science. In the process the Sayyid went much further than Muhammad 'Abduh, further than most Muslims would go today. Muslims went to Aligarh in spite of rather than because of Sayyid Ahmad's views. Many became leading supporters of Muslim separatism and the movement for Pakistan.[20]

The person, however, who brought Sayyid Ahmad's project close to fruition was not a student from Aligarh, although he was subject to Cambridge influence having done graduate work there from 1905–8. This was Muhammad Iqbal (d. 1938), the philosopher-poet of Lahore, who was knighted in 1923. He not only developed a dynamic vision of Islamic history as one of progress but also fitted the nation-state into that progress. At the same time he performed the key service of building a bridge between the Islamic idea of the sovereignty of God on earth and that of the sovereignty of the people as expressed in the modern state. Addressing the Muslim League in 1930 he declared that the Muslims were a separate nation in India and that the north-west of India should be formed into a Muslim state.[21]

By the late 1920s and 1930s groups of Muslims emerged who could neither accept the way forward of the reforming 'ulama because they ignored the facts of life, nor could accept that of the modernists and their nationalist successors because they ignored the facts of Islam. These Muslims formed movements which have been called 'fundamentalist' but which are better called Islamist. They are well represented by the Muslim Brotherhood, founded by Hasan al-Banna (d.1949) in Egypt in 1928, and the Jama'at-i Islami founded by Sayyid Abul A'la Mawdudi (d.1979) in India in 1941. For men such as these the real danger was less British or Western power than the secular culture which came with it. What was needed was to capture the modern state and to use it to impose Islamic law and values on society as a whole. In Egypt in the late 1940s the Brotherhood was to play a leading role in the cause of Palestine and the struggle against British rule. In the subcontinent the Jama'at opposed the Muslim League's campaign for Pakistan; it did not believe that it would be an Islamic state. These movements were the forerunners of those which would, throughout the former British Empire and, indeed, throughout the Muslim world, in the latter half of the twentieth century compete with the nationalists for the control of state power.[22]

We should note that these modernist and Islamist responses were at the level of the state. For the most part Muslims wanted to take over the state structure that British rule had created for them. Where they did not, it was because they felt these structures left them too disadvantaged. In the case of British India, they ended up by creating a separate state, which could embrace most, though not all, of them. In the case of Palestine, they could see no solution from which they would not lose. Of course, Muslims, under their various British regimes, were concerned about events in the wider Muslim world; Palestine was rarely far from their minds. But the prime focus of actions remained the state. As Muhammad Iqbal wrote:

Now brotherhood has been so cut to shreds
That in the stead of community
The country has been given pride of place
In man's allegiance and constructive work.[23]

In spite of the poet's justified complaint there were supra-state responses to the expansion of British Empire across the lands of Islam. There was no shortage of pan-Islamic sentiment. In 1894, the Muslims of Lagos were in correspondence with the Ottoman sultan; in 1910, Friday prayers in Dar es Salaam were still being said in his name; while pan-Islamic sympathies were evident in Malaya from the 1890s.

Such feelings were most powerfully expressed in India where the circulation of Muslim newspapers always shot up when there were crises in the Islamic world, where poets and writers embraced pan-Islamic themes—not least amongst them, the fate of Muslim Spain which carried heavy symbolism for the times—and where there was a powerful emotional identification with the heartlands of Islam. The Khilafat leader, Mahomed Ali, confesses in his autobiography how he contemplated suicide in the autumn of 1912 when he heard that the Bulgarians were within twenty-five miles of Istanbul.[24] It was men of this ilk who sent a Red Crescent mission to Turkey in 1912, founded a society to defend the holy places in 1913, and led pan-Islamist activities throughout the 1920s, focussing in turn on the Khilafat, the fate of the holy places under Ibn Sa'ud, Palestine, and the establishment of a university for the Islamic world.[25]

Against this background there were attempts to organize at a pan-Islamic level in order to strengthen the Islamic world and to resist the West. It was an idea that was always at the mercy of the ambitions of the proposer of the moment. The initiative in the early 1880s came from the romantic Arabophile, W.S. Blunt, who wanted to do for the Arabs what Byron had done for the Greeks; he suggested the founding of a Muslim Congress to elect an Arab to replace the Ottoman caliph. The idea was taken up by Afghani, though not with its anti-Ottoman dimension, it was sustained in the circles around Muhammad 'Abduh and Rashid Rida, and almost realized in Cairo in 1907 by the Crimean Tartar reformer, Isma'il Bey Gasprinski. After the First World War the Turks toyed with the idea of holding a congress to elect a caliph to replace the Ottoman holder of the office. The first two congresses were actually held in 1924 and 1926 with this aim in mind. In the first, however, Sharif Husayn of Mecca found he could get no support for his claim, and in the second the Egyptians were rebuffed in their attempt to bring the office to Cairo. A third congress was held at Mecca in the summer of 1926 where Ibn Sa'ud faced such strong criticism of his custodianship of the holy places that he was put off such meetings for good. A further congress was held at Jerusalem in 1931 by Hajji Amin al-Husayni with the idea of winning support for the Palestinian cause. This established a secretariat which existed for some five years. From then on no major Muslim congress was held until the establishment of the Organisation of the Islamic Conference in 1969 by Sa'udi Arabia in the wake of a serious fire in Jerusalem's al-Aqsa mosque. The charter of the Conference echoes several of the themes of the earlier congresses: the protection of the Muslim holy places, support for the Palestinian cause, and the fostering of Muslim solidarity in relation to the rest of the world. The issue of the Caliphate, however, is ignored.[26]

A supra-state vision also existed in the idea of Arab unity. This had its origin in the first stirrings of Arab nationalism before the First World War. Hopes had been raised by British support for Sharif Husayn during the war and by the establishment of an Arab state at Damascus in 1918. They were dashed by the state system imposed upon the region by the Allies in the post-war settlement. Ideas of Arab unity revived during the interwar period with the writings of Sati al-Husri, a former Ottoman official, and the establishment of the Pan-Arab National Covenant in 1931. They gained extra momentum during the Second World War, as the British declared themselves in favour of unity to win Arab support, as it became the declared policy of the Baath party, and as the Arab League came to be formed in 1945. They were stimulated further by the Palestinian problem and by Egyptian determination to use pan-Arabism to exercise leadership in the region. In the 1950s and 1960s, as Egypt, Syria, and Iraq sought strength in the world of superpower rivalries which had replaced the colonial era, there were attempted unions. Invariably, rivalries between states prevented success; failure to defeat Israel discredited such ideas altogether. Dreams of Arab unity foundered when confronted with the nation-state system in the Middle East which the British Empire had done so much to create.

The impact of Britain's moment in the Muslim world demands more general assessment. It enabled, for instance, some Islamic sects to develop a global presence. British policy, for instance, encouraged the Nizari Isma'ilis to migrate from India to East Africa where they participated in its economic development, becoming in the process a wealthy and highly educated community. British patronage enabled the leaders of this sect, the Aga Khans, to recover their fortunes, stamp their authority on their followers, and become figures in world affairs. In a rather different way the connections of British Empire enabled the Ahmadiyya to carry their proselytizing mission to East and West Africa in the 1920s. Now, despite the bitter hostility of the rest of the Muslim community, they have missions in 120 countries.

The British Empire presided over a more general expansion of the Muslim world. Through sub-Saharan Africa, for instance, although the British brought an end to warlike expansion, apart from special cases like the southern Sudan, it provided an environment in which peaceful expansion could continue to take place as Muslims spread from the hinterland towards the coast in West Africa or from the coast inland in East Africa in search of jobs and commercial opportunities. Moreover, as Muslims, competed with Christian missionaries for pagan souls, they had the advantage of promoting a faith which was different from that of the dominant white man. Economic opportunity brought further expansion of the Muslim world elsewhere. Thus Indian Muslims, using the opportunities provided by indentured labour, came to form communities in the Caribbean. Then too, Muslims, in large part from Pakistan, Bangladesh, India, and East Africa, came to fashion that most distinctive of Imperial legacies—the Muslim community of Britain. Urdu, Bengali, and Gujarati became British tongues, Islamic issues became part of British political discourse, and the domes of purpose-built mosques began to punctuate the skylines of cities such as London, Birmingham, and Bradford.

Through the length and intensity of their encounter with Britain, Muslims from South Asia came to the fore in the Islamic world in terms of new ideas and organization. They had been moving in this direction in the eighteenth century, but the nineteenth and twentieth centuries saw a period of great creativity. In 1928, Indian reformism gave birth to what is regarded in the late twentieth century as the most widely followed movement in the Muslim world—the Tablighi Jama'at or 'Preaching Society'. Indian modernism produced Iqbal whose influence has been felt far beyond the subcontinent; the figure of Mawdudi towers over the development of Islamism; while it was in Pakistan that there has been the most prolonged attempt to build a bridge between understandings of Islam and the requirements of modern society and state. Under British rule Islam in South Asia became less a receiver of influences from elsewhere in the Muslim world and more of a transmitter. This helped shift the centre of gravity of the Muslim world eastwards—a process which is reinforced as East and Southeast Asia become the economic powerhouse of the planet.

Overall strategies of the British Empire helped to shape much of the state system of the modern Muslim world, and left key issues to bedevil subsequent development—amongst them the problem of Palestine, the relationship of the Gulf states to their larger neighbours, and the role of Islam in the identity of modern states from West Africa to Malaya. Styles of rule gave shape to internal politics from the problems of civil war in Nigeria and the Sudan, through to the division of India at independence and the significance of the military in Jordan. The British, along with other European empires, enabled Islam to spread more widely than ever before. In the process Britain became in part Muslim herself.

NOTES

1 C.A. Bayly, *Imperial Meridian: The British Empire and the World 1780–1930* (London, 1989).

2 This was one of two infamous hoaxes involving the impersonation of oriental potentates perpetrated by Horace de Vere Cole, Adrian Stephen, the brother of Virginia Woolf, and others. Adrian Stephen, *The 'Dreadnought' Hoax* (London, 1983), pp. 24–9.

3 For European and British attitudes to Islam and the Muslim world see, Albert Hourani, *Islam in European Thought* (Cambridge, 1991); Maxime Rodinson, trans. R. Veinus, *Europe and the Mystique of Islam* (Seattle, 1987); Kathryn Tidrick, *Heart Beguiling Araby* (Cambridge, 1981); Norman Daniel, *Islam, Europe and Empire* (Edinburgh, 1966); and Francis Robinson, *Separatism Among Indian Muslims: The Politics of the United Provinces' Muslims 1860–1923* (Cambridge, 1974).

4 Daniel, *Islam*, p. 465.

5 Sharif al Mujahid, *Muslim League Documents 1900–1947*, vol. I, (Karachi, 1990), p. 102.

6 Article 2 of the mandatory instrument for Palestine, 1922, in C.H. Dodd and M.E. Sales, *Israel and the Arab World* (New York, 1970) p. 68.

7 Ayesha Jalal, *The Sole Spokesman: Jinnah, the Muslim League and the Demand for Pakistan* (Cambridge, 1985).

8 Avril A. Powell, *Muslims and Missionaries in Pre-Mutiny India* (London 1993), pp. 226–98.

9 Yohanan Friedmann, *Prophecy Continuous: Aspects of Ahmadi Religious Thought and its Medieval Background* (Berkeley, 1989), pp. 1–46.

10 Ralph Russell and Khurshidul Islam, 'The Satirical Verse of Akbar Ilahabadi (1846–1921)', *Modern Asian Studies*, vol. 8, no. 1, January 1974, p. 18.

11 Anthony Milner, *The Invention of Politics in Colonial Malaya: Contesting Nationalism and the Expansion of the Public Sphere* (Cambridge, 1995), p. 210.
12 Part of Muhammad 'Abd Allah's savage poem, 'The Death of Richard Corfield', in B.W. Andrzejewski and I.M. Lewis (eds), *Somali Poetry: An Introduction* (Oxford, 1964), p. 72.
13 Russell and Islam, 'Akbar Ilahabadi', p. 9.
14 Saidul Haq Imadi, *Nawab Imad-ul-Mulk* (Hyderabad, 1975), p. 130.
15 C.C. Stewart, 'Islam' in J.D. Fage and others (eds), *The Cambridge History of Africa*, 8 volumes, (Cambridge 1986, VII, esp., pp. 192–202, and Gail Minault, *The Khilafat Movement: Religious Symbolism and Political Mobilization in India* (New York, 1982).
16 Barbara D. Metcalf, *Islamic Revival in British India: Deoband, 1860–1900* (Princeton, New Jersey, 1982).
17 Albert Hourani, *Arabic Thought in the Liberal Age 1798–1939* (Oxford, 1962), pp 103–244.
18 William R. Roff, *The Origins of Malay Nationalism,* (New Haven, 1967), esp., pp. 56–90.
19 David Lelyveld, *Aligarh's First Generation: Muslim Solidarity in British India* (Princeton, New Jersey, 1978).
20 Christian W. Troll, *Sayyid Ahmad Khan: A Reinterpretation of*
21 Hafeez Malik ed., *Iqbal: Poet-Philosopher of Pakistan* (New York, 1971).
22 Richard Mitchell, *The Society of Muslim Brothers,* (New York, 1969); and Seyyed Vali Reza Nasr, *The Vanguard of the Islamic Revolution: The Jama'at-i Islami of Pakistan* (Berkeley, 1994).
23 Quoted from Iqbal's 'The Mysteries of Selflessness', *Rumuz-i-Bekhudi* (1918), in Wm. Theodore De Bary and others (eds), *Sources of Indian Tradition* (New York, 1958), p. 756.
24 Afzal Iqbal (ed.), *My Life, A Fragment: An Autobiographical Sketch of Maulana Mohamed Ali* (Lahore, 1942), pp. 35–6.
25 Mushirul Hasan, *Mohamed Ali: Ideology and Politics* (New Delhi, 1981).
26 Martin Kramer, *Islam Assembled: The Advent of the Muslim Congresses* (New York, 1986); and for the charter and activities of the Islamic Conference see, Haider Mehdi, *Organization of the Islamic Conference: OIC: A Review of its Political and Educational Policies* (Lahore, 1988).

The British Empire and Muslim Identity in South Asia

British Empire in India saw major transformations in the identities of its Indian subjects. The growth of the modern state, the introduction of new systems of knowledge, the expansion of capitalist modes of production, and the spread of communications of all forms—railway, telegraph, post, press—made possible the fashioning of all kinds of new identities at local, regional, and supra-regional levels. One of the identities which developed most strikingly was the Muslim. Indeed, at independence in 1947 it gained the particular accolade of embracing its own modern state in the shape of Pakistan. This political outcome, however, was just part of an extraordinary series of developments in Muslim identities under British rule which shed light not just on the nature of British rule but also on major changes at work in Muslim society.

That Muslim identity would become a prime theatre of activity did not seem likely in the eighteenth century. Amongst Muslims who were descended from, or who liked to claim that they were descended from, those who had migrated to India to seek service at its many Muslim courts—Turks, Persians, Arabs, Afghans—their Muslim identity was not a matter of overriding concern. At the courts of the Mughals they divided not into Hindu and Muslim factions but into Turkish and Persian ones. They shared their Persian high culture with Hindus, including their poetry which rejected Indian life and landscape as fit subjects for poetic response and found its imaginative horizons in Iran and Central Asia. Family was an important source of identity and this was zealously maintained in family histories, especially if the family claimed descent from the Prophet. Place of settlement was also a source of identity and this was exemplified in the eighteenth century by the custom amongst scholars, poets, and administrators, as they travelled in search of patronage, of adopting the names of their home qasbah hence, 'Bilgrami', 'Mohani', or 'Rudawlwi'. As the eighteenth century progressed, and Shias came to assert themselves—notably in the Mughal successor states of Murshidabad and Awadh—Shia and Sunni came to be, from time to time, significant badges of difference amongst Muslims. Amongst these, and other possibilities, the category 'Muslim' was not of overriding importance. Learned men ('ulama), whose job it was to police the boundaries of community behaviour, would make a point of drawing a distinction between what they considered Muslim religious practice and that of non-Muslims; but this, for the most part, was as far as things went.

Amongst Muslims who were descended from converts to Islam, that is the vast majority of Muslims who expressed themselves through the regional cultures and languages of India—Bengali, Tamil, Malayalam, Gujarati, Sindhi, Punjabi, and so on—the distinctions of language, metaphor, and behaviour between Muslims and the wider society in which they moved have seemed so slight to some that they have referred to an Islamic syncretistic tradition in Bengal[1] or one Indian religion expressed through different religious idioms in the Tamil country of the south.[2] Scholars differ as to precisely what meaning should be attributed to the forms of religious expression of Muslim convert populations. What is clear, however, is that their's was a piety of local Sufi cults in which, more often than not, people of all faiths might participate and which might be expressed as much through regional 'Hindu' idioms as through those classically understood to be Muslim. Such was the nature of Muslim identities in the eighteenth century that many have been able to see them as part of a working 'composite culture'.[3] Such an understanding, nevertheless, should always be qualified by noting that some Muslims had a cultural and imaginative reach that went well beyond the borders of South Asia and that the leading Muslim scholar of the first half of the eighteenth century, Shah Wali Allah of Delhi (d. 1762), was able to declare that 'we are an Arab people whose fathers have fallen in exile in the country of Hindustan, and Arabic genealogy and Arabic language are our pride.'[4]

The period of British rule, which eventually became British empire, brought distinct new strands, indeed firmer edges, to Muslim identities. There was a sharpening of the distinction between Muslim and non-Muslim, which was, in part, an outcome of the impact of British understandings of India and, in part, that of religious revivalism.

There was also the development of a separate Muslim political identity against the claims of an all-inclusive Indian national identity. Parallel with this last process a pan-Islamic dimension to Indo-Muslim consciousness emerged which, for a time between 1919 and 1924, threatened to engulf Muslim politics. The gendering of Muslim identity was a feature as women became a key part of the battlefield across which the discourse of Muslim progress was fought. Finally, there were trends towards individualism, towards asserting individual fulfilment against community obligation, which were arguably part of a process of secularizing Muslim identity and the emergence of Muslims who were purely Muslim by culture.

That such remarkable developments took place in the nature of Muslim identities during the period of the British Empire might suggest that the British presence had a powerful role to play. Certainly, it was influential. But it is crucial not to ignore the powerful element of Muslim agency at work. Each new strand that went to shape Muslim identities under British rule will be examined bearing in mind the questions as to why they emerged and what they meant.

The Sharpening of the Distinction between Muslims and non-Muslims

It has long been part of Indian nationalist historiographical tradition that the British privileged religious identities in India over other possibilities, which inevitably helped to sharpen distinctions between Muslim and non-Muslims. An important part of this process has come to be seen in the British construction of knowledge about India, and the ways in which this construction not only influenced British governance but also Indian ideas about themselves. From the very beginning of the serious study of India in the eigheenth century, Warren Hastings and the orientalists around him—Jones, Halhed, Wilkins—thought of India in terms of Hindus and Muslims. The former were seen to have enjoyed a great classical civilization to AD 1200 while the latter were interlopers in the subcontinent whose empire from the thirteenth century coincided with the decline of classical Indian civilization. The orientalists sought classical texts to guide them in government and in the administration of justice, for instance Halhed's *Code of Gentoo Laws* derived from the Sanskrit *sastras* of the Brahmins or Burhan al-Din Marghinani's *Hidaya* compiled in

Central Asia in the twelfth century, rather than grappling with the complexities of the Indian present. When the British came to place a framework of interpretation over India's past, they divided it into Hindu, Muslim, and British periods. When, from 1871, they began the decennial census of their Indian empire, they tabulated its peoples under religious headings. When they described their empire in imperial and provincial gazetteers, they gave substantial consideration to their Indian peoples as religious groupings down to the level of the district and small town.[5] For much of the nineteenth century, moreover, this tendency to interpret Indian society in terms of religion was reinforced by the committed Christian beliefs of a good number of administrators and the presence of many missionary organizations.

In this context the category Muslim became a major part of the discourse of the colonial state, both within itself and with society at large. Much social action, whether it be competition for jobs in government offices or riots in town and countryside, was interpreted in terms of Muslim and Hindu rivalry. While Muslims, themselves, when they came face to face with the state, more often that not had to define themselves primarily as Muslims. They did so to the census enumerator or when they signed up to join the army; they did so when they went to school or hospital; they did so when they came to vote. The outcome was that men and women, whose Muslimness might not have been prominent in their consciousness of themselves, came to find it increasingly to be so. In the process they became more aware of what might distinguish them from non-Muslims—as for instance, those Bengali Muslims of the late nineteenth century who stopped invoking God as Sri Sri Iswar in favour of Allaho Akbar and who dropped their Hindu surnames (Chand, Pal, Dutt) in favour of Muslim ones (Siddiqui, Yusufzai, Qureshi).[6]

It would, however, be wrong to regard the British as playing the only role in privileging the Muslim category and in sharpening distinctions between Muslims and non-Muslims. Of great importance was the movement of revival and reform which has in various ways striven to vitalize Muslim life on the subcontinent from the early nineteenth century to the present. This was not just an Indian phenomenon but an Islam-wide one, as Muslims strove in various ways to find answers to their loss of power in the world, but it did achieve a particular force and variety of expression in British India. Among the manifestations of the movement were: the jihad movement of the *mujahidin* of Sayyid Ahmad Barelwi (d. 1831) in northern India,[7] that of Sayyid Fadl Alawi in Malabar,[8] and that of Hajji Shari'at Allah (d. 1838) in Bengal;[9] there were the movements of Deoband and the Ahl-i Hadith in the later nineteenth century;[10] and those of the Tablighi Jama'at and the Jama'at-i Islami in the twentieth.[11] Common to all these movements was an attack on all religious practices, which could be conceived of as having a Hindu element, and a concern to assert their understanding of 'pure' Islamic practice. The records of India's learned and holy families speak of the passing of this spirit through the towns and villages of the land, of the debates that were held and of the compromises that were made to accommodate the new boundaries of acceptable 'Islamic' behaviour.[12]

Side by side with the attack on Hindu practices there was also an assault on all behaviour at saints' shrines which suggested that the believer sought the saint's intercession for him with God. At its conception Islam had been profoundly this-worldly, but with the development of its mystical dimensions it had acquired a substantial other-worldly focus. Now, with the assault on intercession, there was to be a profound shift back towards this-worldly piety. Salvation was to be achieved only by action on earth. Particular force was given to this requirement by the colonial context. In the absence of Muslim power to enforce the holy law, Muslims had to use their individual conscience and will to ensure that the law was observed. To achieve this there was a new emphasis on literacy, on the translation of basic works of scholarship on guidance from Arabic and Persian into Indian languages, and on the making of them widely available through the use of the printing press. There began the era of chapbooks and how-to-be-Muslim guides, which can be found down to the present in the bazaars and bookshops of India and the wider Muslim world.[13] When the time came in the early twentieth century to reach beyond the literate, the Tablighi Jama'at or 'Preaching Society' sprang up with the mission to transmit orally its essential Islamic message and to exemplify in the dress and activities of its missionaries the basic standards of 'Islamic' behaviour.[14]

The new 'willed' or quasi-protestant Islam did much to sharpen the distinctions between Muslim and non-Muslim. But for one Muslim, Sayyid Abul A'la Mawdudi, who is arguably the most influential Islamic thinker of the twentieth century, it did not go nearly far enough. Responding, as Syed Vali Nasr has recently shown, to threats in the

1920s and 1930s which Hindu assertiveness seemed to represent to Indian Muslims, he created his vision of a hermetically sealed Islamic world in which all human understanding and all human activity would be subject to revelation. State power, moreover, would be used to put into effect the law derived from revelation.[15]

Of course, the Muslim movement of revival and reform and British rule interacted with each other in shaping definitions of Muslim distinctiveness. Muslim jihad movements and fears of the implacable opposition of so-called Wahhabis were sources of constant concern to the British down to the First World War. 'Fanatical' was the epithet most commonly applied to Muslims, and it was one which only gained force in the late nineteenth century as information flowed into India of British encounters with Muslims elsewhere in the Empire, say in the Sudan or Somaliland.[16] Aspects of Muslim revivalism certainly helped to underpin the British construction of India in religious terms. On the other hand, British rule and the cultural challenges it brought also contributed to sharpening Muslim senses of difference. Not only was there a concern to police the boundaries between Muslim and Hindu behaviour but also those between Muslim and European behaviour. The fatwa literature, the writings of the 'ulama, and the guidance of Sufi pirs were full of responses to society's anxieties as to what European customs and innovations it might be permissible to adopt. Could electric light be used in a mosque? Could European customs of eating at table with knives, forks, and spoons be followed? Could European dress be worn? How far could women be permitted the freedom of their European cousins? The presence of the British and the stream of changes they brought stimulated a continuing debate about where the boundaries of proper Muslim conduct might be.[17]

THE DEVELOPMENT OF A MUSLIM POLITICAL IDENTITY

If for the Indian nationalist historian the British privileged religious identities, in general, and the Muslim identity, in particular, they are regarded as being even more responsible for the emergence and continuance of a Muslim political identity. The case might begin by showing how the colonial construction of knowledge helped to establish religious categories of thought in the mind of the Raj and then show how setting these groupings against each other was a policy some had very much in mind. '"Divide et impera" was the old Roman motto,' declared Elphinstone, the distinguished early nineteenth century governor of Bombay, 'and it should be ours.'[18] And, if such views were thought to be an aberration, they remained very much in the minds of late-nineteenth century administrators, whether it was the vigorous denial of Sir John Strachey in the 1880s that 'nothing could be more opposed to the policy and universal practice of our Government in India than the old maxim of divide and rule...'[19] or Sir Antony Macdonnell's open consideration of the possibilities. 'We are far more interested in [encouraging] a Hindu predominance,' he wrote to Curzon in the 1890s, 'than in [encouraging] a Mahomedan predominance, which, in the nature of things must be hostile to us.'[20]

Most scholars reject a crude 'divide and rule' analysis in favour of noting British concerns to attract powerful allies to their side. Here the focus comes to rest on a particular dynamic which led to the establishment of a Muslim political identity in the developing democratic framework of the Raj. In the 1860s and the 1870s the British were particularly concerned about their failure to attract Muslims to their rule; it was a concern summed up in the title of W.W. Hunter's notorious tract, *The Indian Musalmans* (1871), which was written in response to Viceroy Mayo's question, 'Are the Indian Musalmans bound by their Religion to rebel against the Queen?'. This meant that, when a group of north Indian Muslims, led by the gifted and energetic Sayyid Ahmad Khan, strove to build bridges between Islam and modern science and between Indian Muslims and the colonial state, they were looked upon with approval. When this group went on to found MAO College Aligarh in 1877 and the All-India Muhammadan Educational Conference in 1886 to carry the process forward, it received moral and material support from the government. When this group, known as the Aligarh movement, made a point of not supporting the Indian National Congress, the organization of Indian nationalism, the British were not displeased. Moreover, when representatives of this movement went in deputation to the viceroy in 1906 to ask for special representation for Muslims and recognition of their 'political importance' in the new legislative councils announced by the secretary of state, they were received with sympathy. Furthermore, when they applied enormous pressure as the Morley–Minto council reforms were going through Parliament, they were granted separate electorates for Muslims with extra seats, over and above their proportions of the population, in those provinces where they were 'politically important'.[21]

British understandings of Indian society, British fears and British styles of rule all played their part in making possible the formal recognition of a Muslim political identity in the developing constitution of their Indian empire. Thus Muslims all over India were given a political identity which had been the concern mainly of the Muslims from the north. Separate electorates, moreover, were to remain a feature of the two subsequent devolutions of power in 1919 and 1935. While no direct line should be drawn between the establishment of a Muslim political identity in the constitution in 1909 and the emergence of Pakistan in 1947, it was one of many enabling developments.

The responsibility for the emergence of a Muslim political identity, however, cannot entirely be laid at the feet of the British. Significant attention needs to be given to processes within the Indian society. There was the Hindu movement of revival and reform which, like that of the Muslims, was powered forward by the need to confront colonial rule and Western knowledge. A great ferment of activity was stimulated which in northern India led to the promotion of distinctive Hindu symbols such as the Nagri script (of Sanskrit) as against the Muslim Persian script then used in government, the increasing sanskritization of Hindi so as to differentiate it from Urdu, and the assertion of Hindu preferences in many localities with regard to cows or religious processions as against those of Muslims. Agitation for Hindi led Sayyid Ahmad Khan in 1869 to talk for the first time of working just for Muslims.[22] Recent attempts to make Nagri the script of government, which would put Muslims out of work, and bruising battles over religious preferences on municipal boards were part of the backdrop to the Muslim deputation to the viceroy and its requests for privileges and protection. Indeed, the often close relationship between Hindu revivalism and the Congress was always going to make for a difficult relationship between Muslims and Indian nationalism.[23]

There was also the Muslim movement of revival and reform. Sayyid Ahmad Khan had his intellectual roots deep in the traditions of the Muslim revival. His Aligarh movement is the expression of that revival that has come to be known as Islamic modernism, which achieved its culmination in British India in the thought of Muhammad Iqbal, who succeeded in building a bridge between Islam and the idea of progress, not least in the organization of a modern state. It was suffused with memories of past Muslim glory and the need to restore that glory in the present. The classic statement of its mood was Hali's *Musaddas*—an elegy on the rise and fall of Islam—composed in the 1870s at Sayyid Ahmad Khan's request. Readings from the poem would often be used to introduce educational and political meetings and with verses such as the following leave audiences in tears:

> There is meanness in everything we do. Our ways are worse than those of the most base.
> Our forefathers' reputation has been eaten away by us. Our step makes our countrymen ashamed.
> We have thrown away our ancestors' credit, and sunk the nobility of the Arabs.[24]

Aligarh was designed to deal with this situation. Its alumni were to be the new Muslim elites of British India. They were to form the All-India Muslim League in 1906 which fought for separate electorates and special privileges for Muslims in the Morley–Minto council reforms. They were the key supporters of the League as it strove in subsequent years to preserve the Muslim political identity. Nevertheless, the vicissitudes in the support for this identity must be recorded. In the second decade of the twentieth century the young Muslim elites of northern India were firmly behind it. But in the 1920s support drained away: Muslim landlords joining landlord parties, young professionals joining the nationalist movement, and some leaving politics altogether. In the 1930s it virtually disappeared: only once, between 1931 and 1936, did the Muslim League meet in full session; between 1931 and 1935, Jinnah, the League's key figure, had his main residence in London; while in the first general election after the 1935 Government of India Act it won only 22 per cent of the seats reserved for Muslims. It was only in the special circumstances of the 1940s that the League was able to give the Muslim political identity the broad appeal that enabled it to win over 90 per cent of the reserved Muslim seats in the elections of 1945–6.[25]

BRITISH EMPIRE AND THE PAN-ISLAMIC STRAND

Muslims have always had a special feeling for the idea of their community, their *umma.* At one level this might be acknowledged in the *salam* to neighbours during the act of prayer or in the particular rites performed at a saint's shrine. At another level community might be understood in the fact that all Muslims belonged to a community created by God's grace; they gave alms each year for the support of the community; they endured the privations of the Ramadan fast as one; and that they looked forward to the ultimate celebration of the community in the company of Muslims from all parts of the world during the annual pilgrimage to Mecca.

A feature of the Muslim world all through the twentieth century has been that more and more Muslims have developed a pan-Islamic dimension to their consciousness; more and more have engaged imaginatively and emotionally with the fate of Muslims in faraway lands. In India this development was given a particular intensity, in part, because the British Empire played such a considerable role in the conquest of Muslim peoples and the decline of Muslim power and, in part, because Indian Muslims themselves felt especially insecure.[26]

One development which expanded horizons was the increasing ease of travel that owed much to the shipping routes and railway lines that underpinned the trading and communications network of the Empire. From the 1860s increasing numbers of Muslims went to Britain and to Europe to absorb Western learning or to train as lawyers and doctors. Others went to Cairo or Istanbul to pick up the latest in Muslim ideas. Many seized the opportunities created by the Empire to expand their trading communities around the Indian Ocean shore from Malaysia and Burma through the Gulf to East Africa. Many, too, as they formed half of the Indian army, found themselves fighting the Empire's wars in South Africa or on the western front, but also against Muslims in Mesopotamia or on the North West Frontier. But most important was the way in which improvements in sea travel enabled increasing numbers to perform the pilgrimage to Mecca. In good years tens of thousands performed their holy duty, some coming to settle in the Hijaz as scholars or traders.[27]

A second development of particular note was the construction of the Indo-European telegraph line by a British government which had been made powerfully aware of the strategic benefits of the telegraph in the Mutiny uprising. From 1865 this made possible the rapid transmission of news to and from the subcontinent and gave a massive stimulus to the growth of the Muslim press. Indeed, there was a symbiotic relationship between the growth of pan-Islamic consciousness and the growth of the press which bears comparison with the relationship which Benedict Anderson has noted between the rapid march of print capitalism and the emergence of national consciousness in early modern Europe. The more Indian Muslims discovered about the fate of their brethren elsewhere in the Islamic world, the more they wished to know. When Russia and the Ottoman Empire went to war in the late 1870s, the press boomed. When the British invaded Egypt in 1882, it boomed again. When the Ottoman Empire entered its terminal stages from 1911 onwards, the press boomed as never before. Great newspapers flourished—Abul Kalam Azad's *al-Hilal*, Muhammad 'Ali's *Comrade*, Zafar 'Ali Khan's *Zamindar*.[28]

The new mental horizons were not expressed just in a thirst for news of the Muslim world. They were also expressed in the themes of some of the most successful novels of the time: Sarshar's (1845–1903) *Fasana-yi Azad*, written against the background of the Russo-Turkish war of 1877–8 in which the eponymous hero goes off to the Crimean War to fight alongside the British and Muslims against the Russians,[29] or the many historical romances of 'Abd al-Halim Sharar (1860–1926),[30] which were set in all parts of the Muslim world. The leading Muslim historian of the day, Shibli Nu'mani (1857–1914) devoted his energies to reawakening interest in past Muslim lives and culture, especially the achievements of Arabs and Persians.[31] It was symptomatic that much of the more successful poetry had pan-Islamic themes; Hali's *Musaddas*, for instance, took the world by storm after its publication in 1879, going quickly through six editions.[32] While a vaunting Islam-wide vision pervades the poetry of Muhammad Iqbal. When he wanted to emphasize the decline of Islam, he wrote a tearful poem about the end of Arab rule in Sicily; when he wanted to reflect on human creativity, he wrote his great poem on the mosque at Cordoba; moreover, he wrote much of his verse in Persian so as to reach an audience beyond the confines of India.[33]

Pan-Islamic concerns were also expressed in dress. The Turkish fez was part of the early uniform of Aligarh, as the movement identified with the Ottoman reformers. Muslim scholars in Lucknow followed clothing fashions in Egypt, Syria, and Iran.[34] While at the height of pan-Islamist activism in the second and third decades of the twentieth century Western-educated Muslims made a point of shedding Western dress in favour of Muslim dress bearing distinctive Islamic symbols. Such was the level of identification with the wider Muslim world that men and women were willing to spend huge resources in time and money to further pan-Islamic causes. One, at least, was driven to contemplating suicide when he heard in 1912 that the Bulgarians had advanced to just twenty-five miles from Istanbul.[35]

The most powerful expression of the pan-Islamic dimension to Muslim identity came with the period which stretched from the Balkan wars in 1911 through to the abolition of the Turkish Caliphate in 1924. Great organizations were founded to carry forward pan-Islamic purposes: there was the Red Crescent Mission of Indian Muslim volunteers to provide medical services to Turkish troops in 1912; there was the Anjuman-i Khuddam-i Ka'ba founded in 1913 to protect and otherwise serve the holy places of Islam; there was the Indo-Ottoman Colonisation Society of 1914 which aimed to establish a pan-Islamic settlement at Adana; and there was the Central Khilafat Committee founded in 1919 to protect the temporal and spiritual power of the Turkish caliphs. This last organization swept aside the Muslim League and for two years dominated the Indian National Congress, playing the key role in enabling Gandhi to persuade it to adopt policies of non-cooperation with the government. The Khilafat movement, as it came to be known, had mass appeal not only attracting the Western educated, the traditionally educated but also women and large numbers from the small towns and even the countryside. The movement went into decline from 1922, as the British arrested its leaders and the Turks moved towards abolishing the caliphate. Nevertheless, it was the most substantial mass movement in India since the Mutiny uprising. And, even though it was profoundly bound up with Muslim unease about their position in India as well as being an expression of their opposition to British rule, it was also remarkable witness to their sensitivities to the Muslim world beyond the subcontinent.[36]

The failure of the Khilafat movement led to a reassessment of the pan-Islamic dimension of Muslim identity. Realizing that there was no political salvation to be found in the wider Muslim world, Muslims made their pan-Islamic identity subordinate to a Muslim national identity, or an Indian national identity, or a socialist or even a communist one. Nevertheless, pan-Islam remained an important sub-strand in thought and action. It was expressed in their concern over the future of Arabia in the 1920s, in their support for the Muslim Congress movement—the forerunner of the Islamic Conference Organization—in their ambitions to create a pan-Islamic university, and in their enormous interest in the fate of the Arabs under the Palestine mandate. It was also expressed in the pan-Islamic missions of Indian Muslim organizations, whether the unorthodox Ahmadiyya or the orthodox Tablighi Jama'at.[37]

BRITISH EMPIRE AND THE GENDERING OF MUSLIM IDENTITY

One of the more striking developments in Muslim identity under British rule is its acquisition of a female dimension. Traditionally, if we can risk a brief flirtation with essentialism, Islamic law divided society into public and private realms. The public realm was the key realm. This was the world of the adult man, the place where Islamic social action took place and where the community visibly existed. It was to be distinguished from the domestic world wherein existed the weak—women, children, and slaves. Women, in particular, were seen as sources of *fitna*, social chaos, a threat to the moral order. The man's world was, therefore, the arena of Muslim identity. Here were the distinctive symbols of Muslim identity—mosque, madrasa, and Sufi shrine. Men, too, as Barbara Metcalf tells us, 'learned Arabic and conventionally carried distinctive Islamic names; women knew the regional languages and their names often evoked only beautiful qualities or flowers.'[38] But under British rule women became both guardians of the shrine of Islam in domestic space and moved into public space. Talk about women—indeed, their talk about themselves—increasingly filled public space, and their behaviour and deportment come to range amongst the most potent signifiers of Islamicity. This was a consequence, in part, of the new ideas of womanhood and the status of women which were carried to India by official and non-official Britons and, in part, of the way in which women became the prime site at which the intersecting discourses of colonialism and modernity (at the social level) took place. The role of women became a key issue for Muslims as they considered how they should progress in the world.[39]

From the early nineteenth century the British brought issues regarding women into the public arena with their campaigns against the burning of widows, female infanticide, child marriage, and female seclusion. Once the issues of sati and female infanticide had been addressed by the state, missionaries made much of the running. In the case of Muslims their particular concerns were bringing education to women, attacking seclusion, and improving knowledge about health and the provision for it. There were zenana missions, zenana clubs, and even magazines especially for women. The twentieth century saw the state increasingly concerned to create greater opportunities for women. By the 1930s there were 2.5 million girls in schools of which 0.5 million were Muslims. Substantial attention was being paid to women's health issues, in particular, maternity. Muslim women, moreover, were gaining specific state recognition in the Child Marriage Restraint Act of 1929, the Shariat Application Act of 1937, and the Dissolution of Muslim Marriages Act of 1939. In the Government of India Act of 1935, furthermore, they were acknowledged as having political rights in seats specifically reserved for them. By the 1940s the public existence of Muslim women was widely acknowledged and the business of enlarging the space they occupied was now in the main the task of Muslims themselves.[40]

More important than the ideas that came to India from without in developing a female dimension to Muslim identity was the response of Muslim society to colonial rule. Reformist 'ulama, confronted with the power of non-Muslims in public space, transformed their womenfolk from being threats to the proper conduct of Islamic society to being central transmitters of Islamic values and symbols of Islamic identity. The classic statement of this new position is Mawlana Ashraf 'Ali Thanawi's *Bihishti Zewar*, written in the first decade of the twentieth century, whose volume sales since are probably second only to the Quran. Thanawi's Muslim woman was to be able to read and write Urdu, perhaps to read Arabic, to fulfil her religious obligations, to keep her house in order, to bring up her children with due care, and to be able to sustain appropriate relations with those outside the household. She was regarded as being equal in responsibility and in human potential to men. But in a world in which the Muslim male might well be sullied by the compromises necessary to successful operation under colonial rule, she and her sisters became key sustainers of Islamic values.[41]

In the 1930s Mawlana Mawdudi, the founder of Islamism in India, gave a new twist to the central role of Muslim women. Whereas the reformist 'ulama had generated their new role for Muslim women, as far as can be ascertained, without reference to Western models, Mawdudi, as the classic statement of his position in *Purdah and the Status of Women in Islam* reveals, was obsessed by the freedoms permitted to women in the West.[42] He emphasizes the natural superiority that Islam gave men over women. The task of women was to run the home and their education should be limited to what was necessary to enable them to do so; they should not think of leaving it very much. This home, moreover, in the context of British rule and the films, dress, music, and morals that came with it, had a very special part to play: 'The *harim*,' he declared,'is the strongest fortress of the Islamic civilization, which was built for the reason that, if it ever suffered a reverse, it may then take refuge in it.'[43]

While for the reforming 'ulama and for Mawdudi women and their world became fortress Islam, for those Muslims who made Western standards a key criterion of progress, the 'Western' education of their women and their entry into public space became increasingly a measure of their progress and modernity. This was very much part of the thinking of the Aligarh movement as it developed. If Sayyid Ahmed Khan, himself, thought that men deserved priority, this was less the concern of his followers—Nazir Ahmad, Hali, Shaykh 'Abd Allah, and Begum Shah Jahan of Bhopal. Their efforts led to the foundation of the Aligarh Girls School in 1906 which by 1937 grew to a College offering degree classes. Women in this circle and others carved out for themselves a literary space for themselves in short stories, novels and magazines such as *Khatun*, *Ismat*, and *Tehzib-un-Niswan*. They also began to organize in public. In 1914 the All-India Muslim Ladies Conference was founded. Then for two decades Muslim identities tended to be subsumed within the larger female identities of the leading women's organizations: the All-India Women's Conference, the Women's India Association, and the National Council of Women of India. In the late 1930s, however, the common feminist front was destroyed by the communalization of politics. In the campaign for Pakistan women played an active role on the streets.[44]

Colonial rule both brought Muslim women into public space and led to some Muslims elevating them into the bulwark of their civilization. One way or another women came to represent a substantial part of the Muslim identity. For Muslims and for Westerners the different roles which women filled in their social orders became prime markers of the differences between them. Equally for Muslims the different freedoms they gave their women became key markers of the differences amongst themselves. Of course, this is not a situation confined to British India, but one experienced in societies throughout the Muslim world. It is one, however, which has come to bear particularly heavily on Muslim women in the independent states of India and Pakistan. In the former, women have had to suffer, as in the

Shah Bano case of 1986, because to subordinate Muslim personal law to the common civil code would mean an assault on Muslim identity. Indeed, for Hindu revivalists they have become the very epitome of what is wrong and bad about Muslim society.[45] In the latter, women have had their freedoms sacrificed on the altar of the state's 'Islamic identity'.[46]

BRITISH EMPIRE AND A NEW SENSE OF INDIVIDUALISM

A further development of no little interest was the emergence of a new sense of self, of growing individualism. Of course, this development was mainly restricted to a small elite literate, for the most part, either in English or in Urdu, but it is nonetheless observable. Paradoxically, British rule and the Muslim movement of revival and reform both served to heighten forms of Islamic/Muslim identification which, in principle, should have meant heightened willingness to subordinate individual will to that of the community, but they also created the conditions in which some Muslims increasingly came to assert their desire for individual fulfilment as against the broader claims of the Muslim community and its law. We see these developments in the emergence of Muslims who assert their right to interpret Islam for themselves, as opposed to accepting the interpretations of the 'ulama, through to the emergence of growing numbers of those who were Muslims merely by culture. In the later years of British rule such Muslims often held leftist views as progressive writers, socialists, or communists. Amongst them there were also women who were concerned to raise, and discuss in public, issues which Muslims had traditionally kept concealed.[47]

In a broad sense the contributions of British rule to this development are not hard to discern. It was, of course, the prime channel through which the post-Enlightenment ideas of the West reached India—ideas of the rights of man and of personal fulfilment, vindications of earthly existence and earthly pleasures, and growing tendencies to celebrate not model lives but lives of all kinds. Such ideas were instinct in much Western literature and some of the institutions exported to South Asia. They were also represented in the behaviour and the attitudes of a good number, though certainly not all, of the colonial British. These, however, were not the only sources of incipient Indian Muslim individualism. There was the spread of capitalist modes of production with their erosion of old communal loyalties and their empowerment of individuals. There was the emergence of the modern state with its growing capacity to reach down to each individual citizen. There was also the changes in the technology of communication, in particular the adoption of print, which enabled Muslims to command knowledge as never before and also to begin, as never before, the exploration of their inner selves.[48]

It would be simple to see the emergence of individualism as the outcome of the projection of British power into India. But it is also the outcome of major changes in Islamic culture, which we have already characterized as the shift from 'other-worldly' to 'this-worldly' Islam. The willed or 'protestant' Islam, which was the central feature of 'this-worldly' religion required Muslims to take action for Islam on earth if they were to achieve salvation. The link between salvation and work for Islam on earth, with no chance whatsoever of intercession, helped to set in motion processes that might underpin the development of a more individualistic Muslim self. Many of these processes bear comparison with those that led in the direction of individualism from the Reformation of Christian Europe.

Muslims were empowered by the thought that they and only they were responsible for shaping the earthly world. God gave his guidance, but they were the actors. The overwhelming responsibility placed on Muslims to act on earth runs through all manifestations of their movement of revival and reform. It is well expressed in the challenge which Iqbal makes man throw at God:

You created the night—I lit the lamp.
You created the clay—I moulded the cup.
You made the wilderness, mountains and forests.
I cultivated the flowerbeds, parks and gardens.[49]

Muslims who will their religion make their own choices. The more they do so the more they affirm their own autonomy, their own individuality. Once Muslims move down this path, there must always be the possibility that they will choose to express their individuality by choosing not to believe. With the affirmation of the self, however achieved, there also comes the affirmation of the ordinary things of the self. A striking feature of twentieth-century Indo-Muslim culture has been the increasing valuing of ordinary human things: biographies of the Prophet talk about Him no longer as the Perfect Man but as the perfect family man; women have moved out of seclusion to demand that they and all things to do with them are given respect; even religious philosophers talk of finding God in all the mundane things of life. Then a willed religion had to be a self-conscious one. Muslims had to ask themselves regularly whether they had done all in their power to submit to God and carry out His will in the world. The ground was thus prepared for the 'inward turn'; the self's inner landscape increasingly lay open for exploration.

'This-worldly' Islam made man the chief actor on earth, made his life the prime centre of meaning, and made it clear that he chose either to enjoin the good and forbid the evil or did not. Although designed to reinforce Islam, it also underpinned a valuing of individual desire which might run counter to community requirement. The tension, potential or actual, between individual and community is acknowledged in much twentieth-century Muslim writing. Indeed, the tension is notably expressed in the stridency of some women's writing. It is a tension, moreover, which is broken as from time to time some Muslims burst through the bounds of community to embrace the world of unbelief and other beliefs that lies beyond. In such ways the long-term and unintended outcomes of Islamic reform might work together with influences channelled by the British from the West to bring various 'secular' strands to Indo-Muslim identities.[50]

The period of British rule saw the emergence of new strands of identity among Indian Muslims. For many their religious identity became their prime identity. For a good number, too, their religious identity became their political identity. Muslim imagination expanded to embrace the lives and fate of Muslims elsewhere in the world; for some this became an all-absorbing concern. Increasingly, Muslim identity in public space acquired a feminine dimension. Moreover, individuals were beginning to emerge who wished to be treated as individuals; they rejected the demands made upon them by their 'community' and resisted all stereotyping from without. It should be clear that not all Muslims were affected by all of these processes, and some by none of them. In sum the period of British rule saw a particular privileging of the religious dimension of Muslim identities, but at the same time it also saw other strands emerge which Muslims might choose to emphasize.

In each of the new strands of Muslim identity we have identified, we have discovered processes set going both by British rule and by religious and cultural change within Muslim society. These processes have been independent of each other and have interacted with each other. Thus the sharpening of the distinction between Muslims and non-Muslims was both a consequence of British views of Indian society and of the impact of the Muslim movement of revival and reform; the development of a Muslim political identity was both a consequence of British policies towards Indian society and the fears of the north Indian Muslim elite; the emergence of a pan-Islamic dimension to Muslim identity was the outcome in part of the new world of Muslim communication enabled by the British Empire as also of the values and fears of Indian Muslims; the gendering of Muslim identity owed its development not only to new ideas of women's rights brought to India from the West but also to the new and special role given to women as Muslims sought to respond to British rule; and the new individualism (at this stage of but a few) certainly derived some impetus from the manifold impact of the British Empire on Indian society but was also instinct in the path of individual responsibility which 'this-worldly' Islam set out for Muslims.

Finally, it may be instructive to place the Indo-Muslim experience in the wider context of British interactions with Muslims elsewhere in the Empire. It is arguable that India's Muslims were unique in the intensity of their self-conscious identity as Muslims. They were notable in their development of a Muslim political identity. They were notable, certainly for a short period, in the intensity and impact of their pan-Islamic identity. On the other hand, they were less notable in the gendering of their identity and in the emergence of claims to individual expression as against community obligation. This said, India appears unusual in the extent to which these latter two processes were also underpinned by developments within Muslim society itself.

NOTES

1 Asim Roy, *The Islamic Syncretistic Tradition in Bengal* (Princeton, 1983).

2 Susan Bayly, *Saints, Goddesses and Kings: Muslims and Christians in South Indian Society, 1700–1900* (Cambridge, 1989).

3 Jawaharlal Nehru, *The Discovery of India* (Calcutta, 1946); M. Mujeeb, *The Indian Muslims* (1967); Mushirul Hasan, *Legacy of a Divided Nation: India's Muslims since Independence* (Delhi, 1997). For a recent critique of the composite culture thesis see, Cynthia Talbot, 'Inscribing the Other, Inscribing the Self: Hindu-Muslim Identities in Pre-Colonial

India', *Comparative Studies in Society and History*, vol. 37, no. 4, October 1995, pp. 692–722.

4 Cited in Annemarie Schimmel, *Islam in the Indian Subcontinent* (Leiden, 1980), p. 121.

5 David Ludden, 'Orientalist Empiricism: Transformations of Colonial Knowledge', in Carol A. Breckenridge and Peter Van Der Veer (eds) *Orientalist Empiricism: Transformations of Colonial Knowledge*, (Delhi, 1994), pp. 250–78.

6 Rafiuddin Ahmed, *The Bengal Muslims 1871–1906: A Quest for Identity* (Delhi, 1981), pp. 72–133.

7 Mohiuddin Ahmad, *Saiyid Ahmad Shahid: His Life and Mission* (Lucknow, 1975).

8 S.F. Dale, *Islamic Society on the South Asian Frontier: The Mappilas of Malabar, 1498–1922* (Oxford, 1980).

9 Muin-ud-Din Ahmad Khan, *A History of the Faraìdi Movement in Bengal* (Karachi, 1965).

10 Barbara D. Metcalf, *Islamic Revival in British India: Deoband 1860–1900* (Princeton, 1982).

11 M. Anwarul Haq, *The Faith Movement of Mawlana Muhammad Ilyas*, (1972); and Seyyed Vali Reza Nasr, *The Jama'at-i Islami of Pakistan* (Berkeley, 1994).

12 Altaf al-Rahman Qidwai, *Anwar-i Razzaqiya* (Lucknow, n.d.), pp. 17; C. Liebeskind, 'Sufism, Sufi Leadership and "Modernisation" in South Asia since c. 1800' (Ph.D. thesis, London University, 1995), pp. 317; J.R.I. Cole, *Roots of North Indian Shi'ism in Iran and Iraq: Religion and the State in Awadh, 1722–1959* (Berkeley, 1988), pp. 237.

13 Francis Robinson, 'Islam and the Impact of Print in South Asia', in Nigel Crook (ed.), *The Transmission of Knowledge in South Asia: Essays on Education, Religion, History and Politics* (Delhi, 1996), pp. 62–97.

14 Christian W. Troll, 'Five Letters of Maulana Ilyas (1885–1944); The Founder of the Tablighi Jama'at: Translated, Annotated and Introduced', in Christian W. Troll (ed.), *Islam in India: Studies and Commentaries* (Delhi, 1985), pp. 138–76.

15 Seyyed Vali Reza Nasr, *Mawdudi and the Making of Islamic Revivalism* (Oxford, 1996), pp. 27–46.

16 Francis Robinson, *Separatism Among Indian Muslims: the Politics of the United Provinces' Muslims 1860–1923* (Cambridge, 1974), pp. 126–7.

17 Liebeskind, 'Sufism' (Ph.D. thesis, London University, 1995), pp. 294–308; K.A. Nizami 'Socio-Religious Movements in Indian Islam (1763–1898)', in S.T. Lokhandwalla (ed.) *India and Contemporary Islam* (Simla,1971), pp. 109–10.

18 Robinson, *Separatism*, p. 2.

19 Ibid., p. 131.

20 Ibid., p. 134.

21 Ibid., pp. 84–174.

22 Ibid., p. 98.

23 Francis Robinson, 'The Congress and the Muslims', in Paul R. Brass and Francis Robinson (eds), *Indian National Congress and Indian Society 1885–1985: Ideology, Social Structure, and Political Dominance* (Delhi, 1987), pp. 162–83.

24 Christopher Shackle and Javed Majeed (ed. and trans.), *Hali's Musaddas: The Flow and Ebb of Islam* (Delhi, 1997), p. 147.

25 A. Jalal, *The Sole Spokesman: Jinnah, the Muslim League and the Demand for Pakistan* (Cambridge, 1985).

26 Jacob M. Landau, *The Politics of Pan-Islam: Ideology and Organization* (Oxford, 1990).

27 F.E. Peters, *The Hajj: The Muslim Pilgrimage to Mecca and the Holy Places* (Princeton, 1994), pp. 266–362; C. Snouck Hurgronje, *Mekka in the Latter Part of the 19th Century* (London, 1931).

28 Robinson, *Separatism*, p. 186.

29 Ralph Russell, 'The Development of the Modern Novel in Urdu', T.W. Clark (ed.), *The Novel in India: Its Birth and Development* (London, 1970), pp. 110–17. It should be noted, however, that Sarshar was a Hindu but his work was successful because of the Muslim market for work of this kind.

30 Muhammad Sadiq, *A History of Urdu Literature,* second edition (Delhi, 1984), pp. 430–5.

31 Ibid., pp. 358–68.

32 Ibid., pp. 347–51.

33 Ibid., p. 450.

34 Abdul Halim Sharar, *Lucknow: The Last Phase of an Oriental Culture,* E.S. Harcourt and Fakhir Husain (eds and trans.) (London, 1975), p. 176.

35 Mohamed Ali, *My Life: A Fragment,* Afzal Iqbal (ed.), (Lahore, 1942), pp. 35–6.

36 Gail Minault, *The Khilafat Movement: Religious Symbolism and Political Mobilization in India* (Columbia, 1982).

37 Francis Robinson, 'Prophets without Honour: the Ahmadiyya', *History Today,* 40, June 1990, pp. 42–7; Mumtaz Ahmad, 'Tablighi Jama'at', in John L. Esposito (ed.), *The Oxford Encyclopedia of the Modern Islamic World,* 4, pp. 165–9.

38 Barbara D. Metcalf, 'Reading and Writing about Muslim Women in British India', Zoya Hasan (ed.), *Forging Identities: Gender, Communities and the State* (Delhi, 1994), p 3.

39 Gail Minault, *Secluded Scholars: Women's Education and Muslim Social Reform in Colonial India* (Delhi, 1998); Azra Asghar Ali, 'The Emergence of Feminism Among Indian Muslim Women 1920–47', (Ph.D. thesis, University of London, 1996).

40 Ali, 'Emergence of Feminism'.

41 Barbara D. Metcalf, *Perfecting Women: Maulana Ashraf 'Ali Thanawi's Bihisti Zewar: A Partial Translation with Commentary* (Berkeley, 1990).
42 Abul A'la Maududi, *Purdah and the Status of Women in Islam,* (New Delhi, 1974).
43 Cited in Faisal Fatehali Devji, 'Gender and the Politics of Space: The Movement for Women's Reform, 1857–1900', in Hasan (ed.), *Forging Identities*, pp. 35–6.
44 Ali, 'Emergence of Feminism', pp. 259–381.
45 Paola Bacchetta, 'Communal Property/Sexual Property: On Representations of Muslim Women in a Hindu Nationalist Discourse', in Hasan (ed.), *Forging Identities*, pp. 188–225.
46 Ayesha Jalal, 'The Convenience of Subservience: Women and the State of Pakistan', in Deniz Kandiyoti (ed.), *Women, Islam & the State* (Basingstoke, 1991), pp. 77–114.
47 Francis Robinson, 'Religious Change and the Self in Muslim South Asia since 1800', *South Asia*, vol. XX, no. 1 (1997), pp. 1–15.
48 Ibid.
49 Translation of part of Iqbal's poem, 'God's Talk with Man' in N.P. Ankiyev (ed.), 'The Doctrine of Personality', *H. Malik Iqbal: Poet–Philosopher of Pakistan* (New York, 1971), p. 274.
50 Robinson, 'Religious Change', *South Asia*, vol. XX, no. 1 (1997), pp.13–15.

Living Together Separately: The 'Ulama of Farangi Mahall c. 1700–c. 1950

One day in May 1980, the diners in the ground floor section of the Kwality restaurant in Lucknow's Hazratganj looked up from their meals to see a most unusal sight. A group of traditionally dressed Muslims was moving some what self-consciously through the tables towards the stairs which would take them to the private dining room on the upper floor. They were a striking sartorial vision, wearing a range of styles, some from the nineteenth century particularly, in the form of head wear, some of which would draw attention in the Chawk let alone Hazratganj. These were 'ulama of Farangi Mahall—Matin Miyan, 'Abd al-Rahman Sahib, Mufti Rada Ansari, Fakhir Miyan Bahr al-'Ulum and descendants of the saint of Bansa, Mushir Miyan and Hashim Miyan Razzaqi, who with myself were all guests of the famous Lucknow bookseller, Ram Advani. Ram had been aware of the great hospitality I had been receiving from the Farangi Mahallis and Razzaqis over the past four months and wished to show his gratitude on my behalf.

Once we had sat down and begun to eat I realized that no one seemed willing to talk. I put on my best British good manners and strove to draw everyone into conversation. It quickly became clear that my sallies were unwelcome. The Farangi Mahallis and Razzaqis wished to eat in silence out of respect for their host. It was companionable silence. When the guests had eaten their fill, conversation did develop. But it was not long before the guests said their thanks and their farewells, and descended the stairs to leave to the startled gaze of the diners below. All concluded, as far as I knew, that it had been a most successful event. We all knew, too, how unusual it had been for the Farangi Mahallis and Razzaqis to make the mile and a half journey from the Chawk to dine in the Kwality restaurant, Hazratganj.

This anecdote serves to introduce the Farangi Mahall family of learned and holy men as one which has lived separately from other religious communities but, equally, has been happy to coexist with them. Indeed, for much of its history, family members have seen their past and to some extent their future through a family and a Muslim lens. From time to time they have been concerned to draw clear distinctions between their world and those of others. Of course, it could be argued, and probably rightly, that a family of Muslim learned and holy men was more likely than most to live 'separately' within India. This said, we will note that, when in the twentieth century some shareable public spaces opened up, Farangi Mahallis were able to join other communities, though in small numbers and generally for a restricted time.

Like many of sharif descent, or those who liked to pretend to sharif descent, the Farangi Mahallis traced their line back to the time of the Prophet. It was their ancestor, Ayyub Ansari, who had been the Prophet's host at Medina, and it was he who had been the Prophet's standard bearer and, subsequently, the leader of a naval expedition against Constantinople in c. 638, in which he died.[1] The Farangi Mahallis then traced their descent through the eleventh-century mystic, 'Abd Allah Ansari of Herat, whose descendants migrated to India in the early years of the Delhi Sultanate, establishing themselves in the region of Panipat. In the fourteenth century, one 'Ala al-Din migrated eastwards, settling in the village of Sihali in Awadh. From the mid-sixteenth century, they were able to trace their ancestors in large numbers of documents relating to their rights in land down to the point when their ancestor, the great scholar, Qutb al-din Sihalwi, was murdered by neighbouring zamindars in a squabble over land, and the emperor Awrangzeb in recompense to his four sons made the famous donation of the sequestered *haweli* of a European indigo merchant in Lucknow—Farangi Mahall.[2]

The learned and holy men of Farangi Mahall were also conscious of their various contributions to Muslim rule. They knew that Qutb al-din Sihalwi and his pupils had brought *ma'qulat* scholarship to its peak in the late seventeenth- and early eighteenth-century northern India, a peak which was recognized in West Asia. They knew, too, that Qutb al-Din's son, Nizam al-din, had reformed the madrasa curriculum, which came to be called the Dars-i Nizami, so that it was a much more effective training for administrators. Indeed, not only was it adopted throughout India but it had also been endorsed by the East India Company, when it established the Calcutta madrasa. But Farangi Mahalli contributions did not end with improved forms of education. They also knew that their ancestors had served Indian Muslim rulers: the Mughals themselves, and Mughal successor states, the Nawabs of Farrukhabad, Rampur, Awadh and Arcot, the Begums of Bhopal, and most especially the Nizams of Hyderabad.

Their vision of their past, a classically sharif vision, meant that many Farangi Mahallis would have sympathized with the rhetoric of Muhsin al-Mulk and Imad al-Mulk who drafted the Muslim address to Viceroy Minto in 1906. They had come to India from Arabia and while in India had long been associated with the exercise of Muslim power. Equally, from the mid-nineteenth century onwards, there was a dimension of their consciousness which embraced the Islamic world, but particularly West Asia, and which was especially sensitive to the advance of Western power there. Thus, in 1878, when Russia went to war against the dying Ottoman Empire, 'Abd al-Razzaq of Farangi Mahall founded the Majlis Mu'id al-Islam and compaigned throughout north India to raise funds for the Ottoman cause. His grandson, 'Abd al-Bari, performed the Hajj three times, studied and taught in Mecca and Medina, and visited Baghdad, Damascus, Beirut, Alexandria, and Cairo. He kept a house in Medina so that, as he declared in this will, he might be regarded as being a resident there when he went to heaven, and maintained a correspondence with Muslims of the region, amongst them Young Turks and Sharif Husayn of Mecca. It is hardly surprising that, from the moment that the Ottoman Empire entered its death throes in 1913 to 'Abd al-'Aziz's announcement of this kingship of Sa'udi Arabia in January 1926, most of his energy and imagination should have been focussed in this direction and that, in the process, he should have drawn many members of his family, as well as many Muslims, with him.[3]

Another perspective on the sense of themselves that the Farangi Mahallis had in India is provided by the religious guidance they followed and offered. The Farangi Mahallis paid enormous respect to the Qadri saint Sayyid Shah 'Abd al-Razzaq of Bansa, who died in 1724. In his 1917 essay on the *'urs* at Bansa, 'Abd al-Bari declared that for the 'ulama of Farangi Mahall, however learned they were, 'attendance at his 'urs, has been a means of reinforcing faith'.[4] Indeed, traditionally, at the ceremonies of the 'urs, the Farangi Mahallis were given the place of greatest prominence. On the other side, representatives, of the holy family of Bansa were present at all key moments of the family's life whether official occasions of their madrasa or the death of family members. To bring the saint's blessings, the family always tried to have at least one member of the saint's family staying with them, as they did on the occasion of the dinner in the Kwality restaurant.

In following the traditions of Bansa, as far as it has been possible to discover, the Farangi Mahallis followed only those recorded by their ancestor, Mulla Nizam al-Din (d. 1748). The mulla had been a friend and khalifa of the saint. His narration of the Banswi tradition in his *Manaqib-i Razzaqiyya*[5] places the saint in a world which is clearly populated by Hindus—indeed, on one occasion the saint is attracted to a Hindu boy.[6] The anecdotes that are told, however, are concerned to show Muslim superiority, as a Hindu mystic is revealed to be materialistic,[7] or the distinction between a Muslim and a Hindu position on the transmigration of souls.[8] Equally, the saint is demonstrated to be a strong supporter of those who uphold the law and dignity of Islam, as when he congratulates a disciple who had fasted during a hot monsoon Ramadan when travelling to Bansa,[9] and as when he praises a host at a qawwali concert for upbraiding his guests for going into ecstasy at songs in Hindi but not doing so when they hear verses from the Quran.[10]

There is no hint in the Farangi Mahalli tradition, as represented by the written record, or my personal involvement with the family for over thirty years, of support for the religious practices expressed in Nawab Muhammad Khan Shahjahanpuri's two malfuzat collections, *Malfuz-i Razzaqi* and *Karamat-i Razzaqi*, which belong to the latter half of the eighteenth century. These express concerns not just for the shari'a but for religious harmony in Awadh. The saint shows respect for taziyas and the Muharram processions of Shias. He shows marked respect for the Hindu religious world, and receives it in return. Thus he is present at Diwali celebrations, watches *bakhtiyas* performing the life of Krishna, and has visions of Ram and Lakshman; in turn, Krishna would send his salam to the saint. Such acts, as one might expect, were a step too far for 'ulama. There were important distinctions which had to be maintained.[11] Disciples, however, who belong to this tradition were honoured, nonetheless; Hasrat Mohani, *murid* of 'Abd al-Wahhab and author of poems in praise of Krishna and Mathura, is one of the few non-family members to lie in the family graveyard—in a separate section. Shias and Hindus were always welcome at the family's madrasa.

As far as formal religious guidance is concerned, although the evidence is not considerable, in the late nineteenth century, the Farangi Mahallis seemed rather more accepting of the requirements of living harmoniously in a largely Hindu society than the reformers. Whereas Rashid Ahmad Gangohi of Deoband issued fatawa 'that discouraged social and business intercourse with Hindus, forbade attendance at Arya Samaj lectures (unless one were skilled in debate) and deemed illegitimate the appearance of being Hindu, whether in dress, hairstyle or the use of brass instead of copper vessels',[12] the fatawa of 'Abd al-Hayy of Farangi Mahall declared that, although a Muslim most certainly could not accept a Hindu donation for a mosque, he could eat food prepared by a Hindu, wear clothes washed by a Hindu, and abstain from cow sacrifice, provided it was to avoid a riot and not because he thought the beast was holy.[13]

At this juncture, it is important to reiterate that the Hindu world only seems to have a small purchase on the Farangi Mahalli mind during the eighteenth and nineteenth centuries. Let us look briefly at three works by Farangi Mahallis covering the period from c. 1800 to the early twentieth century. They are: the malfuzat of Anwar al-Haqq (c. 1822) with some additional elements of family history, *al-Aghsan al-Arba'a*, by Wali Allah Farangi Mahalli (c. 1855),[14] the life and malfuzat of 'Abd al-Razzaq, the *Anwar-i Razzaqiyya*, by Altaf al-Rahman Qidwai,[15] and *Salah Falah* by 'Abd al-Khaliq Farangi Mahalli, which was a commentary on the times.[16] The first describes an entirely Muslim world; Hindus do not appear in any way, shape, or form. Apart from the usual mystical and biographical concerns, the main focus is on the problems that this family of Sunni 'ulama had in dealing with the Nawabs of Awadh and their courtiers, and the growing presence of the British both as a source of employment and as a great power in relation to the Nawabi state. The second work covers the life of 'Abd al-Razzaq, including his journey to Madras when young, his involvement in the Mutiny uprising, and after that event his increasingly strong awareness of the British, whom he detested. It also contains substantial coverage of his sayings and miracles. There are only four points in this extensive work where one might gather that 'Abd al-Razzaq lived in a land which was also peopled by Hindus.

Two come as throwaway comments: he recalls that on his journey to Madras in his youth he found blessing in the lands ruled by Hindus which were not present in those ruled by Christians,[17] and he speculates that Muslims came to use fireworks at the festival of Shab-i Barat as a result of the influence of Diwali celebrations.[18] Two come in demonstrations of the spiritual power of the Mawlana. In the first he succeeds in preventing the relations of Hindu Raja, who had secretly converted to Islam from cremating his remains,[19] and in the second he demonstrates to a Muslim, drawn to mysticism by Hindu *jogis*, the greater satisfaction of an Islamic spiritual path.[20] Indeed, 'Abd al-Razzaq saw the future in terms of an almost apocalyptic struggle between Muslims and Christians. The time will come, went one of his sayings, when:

> the world will be divided into two camps, one under the Muslim flag and the other under the Christian flag. The people under the Christian flag will get food cheaply and those under the Muslim flag will pay dearly for it. at that time it will be difficult to protect the faith.[21]

Indeed, it is striking, although we should not really be surprised, how Islamically focussed the Farangi Mahallis were as they considered the future in India. The years after the Muslim address to Viceroy Minto in 1906 saw the beginnings of increasingly intense reflection on the future of Muslims in India and purposeful action. In 1909 'Abd al-Khaliq of Farangi Mahall published *Salah Falah* or his suggestions for the betterment of Muslims. The world view he expresses is substantially changed from that of 'Abd al-Razzaq. It is one which reflects both the press discourse of several decades as well as a view of India expressed in British writings. He regards the British Raj as a good thing; a suppressor of disorder and a source of justice and progress.[22] His world, moreover, is distinctly formed in terms of 'Hindus' and 'Muslims'. He writes of the rise and decline of India in the pre-British period in a language of Hundi–Muslim conflict,[23] of the Mutiny uprising being Hindus versus Hindus and Muslims versus Muslims,24 of how well the *mahajans* have done under British rule,[25] of how Hindu lawyers had all been in favour of Sir Sayyid when he came to Lucknow in 1886 to make his Qaisarbagh speech, and of how the Sayyid had succeeded in offending many through his attitudes to Hindus (in fact, Bengalis).[26] The 'Hindus' have emerged in 'Abd al-Khaliq's consciousness as they have not appeared in family discourse before. His prime concerns, however, remain as purely Muslim as

'Abd al-Razzaq's had been, though his emphases were diametrically opposed; Muslims had slipped behind, he argued, because they had failed to follow the Islamic exhortation that they advance in knowledge. Sayyid Ahmad Khan's Aligarh initiative was just what Muslims should be following.[27] He talks proudly of the presence of Islam in Britain and in the USA, of its rapid advance in Africa, and of a British report which tells of half the population of China being Muslim![28] Islam, he declares, is progressing in India through conversion.[29] The upshot is that, problems of Shia–Sunni rivalry apart, which absorb a quarter of the book, Islam has bright future in India and in the world.

Given this view of a Muslim future in India, in which Hindus appear primarily as the subject of conversion, though to be fair not aggressively so, it was to be expected that the first Muslim organization to be founded in this period by the Farangi Mahallis (apart from their madrasa in 1907) would be focussed completely on a Muslim future. In 1910, responding, in part perhaps, to the great agitation which surrounded the campaign for separate electorates in the Morley–Minto reforms,[30] and, in part perhaps, to the establishment of the Muslim League's headquarters in Lucknow in that year, 'Abd al-Bari presided over the refounding of the Majlis Mu'id-Islam. It aimed, amongst other things 'to try to help the Muslims attain progress in worldly matters, while keeping in mind the injunctions of the shariat'.[31] Its members found themselves subsequently involved in, amongst other things, 'Abd al-Bari's Anjuman-i Khuddam-i Ka'ba organization, the struggle to protect the hold places, and the Kanpur Mosque campaign.

The period of the First World War saw no broadening of their perspective. At this time we are privileged to be able to listen to Farangi Mahallis, and their associates, discussing matters amongst themselves in the pages of *Al-Nizamiyya*, a house journal to which mainly younger members of the family contributed from 1915 to 1919. The purpose of the journal had a specific Muslim focus, and its contributors were Muslims, although it did publish *nath* poetry in praise of the Prophet by a Hindu, Raja Kishen Pershad 'Shad', chief minister of Hyderabad. Amongst its aims were 'the progress of Islam and the encouragement of Muslims to follow its tenets, in all possible ways' and 'the strengthening of unity amongst Muslims'.[32] In subsequent issues we find 'ulama probing into the nature of nationality and how it may be preserved. Ibn Khaldun's idea that it was group solidarity or party spirit (*'asabiyya*) which enabled groups to survive, and in favourable circumstances to dominate others, seems to have been their starting point. 'It was group solidarity,' argued Muhammad Yunus of Farangi Mahall, 'that had enabled both the Aryans to maintain their national existence amongst non-Aryans and the English to maintain their dominion over India.'[33] Later he added that it was high moral principles which enabled a nation to progress. Islam had brought the Arabs to an advanced state, and, when they neglected it, they declined.[34] In the same vein, Sibghat Allah of Farangi Mahall argued that nations survived by protecting their national characteristics (*qawmisi'ar*), and the secret of doing so lay in *ta'assub*, that is bias in favour of one's group, which was precisely what Islam endorsed.[35] In the same issue Sayyid Amin al-Hasan Mohani brought the discussion to the point of action needed in the present. Missionary work (*tabligh*) had enabled a handful of men in the Prophet's time to form and rule a universal community. This was what was needed in the present times to achieve the higher end of nationality (*qawmiyyat*) and democracy (*jumhuriyyat*).[36] There was no sense, he declared, in this wartime period, in which Indian nationalist feeling was growing and in which a Lucknow pact was to be signed, of any nationalist vision that was not purely Muslim. The Shahabad riots of autumn 1917, in which many Muslims were killed by Hindu mobs protesting against cow sacrifice, led Sibghat Allah of Farangi Mahall to reflect on the importance of maintaining the symbols of difference. Muslims must maintain their identity by protecting their chief characteristics of which sacrifice (*qurbani*) was one. Hindus had a sense of solidarity which underpinned their nationalism. They avoided Muslims who they regarded as untouchables or barbarians (*mlecchas*), and despite Muslim rule they had not allowed themselves to be absorbed into Islam.[37]

Similarly, the Farangi Mahallis' focus remained held within a narrow Islamic frame when they had to confront a real issue of devolution of power in India. In 1917, in the aftermath of the Lucknow Pact, but also in that of the Shahabad riots, their Majlis Mu'id al-Islam had an opportunity to present an address to Secretary of State Montagu and Viceroy Chelmsford, who were touring India to gather opinion on constitutional reform. 'Abd al-Bari's telegram calling 'ulama to meet to consider their address made his position on collaboration with Hindus clear: 'Mussalmans nominal leaders and outward co-religionists are in delusion of union with infidels. If 'ulama keep silent Mussalmans will suffer great loss. The matter must be consulted over and a deputation of 'ulema presented before the Secretary of State.'[38] The draft address which emerged from this meeting only confirmed their separate vision, their anger at Hindus, and their need for protection aginst them. It required some very nimble work on the part of Hakim Ajmal Khan and Dr Ansari to remove most of the elements which could be seen as undermining Hindu–Muslim unity and the Lucknow Pact, and to replace them with a formulation that the government was to describe as 'a nakedly impracticable demand for the predomination of priestly influence'.[39]

In the Khilafat period it could be argued that the Farangi Mahallis softened their views towards Hindus, which to some extent they did. It was Gandhi who was the key figure in building a relationship. He had heard of 'Abd al-Bari from Mushir Husayn Qidwai when he was in England, and it is believed that they first made contact when Gandhi attended the 1916 Congress in Lucknow. They came into regular contact as Gandhi campaigned for the release of the 'Ali Brothers and against the Rowlatt legislation. When he came to Lucknow he would stay in Farangi Mahall; to this day Farangi Mahallis point to the room in the Mahalsera in which Gandhi stayed and the papaya tree (though by now surely a replacement) to which the Mahatma would tie his goat. When during 1919 the Khilafat issue became pressing, it was 'Abd al-Bari who courted Gandhi to the extent that in the following year he was able to boast: 'I have made Mahatma Gandhi to follow us in the Khilafat question.'[40] By June 1920 Gandhi was heading a small committee of Khilafatists to put non-cooperation into practice and by September, with Muslim help, the Congress had been won for Gandhi and for non-cooperation.

The remarkable period of political action which followed has been trumpeted as a period of Hindu–Muslim unity, which it was, and Hindu–Muslim friendships which were to endure the nationalist struggle were made in it. But for the vast majority of Farangi Mahallis it was not seen thus. Just as 'Abd al-Bari thought of Gandhi being won for the Khilafat so they saw the Congress in general being won for the cause. Everything, moreover, was fine so long as the tensions between the nationalist movement's search for power in India and the 'ulama's pan-Islamic dreams did not clash. But, of course, they were bound to do so.

As in 1922 and 1923, the prospect of elections to the Montagu–Chelmsford councils became closer, many politicians began to focus on the prospect of real power; the direct action favoured by 'ulama in pursuing their pan-Islamic causes became less attractive. At the same time, the new assertiveness of Muslims in the towns and cities of India, and their prominence in Congress affairs, had galvanized Hindus into acting as Hindus. In the autumn of 1922, the Hindu Sabha was refounded as the Hindu Mahasabha. In spring 1923 Swami Shraddhanad launched the Shuddhi movement amongst the Meos, and in the summer of 1923 northern India was wracked by Hindu–Muslim riots. 'Abd al-Bari, along with several Muslim organizations, leapt to the defence of their co-religionists. The erstwhile protagonist of Hindu–Muslim unity now told his followers to forget about trying to accommodate Hindu feelings. He urged them to sacrifice cows, declaring that:

> if the commandments of Shariat are to be trampled underfoot then it will be the same to us whether the decision is arrived at on the plains of Delhi or on the hilltops of Simla. We are determined to non-cooperate with every enemy of Islam whether he be in Anatolia or Arabia or in Agra or Benares.[41]

By the end of the Khilafat period, arguably the first really intense north Indian Muslim engagement in the public sphere at the national level, Hindus were firmly in the Farangi Mahalli consciousness.

In dealing with the Farangi Mahallis we have tended to treat them as an undifferentiated group. But it should be clear that we have been dealing in large part, though not wholly, with those in the dominant (in numbers at least) line of descent from Qutb al-Din Sihalwi—that of Mulla Sa'id—and, in particular, those attracted by the leadership of 'Abd al-Razzaq and his grandson, 'Abd al-Ḅari. Until the 1937 elections, the politically minded of these, like the influential Mawlana 'Inayat Allah, head teacher of the Madrasa Nizamiyya, tended to be supporters of the Congress. But, at this point, they began to turn to the Muslim League of which, in 1942, 'Abd al-Bari's son, Mawlana Jamal Miyan, became the honorary assistant secretary.

Others, however—for instance, the younger brothers of 'Abd al-Khaliq, the author of *Salah Falah*, Mawlanas 'Abd al-Hamid and 'Abd al-Majid, from the side of the family descended from Qutb al-Din's third son, Mulla Nizam al-Din, through the great eighteenth-century scholar 'Abd al-'Ali Bahr al-'Ulum—took a pro-British and anti-nationalist line. There was a history of ill-feeling between the descendants of Mulla Sa'id and Mulla Nizam al-Din going back to the time in the early nineteenth century when 'Abd al-Bari's great-grandfather, Mulla 'Ala al-Din, had been preferred as successor to Bahr al-'Ulum as sajjadanashin over the great man's son 'Abd al-Rab. In 1912 ill feeling broke out again when 'Abd al-Hamid and 'Abd al-Majid resigned as teachers from the Madrasa Nizamiyya in protest over 'Abd al-Bari's anti-government stance on pan-Islamic issues. In 1918 they were rewarded with a government grant to set up their own madrasa in opposition to Madrasa Nizamiyya. Throughout the First World War and the Khilafat Movement they issued fatawa in support of the government and against the pronouncements of 'Abd al-Bari. Both were awarded medals of Shams al-'Ulama.

From the 1930s, one or two others, inspired in large part by the Progressive Writers Movement, broke with their family's sharif Muslim view of the world. Hayat Allah Ansari, for instance, founded a communist study circle, published a pro-Congress Urdu socialist weekly, *Hindustan*, from 1937 until it was closed by censorship in 1942. He edited the Congress *Qawmi Awaz* newspaper from 1945 to 1972, won the Sahitya Akademi Award for the best Urdu novel for this *Lahu ke Phul* (Flowers of Blood), and was President of the Anjuman-i Taraqqi-i Urdu. A staunch Nehruite, he was nominated to the Rajya Sabha. There was also Mufti Rada Ansari, who taught at the Madrasa Nizamiyya from 1936 to 1943 until his radical nationalist activities forced him to resign. He was secretary of the Lucknow branch of the Progressive Writers Association, holding meetings at Farangi Mahall. A communist, he strongly opposed the Muslim League. From 1948 to 1969 he was on the staff of *Qawmi Awaz*, leaving it to become a lecturer in Sunni theology at Aligarh Muslim University. In later life he used to refer to his communist days as 'the time when I was misguided'. There was also Nasim Ansari, son of the active Khilafatist and dedicated teacher, Mawlana Shafi, who joined the Progressive Writers association and supported communism, though not actively, before becoming Professor of Surgery at Aligarh Muslim University. Two of his sisters took the unprecedented step for Farangi Mahallis of marrying Hindus: Wasima married Keshwant Singh and was active in communist circles in Lucknow in the 1950s and 1960s, Khadija married Professor Anrud Gupta, and at least up to the 1980s both were known to be communist sympathizers.

From their arrival in Lucknow in the later seventeenth century down to the early twentieth century, the Farangi Mahallis had been able largely to ignore the Hindu world about them. Part of the sharif world of Muslim governing traditions, they taught in madrasas and served at the courts of Muslim princes. Only two Hindus appear in their record in positions of honour, both in the early twentieth century. One was Raja Kishen Pershad who, like many of his fellow Kayasths, Khatris, and Kashmiri Brahmins, influenced by the world of Muslim courts, was able to contribute to sharif literary culture. The second was, of course, Gandhi, 'Abd al-Bari's key ally in the Congress. It is important to note, however, that throughout 'Abd al-Bari's intense engagement with the nationalist movement, in which thousands of letters and telegrams were received and sent, he had only one Hindu correspondent—Gandhi.[42] When Hindus appear in the record the Farangi Mahallis themselves keep, it is as benchmarks—for instance, as better rulers than the British, or as presenting examples of behaviour Muslims should avoid as in the *Manaqib-i Razzaqiyya*, or as the mirrors in which Muslim superiority might be revealed as in the *Anwar-i Razzaqiyya.* The Hindu presence seems detached from their consciousness, as detached as that of the Farangi Mahalli 'ulama from the world of Hazratganj when they came to dine in the Kwality restaurant.

From the beginning of the twentieth century, it was increasingly clear that the structures of power which sustained the sharif world view were crumbling. In British India the remnants of Muslim court culture were steadily being stripped out of the state machinery; Persian had been replaced by the vernaculars and now Urdu itself, in the Persian script, was under threat from Hindi in the Devanagri script. At the same time, a madrasa education was no longer a route to government service; qualifications from the state system of education were needed and, for the levels of government to which the sharif aspired, these had to be in English. Only by taking service at the courts of Muslim princes was it possible, for the most part, to remain insulated from the new non-sharif world.

Those who remained in British India were confronted not just by a state machine in which Muslims would have to engage with other peoples and cultures on terms not of their own making, but also by a growing public sphere in which they failed to engage with others at their peril. This sphere was there in the press, in the local, provincial, and national arenas of politics, in the political organizations that formed to compete in these arenas, and in the new associations which formed to pursue activities ranging from film and literature to tennis and cricket. Here were opportunities to work together in public, even if they did not do so in private. A few took these opportunities, and it helped to have an income to enable them to do so. Most, however, either continued to live together separately in the new India, sustaining fragments of the once all-powerful sharif culture, or largely for financial reasons left India for Pakistan, West Asia, Britain, and North America.

NOTES

1 The seventeenth-century Ottoman chronicler, Evliya Chelebi, has a marvelously sardonic description of how Mehment Fatih with the help of a dream of his Shaykh al-Islam discovered Ayyub Anasari's tomb at Eyup.

2 This profoundly sharif vision of the Farangi Mahalli past is set out in Mawlana Mawlwi Muhammad 'Inayat Allah, *Tadhkira-yi 'ulama-i farangi mahall* (Lucknow, 1928).

3 For 'Abd al-Bari's life and his focus on West Asia, see 'Abd al-Bari and the Events of January 1926', in Robinson, *'Ulama of Farangi Mahall*, pp. 145–76.

4 'Abd al-Bari, *'Urs-i Hadrat-i Bansa* (Lucknow, n.d., but internal evidence suggests 1926), p. 10.

5 Mulla Nizam al-din's *Manaqib-i Razzaqiyya* was originally in Persian. The edition used here is the Urdu translation made by Sibghat Allah Shahid Farangi Mahalli (Lucknow, n.d., but probably in the 1930s or 1940s). The translation was made at the request of the *sajjadanashin* at Bansa, Sayyid Shah Mumtaz Ahmad Razzaqi.

6 Nizam al-Din, *Manaqib*, p. 64.

7 Ibid., p. 19.

8 Ibid., p. 38.

9 Ibid., p. 24.

10 Ibid., p. 19.

11 For a discussion of this point, see Robinson, *'Ulama of Farangi Mahall*, pp. 64–6.

12 Barbara D. Metcalf, *Islamic Revival in British India: Deoband, 1860–1900* (Princeton, 1982), p. 153.

13 'Abd al-Hayy Farangi Mahalli, *Majmua-yi Fatawa Hadrat Mawlana 'Abd al-Hayy Marhoom, Farangi Mahalli*, tenth edition (Lucknow, 1985), vol. 1, pp. 57, 149, and 170.

14 Wali Allah Farangi Mahalli, *al-Aghsan al-Arba'a*, Nadwa ms. (Lucknow, n.d.).
15 Altaf al-Rahman Qidwai, *Anwar-i Razzaqiyya* (Lucknow, n.d.). It is family tradition that 'Abd al-Bari dictated this text to Qidwai, who acted as his amanuensis.
16 Muhammad 'Abd al-Khaliq, *Salah Falah* (Lucknow, 1909).
17 Qidwai, *Anwar*, p. 61.
18 Ibid., p. 45.
19 Ibid., pp. 88–90.
20 Ibid., p. 93.
21 Ibid., p. 128.
22 Khaliq, *Salah*, pp. 16–40.
23 Ibid., pp. 12–15.
24 Ibid., pp. 26–8.
25 Ibid., pp. 33–4.
26 Ibid., pp. 41–2.
27 Ibid., pp. 43–4.
28 Ibid., pp. 71–5.
29 Ibid., pp. 76.
30 'Abd al-Bari had been a strong supporter of separate electorates in the great campaign for them in 1909.
31 Francis Robinson, *Separatism Among Indian Muslims: The Politics of the United Provinces' Muslims 1860–1923* (Cambridge, 1974), p. 276.
32 *Al-Nizamiyya*, 1:1 (March 1915).
33 Muhammad Yunus, 'Tarikhi qawmen kyonkar banti hayn', ibid., pp. 19–24
34 Muhammad Yunus, 'Hamari taraqqi ke raz', *Al-Nizamiyya*, 1:3 (May 1915), pp. 23–7.
35 Sibghat Allah Shahid, 'Qawmi si'ar ka tahaffuz', *Al-Nizamiyya*, 1:3 (May 1915), pp. 29–30.
36 Sayyid Amin al-Hasan Mohani, 'Tabligh', *Al-Nizamiyya*, 1:3 (May 1915), pp. 15–22.
37 Sibghat Allah Shahid, 'Islam ka sab se aham usul: "qurbani"', *Al-Nizamiyya*, 3:8–9 (October/November 1917), pp. 49–57.
38 'Abd al-Bari to Tajuddin, 13 Oct. 1917, copy of the text of a telegram, 'Abd al-Bari Papers, File 10, (English) Farangi Mahall.
39 For how Ajmal Khan and Ansari worked the changes, see Robinson, *Separatism Among Indian Muslims*, pp. 284–6.
40 Ibid., p. 293.
41 For this statement and the strength of 'Abd al-Bari's feelings at this time, see ibid., p. 339.
42 From c. 1912 to 1926 'Abd al-Bari's correspondence and telegrams were carefully kept in letter books from which the range and intensity of his correspondence may readily be ascertained. Farangi Mahall papers, Lucknow and Karachi.

Women as Patrons of Art and Culture: The Begums of Bhopal[1]

For most of the period from 1819 to 1926 Bhopal was ruled by four forceful women. The Begums, as they were known, ruled a state of roughly 7,000 square miles in central India which had been carved out of the decaying body of the Mughal Empire in the eighteenth century by the Afghan soldier–administrator, Dost Muhammad. Their state was the most important Muslim-ruled state after Hyderabad. Their reigns offer a rare opportunity to observe their patronage across a wide range of artistic activity and to seek its distinguishing quality.

That the Begums had such an opportunity was the outcome, in part, both of the early deaths of their husbands and their failures to conceive male heirs and, in part, both of the support they received from the British and their own considerable abilities. The first Begum, Qudsiyya, came to power in 1819, aged seventeen, as regent for her daughter, Sikandar Begum, after her husband had been accidentally killed. She clearly enjoyed ruling, delaying the marriage of Sikandar Begum as long as she could and, when Sikandar's husband, Jahangir Muhammad Khan, tried to seize power, she had the better of the military struggle until the British stepped in and forced her to retire. In compensation she received a jagir of Rs 5 lakhs per annum for life (at this time the total revenue of Bhopal state was only Rs 11 lakhs), which enabled many acts of patronage until her death in 1881.[2]

After the death of her husband in 1844, Sikandar was appointed co-regent with her maternal uncle on behalf of her daughter, and sole regent in 1849 when her uncle had proved himself incompetent. Like her mother she, too, enjoyed power. In 1859, she successfully demanded from the British that she be made ruler in her own right on account of her loyalty to them during the Mutiny uprising. She transformed the administration of Bhopal, more than doubling its revenues during her reign, and was described by her fond granddaughter, Sultan Jahan, as having performed for her state the services of Akbar for the Mughal Empire.[3]

In 1868, Sikandar was succeeded by her only child, Shah Jahan. She did not have to assert herself as her mother and grandmother had done. Rather, she had to be saved from the consequences of her affections. In 1871, a widow, she married one of her officials, Siddiq Hasan Khan, who was an able scholar and leading figure in the Ahl-i Hadith movement of Muslim religious reformers. Much loved by his wife, Siddiq Hasan quickly came to assert himself over the administration of the state, overreached himself, and was deposed by the British.[4]

Sultan Jahan succeeded as ruler on her mother's death in 1901. Initially, the British wondered if she had the ability to rule Bhopal whose affairs had suffered badly in the last years of her mother's life. But Sultan Jahan quickly demonstrated her administrative skills and ruled for a quarter of a century with conspicuous success, abdicating in 1926 in favour of her son Hamid Allah Khan.[5]

Several strands run through the characters of these four women. There was a strong streak of practicality which meant that much of their patronage was used for the public good. There is no better example of this than the great benefactions of Qudsiyya to the people of Bhopal. For instance, spurred by the great loss of life from famine in the late 1860s she donated Rs 15 lakhs from her private purse towards bringing the Indian Midland Railway through Bhopal. She also paid around Rs 6 lakhs to bring pure drinking water into Bhopal city, erecting pumping stations and a network of pipes, with the result that cholera was wiped out.[6]

In all the Begums except Qudsiyya there was a strong strand of scholarship. They wrote books. Indeed, it is from their writings about their family that we come to know so much about them. They enjoyed the company of scholars, supported them, and would exchange copies of their works with Viceroys who were of a literary bent, such as Lytton and Curzon.

The Begums were without fail pious, although their piety could be expressed with a markedly different nuance. In the case of Qudsiyya, whose beliefs were of an unreformed kind, it meant strong opposition to widow remarriage, which led to some estrangement from her granddaughter. Shah Jahan, on the other hand, seems to have shared the reformist views of her second husband; she was strongly opposed to Sayyid Ahmad Khan's educational policies at Aligarh and would only donate funds towards the college mosque.[7] Sultan Jahan, on the other hand, was a strong supporter of all that Aligarh stood for—sending her youngest son there, contributing greatly to its initiatives in women's education, and becoming the university's first chancellor.[8]

In their own lives the Begums displayed a strong belief in the capacity of women to live on their terms. Qudsiyya, Sikandar, and Shah Jahan went without purdah, when it suited them; Sultan Jahan made a virtue of adopting it, when it suited her. The first three actively enjoyed hunting.[9] Sikandar was the first ruler of a native state to perform Hajj, which was not a safe thing to do as her granddaughter discovered when she came under gunfire on her Hajj in 1903.[10] The latter, moreover, was explicit about the superiority of women rulers.[11]

Like most rulers with half an eye on posterity the Begums patronized architecture. Qudsiyya built Bhopal city's Jama Masjid, the minarets of which in purple-red sandstone tower above the bazaar. An inscription on the north doorway tells of her act of charity.[12]

Sikandar led the process of converting Bhopal into a city of 'pukka' buildings. The erection of mud structures was forbidden, artisans were attracted from all over India, many houses, shops, and mosques of brick and stone were built. The most striking of her buildings is the Moti Masjid, or Pearl Mosque, which was inspired by Delhi's Jama Masjid and uses a similar mixture of white marble and red sandstone.[13]

The desire to respond to, perhaps even to outdo, aspects of the Mughal architectural achievement should be noted. This theme runs through some of the major buildings of Shah Jahan, whom her daughter describes as having 'a passion for building'.[14] It is wholly appropriate that she bore the name of the greatest of the Mughal builders and that the new area of Bhopal city in which most of her buildings are to be found was called Shahjahanabad.

'Money flowed like water', declares her daughter, in the construction of the 'Ali Manzil, Benazir, and Taj Mahal palaces for Shah Jahan's own use.[15] The Taj Mahal was built after the models of the Mughal palaces of Delhi. To this the Begum added a personal touch by giving every room, and there were hundreds of rooms, a different colour which was repeated in everything from the doors to its walls and its furnishings. But, having built the palace, the Begum found little comfort in its spacious halls and broad doorways built to the Mughal standard and had them all altered so the overall effect was destroyed.[16] Subsequently, the Taj Mahal Palace came to house the Sultaniyya School for girls and the Benazir, the Alexandria High School for boys.

Shah Jahan's major statement, however, was the Taj ul-Masajid, or Crown of Mosques. This boasts similar dimensions to Delhi's Jama Masjid with a courtyard area of 325 by 325 feet; it also uses a similar red-and-white colour scheme. Its minarets, however, at 270 feet high are more than twice the height of those of its Delhi rival. Construction was started in 1887. By Shah Jahan's death Rs 16 lakhs had been spent and vast sums wasted; for instance, Rs 7 lakhs worth of crystal floor slabs made in England had to be discarded when it was discovered that they reflected the image of worshippers. Further work stopped until the 1970s when the trustees of the Dar al-'Ulum placed in the building set about raising funds to complete it. Now it is a landmark which dominates the skyline for miles and each winter hosts the three-day *ijtima* congregation of the Tablighi Jama'at.[17]

That Sultan Jahan had reservations about her mother's ambitions is clear from the tone in which she writes of them. Her actions were no less eloquent; construction of the Taj ul-Masajid was stopped as soon as she came to the throne. Nevertheless, she too had desires to build. Her husband, Nawab Ehtisham al-Mulk was an architect himself. A good number of public buildings were started in her reign. Moreover, soon after she came to the throne, she commissioned a new palace on a spur running down to the lake outside the city, the Ahmadabad Palace.[18]

Many builders tend to be interested in gardens and garden design, and the Begums were no exception. All four laid out gardens. Qudsiyya's was Aysh Bagh (Garden of Delight), which had many fine trees, a small mosque and a much-admired stepped well. Sikandar's was the Farhat-Afzal Bagh (Increase of Joy Garden). Both still exist. Shah Jahan's was the 'Ali Manzil garden of two terraces attached to the Benazir Palace with magnificently laid out grounds, stonework, and fountains. Here the Begum was accustomed to hold a 'Bazaar'. Sultan Jahan laid out gardens at the Ahmadabad Palace. Her joy in their beauty can be seen in her paintings.[19]

Patronage of literature was expected of any ruler and not least because rulers needed poets to laud their qualities and achievements in *qasidas*. Notable patronage began under Sikandar, who had tried to bring Ghalib to Bhopal but had to settle for sending him gifts. She also commissioned Rajab Ali Beg Suroor to write his story, 'Sharar-e-Ishq' in the style of his *Fasana-yi-Ajayb*. Patronage reached its peak under Shah Jahan. She was a poet herself (under the pen name of, first, 'Shirin' and, later, 'Tajrur') with two diwans and a mathnawi to her name. Love of literature was one of the particular joys she shared with her second husband, Siddiq Hasan Khan. Between them they attracted many poets to Bhopal, of whom the most distinguished was Amir Minai, whose *Amir-i Lughat* was published under the Begum's patronage. Of especial note, however, is the Begum's support for women poets. Amongst the gifted women poets of her circle were Hasanara Begum 'Namkeen', who published a diwan and two prose works, and the two daughters of Nawab Mustafa Khan 'Shefta', the correspondent and literary companion of Ghalib, Munawwar Begum and Musharraf Jahan Begum, both of whom published a diwan. Sultan Jahan's literary patronage was altogether a different matter. Educated on modern lines she disapproved of court poets and favoured men of letters who wrote on 'improving' matters such as science, social reform, and ethics. Among the prominent authors of her day, whom she employed in her secretariat, were Muhammad Amin Zuberi, Niyaz Fatehpuri, and Dr 'Abd al-Rahman Bijnori.[20]

With support for literature there was also support for learning. As we might expect of a family of scholarly tastes, all four Begums patronized learned men. When Sikandar Begum toured northern India in the 1860s, she made a point of going to the Farangi Mahall family of Lucknow, the leading Sunni scholars of the day, to engage in discussions.[21] When her daughter visited Calcutta in 1882, her donations targetted hospitals and places of learning, among them the Calcutta Madrasa and the Asiatic Society of Bengal.[22] In time, Bhopal became a source of patronage for 'ulama not just from within India but also from abroad. Two important presences in the state in the second half of the nineteenth century were those of two Yemeni scholars, Shaykh Husayn 'Arab and Shaykh Zayn al-Abidin, the qadi of Bhopal. These men and others brought with them the teachings of Muhammad Ibn 'Ali al-Shawkani (d. 1834), who followed the great fourteenth-century Hanbali scholar, Ibn Taymiyya. It was not surprising that, when Sultan Jahan performed Hajj, she found herself greeted in the Hijaz by Arabs who were Bhopal state pensioners.[23]

The most striking piece of patronage for scholarship and, ultimately, one of a very personal nature for Shah Jahan, was support for Siddiq Hasan Khan. Hailing from a poor Sayyid family, Siddiq Hasan had been hired by Sikandar Begum to write the history of Bhopal. His rise to become, first, private secretary to Shah Jahan and, then, her second husband, alongside the presence of followers of al-Shawkani, helped Siddiq Hasan make Bhopal into a major centre of the Ahl-i Hadith movement. From here he pressed forward the movement's opposition to taqlid, that is, following the established legal judgements of scholars of the past, and asserted the Quran and Hadith as the only sources of authority. So, within Bhopal, he banned Shia celebrations of mohurrum and Sunni celebrations of mawlud, as well as lesser customs such as the firing of a gun at the birth of a child. Outside the state he indulged in vituperative assaults on leading Hanafi 'ulama, such as Mawlana 'Abd al-Hayy Farangi Mahalli. And with the support of a team of assistants, published between 97 and 222 books (scholars differ as to the precise number). That they were published in Arabic and Persian as well as in Urdu, and from Istanbul and Cairo as well as Bhopal and elsewhere in India, indicates how he wished to address the Islamic world at large. His position in the Bhopal state most certainly gave a boost to his Ahl-i Hadith brand of Muslim reformism.[24]

One area of Muslim culture to which Sultan Jahan gave particular care was Unani Tibb, or Greek medicine, which she noted 'the Mussalmans have in the past identified themselves with ... completely'. Early in the twentieth century it had become clear that this medical system was under major threat from Western biomedicine. Among the system's weaknesses were that surgery—where Western medicine had made great advances—had long been neglected, and that there were no professionally-assured standards of skill. Leading hakims, such as Hakim Ajmal Khan of Delhi and Hakim 'Abd al-'Aziz of Lucknow, were beginning to take steps to enable Unani Tibb to meet these challenges. Sultan Jahan was moved to act for at least two reasons. On the one hand, there was family interest; her father had been extremely knowledgeable in the field and her husband particularly interested in it. On the other hand, it appealed to her sense of practicality; it was much cheaper and more accessible to the poor than Western medicine. To revive and sustain the system she founded a Unani medical school named after her daughter, Asif Jahan, which included surgery in its curriculum. Hakims, too, were required to be registered. Thus, Bhopal was enabled to play a role in the modernizing of a great medical tradition and in enabling it to survive to the present.[25]

The most striking contribution to Muslim culture, and one in which the personal leadership of the Begums was most distinctive, was in the furthering of feminism. All the Begums except Qudsiyya did so by specific action. Sikandar founded the Victoria Girls School at a time when it was most unusual for Muslim women to be educated outside the home. Shah Jahan not only encouraged women poets, but also held women's discussion groups and founded the Lady Lansdowne hospital for women. Her most distinctive contribution, however, was the publication of her *Tehzib un-Niswan* in 1889. This large book was the first woman's encyclopaedia in India. It was eminently practical, after the style of the Begums, in that it dealt with issues that really mattered to women—such as health—and did so in a most accessible form of Urdu. Furthermore, its approach as markedly different from works produced for women by men, not least the classic of the genre, Ashraf 'Ali Thanawi's *Bihishti Zewar*, published nearly two decades later. Whereas the latter reflected his patriarchal views in talking of the submissive and constrained role of women, Shah Jahan focussed on general guidance for women in pregnancy, child-rearing, marriage, and divorce within the framework of the Quran and Hadith.[26]

Sultan Jahan made major steps forward in the patronage of women's causes but with a shift of emphasis away from her mother's Ahl-i Hadith-influenced vision to a modernist one which stood right at the forefront, in social terms, of the Aligarh enterprise. Within Bhopal she made pioneering moves in women's health care by establishing schools for nurses and for midwives. She killed two birds with one stone with the establishment of the Asifiyya Technical School for destitute women. On the one hand, she helped women support themselves by teaching them a useful craft, on the other, the school became the framework within which both the *zari* industry (the decoration of shoes and handbags of various shapes and colour with zari thread and beads on velvet) and new Arab forms of embroidery, such as *kalabattu* (gold threadwork), *poth* (beadwork) and *zanjeeva* (drawn threadwork), came to be introduced to Bhopal and for which the state gained a reputation.[27]

By far the most important influence of Sultan Jahan lay in the education of girls. She had a clear view that to teach girls the Quran and some Urdu was not nearly enough. 'Imperfect education', she declared, 'is worse than none at all.'[28] As good as her word, and not without difficulty, she established the Sultaniyya Girls School in 1902 in an annex to the Taj Mahal Palace. This came to teach a broad modern curriculum as compared with the Quran and Urdu of the Victoria Girls School. In 1907, she opened a similar school for Hindu girls, the Birjisiyya Kanya Pathshala.

At the same time Sultan Jahan was able to carry her vision into the all-India context of the Aligarh movement. From the early 1890s the Muslim Educational Conference had passed resolutions in support of women's education, and from 1896 a Women's Education section had been founded within the Conference.

Nothing, however, was achieved until Shaykh 'Abd Allah, with strong support from his wife, Wahid Jahan, approached Sultan Jahan for a grant to found a school for girls at Aligarh. The Begum promised Rs 1200 per annum and, in 1904, the Educational Conference resolved to found the school. A further generous donation of Rs 20,000 in 1912 secured the construction of a boarding house, thus giving the school the all-India cachet of its neighbouring college. How far the Shaykh and the Begum were ahead of the thinking of the Muslims of their time is clear from the fact that the first pupils were drawn almost entirely from Shaykh 'Abd Allah's family.[29] Sultan Jahan's practical work, however, did not end here. In 1914, she was to found the All-India Muslim Ladies Conference. On the one hand, it was to set up more schools for girls on modern lines and, on the other, it was to give birth in 1917 to the Indian Women's Association, which was to play a major role in the struggle for the extension of female franchise in the 1930s.[30]

The impact of the four Begums on art and culture was greater than can reasonably be expected from the rulers of a state of Bhopal's size. In some ways they used their patronage like any ruler of their time—on poetry and public works, and on scholarship and architecture. In some ways, too, they supported their particular taste, whether it be in gardens or embroidery, or embraced a particular cultural cause, such as the preservation of Unani Tibb. In other ways, however, their patronage reflect their especial concern for women to be able to fulfil themselves not just at home but, increasingly, in the public realm. Here their leadership was most distinctive and their patronage, most important.

NOTES

1 I am most grateful to Siobhan Lambert-Hurley for comment on this article. Her book on Sultan Jahan Begum is due to appear soon as *A Muslim Women's Movement in India: The Begum of Bhopal* (Routledge/Royal Asiatic Society Books, forthcoming).

2 H.H. Nawab Sultan Jahan Begum, *Hayat-i-Qudsi: Life of the Nawab Gauhar Begum alias The Nawab Begum Qudsia of Bhopal*, trans. W.S. Davis (London, 1918), pp. 11–96; and K. Mittal, *History of Bhopal State* (New Delhi, 1990), pp. 18–21.

3 H.H. Nawab Sultan Jahan Begam, *An Account of My Life*, vol. I, trans. C.H. Payne (London, 1910), pp. 5–15.

4 The affection between the two is well-expressed in Shah Jahan's history of Bhopal which has an epilogue by Siddiq Hasan. H.H. Nawab Shajahan Begum of Bhopal, *The Taj-ul Ikbal Tarikh Bhopal or the History of Bhopal*, trans. H.C. Barstow (Calcutta, 1876), p. 150ff, pp. 231–3.

5 Mittal, *Bhopal*, pp. 33–97.

6 Qudsiyya's practical bent is underscored by her will in which she deposited money with the British to cover the costs of maintaining her water supply system without taxation being raised for that purpose from the people. Qudsiyya made two wills, both of which mark her out as a woman of wisdom, piety, and charity. Sultan Jahan, *Hayat-i-Qudsi*, pp. 155–60.

7 H.H. Nawab Sultan Jahan Begum, *Hayat-i-Shahjehani: Life of Her Highness The Late Nawab Shahjehan Begum of Bhopal*, trans. B. Ghosal (Bombay, 1926), p. 235.

8 For Sultan Jahan's key role in enabling the foundation of the Girl's School at Aligarh see, Gail Minault, 'Shaikh Abdullah, Begum Abdullah, and Sharif Education for Girls at Aligarh', in I. Ahmad (ed.), *Modernization and Social Change Among Muslims in India* (New Delhi, 1983), pp. 207–36.

9 The Political Agent, Charles Macpherson, described Qudsiyya, Sikandar, and Shah Jahan thus in 1854:

> The grandmother and mother ride, spear, and shoot grandly or have been used to do so... The Regent [Sikandar] is a wonderful woman in the way of government ... talks exactly in her way like the fastest European woman you may happen to know....

10 H.H. Nawab Sultan Jahan Begam, *The Story of a Pilgrimage to Hijaz* (Calcutta, 1909), pp. 248–57.

11 Reflecting on the achievements of Muslim women rulers, Sultan Jahan declared:

Men are given bodily strength to earn their living and to enable them to fight in battle. Women have been granted the qualities of mercy, sympathy, toleration, fidelity and firmness. These render them especially suitable as rulers of kingdoms though no doubt education and careful upbringing are necessary for both sexes. Given these, women are superior to men.

Sultan Jahan, *Hayat-i-Qudsi*, p. 103.

12 'The construction of the Jama Masjid was commenced in the beginning of the year 1248 AH (AD 1832) corresponding to 1240 by the Fasli calendar, by the generous and virtuous Nawab Gauhar Begum Saheba, daughter of the Nawab Ghaus Muhammad Khan, wife of the Late Nawab Nazir ud-daulah Nazar Muhammad Khan Bahadur. It was finished in the end of the year 1273 AH (AD 1857) corresponding to 1264 Fasli. Eminent architects have given it strength and beauty, and by careful management of honest persons it cost five hundred and sixty-five thousand rupees two annas and nine pies. This inscription is by the hand of Muhammad Abbas Sherwani.'

Ibid., p. 134.

13 Shah Jahan writes with evident pride of her mother's building activities, *Taj-ul Ikbal*, pp. 224–7.

14 Sultan Jahan, *An Account of My Life*, vol. I, p. 198.

15 Sultan Jahan, *Hayat-i-Shahjehani*, pp. 80–1.

16 H.H. Nawab Sultan Jahan Begam, *An Account of My Life*, vol. II, trans. Major Abdus Samad Khan (Bombay, 1922), p. 3.

17 S. Ashfaque Ali, *Bhopal Past and Present* (Bhopal, 1881), Appendix 3; and Sultan Jahan, *An Account of My Life*, vol. I, pp. 198–9.

18 Sultan Jahan, *An Account of My Life*, vol. II, pp. 214–15.

19 Copies of some of these paintings can be found in vol. II of her autobiography and in the Ranken papers (Mss. Eur. F 182) in the India Office Records.

20 Ali, *Bhopal*, Appendices 12 and 13.

21 Shahjahan, *Taj-ul Ikbal*, p. 84.

22 Her donations in Calcutta went as follows: Zenana Hospital Rs 1,000, Bengal Asiatic Society Rs 500, Calcutta Madrasa Rs 300, The Rest House Rs 250, Mayo Hospital Rs 250, Campbell Hospital Rs 250, Indian Agricultural Society Rs 250, The Zoological Gardens and Museum Rs 1,000. Sultan Jahan, *Account of My Life*, vol. I, p. 107.

23 Sultan Jahan, *Pilgrimage*, pp. 270–1.

24 For the Ahl-i Hadith movement and Siddiq Hasan's ideas and circle in Bhopal see Saeedullah, *Life & Works of Nawab Siddiq Hasan Khan of Bhopal* (Lahore, 1973); and Barbara D. Metcalf, *Islamic Revival in British India: Deoband, 1860–1900* (Princeton, 1982), pp. 264–96.

25 Sultan Jahan, *Account of My Life*, vol. II, pp. 142–7.

26 For this comparison I am indebted to my postgraduate student, Azra Asghar 'Ali who, when this article was written, was completing her thesis 'The Emergence of Feminism Among Indian Muslim Women, 1920–47' (Ph.D. thesis, University of London, 1996).

27 Ali, *Bhopal*, Appendix 11.

28 Sultan Jahan went on to say:

> The sweet waters of this spring should either be drunk deep or not tasted at all: hence the necessity of regular schools for communal education. It is a stupid thing, to my mind, to teach the girls to read and write, and then leave them to their fate.

Sultan Jahan, *Account of My Life*, vol. II, p. 150.

29 Minault, 'Shaikh Abdullah', in Modernization and Social Change (New Delhi, 1983).

30 Asghar Ali, 'Emergence of Feminism', chapter 1 (Ph.D. thesis, University of London, 1996).

*Other-Worldly and This-Worldly Islam and the Islamic Revival**

In his *Islam in Modern History*—which was published in 1957, and which remains, till today, a work remarkable for its insights—Wilfred Cantwell Smith refers to the extraordinary energy which had surged through the Muslim world with increasing force in the nineteenth and twentieth centuries. He talks of:

> dynamism, the appreciation of activity for its own sake, and at the level of feeling a stirring of intense, even violent, emotionalism ... The transmutation of Muslim society from its early nineteenth-century stolidity to its twentieth-century ebullience is no mean achievement. The change has been everywhere in evidence.[1]

This surge of energy is closely associated with a shift in the balance of Muslim piety from an other-worldly towards a this-worldly focus. By this I mean a devaluing of a faith of contemplation of God's mysteries and of belief in His will to shape human life, and a valuing instead of a faith in which Muslims were increasingly aware that it was they, and only they, who could act to fashion an Islamic society on earth. This shift of emphasis has been closely associated with a new idea of great power, the caliphate of man. In the absence of Muslim power, in the absence, for the Sunnis at least, of a caliph, however symbolic, to guide, shape, and protect the community, this awesome task now fell to each individual Muslim. I hazard to suggest that this shift towards a this-worldly piety, and the new responsibilities for Muslims that came with it, is the most important change that Muslims have wrought in the practice of their faith over the past one thousand years. It is a change full of possibilities for the future.

* This lecture was given at the Royal Asiatic Society, London, on 10 April 2003, in memory of the great scholar of comparative religion, Wilfred Cantwell Smith.

Throughout Islamic history there has been a tension between other-worldly and this-worldly piety. This said, dependent on time and on context, the broad emphasis in piety has swung first one way and then the other. Amongst the early Muslims the emphasis was this-worldly. In Mecca and Medina, the Prophet and his companions promoted an activist this-worldly socio-political ethic. The community they created was the most successful in worldly terms that the earth had seen. In little over a hundred years it came to rule a huge swathe of rich and fertile lands from Central Asia and the Indian Ocean in the east to the Atlantic Ocean in the west. For the following thousand years, from the eighth to the eighteenth century of the common era, the worldly success of the community helped to underpin the authority of God's revelation to man through Muhammad. The possession of power was seen to be essential to upholding the shari'a, the holy law, the systematized form of guidance for man which Muslim scholars had derived from the Quran and Hadith.

From early on, however, this activist community of Muslims came to develop an other-worldly strand in its piety. This was Islamic mysticism, or Sufism, which was inspired by the Quran, the religious practice of the Prophet, and that of the early Muslim community. It grew, in part, as Arab Muslims came into contact with the Christian and other mystical traditions of the lands they conquered and, in part, as a reaction to the moral laxity and worldliness of the Umayyad and Abbasid courts. Early Sufi feeling was inspired by fear of God and Judgement, then by love, and, in the third Islamic century, by the doctrine of the 'inner way', or the spiritual journey towards God. The mystic progressed along this way through processes of self-abnegation and enhanced awareness of God. The final stage was reached when the self was annihilated and totally absorbed in God. It was this, of course, which led al-Hallaj in 922 to declare, 'I am the Truth', and be brutally put to death for his pains. Side by side with the mystical way there also developed a metaphysical understanding of God and his relationship to humankind. Sufis proposed a transcendent God whose spiritual radiance was reflected in humanity. To discover the divine essence that lay within them, human beings had to overcome their worldly nature.

Thus Sufis fostered an other-worldly piety. Many came to rely on *futuh*, unasked for charity, in order to survive; they glorified poverty; they made much of their complete trust in God; they stood apart from power, as for the most part Indian Chishtis did, and avoided family life. 'When a Sufi gets married,' declared Ibrahim bin Adham in the eighth century, 'it is as if he has boarded a boat; when a child is born to him, it means he has drowned.'[2] On the other hand, there were Sufis who felt bound to engage with the world. Some embraced the powerful. Thus, the shaykhs of the Yasaviyya in Central Asia engaged with the Timurid princes, and the shaykhs of the Naqshbandiyya engaged with the Mughals. Others made it clear that waiting around for God to provide was just not good enough. Men must follow the Prophet's example and be active in society; they must earn their living as traders, they must cultivate the earth.[3] Few were as strong on this point as Abu Hamid al-Ghazzali (d. 1111), for many the greatest Muslim after the Prophet. In his *Revival of the Religious Sciences* he makes a strong case for men earning their living within the framework of the shari'a and cites the Prophet's saying that, 'the honest traders will have the same position on the Day of Judgement as the most truthful persons and as martyrs in the path of God.'[4] Indeed, al-Ghazzali's own life, which is most wonderfully told in his autobiography, *The Deliverance from Error*, makes manifest the tensions he experienced in his own life between other-worldly and this-worldly pulls, and which he resolved eventually in favour of the latter. He began as a teacher in Baghdad's Madrasa Nizamiyya, whose aim was to gain an influential position and widespread recognition. Then, he realized the error of his motivation and retired to live the life of a Sufi for ten years. But finally he realized that it was not right that he should cling to retirement because of, as he puts it, 'laziness and love of ease, the quest for spiritual power and preservation from worldly contamination.'[5] He must return to the work of teaching, not for worldly success, but in order that men should recognize the 'low position' of such success 'in the scale of real worth.'[6]

From the fourteenth century CE the emphasis in Muslim piety began to swing firmly in the other-worldly direction. The main source of this shift was the extraordinary influence of the Spanish Sufi, Ibn 'Arabi, who died in 1240. On a pilgrimage to Mecca Ibn 'Arabi had a vision of the divine throne in which he was told that he stood foremost amongst the saints. This led him to develop his doctrine of *wahdat al-wujud*, the 'unity of being'. God, Ibn 'Arabi argued, was transcendent. But, because all creation was a manifestation of God, it was identical with him in essence. It followed that God was necessary for men and women to exist but, equally, they were necessary for God to be manifest. In expressing his vision he both generated a rich symbolic vocabulary and produced a masterly synthesis of Sufi philosophic and neo-Platonic thought.

From the fourteenth century mystical discourse increasingly focussed on Ibn 'Arabi's 'unity of being'. One of the main vehicles of his ideas was poetry. This was as much the case for poetry in Arabic and the African languages, and for the poetry of Yunus Emre in Turkish, of Bullhe Shah in Punjabi, or 'Abd al-Latif in Sind, as it was for poetry in the higher Persian tradition, that of Jalal al-din Rumi, or of Hafiz Shirazi, or of Mulla Jami of Herat. The outcome of such widespread absorption of the idea of the 'unity of being' was to lessen the importance of observing the shari'a. If everything was God, if achieving ecstatic union with Him was enough, it made it less important to put into practice one earth His revelation. The emphasis on this-worldly performance was lifted.

A second vehicle of Ibn 'Arabi's ideas was, of course, Sufis themselves. The period from the fourteenth to the eighteenth century was one of immense expansion of the Islamic world—into sub-Saharan Africa and into South and Southeast Asia. It was in this period that the foundations of the Muslim community, as it is in the world today were laid, in which as many live east of the Hindu Kush as to the west. Sufis were the prime agents in the long process of slowly drawing people of a myriad local religious traditions into an Islamic milieu. This meant accommodating local needs and customs. It meant incorporating worship of trees, or fish or crocodiles, or cults relating to St. George or Khwaja Khidr, into local Sufi piety. It meant tolerating a range of ritual practices: the lighting of candles, the smearing of sandalwood paste, the tying of a piece of cloth to a shrine to remind a saint of a request. In enabling Sufis to build bridges between their Islamic messages and local religious practice, in enabling them to help to fashion an expansion of the Muslim world of enormous geo-political significance, Ibn 'Arabi's central idea of the 'unity of being', and the profound other-worldly focus it gave to piety, was of the first importance.

From the beginning there was a running critique of Ibn 'Arabi, particularly of those ideas that appeared to permit Muslims to flout the shari'a. There was the fourteenth-century Hanbali scholar, Ibn Taymiyya of Damascus. When Ibn Battuta, who accepted most Sufi practices, heard him preach in 1326, he thought Ibn Taymiyya had 'a kink in his brain'. The Mamluks appeared to agree because they threw him into prison, where he died.[7] But, from the seventeenth century, there was growing sympathy for his uncompromising attitude to Ibn 'Arabi, and today he is regarded as embodying the spirit of the Islamic revival.[8] There was the famous dispute in seventeenth-century Sumatra over the interpretation of Ibn 'Arabi, which was only resolved by a magisterial intervention from Ibrahim al-Kurani, the great scholar of Hadith in Medina.[9] In the same century, there was in India the Naqshbandi Sufi, Shaykh Ahmad Sirhindi, who proposed to counter Ibn 'Arabi's 'unity of being' with the concept of the 'unity of witness' *wahdat al-shuhud.* Instead of Sufis saying that 'all was God' they should now say that 'all was from God'. God had created the earth. He had also sent down, through his Prophet, guidance as to how his community should be fashioned on earth.[10] Sirhindi's ideas were taken up by his followers, the Mujaddidi branch of the Naqshbandi Sufi order, and from the eighteenth century they were to be widely followed in South and West Asia.[11] Then, around 1740, Muhammad Ibn 'Abd al-Wahhab, strongly influenced by Ibn Taymiyya, began to preach against all Sufi innovations. His puritan message, which went as far as to oppose any form of reverence for the Prophet's tomb in Medina, gained added force from 1744 when he hitched his fortunes to those of the house of Muhammad ibn Sa'ud of the Najd.[12] This said, having noted the continuing opposition to Ibn 'Arabi's doctrine of the 'unity of being', we must accept that his other-worldly piety was that of most Muslims from the fourteenth to the eighteenth century.

The nineteenth and twentieth centuries saw the emphasis in Islamic piety swing firmly in a this-worldly direction. The prime cause was the assertion of Western power throughout the Muslim world. It is worth noting the spread and nature of the change. The symbolic beginning was Napoleon's invasion of Egypt in 1798, followed in 1799 by the snuffing out of Mysore, the last significant Muslim opponent of British power in India. Between 1800 and 1920, the British, the French, the Russians, the Dutch, the Italians, and the Germans annexed or asserted influence over almost the entire Muslim community. In 1920 the only areas largely free of European influence were Afghanistan, the Yemen, the Hijaz, and Central Arabia. Iran enjoyed a much-qualified freedom; Ataturk was fighting for Turkish freedom and self-respect in Anatolia.

From the 1920s to the 1960s, with the exception of the Muslims of Central Asia who had to wait until the 1990s, Muslim societies achieved their freedom from direct foreign rule. But for many it was freedom of a limited kind, if freedom at all. First the departure of their Western rulers did not mean that the West would not still wish to have a say in their affairs, whether it be for continuing reasons of empire, or in pursuing Cold War rivalries, or, after the Iranian revolution, in striving to limit the spread of Islamic revivalism in political form. The process of meddling in the Muslim world continued, whether it be in the politics of Pakistan, of Iran, or of Algeria. It is a process which has been interlarded with some notable acts of bullying and adventurism, whether it be the British and the USA in Iran in 1953, the British and French in Egypt in 1956, the British and the USA in Iraq in 2003, or the Russians, who for these purposes are part of the West, in Afghanistan and Chechnya in the late twentieth century. Second, the end of Western rule did not bring an end to transformative Western influences in Muslim societies. In many cases their impact was redoubled. The penetration of Western trade and capital continued, fashioning local economies to their purpose. New elites continued to emerge to manage the new economic and political structures—technocrats, bureaucrats, bankers, intellectuals, industrial workers, all people who belonged to an existence outside the old urban communitarian world of the artisan workshop, the bazaar trader, the caravansarai, and the quarter, which had long sustained Muslim societies and their distinctive worldviews. Foremost amongst these new elites were the new political elites—the Zulfiqar 'Ali Bhuttos, the Abbas Hoveidas, the Habib Bourguibas—more often than not trained in the West, subscribing to Western values, supporters of Western culture, and happy to see it given substantial freedom to flourish in Muslim societies.

The onset of Western power in Muslim societies, and the continuing blows it has delivered to Muslim self-esteem right down to the present, has led to a major process of self-questioning and reflection. How could Islam, which for 1,200 years had walked hand in hand with power, become divorced from its exercise? Was it, perhaps, because Muslims had not been good enough Muslims? Was it because they had not tried hard enough to relate the guidance they had received from God to changing human circumstance? And how were they to sustain Muslim societies without power, a question which was as relevant in an independent Egypt, Iran, or Turkey, as it was in an India ruled by the British or an Indonesia ruled by the Dutch? Indeed, the onset of Western power created circumstances in which critics of other-worldly piety were to be heard with much greater sympathy. These were circumstances in which attacks on Ibn 'Arabi's hold on Sufi thought were likely to increase and be successful, in which the Quran and Hadith and the early community at Medina gained new prominence as sources of Muslim guidance, in which there was redoubled interest in the life of the Prophet as a model to follow, and in which there was a new emphasis on ijtihad—individual enquiry or reasoning—to renew the faith. The outcome was the emergence of an activist—willed or, as for some, a protestant—Islam. The outcome was the dynamism which Cantwell Smith saw sweeping through the twentieth-century Muslim world. At the heart of this activism, and the energy which it created, was the placing of the responsibility of fashioning Islamic society on each individual Muslim—the caliphate of man.

It is well understood that this move to an activist this-worldly Islam was expressed differently in different Muslim societies with their distinctive social, economic, political, and cultural formations. Acknowledging this, let us see how the move towards a this-worldly Islam was expressed in British India. Here, under a British rule, which in the early nineteenth century began vigorously to hack away the financial and institutional structures which sustained Islamic society, the issue was how to create a Muslim society without power. A concern to elevate the principle of tawhid, the oneness of God, ran through most of the movements of the age. There was a running attack on all Sufi customs which, following Ibn 'Arabi, suggested that God might be immanent rather than purely transcendent, which was expressed most frequently and forcibly in attacks on any practices which suggested that Sufi saints might be able to intercede for man with God. At their most extreme these attacks aimed to wipe out Sufism altogether. By the same token there were assaults on indigenous customs which had come to be incorporated into Islamic practice. Some Muslims, for instance, followed the Hindu custom of not marrying widows. In some cases this led to overzealous reformers engaging in widow-rustling to ensure that Muslim preference was observed.[13]

A Muslim community which was going to sustain itself needed teachers and scholars to transmit knowledge and make it work in society. The Deoband madrasa, founded in 1867, and supported by public subscription alone, was the model for this. By 1967, it claimed to have founded over 8,000 madrasas on this model. The reforming movement as a whole favoured a madrasa curriculum which gave little weight to theology and philosophy and the triumphs of medieval Persianate scholarship, preferring instead to elevate the Quran and Hadith—the unadulterated record of the activist days of the early Muslim community. Whereas some elements of the reforming movement favoured taqlid, or the following of legal rulings handed down from the past, the more extreme reformers, for instance the Ahl-i Hadith, favoured ijtihad, and as the revival progressed the demand for ijtihad was to get stronger and stronger. This shift towards a self-sustaining this-worldly community of believers was powerfully supported by the introduction of print and the translation of the Quran and large numbers of key texts into vernacular languages. The reforming 'ulama were the great supporters of the printing press; they saw it rightly as the means of creating a new constituency for themselves outside the bounds of colonial power. But they also helped to breed something totally new in Muslim history—a growing body of Muslims, trained outside the madrasas, who could reflect upon the sources of their faith and interpret them for themselves.[14]

These processes were only enhanced by the way in which the reforming movement made it clear that there was no intercession for man with God. Muslims were personally responsible to God for the way in which they had put His guidance to them into practice on earth. We are fortunate in having the guidance which a leading reformer, Ashraf 'Ali Thanawi, prepared for women in his tradition, though it could equally have been for men. Entitled, *Bihishti Zewar*, or 'The Jewels of Paradise', it is said to be the most widely published Muslim publication in the subcontinent after the Quran. Should anyone consider backsliding in performing their duties, Thanawi paints a horrific picture of the Day of Judgement and the fate that will befall those who have not striven hard enough to follow God's guidance. To help believers avoid this awful fate, Thanawi instructs them in a process of regular self-examination, morning and evening, to ensure purity of intentions and to avoid wrongdoing. Thus, the Deobandi tradition, which was at the heart of the Indian reforming movement set about fashioning Muslim individuals who were powerfully conscious that they must act to sustain Islamic society on earth in order to achieve salvation.[15]

The feeling of personal responsibility before God, and the need to act on earth to achieve salvation, ran through the many manifestations of reform in India. It was a central issue for Sayyid Ahmad Khan (d. 1898) who hailed from the reforming tradition but, in his development of the principles of Islamic modernism, travelled way beyond it. Listen to what he has to say about the driving force behind his educational mission:

> I regard it as my duty to do all I can, right or wrong, to defend my religion and show the people the true, shining countenance of Islam. This is what my conscience dictates and, unless, I do its bidding, I am a sinner before God.[16]

This sense of personal responsibility, if anything, was even more an issue for Muhammd Ilyas (d. 1944), the founder of the Tablighi Jama'at or 'Preaching Society', which is now, we are credibly informed, the most widely-supported movement in the Islamic world. He was constantly oppressed by fear of Judgement and whether he was doing enough to meet God's high standards. 'I find no comparison between my anxiety, my effort and my voice,' he wrote, 'and the responsibility of Tabligh God has placed upon my shoulders. If He shows mercy, He is forgiving, merciful, and if He does justice, there is no escape for me from the consequences of my guilt.'[17] The members of the Tablighi Jama'at make manifest the need to act on earth, following the precept of Ilyas' 'knowing meaning doing.'[18] Every year members of the Tabligh form groups of ten, jama'ats as they are known, to go out and preach their faith.[19]

The sense of personal responsibility, and the centrality of action on earth to the Muslim life, was expressed most completely by that sensitive and remarkable thinker, Muhammad Iqbal (d. 1933). For Iqbal, man was chosen by God, but was free to choose whether he would follow God's guidance or not. Man realized himself in the creative work of shaping and reshaping the world. The reality of the individual was expressed most explicitly in action. 'The final act', he declares in the closing sentences of his *Reconstruction of Religious*

Thought in Islam, 'is not an intellectual act, but a vital act which deepens the whole being of the ego and sharpens his will with the creative assurance that the world is not just something to be seen and known through concepts, but to be made and remade by continuous action.'[20] Man was the prime mover in God's creation, as Iqbal makes so clear in man's response to God in his poem 'God's Talk with Man':

You created the night—I lit the lamp
You created clay—I moulded the cup
You made the wilderness, mountains and forest
I cultivated flowerbeds, parks and gardens.[21]

As the prime mover, man was God's representative on earth, his vice-regent, the Khalifat Allah. Thus Iqbal draws the Quranic reference to Adam as his vice-regent, or successor, on earth, which had been much discussed by medieval commentators on the Quran, and not least among them Ibn Taymiyya and Ibn 'Arabi, into the modern politico-Islamic discourse of South Asia. In doing so he both emphasizes the enormous responsibility of each individual human being in the trust that he/she received from God and encapsulates that relationship in the concept of the caliphate of each individual human being.[22] The idea was further taken up by Mawlana Mawdudi (1903–79), founder of the Jama'at-i Islami, who added his considerable weight to its presence in Islamic thought on the subcontinent, and beyond.[23]

The sense of the personal responsibility of each human being is no less present in the thought of other Muslim reforming traditions, which of course intermingled with that of India. It is there in the grand narrative of the Egypto-Arab tradition. It is there in Jamal al-Din Afghani's (1838/9–97) admiration for the achievements of the European Protestants in Christianity, for their willingness to ignore the advice of their priests, in going back to first principles, and making up their minds, as he urged Muslims to do, using their own efforts. 'Verily,' he was to say many times quoting the Quran, 'God does not change the state of a people until they change themselves inwardly.' He identified himself, of course, with Martin Luther.[24] This activism for individuals was present in his friend and pupil, Muhammad 'Abduh (1849–1905), who was probably the first major thinker in the modern Arab world to emphasize the caliphate of man. Because of the power of reason with which God endowed him, 'Abduh argued, man 'has unlimited capacities, unlimited desires, unlimited knowledge and unlimited action.' Man was required to use these capacities to break the bonds of taqlid and demonstrate that Islam was fully compatible with the demands of modernity.[25] This activism was present, too, in the emphasis of 'Abduh's leading disciple, Rashid Rida (1869–1935) on jihad, or positive effort, being the essence of Islam. This was, he argued, a principle contained both in Islam and in modern civilization. If the Europeans manifest this quality more than anyone else in the world, it was for Muslims to recapture it and regain their true position.[26]

This activism was there, of course, when the movement for reform, shocked by the corruption and complacency of Egypt's elites, both 'ulama and layfolk, began to be manifest as a radical popular movement, an Islamist movement, the Muslim Brotherhood, which would morally regenerate society from within. Its founder, Hasan al-Banna (1906–49), appealed for personal and individual reform which would create a leaven of spiritually-inspired individuals in society, who would actively execute a programme addressing modern problems.[27] It was there, too, in the second phase of the Brotherhood's existence in the call of Sayyid Qutb (1906–66) for Muslims to commit themselves to jihad against the *jahili*—Islamically ignorant—elements which pervaded it. He, following the lines of argument of 'Abduh, emphasizes the role of man as the khalifa of God on earth:

> It is thus the supreme will intending to give to the new being the reins of the earth, and a free hand in it; and entrusting him with the task of revealing the Creator in innovation and formation, in analysis and synthesis, in alteration and transformation; and of discovering the powers and potentialities, and treasures and resources of this earth, and makes all this—God willing—subservient to the great task with which God entrusted him.[28]

If we move away from the grand narrative of reform and revival in the Arab context to address it in the Iranian context, while acknowledging the distinctive differences of the Shia tradition, we nevertheless find a similar emphasis on personal responsibility and action in this world. It is there in the thought of two of the most important players in the ideological build-up to the Iranian revolution—Ayat Allah Murtaza Motahhari and 'Ali Shari'ati. They were ideological rivals, the one protecting the position of the 'ulama, the other attacking it, while both sought to develop a constituency amongst the young. For Motahhari, pupil, friend, and confidant of Khomeini, whom the Ayat Allah described as the 'fruit of my life' as he wept at his funeral in May 1979, man was not so much the vice-regent of God but, using that classical term from Iranian religio-political discourse,'the shadow of God on earth'.[29] God, moreover, in his creation of man had bestowed upon him the potential to gain perfection and return to Him. But Motahhari's route to God lay very firmly through this-worldly activity:

> this and the other world are connected together. This world is the [cultivating] field for the other ... What gives order, prosperity, beauty, security, and comfort to this world is to bear other worldly-standards upon it; and what secures other-worldly bliss is to perform this-worldly responsibilities properly, combined with faith, purity, prosperity, and piety.[30]

For 'Ali Shari'ati, models for contemporary Muslims were the Prophet and the men trained by Him—'Ali, Abu Dharr, and Salman, all of them men of action in this world but also men of piety and devotion. As is his wont, in his essay, 'The Ideal Man—the Vice-regent of God', he paints a daunting picture of the ideal. Amidst an amazing array of qualities and achievements:

> He has accepted the heavy Trust of God, and for this very reason he is a responsible and committed being, with the free exercise of his will. He does not perceive his perfection as lying in the creation of a private relationship with God to the exclusion of men; it is rather, in struggle for the perfection of the human race, in enduring hardship, hunger, deprivation and torment for the sake of liberty, livelihood and well-being of men, in the furnace of intellectual and social struggle, that he attains piety, perfection and closeness to God.[31]

So far we have been concentrating on the central shift in Muslim piety over the past two hundred years, the shift towards individual personal responsibility for working to create an Islamic society on earth in order to achieve salvation—a this-worldly Islam. This was a key element in the packages of ideas developed by Islamic reformers and revivalists from the mid-nineteenth century onwards. By the second half of the twentieth century these reformers and revivalists had, by and large, transformed themselves into what we now know as Islamists—the Muslim Brotherhood in its various forms in the Arab world, Mawdudi's Jama'at-i Islami in South Asia, some of the makers of the Iranian revolution; men concerned to fashion a vanguard of the morally pure to rearm society, men who created an understanding of Islam as an all-embracing ideology, men concerned to lead organizations which might capture the state so that they might use its power to impose their ideology of *nizam-i Islam* on society and keep out corrupting influences from the West. The leaders of Islamist movements were typically teachers, lawyers, doctors, engineers, government servants—people commanding modern science and technology and modern legal and bureaucratic systems, but who were concerned that these should serve Islamic ends. Islamism was essentially the ideology of a middle and lower middle class, which was opposed to the culture and corruption of their elites, and their close association with the ideas, values, and interests of the West. They wanted, and still seek, to fashion the world in their own (bourgeois) image.

From the 1960s support for Islamist movements grew rapidly. This was in part the outcome of the expansion of the state, of business, and of service infrastructure—of the expansion of those social locations in which the Islamist ethic might thrive, with its concern for setting and meeting targets, the rule of law, promotion by merit and so on. It was in part, too, an outcome of the huge increase in the consumption of oil, accompanied by the great oil price rise of the 1970s, and the vast new resources it brought to many Muslim societies. It was also in part due to the massive movement of population from the countryside to the cities in this period. This last development brought mass support to Islamists, as they stepped in where the state frequently failed—that is, providing the schools, hospitals, and clinics, the social and psychological support, which these new entrants to the urban environment often desperately needed. We should note, in addition, the capacity of Islamist movements to mobilize mass support by constructing and transmitting an understanding of Islam as the answer to modernity.[32] As we know, this process has greatly enhanced Islamist influence in all Muslim societies, leading of course to the Iranian revolution, but also to substantial Islamist advances through the ballot box as, for instance, in Turkey, or Pakistan, or Algeria—although this last victory was aborted by the intervention of the army—and also to an Islamist hollowing out of a secular Egypt from within, as has been brilliantly described recently by Geneive Abdo.[33] In the twenty-first century, as compared with the nineteenth, the numbers of Muslims who feel a strong personal responsibility to act on earth to achieve salvation has been greatly increased.

I want to end by reflecting briefly on what this great shift in the emphasis of Muslim piety—which Iqbal in particular, but also other observers, described as being similar to the Protestant Reformation in Christianity—might mean. In particular, what significance should be given to the emphasis on personal responsibility and action on earth.

In another place I have argued that, in British India in the first half of the twentieth century, this new sense of personal responsibility led to increasing manifestation of aspects of individualism. There was increasing consciousness of the self being instrumental in the world, of the self, as Iqbal stated, making and remaking the world by 'continuous action'. There was a sense of self-affirmation and personal autonomy which came from adopting the way of faith as a result of personal choice. There was an affirmation of the ordinary things of the self, the ordinary things of daily life—family, domestic life, children, love, sex. This is a change which can be witnessed in the changing representations of the Prophet in the *sirat* literature, the biographies of the Prophet. Less attention is given, as Cantwell Smith has pointed out, to his intelligence, political sagacity and capacity to harness new social forces in his society, and more to his qualities as a middle-class family man: his sense of duty and his loving nature, his qualities as a good citizen, his consideration for others and, in particular, for those who are less fortunate. And finally there has been the growth of self-consciousness and the reflective habit. Reflectiveness, you will recall, was urged by Thanawi's *Bihishti Zewar*. Its impact can be seen in the creative and biographical literature of the time. As we might expect, the growth of individualism was bound to lead to tensions with the requirements of the community. And, because Muslim women in British India were given the particular role of preserving an Islamic private space in a world in which public space was dominated by Western values, it was a burden particularly felt by them. The relationship between this-worldly Islam and the growth of individualism in Muslim South Asia is an exciting line of enquiry.[34]

In a recent article designed to demonstrate the modernizing aspects of Islamism in Egypt, the Norwegian scholar Bjorn Utvik, draws attention to the individualizing impact of the Islamists' central idea of the personal responsibility of the believer to struggle for the cause of God on earth. He emphasizes, as we might expect, the crucial importance of this being a personal choice. It is associated with ideas of work as a calling, of the value of time, indeed, of an Islamic work ethic, with a demand for the impersonalisation of public life and an end to bribery and patronage, and for merit to be the sole criterion for promotion to posts of responsibility in society. 'Together', he says:

> these aspects of Islamism work to open the road for the idea of individual career, individual life projects. This has been shown to be a characteristic setting young Islamist students in the 1980s off from their parent generation. It means that the choice of partner and line of work is something the young Islamists expect to do for themselves and not be decided by the family or some other communal entity.[35]

In a remarkable book, *Being Modern in Iran*, the brilliant French anthropologist, Fariba Adelkhah, discovers increasing individualism to be the outcome of the interactions between the Islamist project, the emergence of a significant public sphere and the rationalization, bureaucratization, and commercialization of Iranian society. She notes the huge popularity of self-help books and magazines of all kinds, the new importance of going to the gym and other forms of body care for men and women, the great attention given to individual achievement in sport, the popularity of game shows, the public rewards given for academic success in school, the films which approvingly depict women of independent spirit and behaviour, and the move towards the nuclear family, and respect for individual space within that family.[36]

I put it to you that the shift to a this-worldly Islam, with its emphasis on personal responsibility to achieve salvation, and with its emphasis on the caliphate of man, which was adopted to help give Muslim societies the strength to resist the Western onslaught, has played, and is playing, a significant role in underpinning the growth of individualism. This growth of individualism is accompanied by self-discipline and the work ethic, respect for law, support for promotion by merit and opposition to patronage and corruption. Last year Bernard Lewis published a most tendentious book entitled, *What went Wrong? The Clash between Islam and Modernity in the Middle East*. In it he declared that the problem with Middle Eastern countries, indeed all Muslim countries, was Islam.[37] Whatever one's view of the role of

Islam in what might or might not have gone wrong in Muslim societies, I suggest to you that this-worldly Islam may also be part of what is going right.

NOTES

1 W.C. Smith, *Islam in Modern History* (Princeton, 1957), p. 89.

2 Statement attributed to Ibrahim bin Adham in the *Kitab al-Luma* of Abu Nasr Sarraj cited in Riaz ul-Islam, *Sufism in South Asia: Impact on Fourteenth Century Muslim Society* (Karachi, 2002), p. 216; for a discussion of the futuh system, see ibid., pp. 87–150.

3 For Sufi ideas on engagement with this world, see ibid., pp. 151–215.

4 Ibid., p. 163.

5 W. Montgomery Watt, trans., *The Faith and Practice of al-Ghazali* (Oxford, 1994), p. 80.

6 Ibid., p. 82.

7 H.A.R. Gibb, *The Travels of Ibn Battuta A.D. 1325–1354*, Part I (New Delhi, 1993), pp. 135–37.

8 K.A. Nizami, 'The Impact of Ibn Taimiyya on South Asia', *Journal of Islamic Studies*, I (1990), pp. 120–49; H. Algar, *Wahhabism: A Critical Essay* (New York, 2002), pp. 8–10; E. Sivan, *Radical Islam: Medieval Theology and Modern Politics* (New Haven, 1985), pp. 94–107.

9 A.H. Johns, 'Islam in the Malay World: An Exploratory Survey with Some Reference to Quranic Exegesis' in R. Israeli and A.H. Johns, *Islam in Asia: Volume II South and Southeast Asia* (Boulder, Colorado, 1984), pp. 115–61; P. Riddell, *Islam and the Malay-Indonesian World: Transmission and Responses* (London, 2001), pp. 125–32.

10 B.A. Faruqi, *The Mujadid's Concept of Tawhid*, second edition, (Lahore, 1943) and Y. Friedmann, *Shaykh Ahmad Sirhindi: An Outline of His Thought and a Study of His Image in the Eyes of Posterity* (Montreal, 1971).

11 A. Hourani, 'Shaikh Khalid and the Naqshbandi Order', in S.M. Stern, A. Hourani, and V. Brown (eds) *Islamic Philosophy and the Classical Tradition* (Columbia, S.C., 1972), pp. 89–101; H. Algar, 'The Naqshbandi Order: a Preliminary Survey of its History and Significance', *Studia Islamica,* XLIV, pp. 123–52; M. Gaborieau, *et al.*, *Naqshbandis: Historical Developments and Recent Situation of a Muslim Mystical Order* (Istanbul and Paris, 1990), in particular, the articles by Algar, Adams, Friedmann and Damrel; and for the reach of Sirhindi's ideas into twentieth-century Turkey, S. Mardin, *Religion and Social Change in Modern Turkey: The Case of Bediuzzaman Said Nursi* (Albany, New York, 1984).

12 Algar, *Wahhabism.*

13 Barbara D. Metcalf, *Islamic Revival in British India: Deoband, 1860–1900* (Princeton, New Jersey, 1982), pp. 3–86.

14 Ibid., pp. 87–296; 'Islam and the Impact of Print in South Asia', in F. Robinson, *Islam and Muslim History in South Asia* (New Delhi, 2000), pp. 66–104.

15 Barbara D. Metcalf, *Perfecting Women: Maulana Ashraf 'Ali Thanawi's Bihishti Zewar: a Partial Translation with Commentary*, (Berkeley, 1990), pp. 221–30, 233–6.

16 Speech of Sayyid Ahmad Khan to the students of Aligarh College, undated, but made after he began his commentary on the Quran c. 1876, quoted in Altaf Husain Hali, *Hayat-i Javed*, trans. by K.H. Qadiri and D.J. Matthews (New Delhi, 1979), p. 172.

17 S.A.H.A. Nadwi, *Life and Mission of Maulana Muhammad Ilyas,* translated by Mohammad Asif Kidwai (Lucknow, 1979), p. 108.

18 C.W. Troll, 'Five Letters of Maulana Ilyas (1995–1944), the Founder of the Tablighi Jama'at', translated, annotated, and introduced, in C.W. Troll (ed.), *Islam in India: Studies and Commentaries 2: Religion and Religious Education* (Delhi, 1985), p. 143.

19 M.K. Masud, *Travellers in Faith: Studies of the Tablighi Jama'at as a Transnational Islamic Movement for Faith Renewal* (Leiden, 2000), especially pp. 3–42.

20 M. Iqbal, *The Reconstruction of Religious Thought in Islam* (Lahore, 1954), p. 154.

21 Translation of part of Iqbal's poem 'God's Talk with Man' in N.P. Ankiyev, 'The Doctrine of Personality', H. Malik (ed.), *Iqbal: Poet–Philosopher of Pakistan* (New York, 1971), p. 274.

22 Iqbal, *Reconstruction*, p. 95. The particular verse is 2.30.

'And when thy Lord said to the Angels, I am going to place a ruler [*khalifa*] in the earth, they said: Wilt thou place in it such as make mischief in it and shed blood? And we celebrate Thy praise and extol Thy holiness. He said: Surely I know what you know not.'

Maulana Muhammad Ali, *The Holy Qur'an'*, fifth edition, (Lahore.1973). Jaafar Sheikh Idris provides an excellent discussion of the views of early commentators on the meaning of this and other verses using the term khalifa. He notes that the interpretation favoured by thinkers of the Islamic revival is closer to that of Ibn 'Arabi than that of Ibn Taymiyya, but it nevertheless remains distinct. He explains the modern understanding of the caliphate of man in terms of the idea 'that man is master of this world and of his own destiny, and of material development, which material development is not desirable only because it satisfies human needs, but also, and perhaps more importantly, because it is a reflection of man's great abilities' as the outcome of Western influences. J.S. Idris, 'Is Man the Viceregent of God?', *Journal of Islamic Studies*, I (1990), pp. 99–110.

23 S.A.A. Maudoodi, *Fundamentals of Islam* (Delhi, 1979, p. xviii, and for a disquisition on the role of man as God's trustee on earth, pp. 29–30.

24 N.R. Keddie, *An Islamic Response to Materialism: Political and Religious Writings of Sayyid Jamal ad-Din al-Afghani* (Berkeley, 1968), pp. 81–4.
25 Idris, Ibid.
26 A.H. Hourani, *Arabic Thought in the Liberal Age 1789–1939* (Cambridge, 1983), pp. 228–9.
27 B. Lia, *The Society of the Muslim Brothers in Egypt: The Rise of an Islamic Mass Movement* (Reading, 1998), pp. 83–4.
28 Qutb's *Fi Dhilal al-Qur'an* quoted in Idris, p. 107; for the second phase of the Brotherhood's development and the particular influence of Qutb, see Sivan, *Radical Islam*.
29 V. Martin, *Creating an Islamic State: Khomeini and the Making of a New Iran* (London, 2000), p. 83.
30 H. Dabashi, *Theology of Discontent: The Ideological Foundations of the Islamic Revolution in Iran* (New York, 1993), p. 194.
31 'Ali Shari'ati, *On the Sociology of Islam*, trans. H. Algar (Berkeley, 1979), p. 123.
32 The role of Islamist interpretations of Islam in mobilizing support for action has been most effectively analysed from the standpoint of theories of political mobilization by C.R. Wickham in *Mobilizing Islam: Religion, Activism, and Political Change in Egypt* (New York, 2003) and from that of comparative political theory by R.L. Euben, *Enemy in the Mirror: Islamic Fundamentalism and the Limits of Modern Rationalism* (Princeton, 1999).
33 G. Abdo, *No God but God: Egypt and the Triumph of Islam* (Oxford, 2000).
34 F. Robinson, 'Religious Change and the Self in Muslim South Asia since 1800', *South Asia*, vol. XX, no. 1 (1997), pp. 1–15.
35 B.O. Utvik, 'The Modernizing Force of Islamism', in J.L. Esposito and F. Burgat (eds), *Modernizing Islam: Religion in the Public Sphere in the Middle East and Europe* (London, 2003), p. 59.
36 F. Adelkhah, *Being Modern in Iran* (London, 1998), pp. 139–78.
37 B. Lewis, *What Went Wrong? The Clash between Islam and Modernity in the Middle East* (London, 2002).

Islam and the West: Clash of Civilizations?

In 1993, the journal, *Foreign Affairs*, published an article entitled 'Clash of Civilizations' by Samuel Huntington, Harvard Professor, former Director of Security Planning for the National Security Council, and president of the American Political Science Association. By 1996, Huntington had developed his article into a book and it was published under the title, *The Clash of Civilizations and the Remaking of World Order*.[1] The argument was that in a post-Cold War world, the crucial distinctions between people were not primarily ideological or economic, but cultural. World politics was being reconfigured along cultural lines, with new patterns of conflict and cooperation replacing those of the Cold War. The hot spots in world politics were on the faultlines between civilizations: Bosnia, Chechnya, West Asia, Tibet, Sri Lanka, etc. The civilization with a particularly large number of hot spots was Islam. It had bloody borders and represented the greatest danger to world peace.

The argument has influenced, indeed, helped to frame the debate about the future world order to an extent which even distresses Huntington himself. It has not been well-received amongst professional scholars of Islam, who have objected to the way in which it has assisted in demonizing Muslims and to the way in which, by generalizing about Muslims, it has brushed over the many differences of economic and political status, outlook and understanding which the Muslim world embraces. Huntington's argument has been assessed by several scholars, so it needs no further elaboration here.[2] However, the events of September 11 and the widespread realization of the existence and purposes of Osama Bin Laden and his al-Qaeda organization created a new dimension by which to examine this thesis.

First it is necessary to summarize the historical, particularly, Islamic, background to the events of September 11 and the great change in power relationships between Muslim peoples and the West over the past two hundred years. For a thousand years, that is, for much of the period from the eighth to the eighteenth century, the leading civilization on the planet in terms of spread and creativity was Islam. It was formed in the seventh century when Arab tribesmen, bearing the prophecy of Muhammad, or so the traditional story goes, burst out of the Arabian Peninsula. Within a decade they defeated the armies of two rival empires to the north, those of Christian Byzantium and Sassanian Iran. A great new cultural and economic nexus came to be developed which was able to draw on the knowledge and commodities of lands from China and India in the east to Spain and Africa in the west, as well as those of the West Asian lands in which it was based. This new civilization commanded a substantial slice of the world's area of cities and settled agriculture. In this region there was shared language of religion and the law. Men could travel and do business within a common framework of assumptions. In its high cultures they could express themselves in symbols to which all could respond. Arguably, it is the first world system, the one which preceded that of Immanuel Wallerstein.[3] The first notable centres were found in the Arab worlds of Damascus, Baghdad, Cordoba and Cairo from the eight to the twelfth centuries, the second in the Turco-Iranian worlds of Istanbul, Isfahan, Bukhara, Samarqand, and Delhi from the fourteenth to the seventeenth centuries. There were great achievements in scholarship and science, in poetry and prose, and in the arts of the book, building, and spiritual insight, which are precious legacies to all humankind. For about half of what is termed the Christian era Muslims could regard themselves as marching at the forefront of human progress. Over the same period, the odd crusade or loss of Spain aside, they could regard the community of believers created by God's revelation to man through the Prophet Muhammad as walking hand in hand with power.

Over the past two hundred years the Islamic world system has been overwhelmed by forces from the West, forces driven by capitalism, powered by the Industrial Revolution and civilized, after a fashion, by the Enlightenment. The symbolic moment, when the leader's standard overtly passed to the West, was Napoleon's invasion of Egypt in 1798. From this moment Western armies and Western capital overran the lands of the Muslims: the British took India; the British and Dutch took Southeast Asia; the British, French, Germans, and Italians occupied North, East, and West Africa; the Russians swamped Central Asia; and the British and French carved up West Asia between them. By the 1920s Afghanistan, Iran, Turkey, Central Arabia, and the Yemen were the only Muslim countries free from Western control, and even some of these were subject to influence. The caliphate, the symbolic leadership for the community of believers, which reached back to the Prophet, had been abolished. For a moment it was feared that the holy places of Islam—Mecca and Medina—might fall into the hands of the infidel. The community of believers, which for so many centuries had walked hand in hand with power, had good reason to believe that history—if not God—had deserted it.

For the remainder of the twentieth century matters did not seem a great deal better. Certainly, from the emergence of modern Turkey in the early 1920s to that of the Muslim republics of the former Soviet Union in the 1990s, we could talk of a steady decolonization of the Muslim world—at least in the formal sense. But for many this has seemed a Pyrrhic victory. More often than not they have found Western rule replaced by that of Muslims with secular Western values, while Western capital and Western culture have come to be even more corrosive of their customs and their standards than before. This challenge has elicited from many Muslims the assertion of an Islamic, and for some a totalitarian Islamic, future for their people. Such views have not been shared by all Muslims but have come to be shared by enough of them to represent a significant threat to the secular leaders of their societies, and on occasion, as in the revolution in Iran, to drive their upholders to power. These Muslims, who are popularly known as 'fundamentalist' in the West, are more appropriately known as 'Islamists'. I shall elaborate on these 'Islamists' when I address the significance of the Islamic revival. For the moment it is enough to note that they represent the major opposition to the leadership of Muslim states—many of which have relations of greater or less strength with the USA—among them Sa'udi Arabia, Pakistan, Algeria, Tunisia, Turkey, Egypt, Jordan, Kuwait, and also, of course, the Palestinian Authority. In this situation, lack of fairness or evenhandedness on the part of non-Muslim states is an irritant which helps to radicalize Muslim populations not just in the states concerned but also across the Muslim world. There are the problems of Muslim minorities in the Balkans and the resistance of the people of Chechnya to Russian military might. Indian Muslims experienced a sense of threat as they were first demonized by Hindu revivalism and then, in 1992, saw Emperor

Babur's mosque torn down by Hindu revivalists. The Muslim majority in Kashmir feel oppressed as they are held down by India's martial rule, while the peoples of Iraq suffer on account of their rogue regime. The Muslim and Christian peoples of Palestine have experienced the greatest injustice during these past fifty years and more. These are all complicated issues, but from the point of view of many Muslims in the streets and bazaars of Muslim towns and cities across the world they represent symbols of injustice and oppression. They represent a world order in which Muslims are victims. They constitute a world order in which Muslims must organize to resist.

There are three significant developments which accompanied the transformation of the Muslim position in the world in the nineteenth and twentieth centuries. They form strands in the long-term background to the events of 11 September. First, Muslim peoples have long suffered a range of feelings from a tremendous sense of loss through to a deep bitterness and rage at their powerlessness in the face of the West. This was particularly strong in the Indo-Pakistan subcontinent—now the home of over 350 million Muslims—originally because of the speed with which the Mughal Empire lost power in the eighteenth century. Then it grew because of the new competition for power this brought with rival peoples, and finally because this was the area of the Muslim world most heavily exposed to rule from the West. This was expressed in the most powerful artistic form of culture—poetry.

The eighteenth- and nineteenth-century poetic genre of *Shahr Ashob* mourned the passing of great cities, of great centres of Muslim civilization. One of the greatest works of the nineteenth century, the *Musaddas* or Elegy of Altaf Husayn Hali entitled, *The Flow and Ebb of Islam*,[4] was a great set-piece poem on the rise and decline of Islam and its causes. It was highly popular and came to be used almost as a national anthem for the Pakistan movement. It would be recited at the opening of political meetings and have everyone in tears as they contemplated the fate of Islamic civilization:

When autumn has set in over the garden,
Why speak of the springtime of flowers?
When shadows of adversity hang over the present,
Why harp on the pomp and glory of the past?
Yes, these are things to forget; but how can you with
The dawn forget the scene of the night before?

The assembly has just dispersed;
The smoke is still rising from the burnt candle;
The footprints on the sands of India still say
A graceful caravan has passed this way.[5]

Of course there was admiration for the achievement of Europe, even if of a despairing kind. The secretary of the Moroccan envoy to France wrote, in 1846, after watching a review of French troops:

So it went on until all had passed leaving our hearts consumed with fire for what we had seen of their overwhelming power and mastery ... In comparison with the weakness of Islam ... how confident they are, how impressive their state of readiness, how competent they are in matters of state, how firm their laws, how capable in war.[6]

But as Western power enveloped the Muslim world, there was growing protest against the West. From 1926 to 1957 Husayn Ahmad Madani was principal of the great reformist school of Deoband, whose organization and influence in Pakistan was to create the network of madrasas in which the Taliban were bred. 'The British and the European nations do not consider Asians and Africans as human beings, and thus deny them human rights', he asserted in his autobiography written after his internment in Malta during the First World War, 'The British are the worst enemies of Islam and the Muslims on the earth.'[7] Muhammad Iqbal, a man who intellectually owed much to the West, accepted a knighthood from the British, and was the poet–philosopher behind the concept of Pakistan—a Muslim modernist, in no way radical. In his *Persian Psalms,* published in 1927, he declared:

Against Europe I protest,
And the attraction of the West.
Woe for Europe and her charm,
Swift to capture and disarm!
Europe's hordes with flame and fire
Desolate the world entire.[8]

The rejection of Europe—or by now the West, in general—both as a destructive force and a false model of progress was a theme of many of the leading ideologues who prepared the way for the Iranian revolution. 'Come friends', said 'Ali Shari'ati in the 1960s, 'let us abandon Europe; let us cease this nauseating apish imitation of Europe. Let us leave behind this Europe that always speaks of humanity, but destroys human beings wherever it finds them.'[9] By this time, as the

USA replaced Europe in the demonology of the Islamic world, it became the focus of bitterness and resentment, which was all the greater because it affected the lives of supposedly free peoples. Ayat Allah Khomeini's howl of rage when, in 1964, the Iranian Parliament granted US citizens extraterritorial rights in Iran in exchange for a $200m loan, spoke for all Muslims who had felt powerless in the face of a bullying West from the bombardment of Alexandria in 1882 to the plight of the Palestinians in the present crisis: 'They have reduced the Iranian people to a level lower than that of an American dog'.[10]

Such feelings were no less strongly held in the Arab world. Here a key focus was the Crusades, which Carole Hillenbrand explores in the epilogue to her brilliant book, *The Crusades: Islamic Perspectives.* They permeate, she declares, 'many aspects of modern life in the Arab and wider Muslim world',[11] where they have left psychological scars. They frequently referred to the Crusades and drew parallels as they felt the weight of European colonialism. The myth of Saladin as the great leader of resistance to the West and his victory over the Crusaders at Hattin was a central theme in the Palestinian struggle under the British Mandate.[12] Indeed, the Israeli state has come to be seen as a modern version of the Latin Kingdom of Jerusalem, which was established by what Sayyid Qutb, the leader of the second phase of the Muslim Brotherhood called 'the Crusader spirit which runs in the blood of all Westerners'.[13] In his pronouncements Osama Bin Laden, along with his fellow Islamist leaders, conjured up this spirit of the Crusaders in Arab and Muslim minds. In a fatwa of 20 February 1998 he proclaimed the formation of a 'world front for *Jihad* against Jews and Crusaders':

> The rule to kill Americans and their allies—civilians and military—is an individual duty for any Muslim ... to liberate the al Aqsa Mosque [in Jerusalem] and the Holy Mosque [in Mecca] from their grip, and in order for their armies to move out of all the lands of Islam, defeated and unable to threaten any Muslim...[14]

Bin Laden belongs to a long tradition of protest against Western power in Muslim lands, though in this case his words have been followed by action.

The second development is that of an increasingly active pan-Islamic consciousness in the Muslim world since 1800. There are reasons for this pan-Islamic sentiment which derive from Islam itself. Muslims believe that theirs is a community, an umma, created by God's revelation to man through Muhammad. Moreover, that revelation tells them that they are the best community produced for mankind. They believe that it is an especial blessing to belong to this community. The brotherhood of all those who belong to the community, in total equality before God, is a strong concept which is widely celebrated from the salam in communal prayer through to the shared experience of the pilgrimage to Mecca. A concern to cherish and sustain the community against all forms of divisiveness is the underlying spirit of the shari'a, the holy law. The classical traditions of biography, moreover, were always designed to show the role of individuals, first, in sustaining and enriching the community in their time and, second, in transmitting that precious knowledge to future generations as continuing manifestations of the community. There is a special magic in the community as expressed by Muhammad Iqbal, writing at a time when it was threatened by the growth of nationalism. In his *Secrets of Selflessness*, published in 1918, he declared:

Our essence is not bound to any place;
The vigour of our wine is not contained
In any bowl; Chinese and Indian
Alike the shard that constitutes our jar,
Turkish and Syrian alike the clay
Forming our body; neither is our heart
Of India, or Syria, or Rum,
Nor any fatherland do we profess
Except Islam.

But twentieth-century realities were destroying this charismatic community:

Now brotherhood has been so cut to shreds
That in the stead of community
The country has been given pride of place
In men's allegiance and constructive work;
The country is the darling of their hearts
And wide humanity is whittled down
Into dismembered tribes..[15]

Iqbal, however, need not have been quite so concerned. The community was being re-created in a very special way in the age of the modern nation-state, using basic religious building blocks. One pillar has been the great increase in the numbers of those performing the pilgrimage to Mecca in the nineteenth and twentieth centuries—from under one million in the 1920s to over ten million in the 1970s. Growing wealth and the great improvements in transport by land, sea, and air have facilitated this community-affirming ritual. But most important has been the growth of global news and communications systems, from the expansion of the press in the mid-nineteenth century to the development of global radio and television in the second half of the twentieth. The press flourished in British India as West Asia came under European domination from the 1870s: when Russia and the Ottoman Empire went to war in the late 1870s; when the British invaded Egypt in 1882; when the Ottoman Empire began to decline, from 1911 to 1924.[16] Such was the fervour and excitement that many Muslims came to dream about the wider Islamic world. Muslims adopted headgear and other forms of dress to indicate their identification with West Asia. For the same purpose they stopped giving their children names from regional languages in favour of classical Islamic ones. Their writings revealed how they identified with Muslims of other countries.[17]

During the second half of the twentieth century this process has intensified, with an especial focus on Iran, Iraq, and Palestine. Some of the crowds that have protested against allied action in Afghanistan or Israeli action in the West Bank may have been organized, but large numbers have protested spontaneously out of fellow feeling for their Muslim brothers.

What this strong sense of community, of Islamic brotherhood, means is that, although there are many differences and distinctions amongst Muslims, there is a level at which they will unite, especially when confronted by bullying, interference, or invasion from outside. This is reflected in the local press throughout the Muslim world and among people talking on buses and trains, in bazaars and villages. Of course, power players in the Muslim world have from time to time tried to hijack this sentiment for their own purposes, as the Ottoman Empire did with its pan-Islamic policies in the late nineteenth century, as Sa'udi Arabia has tried to do through their Islamic Conference Organization and the World Muslim League from the 1960s, and as Osama bin Laden did during 2001, harnessing global communications technology to his cause with no little skill.

The third development, and in many ways the most important, has been the worldwide movement of Islamic revivalism which, from the eighteenth century, has been expressed in many different ways through differing social, economic, cultural, and political circumstances. It is important to recognize that this movement has profound Islamic roots and precedes the assertion of Western power in the Muslim world. From the nineteenth century onwards the movement has interacted powerfully with the Western presence and is in varying ways shaped by it. All the Islamic organizations that have gained attention through the events of 11 September have their roots in this revival and this reaction. The fundamental concern of this extraordinary movement has been the renewal of Islamic society from within and not assault on outside forces—an internal struggle or jihad, not an external one.

At the heart of this Muslim revival lay a return to first principles. In the spread of Islam from West Africa to China and Southeast Asia too many concessions had been made to local religious practice, which compromised the monotheism of God's message to humanity through Muhammad. It was necessary to go back to first principles, to abandon much of the medieval superstructure of learning and concentrate on the Quran and the traditions of the Prophet, to try to recreate the perfection of the Prophet's community in the oasis of Medina. At the same time, there was an attack on all ideas about the intercession of God in the affairs of mankind, as represented by the shrines of saints. From the late eighteenth century, the concept that man alone was responsible for his salvation—indeed, that he must act on earth to achieve it—steadily spread to many parts of the Muslim world. This, as is the case with the Protestant Reformation in Christianity, has released vast amounts of energy. It represents a shift in emphasis in the forms of Muslim piety from an other-worldly to a this-worldly Islam.[18]

There are three manifestations of this worldwide Islamic movement which link directly to the present. The first is the Wahhabi movement of Arabia. This was the creation of an eighteenth century scholar, Muhammad ibn 'Abd al-Wahhab, who preached a return to the Quran and the traditions and removal of all religious practices suggesting God's intercession. His preaching is the *locus classicus* of the Islamic revival and the name Wahhabi is given to similar forms of Islamic purism down to the present. The message of this scholar, however, would not have made much impact had he not teamed up in 1744 with a petty chieftain of Central Arabia, Muhammad ibn Sa'ud. His message and Sa'ud's ambitions proved an explosive mixture. They underlay the creation of the first Sa'udi empire, which was brought down by the armies of Ibrahim Pasha of Egypt in 1818. They subsequently inspired the creation of the second Sa'udi empire, the Kingdom of Sa'udi Arabia, which emerged in the 1920s.

This Sa'udi state became the corporate venture of the Sa'udi family, dependent on the legitimization of Wahhabi 'ulama that we know today. There has developed a constant and increasingly abrasive tension between the family and state interests of the Sa'udi family and the concerns of the Wahhabi 'ulama to promote their Islamic understanding and to assert their authority. This situation has been exacerbated both by the Western lifestyle and corruption of many members of the royal family and by the states close association with the USA. The presence of large numbers of Westerners in Sa'udi Arabia since the Gulf War of 1990 has made matters much worse. Other important factors are the growing Sa'udi middle class who have no representation and a growing population without jobs. As the median age in Sa'udi Arabia is 19.7, the situation will get worse, and the annual per capita income has fallen from $28,000 in the early 1980s to $7,000 today.

The Sa'udi regime could not afford to permit the USA to use the Prince Sultan airbase during the 2001 campaign in Afghanistan. It should be no surprise that the Sa'udis should have tried to gain Islamic credentials by supporting Hamas, the Palestinian Islamist organization, or the Jama'at-i Islami of Pakistan, the Islamic Salvation Front of Algeria or the Muslim Brotherhood of Egypt. Nearly half of the hijackers of 11 September were of Sa'udi origin, and one of the stated objectives of Osama bin Laden, that Sa'udi citizen banished from his country, was the overthrow of the current Sa'udi regime.

The second manifestation of the Islamic revival connected with the present is the emergence of 'reformist Islam' in South Asia in the nineteenth century. This is a movement whose ideas and organization can be linked directly through time to the Taliban. At the heart of South Asia's 'reformist Islam' was the Deoband madrassa, founded in 1867 and called by some the most important traditional Muslim university in the world after Egypt's al-Azhar. Deobandis were tackling the problem of how to sustain an Islamic society under British rule. They debated how to sustain Islam in the relatively novel situation in which they did not have, and would not wish to have, state support. The individual human conscience in search of salvation, knowing how to act properly as a Muslim, was to be the driving force sustaining a Muslim society. They embarked on a concerted effort to translate the Quran and other key texts into Indian languages. For the first time in the Muslim world the printing press was harnessed seriously and with enormous vigour to make these texts as widely available as possible. Schools were set up on the Deoband model; by 1967 there were said to be over 8,000 worldwide, all supported by private subscription. This movement has come to be seen as a form of 'Islamic Protestantism' in which Muslims without power developed their Muslim community by themselves. It was a self-sufficient form of Islam which could operate outside the colonial state, indeed, outside any state at all.[19]

The reformist Muslims, the Deobandis, largely opposed the creation of Pakistan—they did not need a Muslim state to create their Islamic world. Once it was created, they carried forward their message both in Pakistan and Afghanistan, where they had long-established madrasas. By the 1980s and 1990s hundreds of Deobandi madrasas had been established in Pakistan. From at least the 1970s they were assisted from outside by funds, in particular, from the Persian Gulf states and Sa'udi Arabia, and also by revenue remitted by Pakistanis working in the Gulf. The process was assisted, too, by the Islamic government of General Zia ul-Haq and by a Sunni Muslim urban elite concerned to consolidate its hold over the many Pakistanis who were moving from the countryside to the towns. Given their long-term connections with Afghanistan, it was natural after the Soviet invasion of 1979 that the Deobandi madrasas should perform a major role in assisting the large numbers of refugees who fled to Pakistan. Thus began the militarization of the madrasas as the Afghans, but also Pakistanis and Arabs, fought their jihad against the Russians. Once the Russians had been defeated, it was but a short step from this to the next stage: Pakistan's Inter-Services Intelligence agency used the students from these madrasas, the Taliban, to create a favourable regime in Afghanistan and give Pakistan the strategic depth to the North West that it had long sought. The Taliban were armed and trained and, in 1994, they invaded Afghanistan; by 1997 Pakistan recognized the Taliban as the rulers of Afghanistan.[20]

The irony is that the Taliban, the heirs of a revivalist movement designed specifically to fashion an Islamic society which could exist without state power, should have been the very first group of Sunni Muslim 'ulama to achieve total and unfettered control of a state—or at least the shattered remains of what was the Afghan state. Pakistan has been forced to assist in the destruction of the monster it helped to create, as it is now being pressed to curb the guerilla groups whose action it has supported in Kashmir. These are not actions which it will be easy for the Jami'yat al-'Ulama-yi Islam (the Deobandi party in Pakistani politics) and its sympathizers to forgive.

The third aspect of the great Islamic movement of revival and reform which reaches into the present is the ideology and organization of Islamism. Islamists are very much a twentieth-century phenomenon. They find the solutions of the reformers to the challenges of the West and modernity unsatisfactory because, by and large, they ignored modernity and dodged the issue of power. The responses of Muslim modernists, many of whom led nationalist movements, were no less satisfactory. Certainly they understood the issue of power, but in engaging with the West they were deemed to be willing to sacrifice too much that was essential to Islam and Muslim culture. Islamists saw the real danger as Western civilization itself. Their real enemies were the secular or modernist elites in Muslim societies who collaborated with Western political, economic, and cultural forces, and enabled Western influence to flourish in their societies. Their prime aim was to take power themselves so that their societies could be sealed off from these corrupting influences. They would then be able to introduce their Islamic system in which the Quran and the shari'a were sufficient for all human purposes. This was a system to match capitalism or socialism; it envisaged the Islamization of economics, knowledge, and so on—it was an ideology.

The founders of the Islamist trajectory in Islamic revivalism were Mawlana Mawdudi of India and Pakistan (1903–79), whose organization was the Jama'at-i Islami, and Hasan al-Banna of Egypt, assassinated in 1949, who founded the Muslim Brotherhood. From the 1970s Islamist organizations had spread widely in the Muslim world. Among the more notable organizations were the Islamic Salvation Front of Algeria, Hamas of Palestine, and the Rifa Party of Turkey. Amongst their notable successes were the dramatic assassination in 1981 of Anwar Sadat, the president of Egypt, the steady Islamization of the Pakistani constitution and law, and, of course, the Iranian revolution.

It is important to understand that Islamism is in its way a profoundly 'modern' movement, concerned to chart an Islamically-based path of progress for Muslim societies. While concerned to resist the West, its leaders have been influenced by Western knowledge. Sayyid Qutb who took over the leadership of the Muslim Brotherhood from Hasan al-Banna was much influenced by the French fascist thinker, Alexis Carrell, and a visit to the USA. 'Ali Shari'ati, ideologue of the Iranian revolution, was much influenced by Sartre, Fanon, and Louis Massignon. Erbakan, the leading Turkish Islamist politician, was an engineer. Bazargan and Banisadr, early leaders of the Iranian revolution were an engineer and an economist, respectively.. The followers of Islamist movements are the displaced. More often than not they have moved from the countryside to the city and look for medical, educational, and psychological support, often in areas where the state is failing. Anthropological studies have shown that Islamism and its organizations often provide the means by which both men and women can come to participate in the modern economy and state.

Classically, the prime concern of Islamist groups has always been to effect change in their own societies, to seize power if possible. The one exception to this rule has been a concern from the beginning with the fate of Palestine. However, we are told that Osama bin Laden's al-Qaeda network contains members of former Islamist groups and is in contact with Islamist groups throughout the world. This network, moreover, seems to have been that which, from the early 1990s, has consistently waged war on US targets in West Asia and on the USA itself. We need to know why this change has taken place. Is there, for instance, a new strand of Islamism which sees the struggle for power in Pakistan, Sa'udi Arabia and Egypt as one which can only be won by assaults on the USA? Or are we dealing with the personal vendetta of an evil genius brilliantly able to make the anger and hunger for justice in the Islamic world serve his purpose?

How far, then, does this scenario represent the makings of a clash of civilizations, of Islam and the West? It is possible to portray the 1,400 years of interaction between the Islamic world and the West as a clash of civilizations, of world views. We can refer to our Crusades against Islam in West Asia and in Spain. We can refer to the annual Ottoman campaign in Europe, which took the form of holy war. We can be blinded by the legacy of hundreds of years of polemic against Islam just as Muslims belittled European civilization until the nineteenth century. But, alternatively, we could, as more and more scholars are doing today, note how much Christian and Islamic civilizations have fruitfully interacted through history and played a part in shaping each other.

The roots of Islamic civilization lie in the monotheistic and Hellenistic traditions of the eastern Roman Empire. Indeed, its universalism is directly derived from the political and religious universalism of Constantine's Byzantine Empire. Medieval Europe was hugely enriched by the Arab–Muslim knowledge which was transmitted through Italy and Spain. Down to the nineteenth century Europeans measured themselves in various ways against the world of Islam. During the nineteenth and twentieth centuries, as we have seen, the Muslim world came to be shaped by Europe. And now, of course, Muslims play their part in shaping the West both as communities within, as well as from without. These two worlds—Christian and Muslim—have shared much and have much to share.[21] In a most important statement the Second Vatican Council asked Christians to reflect on what they shared with Muslims:

> The Church regards with esteem also the Moslems. They adore the one God, living and subsisting in Himself, merciful and all-powerful, the Creator of heaven and earth, who has spoken to men; they take pains to submit wholeheartedly to even His inscrutable decrees, just as Abraham with whom the faith of Islam takes pleasure in linking itself submitted to God. Though they do not acknowledge Jesus as God, they revere him as a prophet. They also honour Mary, His virgin Mother; at times they even call on her with devotion. In addition they await the day of judgement when God will render their deserts to all those who have been raised up from the dead. Finally, they value moral life and worship God especially through prayer, alms-giving and fasting.[22]

Arguably, if there is a clash of civilizations, it is between those who believe in God and those who do not.

Do the howls of rage and protest at the dominance of the West speak for all Muslims? No. Throughout the period of Western dominance in the world, there have been Muslims who have felt that Western power and dominance was not a cause for complaint but a call to constructive action. Western power and dominance was based on knowledge from which they should benefit. This goes as much for leading figures such as Sayyid Ahmad Khan, the creator of Islamic modernism, or Mustafa Kemal Ataturk, who gave modern Turkey such distinctive direction, as it does for the tens of thousands of Muslims every year who come to the West to be educated in its universities. These expressions of protest, moreover, stem less from an intrinsic hatred of the West than from the impact of the West on Muslim societies. Often it is part of a discourse within Muslim societies about how they should progress, a discourse in which Western influence is felt to be a constraint. It is worth reflecting on the sense of self-confidence which Iran has gained from its revolution, a revolution which has allowed it to chart its own destiny. 'What has your revolution achieved, what has it given the Iranian people who are suffering from the ravages of war?' a journalist asked an Iranian leader in 1989, as ten years of the revolution were celebrated. He replied: 'We have given the Iranian people a sense of self-respect and dignity. Now Iranians in Tehran, and not [people] in Washington or in London, make decisions about the destiny of Iran.'[23]

In considering the clash of civilizations, how much weight should we give to pan-Islamic consciousness, to Islamic solidarity? Traditionally, Islamic solidarity has tended to founder on the other affinities which bind groups of Muslims: the differences between major ethnic groups—Arabs, Persians, Turks, South Asians, and so on. There are the subnational affinities which bedevil the politics of many states: Kurds, Berbers, Azeris; the differences between the Punjabis and the rest in Pakistan, those between the Pathans and the rest in Afghanistan. We have the great religious distinctions between Shia and Sunni. There are the often bitter sectarian distinctions generated by the process of Islamic revival on the Indian subcontinent: Deobandi, Barelwi, Ahl-i Hadith, Ahl-i Quran, Ahmadi, Jama'at-i Islami, Tablighi Jama'ati, and others. Then on top of this there are the often-competing interests of Muslim states. For a moment, iconic issues such as Palestine can bring Muslims together, but in the long term solidarity is always likely to be broken by local affinity, local antagonism, state interest, and the mundane.[24]

What weight should we give to the issue of Islamism? Islamist parties form the chief opposition to current governments in many Muslim states. Moreover, given the weakness of these states, given their economic problems, and, in particular, given their age structures—most Muslim societies are experiencing or about to experience massive youth bulges (the Muslim population of the world which was 18 per cent in 1980 is due to become 30 per cent by 2025)[25]—it is likely that a number of Islamist parties will come to power. Will the accession to power of parties, which more often than not see Western civilization as the enemy, bring us closer to a clash of civilizations? Certainly, in the first flush of victory we might expect some hardening of attitudes towards Israel, a revision of oil policy, or a withdrawal of support for UN resolutions supporting interventionist policies. However, as Anthony Parsons, HM Ambassador to Iran at the time of the revolution, always used to maintain, and Fred Halliday does now, these regimes will be swiftly constrained by the political economies of their societies and by the geo-politics of their environment. It is remarkable how increasingly pragmatic the revolutionary regime in Iran has become, whether it be over allied intervention in Afghanistan, sending its students to Europe, or talking to the 'Great Satan' itself. Deputy Foreign Minister Kharazi had to resign, not because he was talking to the USA, but because he revealed the fact in public.

The final issue is whether Osama Bin Laden's al-Qaeda represents a new strand of Islamism which has broader objectives. By his own account it does. He is no longer concerned just to take power in Muslim societies but to wage war on Western hegemony. In his book, *America and the Third World War*, for instance, which became available in 1999, he calls on the entire Muslim world to rise up against the existing world order to fight for their rights to live as Muslims, rights which he says are being trampled on by the West's intentional spreading of Westernization.[26] In Bin Laden we have a Muslim who sees the current situation in terms of a clash of civilizations, and who has created a global terrorist network to resist Western hegemony. In addressing this threat, it will not be enough to focus on the terrorist network itself, the West must address and be seen to be addressing, the many issues of injustice from Palestine onwards which drive young Muslims into the Bin Laden camp. The prize is Muslim public opinion, that third of the world's population by 2025. If we act so as to alienate—or sustain the existing alienation of—that public opinion, we might just begin to have a real clash of civilizations.

NOTES

1 S.P. Huntington, *The Clash of Civilizations and the Remaking of World Order* (New York, 1996).

2 See, for instance, the critique of Huntington in G.E. Fuller, and I.O. Lesser, *A Sense of Siege: The Geopolitics of Islam and the West* (Boulder, Colorado, 1995), and F. Halliday, *Two Hours that Shook the World: September 11, 2001: Causes and Consequences* (London, 2002).

3 I. Wallerstein, *The Modern World System*, vol. I–III (New York, 1974–89).
4 For a translation and commentary on this most influential work in the lives of Urdu-speaking Muslims in South Asia see: C. Shackle, and J. Majeed, trans. and intro., *Hali's Musaddas: the Flow and Ebb of Islam* (Delhi, 1997).
5 Translation by Gail Minault in G. Minault, 'Urdu Political Poetry during the Khilafat Movement', *Modern Asian Studies*, vol. 8, no. 4 (1974), pp. 459–71.
6 S.G. Miller, trans. and ed., *Disorienting Encounters: Travels of a Moroccan Scholar in France in 1845–1846: The Voyage of Muhammad As-Saffar* (Berkeley, 1991), pp. 193–4.
7 *Safarnamah-i Malta*, H.A. Madani, Deoband (1920), quoted in R. Malik, *Mawlana Husayn Ahmad Madani and Jamiyat 'Ulama-i Hini 1920–1957:* 'Status of Islam and Muslims in India' (Ph.D. thesis, University of Toronto, 1995), pp. 44–5.
8 A.J. Arberry, trans., *Persian Psalms (Zabur-i Ajam) ... from the Persian of the late Sir Muhammad Iqbal* (Karachi, 1968).
9 Quoted in Hamid Algar's introduction to H. Algar, trans., *On the Sociology of Islam: Lectures by Ali Shari'ati* (Berkeley), p. 23.
10 H. Algar, trans., *Islam and Revolution: Writings and Declarations of Imam Khomeini* (Berkeley), California, 1981, p. 182.
11 C. Hillenbrand, *The Crusades: Islamic Perspectives* (Edinburgh, 1999), p. 590.
12 Ibid., pp. 592–600.
13 Ibid., p. 602.
14 Y. Bodansky, *Bin Laden: The Man who Declared War on America* (Roseville, California, 1999), pp. 226–7.
15 W.T. de Bary, (ed.) *Sources of Indian Tradition* (New York, 1958), p. 756.
16 F. Robinson, 'Islam and the Impact of Print in South Asia' in F. Robinson, *Islam and Muslim History in South Asia* (Delhi, 2000), pp. 66–104.
17 F. Robinson, *Islam and Muslim History*, pp. 66–104.
18 For a sketch of the overall development of this process see: F. Robinson, *Atlas of the Islamic World since 1500* (Oxford, 1982), pp. 110–75; and for its impact on the individual see: F. Robinson, 'Religious Change and the Self in Muslim South Asia since 1800', *South Asia*, vol. XXII, Special Issue (1999), pp. 13–27.
19 For an authoritative analysis of the Deobandi movement see: B.D. Metcalf, *Islamic Revival in British India: Deoband, 1860–1900* (Princeton, New Jersey, 1982).
20 For the growth of madrasas and their significance in Pakistan see: M.Q. Zaman, 'Sectarianism in Pakistan: The Radicalization of Shi'i and Sunni Identities', *Modern Asian Studies*, vol. 32, no. 3 (1998),

pp. 689–716, and S.V.R. Nasr, 'The Rise of Sunni Militancy in Pakistan: The Changing Role of Islamism and the Ulama in Society and Politics', *Modern Asian Studies,* vol. 34, no. 1 (2000), pp. 139–80; and for the relationship between the Taliban and the madrasas, see A. Rashid, *Taliban: Islam, Oil and the New Great Game in Central Asia* (London, 2000).

21 F. Robinson, 'The Muslim and the Christian Worlds: Shapers of Each Other', in Robinson, *Islam and Muslim History,* pp. 28–43.

22 *Nostra Aetate,* proclaimed by Pope Paul VI on 28 October 1965.

23 M. Hussain, 'Roots of anti-Americanism', *Herald,* October 2001, pp. 50–4.

24 G.E. Fuller, and I.O. Lesser, *A Sense of Seige,* pp. 109–36.

25 Huntington, *The Clash of Civilization,* pp. 102–21.

26 Bodansky, *Bin Laden,* p. 388.

Responses to Major Contributions on Islamic and South Asian History

*Modern Islam and the Green Menace**

There is much that is unhealthy in popular attitudes to those human beings who call themselves Muslims. They are thought to be irrational, fanatical, violent and, in the male form, oppressors of women. Their faith is regarded as opposed to modernity, secularism, capitalism, and democracy. They are seen to inhabit a monolithic Islamic world which thinks as one and moves as one, and is so unlike the diverse and highly differentiated 'West'. They are, moreover, feared to be in a global Islamic uprising against the West. Whereas once as a dinner-party guest known to be sympathetic to the Muslim world one was likely to be on the receiving end of a tirade against Islamic oppression of women now, more often than not, one gets a worried quizzing about the dangers of Muslim 'fundamentalism'.

Such attitudes and such cultural stereotyping have a long pedigree in our past, from the Middle Ages, when Muslims were regarded as following a prophet who was an impostor motivated by lust and ambition, and as the rightful recipients of crusades which were conducted in a language of hate, down to the post-Enlightenment era of the nineteenth and twentieth centuries, when they might be regarded variously as the denizens of an exotic world in which European sexual fantasy could run riot or as the unreasoning opponents of European imperialism bent upon a *mission civilisatrice.* But now such attitudes have become particularly salient as people wonder if a green menace might not be surging forward to replace the red menace of yore.

Some Muslims, on the other hand, have developed pretty unhealthy attitudes towards the West. Once there was a chorus of admiration. 'All good things, spiritual and worldly, which should be found in man,' declared the Indian reformer Sayyid Ahmad Khan on

* Aziz Al-Azmeh, *Islams and Modernities*, Verso, extent 157pp.

his visit to London in 1869, 'have been bestowed by the Almighty on Europe, and especially on England.' Now voices of hatred and rejection are heard more prominently. Take the words of 'Ali Shari'ati, ideologue of the Iranian revolution and barely less important than Ayat Allah Khomeini: 'Come, friends, let us abandon Europe; let us cease this nauseating, apish imitation of Europe. Let us leave behind this Europe that always speaks of humanity, but destroys human beings wherever it finds them.' There is contempt for western ways and customs, from its materialism through to attitudes to women. There is bitterness at unfair treatment at the hands of Western power: imperialism and its legacies; support for Israel at the expense of Arabs; a willingness to use force to halt the Iraqi aggressor in the Gulf but not the Israeli aggressor in the Lebanon or the Serbian in the Balkans. Some even talk of a continuing Christian crusade against the Islamic world in which support for the publication of Salman Rushdie's *Satanic Verses* forms a part.

Crusades and green menaces or not, given that Muslims represent a fifth of the world's population, given that several western European countries contain significant Muslim minorities, and given that the globalization of the world's economy and its media mean that western and Muslim societies are likely to interact more and more as time goes on, such attitudes of cultural stereotyping and hostility are sources of abrasiveness and hurt that we could do without. Over the past seven years Aziz Al-Azmeh, who is a professor of Islamic Studies at the University of Exeter, has published a series of reflections on the West, the Muslim world, and interactions between them. These reflections come together well as a book. Two themes play a linking role. There is Al-Azmeh's anger at the damage done by orientalist perceptions, that is those which see the Orient as partaking of some unchanging essence and which fail to see that it might be as highly differentiated as the Occident and no less subject to processes of economic, social, ideological, and political change. There is also what seems to be his anger at the way Arab nationalism and its secular and socialist visions of progress, has been displaced as the leading ideology in many Middle Eastern societies by Islamisms (forms of Islamic ideology often called 'fundamentalist' in the West) with their unworkable Utopian visions. The shade of Edward Said stalks through the essays. Indeed, that presence is announced from the very beginning in the anti-essentialist title *Islams and Modernities.*

Al-Azmeh targets first a quite unintended and somewhat ironical alliance he perceives to exist between Western orientalism and Islamism. Looking at Britain he observes how the old orientalist ways of discussing difference have been worked into a discourse of culturalism. So all Muslims, whatever part of the world they come from, are assumed to share a homogeneous Muslim culture, even though a Bengali Muslim is likely to have as much in common with a Bengali Hindu as with a Mirpuri Muslim from Kashmir, let alone a Turkish Muslim from Cyprus. Such an approach to ethnic diversity, he points out, plays neatly into the hands of Islamist groups that wish to create communalist organizations in British society, separate Muslim schools, a Muslim Parliament, indeed, a whole set of institutions which will allow Muslims to live exclusively and apart from the mainstream of British life.

This unholy alliance between orientalism and Islamism, however, is not restricted to the British arena; it is at work in global interactions between Muslim and western societies. Islamists who aim to capture the modern state and use its powerful machinery to impose the shari'a in full are trying to fashion precisely the Muslim world which orientalism always imagined existed, one in which everything—agriculture, technology, science, warfare, dress, and so on—somehow contained an Islamic essence and could therefore could be called Islamic. 'The discourse of political Islamism,' he states, 'shares many features with the category of Islam in the social imaginary of "the West".' Not everyone is going to accept the role of the orientalist as whipping boy, and certainly not everyone is going to accept that the achievements of orientalist scholarship underpin the visions of contemporary Islamists. Nevertheless, it remains important to note that the claims of Islamism are supported by images of Islam long established in the West and to note, too, that just as these traditional Western images veil a host of Muslim realities so do the claims of the Islamists.

Most of Al-Azmeh's essays are devoted to examining the origins and claims of Islamism. One concern is to explore its social location, which is found in the petty producer and trading classes of Middle Eastern towns. Once these were in large part protected from the play of power by local notables but in the twentieth century they have come to be exposed to an increasingly demanding state in a context of increasingly intense economic change. Precisely the same groups supported Arab nationalism; they deserted it because nationalist regimes failed them economically and politically. 'Islamism as political ideology,' declares Al-Azmeh:

> is not some ersatz nationalism, but the attempt of moribund social structures to perpetuate themselves in spite of and as against nationalist regimes under the aegis of which they first lost their patrimonial leadership and hence their political cover which shielded them as much as possible from the vagaries of development and then lost their economic position through progressive declassment and relative pauperization.

Mark Islamism for the political ideology that it is. Mark, too, that its future is going to depend not on waves of religious feeling passing through the Muslim world, but on the progress of state–society relations in many differently situated Muslim countries. This said, Al-Azmeh does seem to draw the boundaries of the Islamist constituency too tightly. For Islamism finds significant support in other groups both dislocated and particularly sensitive to dislocation: in the masses which have moved over the past three decades from countryside to town, in students who pass through universities with little hope of employment, and in young professionals who wish to bridge the gulf between the worlds of science and technology they inhabit and the aspirations and values of their communities.

A second concern is to investigate the influence of European ideas on Islamism. Here Al-Azmeh turns the spotlight on the thought of the charismatic Jamal al-Din al-Afghani, who lived in Tehran, Kabul, Hyderabad, Calcutta, Cairo, London, Paris, and St. Petersburg before his death in Istanbul in 1897, and who has acquired cult status in Islamist circles since the 1970s. He notes Afghani's romanticism, his concern to revive the 'authentic Islamic essence,' and his vision of the nation as a body united by religion. He records the specific influences of Ernest Renan and Martin Luther and speculates on the probable influence of Herder of the German romantic school and the like-minded Gustave le Bon of France. He enjoys the ironic spectacle of Islamists, who wish to seal themselves off from the corrupting West, idolizing a thinker who was so powerfully influenced by European thought.

What can be said for Afghani, moreover, can be said for many Islamist ideologues. Recent research has revealed, for instance, the influences of the French fascist thinker, Alexis Carrel on the Egyptian, Sayyid Qutb, who led the development of the second phase of the Muslim Brotherhood until his execution by Nasser's regime in 1966.

Again, the very importance of 'Ali Shari'ati to the Iranian revolution was his capacity to place the ideas of Marx, Sartre, and Fanon in an Islamic frame. Even the traditionally learned scholar does not escape the influence of Europe. As far as we know Ayat Allah Khomeini was free from the influences of modern Western philosophy, but there can be no doubting the effect of Plato, who has been studied in Muslim madrasas for a thousand years or more and whose concept of the philosopher-king has been translated through time into the Islamic mystical concept of the 'perfect man'. It was this Islamized philosopher-king who was the supreme figure of authority in Khomeini's theory of Islamic government. In the absence of the Hidden Imam of the Shias this man, just and learned in divine law, was the only person entitled to rule.

There is an important general point, and one too often ignored, which emerges from the influence of European thought upon the Islamists. Not only do Muslim and Christian civilizations draw upon the same semitic traditions of prophecy but they have shared and will continue to share in and be enriched by each other's learning. Under the Abbasid caliphate at least eighty Greek authors in fields such as philosophy, medicine, mathematics, physics, astronomy, geography, and the occult sciences were translated into Arabic. Many of these subjects, notably mathematics, astronomy, and medicine, made great advances in Muslim hands and, in the Middle Ages, the product of Muslim scholarship, plus many classical texts, which had been lost, passed back to Europe. Indeed, the debt of Europe and western civilization to the Islamic world is rather greater than is often supposed, though it is to be hoped that the pioneering work of scholars such George Makdisi (*The Rise of Colleges: Institutions of Learning in Islam and the West*, 1981, and *The Rise of Humanism in Classical Islam and the Christian West*, 1990) will help to set the record straight. In the same way the debt of modern Islamic thought to Europe is rather greater than generally supposed. Much of it represents, as Al-Azmeh tells us, local adaptations of, or responses to, European intellectual traditions such as Marxism, naturalism, liberalism, and nationalism. Is it really feasible for Muslims and westerners to represent each other as so profoundly different and separate when so much has been shared over so long?

Al-Azmeh is further concerned to show that the Islamist Utopia in which all of life is subject to divine law has no substantial precedent in Muslim history. Muslims have traditionally drawn a distinction between the ideal of the caliphate as the overseer of the shari'a and political reality. It is the position classically expressed by al-Mawardi in the eleventh century as he strove to bridge the gulf between the claims of the Abbasid caliphate and the limitations of its power. Indeed, it was widely accepted by the learned men of Islam that even unjust and impious rulers should be obeyed on the grounds that any form of order was better than anarchy.

Islamic Utopias are, like all Utopias, impracticable. To make the point Al-Azmeh examines the history of Sa'udi Arabia where for much of the twentieth century the ideas of the leading figure in the Islamic revival of the eighteenth century, Muhammad ibn 'Abd al-Wahhab, have been used as the ideology of the state. He finds the state, on the one hand, requiring a severe devotional puritanism in public life and enforcing its observance with religious police, but on the other, allowing substantial room for royal discretion, whether it be in marriage practices, economic legislation, or contact and cooperation with Christians. Both risings against the Sa'udi state, those of the Ikhwan in 1927 and of Juhayman al-Utaybi in 1979, were of groups which felt that its political leadership was failing to implement the Wahhabi ideal.

The message to those who worry about the so-called Green Menace is, don't, or at least not too much. Islamist regimes sooner or later have to adjust to political reality. Revolutionary Iran has been going through just such a process, exemplified by the constitutional changes of July 1989, in which provisions reflecting Khomeini's theory of Islamic government were diluted by men keen to get important legislation in the fields of labour and agrarian reform on to the statute book.

Overall, this book should bring some comfort to those in the West who fear developments in Islamic lands. Fear, as so often, stems from ignorance; in this case, ignorance of how much is shared by Muslims and Westerners, of how great the constraints are on realizing Islamist Utopias, and how far perceptions of 'Islam' have come to be distorted by attitudes long established in Western societies and by the influence of orientalist scholarship. It is just a pity that a book which deserves to be widely read for its learning and its intelligence, as well as its argument, should in places be written in language which challenges comprehension.

*Never Argue with the Camel-driver**

The Hajj, as the Muslims call the pilgrimage to Mecca, is the fifth pillar of Islam. In the first pillar Muslims affirm their faith by saying the creed; in this last pillar they reaffirm their faith by visiting the house of God. In doing so they put off their daily clothes and don a garment of two seamless sheets. Thus, symbolically they shed their distinctions of wealth, birth, and race and celebrate the shared community of all Muslims before their maker.

The roots of the Hajj lie deep in the pagan past of Arabia. Over the centuries it has come to be the greatest communal gathering of mankind, numbering in recent years over two million pilgrims. As such it is not just of great religious but also of great political, commercial, and social significance. An object of curiosity for many years, it is now coming to be the subject of serious academic study.

This book, which is one of at least three major books on the topic to appear this year [1995], surveys the Hajj from its pre-Islamic origins down to 1925, when the Hashemites, the hereditary guardians of the holy places for over a thousand years, were expelled by the Sa'udis. The various routes to Mecca are discussed, as is the practice of the pilgrimage in the high Middle Ages. Considerable attention is given to the careful Ottoman management of the process in the sixteenth and seventeenth centuries. Considerable attention, too, is given to the transformation of the Hajj in the nineteenth and early twentieth centuries by the advent of steamship and rail travel, which brought new numbers of pilgrims and new health hazards. The book ends with the Sa'udi takeover: this is seen to bring about a major change

* F.E. Peters, *The Hajj, The Muslim Pilgrimage to Mecca and the Holy Places*, Princeton University Press, distributed in the UK by Chichester: Wiley, extent 399pp.

both in the style of management and in the religious sensibilities of those in charge.

In developing his presentation Peters draws in the main on literary texts. The accounts of the pilgrims themselves, often in substantial quotation, play the major role, supported by the works of chroniclers, geographers, and European travellers. Some recourse is had to Ottoman and British archives where relevant. Unfortunately, no recourse may be had to archaeological evidence, which could possibly do much to unlock the origins of the rites; it does not exist for Mecca and Medina and is unlikely to exist in the foreseeable future. There are, however, excellent photographs from the late-nineteenth and early-twentieth centuries, which have been drawn from the thousands assembled over the past two decades to form a comprehensive visual encyclopaedia of the holy cities of Islam.

One thing is clear; the Hajj has always been a considerable feat of organization. If the problems now tend to be focussed on the Hijaz itself—on dealing with the 400 planes that land at Jiddah each day during the pilgrimage period, on moving millions many of whom are old and infirm around the forty-kilometre pilgrimage circuit without incident, on managing the sacrifice of over a million sheep at Mina within three days, and on coping with the recent politicization of some Hajjis—in the past the main feat was getting pilgrims to the Hijaz and back, and the greatest part of that was travelling across the Bedouin-infested wastes of Arabia.

Right down to the present century, pilgrims travelled in caravans, for instance, the Baghdad, the Damascus, or the Cairo caravans. One element of organization involved the establishment of networks of fortified posts, water cisterns, and resting places along the various routes. By the end of the eighth century these had come to be well-established, amongst the most famous being 'Zubayda's Way' stretching from Kufa to the Hijaz, which was named after the consort of the caliph, Harun al-Rashid. No less organization was bound up in the caravans themselves. Handbooks for the guidance of the caravan commanders still exist. From one of these we learn that in the fifteenth century the Cairo caravan travelled in parallel columns and in the following order: advance party, notables, strong boxes with treasure, Turkish band, women, merchants, ordinary pilgrims, rearguard. On the other hand, in the Persian caravan of the nineteenth century pilgrims travelled in order of city and of tribe. Such caravans, moreover, often involved a multitude of people and animals: a French observer watching the pilgrims return to Damascus in 1432 reckoned it took the 3,000 camels two days and two nights to enter the city.

Some pilgrims were greatly impressed by the caravan experience. Ibn Jubayr (Hajj of 1184), who has left us an unusually rich and detailed narrative, marvelled at the meticulous planning of his caravan and the speed with which everyone obeyed the orders of the commander. Both Ibn Jubayr and that inveterate traveller, Ibn Battuta (Hajj of 1326), revel in the pleasures of night marches: all carried lighted torches and thus 'people travel as it were among wandering stars which illuminate the depth of the darkness and which enable the earth to compete in brightness with the stars of heaven.' A nineteenth century Westerner, her romantic view of camel travel sharpened, doubtless, by an era of orientalist painting, warmed to the sight of the caravan on the march: 'Crossing this [mirage], and apparently wading in the water,' declared Lady Anne Blunt as, greyhounds at her side, she watched the Persian caravan cross the Jebel Shammar, 'was the long line of pilgrim camels, each reflected exactly in the mirage below him with the dots of blue, red, green, or pink, representing the litter or tent he carries. The line of the procession might be five miles or more in length; we could not see the end of it ... a lovely vision.'

In fact, for many the caravan experience was harsh, dangerous, often deadly. The great problem was the Bedouin who saw pilgrims as fair game and, if not bribed to stay away, hunted them. The Persian, Nasir-i Khusraw (Hajj of 1049), recalls how 2,000 Moroccans were killed outside the gates of Medina for refusing to pay protection money. Nearly 900 years later the Ottoman managers of the Hijaz railway found their trains the constant object of attack until they had paid their predators off, levying a surcharge on tickets of those travelling through Bedouin territory. Even when the appropriate bribes had been paid, danger was ever present. A Turkish Hajj guide of c. 1910 is full of rules to follow to avoid being robbed or having one's throat slit: 'During the march never dismount from your camel ... when you do dismount do not leave your luggage ... if you wish to sleep it should be done in shifts ... never argue with the camel-drivers.'

It was not just the Bedouin but everyone who saw pilgrims as sheep to be fleeced. Some made their money from a distance, like the Damascus agents who could be chartered to manage a whole Hajj, or the authorities of the Red Sea port of Aydhab who used to hang pilgrims by the testicles for refusing to pay their toll (Saladin earned a fragrant reputation for putting an end to this practice), or Thomas Cook and Son to whom the British awarded the monopoly of pilgrim transport in the Indian Ocean. But for the inhabitants of the Hijaz mulcting pilgrims was a serious business; the Hajj was, after all, their one big opportunity to make money each year. Pilgrim guides were renowned for their rapacity; one reckoned that the profit from twelve Turkish pilgrims would be enough to keep him for a year. Camel-broking was a tightly-guarded monopoly which made a few men very rich. The Sharif of Mecca got his cut by licensing guides and levying a fee on each camel hired. He could, however, go too far; when in 1922 he began to charge customs duties on pilgrims' effects at Jiddah, there was uproar. Even Meccan women got into the act. According to Snouck Hurgronje, the Dutch orientalist who stayed in the city as a Muslim during 1884–5, they targetted pilgrims who aimed to be there a longer period. Such men usually sought wives. Once married the women would aim to relieve their victims of their wealth within six months or so, and then behave so badly that they were divorced.

In the nineteenth century the Hajj came to be of more than purely Muslim interest. The leading colonial powers, the British, the French, and the Dutch, became concerned during this time of Islamic revival about its role in spreading subversive ideas to their Muslim peoples. But what brought international concern sharply into focus was the Hajj's role in spreading disease. In 1831 cholera made its first appearance in Mecca. In 1865, 15,000 out of 90,000 pilgrims died from cholera, a further 60,000 Egyptians died in Alexandria, and the epidemic was carried to most cities in Europe. There were a further eight epidemics between 1865 and 1892, and then the most terrible of all in 1893 when 33,000 out of 200,000 pilgrims died at Jiddah, Mecca, and Medina. International action was taken to protect Egypt, in particular and Europe, in general. Sanitary conferences were held on the Meccan pilgrimage. Pressure was brought to bear on the Ottomans to improve pilgrim controls and the implementation of quarantine regulations. By the 1920s the days of cholera epidemics were over but these measures had become bureaucratized as the International Health Convention with its office in Paris, which became the World Health Organization in 1948. In 1957 the Sa'udi government won a singular victory when it gained sole responsibility for the health administration of the Hajj.

The last era of the old-style pilgrimage began in June 1916 when Sharif Husayn raised the flag of Arab revolt in Mecca and with the help of the British threw off the Ottoman yoke. The first Hajj under his control hinted at the subsidies he now received from the allies. Pilgrims were reminded of French achievements at Verdun from the very spot in the great mosque from which Muhammad had preached; the Marseillaise was played as the pilgrims presented themselves at Mt. Arafat. In the following years, to the despair of the British consul at Jiddah, the Hajj continued its pattern of licensed extortion. But the days of such activities were numbered. Already 'Abd al-'Aziz ibn Sa'ud had established his Wahhabi regime in the Najd and in 1924 and 1925 the Wahhabis took the holy cities. They mocked the old Sharif, parading a donkey around Mecca in his turban, and imposed their puritan preferences on religious and social behaviour.

Much of this most informative book deals with the Hajj in its wider ramifications. But it does not neglect its essential religious purpose. We are given a strong impression of the powerful impact of the pilgrimage on all who witnessed it. 'I have seen the religious ceremonies of many lands,' declared Richard Burton (Hajj of 1853—illegal), 'but never—nowhere—aught so solemn, so impressive as this.' Many pilgrims, like 'Ali Bey (Hajj of 1807), have been overwhelmed by the rites at Mt. Arafat as a celebration of the brotherhood of man:

> The native of Circassia presents his hand in a friendly manner to the Ethiopian, or the Negro of Guinea: the Indian and the Persian embrace the inhabitants of Barbary and Morocco; all looking upon each other as brothers, or individuals of the same family united by the bands of religion; and the great part speaking or understanding, more or less the same language, the language of Arabic. No, there is not any religion that presents a spectacle more simple, affecting and majestic!

The responses of Malcolm X (Hajj of 1964) were exactly the same.

*Through the Minefield**

For more than fifty years Bernard Lewis, who held a chair at the School of Oriental and African Studies from 1949 to 1974 and subsequently at Princeton University, has been a leading authority on the Middle East. It is no surprise that his treatment of this region, whose past and present harbour so many grievances, and whose myths and histories are often thought too important to be left to the mere historian, has not been without controversy.

For the Palestinian literary critic, Edward Said, Lewis is the typical 'orientalist', condescending to Arabs, 'essentialist' towards Muslims—that is ascribing to them some unchanging essence wherever and whenever they may be found—and too close to the Israeli cause to be regarded as capable of impartial judgement. Indeed, he is accused of being over-selective in presenting evidence. Lewis has given in return as good as he has got. Nevertheless, Said's critique has found a body of support amongst Western scholars, while it has been echoed with relish by Islamists and others in the Middle East.

Recently Lewis has been fined $2,000 by a Paris court on charges of having insulted the Armenian nation. His crime was to have expressed doubt in an interview with *Le Monde* as to whether genocide was a the proper term to describe the Armenian massacres of 1915, asserting that there was 'no serious proof of a plan by the Ottoman government to exterminate the Armenian nation'. This is, of course, an outrageous judgement on a scholar whose knowledge of the Ottoman archives places him in a much better position to form a view on the subject than a Paris court or the unfortunate Armenians themselves, whose great suffering is not denied. It serves to remind us yet again of the minefield which Lewis traverses as he guides us through this region's contested past.

* Bernard Lewis, *The Middle East, 2000 Years of History from the Rise of Christianity to the Present Day*, Weidenfeld and Nicholson, extent 433pp.

Lewis begins his history of the Middle East with the advent of the Christian era. In doing so, he has two concerns: he wishes to rescue the Byzantine and Sasanian empires from the humble positions they are usually given, alongside pre-Islamic Arabia, as the backcloth to the rise of Islam; and he aims to make connections between the contemporary Middle East and its ancient civilizations which we have only recently come to know through the work of archaeologists and orientalists. As the political story has been told a good number of times, he gives more attention to social, economic, and, particularly, cultural change. Not least amongst the cultural changes he wishes us to savour is that brought about by the impact of the West. Indeed, this is heralded right from the beginning with a splendid conceit involving the deconstruction of a Middle Easterner in a coffee-house, sitting in a chair, by a table, reading a newspaper. The telling, however, of 2,000 years of history in 400 or so pages must involve a great deal of selectivity. In this case, the Byzantines, Persians, and Mamluks get short shrift, while the worlds of the Arab caliphate and Ottoman Empire do rather well.

The emergence of the Arab Muslims in the seventh century to rule an area which stretched from Central Asia and the Indus Valley in the east to the Atlantic Ocean in the west is one of the great events in world history. Eighty years after the death of the Prophet, the Umayyad caliphs had a clear view of the world supremacy they had achieved. At Qusayr Amra, a hunting lodge in the Jordanian desert, they had a mural painted in which six rulers of the infidels paid homage to the caliph. They were the Byzantine emperor, the last Visigothic king of Spain, Chosroes the last notable Persian emperor, the Negus of Ethiopia, while the two remaining figures, now defaced, may represent the Chinese emperor and a Turkish or Indian prince. Nevertheless, Lewis is concerned to remind us that it is not the conquests of the Arabs but the Arabization and Islamization of their conquered provinces 'that is the wonder of Arab empire'. This more than anything else transformed the history of the Middle East.

One outcome of the spread of Islam was the creation of what some scholars have come to call an Islamic World system. Its basis was a long-distance trading network which stretched from Fez in Morocco to the Great Wall of China. Arabic was the language of international communication and Islamic law in many areas governed the process of exchange. The major cities of the Middle East, a Baghdad or a Cairo, were great trading entrepôts. Here the Islamic civilization of the high Middle Ages flowered, nourished by the wealth of commerce. This was a world which far surpassed Europe in resources and sophistication; in fact, it was to contribute much to the development of its western neighbour in science, medicine, philosophy, and material culture. There was nothing it wanted from Europe, a demonstrably backward region. The Crusades, though much vaunted in European history, were mere pin-pricks. Much more important were the Mongol invasions of the thirteenth century which, although not as destructive as once thought, rearranged the location of power. The cultural centre of gravity among Arabic-speaking peoples moved from Baghdad to Cairo, the old seat of the caliphate acquiring a provincial status which it maintains to this day. Within a couple of centuries, the lead in the region was to be in the hands of the gunpowder empires of the Ottomans and Safavids in the north and east of the region.

Lewis has much respect for the Ottoman achievement. This empire, which at its height in the mid-sixteenth century, stretched from North Africa to the plains of Hungary and from the Black Sea to the Indian Ocean, was ruled by 'a perfect machine of absolutist government'. Busbecq, the ambassador of the Holy Roman Emperor at the court of Sulayman the Magnificient, was deeply worried about the capacity of Christian Europe to survive the Turkish threat. Moreover, these were real concerns right down to 1683, when the second Ottoman siege of Vienna was lifted. Much of the literature produced in Europe on the Ottomans deals with the merits of their system and the advantages to be gained from imitating them.

Naturally, therefore, a key question is how did Europe come to get the better of the Ottoman Empire, and at last advance ahead of the Middle East? Lewis points to the rise of the European maritime economies, the colonization of the Americas and South and Southeast Asia, the flows of bullion from the Americas, the possibilities of credit far beyond anything the Ottomans could achieve, and states which were prepared to put their weight behind their trading companies as compared with the free market operations of the Ottoman world. He also points to vitality-sapping changes within the empire: the growth of tax farming, for instance, to pay for constantly rising costs of warfare, and the emergence of the hereditary principle in the army and the administration. The major problem, however, was not absolute but relative decline. The Ottomans just could not keep pace 'with the rapid advance of the West in science and technology, in the arts both of war and peace, and in government and commerce'. A well-chosen example shows how the shift of economic power was taking place: in the seventeenth century, the Ottoman Empire exported coffee and sugar to the West; by the late eighteenth century most coffee and sugar used in the empire itself was grown in European colonies and imported by Europeans.

Lewis invokes a comparison—which has often been made—between the rivalry of the Ottoman Empire and Europe, on the one hand, and that of the Soviet bloc and the West, on the other. In both cases, different ideologies and systems confronted each other. In both cases, the assault from the enemies of the West faltered and died because their economies could not sustain their military effectiveness and they themselves could not withstand the nationalist demands of their subject peoples. We are cautioned, however, against taking the comparison too far. In the Cold War the flow of refugees was to the West. In the earlier confrontation the flow was the other way: Jews expelled from Spain in 1492 and dissident Christians persecuted by the dominant Churches in their lands went East.

The past two centuries have brought changes to the Middle East without precedent since the rise of Islam; powers from the West and their civilization have become established in the region. By the mid-nineteenth century, fear of Ottoman expansion in Europe had been replaced by fear that they would not be strong enough to prevent Russian expansion in the Middle East—the famed Eastern Question. By the settlement of the region after the First World War, only the emergence of two strong men, Atatürk and Reza Shah Pahlavi prevented the continuing humiliation of Turkey and Iran by Western power, while the remainder of the area was under some form of European rule with the exception of the Yemen and what was to become Sa'udi Arabia.

By the 1970s, all countries in the region had achieved final independence from the West, but the impact of Western civilization only increased as Middle Easterners continued to respond to its culture, ideas, values, and consumer goods. Arguably, the period of Western hegemony, understood in its widest sense, has brought about the greatest transformation of the Middle East since the rise of Islam. Certainly, many Middle Easterners regard the impact of Western civilization as the greatest disaster ever to befall their society. Indeed, many are currently mobilized against its influence in various Islamist organizations such as the Rifa party of Turkey, and the Muslim Brotherhood and Hamas of the Arab world, even though ironically they are themselves products of that influence. It is with good reason, as Lewis points out, that Khomeini referred to the USA as 'the Great Satan', the great tempter of the righteous from the paths of virtue.

The book is enlivened by much memorable detail. Who would have thought that seventeenth-century Egyptians incubated poultry eggs in ovens or that the first coffee house in Christian Europe was opened in Vienna after the siege in 1683 by an Armenian who was given exclusive rights to trade as a reward for his espionage work behind Ottoman lines? Many Middle Eastern voices are made to speak and remind us of how little the human condition changes: 'The basis of government is jugglery,' declared an official of Abbasid Baghdad, 'if it works, and lasts, it becomes policy.'

Striking observations give food for thought. There have been two occasions in the period when Middle Easterners have adopted the dress of the outsider. The first was after the Mongol conquest, when they began to wear Mongol-style dress and let their hair grow long. Only when the Mongols converted to Islam did they go back to traditional Muslim attire. The second was the adoption from the nineteenth century of the Western military uniform of tight tunic, trousers, and a peaked cap by Middle Eastern armies. In both cases the Middle Easterner was adopting the garb of power. In the latter case, Western dress has spread to most of urban society, although rather more slowly among women, and after the Iranian revolution with an increasing rejection of the tie, which is thought to represent the cross. 'This change of style,' observes Lewis, 'remains as a continuing testimony to the authority and attraction of Western culture, even amongst those who explicitly and vehemently reject it.'

Having 2,000 years of Middle Eastern history to cover enables Lewis to make some important general observations about the region. It is, for instance, one of the three areas of ancient civilization in the world, but is distinctly different from the other two, namely China and India, in that its civilization has been diverse and its history discontinuous. Middle Eastern civilization has never had the levels of homogeneity of China or even the lesser levels of India. And, while the Chinese and Indians can study the records of their ancient past, and have done so in an unbroken tradition, much of the learning and languages of the Middle East were lost in successive processes of Hellenization, Romanization, Christianization, and Islamization, which swept away ancient written cultures. Only recently have they been unearthed and come to play a part in the struggle to define the political identities of the peoples of the region.

Another observation sums up so much about the Middle East and so well that it is worthy of quotation in full:

> The picture which emerges is of a region of ancient and deep-rooted culture and tradition. It has been a centre from which ideas, commodities, and sometimes armies have radiated in all directions. At other times it has been a magnet which attracted many outsiders, sometimes as disciples and pilgrims, sometimes as captives and slaves, sometimes as conquerors and masters. It has been a crossroads and a marketplace where knowledge and merchandise were brought from ancient and distant lands, and then sent, sometimes much improved, to continue their journey.

With regard to the present, Lewis justly marks down the Iranian revolution as one of the great revolutions of modern times, to be compared with the French and the Russian ones, but strangely does not go on to analyse in any substantial way the phenomenon of radical religious activity in the region, both Muslim and Jewish, about which many readers would wish to understand more. On the other hand, the steady march of women into the public arena, as important players in the economy and increasingly important players in politics, is noted as irreversible and of enormous significance. The 1990s, moreover, offer special new opportunities to Middle Eastern regimes. The ending of the Cold War and the aftermath of the Gulf War signalled an era in which local powers would be freer to settle their disputes without outside interference. Furthermore the growing influence of local religious extremism has impressed upon them the urgency of doing so. It is in this context that the Israelis, the PLO, and various Arab governments have made significant moves towards peace.

Given the stir surrounding Lewis's work in recent decades, we are bound to ask if this book will attract critical fire. As ever, he is not slow to explode myths, to offer provocative judgements, and to remind readers of inconvenient facts: whatever nineteenth-century missionaries might have wished to think, Islam was not spread by the sword; in 1800, the Ottoman Empire offered a career more open to talents than even post-revolutionary France; there were Greeks in the nineteenth century proud to serve the Ottoman Empire and content with the 'supremacy of Islam'; detailed study of the Ottoman archives reveals nearly 1,400 courts martial in the First World War, in which Ottoman civil and military personnel were tried and sentenced, some of them to death, for offences against the Armenian deportees.

This said, does he needlessly cause offence by commission or omission? The term, the 'Middle East' is a classic trope of orientalism; it is, after all only the Middle East of the 'West'. However, this is how the region is known even to numbers of those who live within it. Were he to adopt the neutral 'West Asia', as the Indians do, most would wonder what he was writing about. Some Muslims are bound to be offended by his insistence that much of the traditional Muslim narrative of the first century of Islam is highly problematic. But, in stating this, he only echoes the consensus of modern Western scholarship.

There are areas, on the other hand, in which Lewis's position seems less secure. Most Western scholars would now avoid publishing, as he does, a picture of the Prophet Muhammad, unveiled and full face, even if it does come from a well-known Muslim source. Equally, many will have difficulty with an essentially favourable assessment of the British impact on the Middle East, which leaves out the role of British policy in facilitating the creation of a Jewish national home—the basis of the Israeli state. The British are congratulated for fostering higher standards of living, for bringing the English language, for introducing modern science, and for presiding over a period of liberal economy and limited political freedom. But, in drawing up the balance sheet, no mention is made of the policy which, whatever the rights and wrongs of the Zionist cause, was ultimately to bring so much grief to Arab peoples in Palestine and elsewhere.

Here is a clear case of selectivity in forming a judgement. At least one of the accusations of Said and his followers would appear to be justified. What of their other accusations? Is Lewis condescending towards Arabs? Perhaps. He notes that the Mufti of Jerusalem, Hajji Amin al-Husayni, declared his support for Hitler as soon as the Nazi leader came to power in 1933. He notes, too, that the young Nasser and Anwar Sadat Both supported Germany during the Second World War, the latter to the extent of engaging in espionage. But he also points out that such preferences were perfectly natural for Arabs who had come to hate British imperialism and the growing Jewish presence it had brought to Palestine.

Lewis enjoys the irony of Arab support for Nazi Germany, whose policies were bringing about the increasing Jewish presence in Palestine, as opposed to their hostility to the British, who were trying to limit that presence. It is, however, the historian's job to point out such ironies, to reveal the complex interaction of events, and to show how at times the right hand may work at cross purposes with the left.

Lewis comments on the failure of Arab policies: the vision of pan-Arabism, which was to make the Arabs great again, but which foundered against the rocks of lesser loyalties to the state system left by the colonial powers; and the programmes of Arab socialism, which not only failed to provide the economic advances sought by Arab peoples, but also helped to keep ruthless dictatorships in power. But all these points which Lewis raises are facts; they cannot be denied. If there is a problem, it is in an angle of vision, which passes judgement rather more on Arabs than on Israelis, Turks, or even Iranians, and in a tone, which betrays little sympathy for Arab predicaments.

Are there any signs of 'essentialism', that dire affliction of the orientalist? Coming across phrases such as 'Muslim government and society' and 'Muslim belief', the reader might smell an essentialist rat. But there is little need to fear. Lewis constantly emphasizes variety and change in Muslim civilization. In discussing the shari'a, or holy law, he is at pains to point out that, despite the constraints of the unchangeable text of the Quran and the accepted corpus of the traditions, Muslims did to a considerable extent modify and develop their laws in accordance with the juristic principle the 'the rules change as the times change'. Again, in a discussion of holy war he demonstrates that the concept was interpreted in different ways and even in its classical form of war against the infidel did not have universal support. 'Hey, you fools, why do you squander your lives for nothing?,' he quotes a Sufi wandering among Ottoman soldiers on the Austrian front in 1690. 'All the talk you hear about the virtues of holy war and martyrdom in battle is so much nonsense.'

Such is the prejudice against Lewis, particularly in the Third World, that he is dismissed, as one postgraduate student of mine from India did recently, with barely the courtesy of a reading. Like all historians, he should be read with a degree of scepticism, but those who choose not to do so because of his Zionist sympathies or his apparent pleasure in the failure of the socialist experiment will be making a mistake. This book is rich in historical knowledge and full of insight. It both demonstrates and asserts that 'the Islamic civilization of the Middle East, at its peak, presented a proud spectacle—in many ways the apex of human civilization achievement to date'.

*House of Mirrors**

Between 1798 when Napoleon invaded Egypt, and the end of World War One, the fortunes of the Muslim world were utterly transformed. In the eighteenth century Muslims completed a period of over one thousand years in which Islam had walked hand in hand with power. By 1920 all the Muslim world except Central Arabia, the Yemen, and Afghanistan, was either under colonial rule or, like Turkey and Iran, struggling to resist dismemberment by colonial powers. This transformation spurred creative responses, many of which influence the Muslim world today.

One context in which the loss of power was felt most keenly was northern India. In the first half of the nineteenth century Delhi was a great cultural centre; the British administered, Hindus did business, and the Mughal court patronised the arts. All was brutally destroyed by British retribution after the Mutiny uprising: the emperor was deposed, the people were driven out of the city, the Friday mosque, the Jama Masjid, was turned into a barracks, the quarters of the city between this mosque and the Red Fort, where the Mughal aristocracy had lived, were razed to the ground. 'Do not go into the ruins of Delhi,' the poet Hali told an audience in 1874, 'at every step priceless pearls lie buried beneath the dust ... times have changed as they can never change again.'

Within a generation this shattering experience had drawn two major responses. Both were led by Muslims who had lived or worked in pre-Mutiny Delhi. The first was the Deoband movement which developed a form of willed or 'protestant' Islam which enabled Muslims to live to a large extent outside the confines of the colonial state. It has given birth to a most important traditional Muslim university at Deoband and arguably in the Tablighi Jama'at (Preaching Society)

* Christopher Shackle and Javed Majeed, trans and eds, *Hali's Musaddas: The Flow and Ebb of Islam*, Oxford University Press, extent 262pp.

the most widely followed Muslim movement today. The second was the Aligarh movement founded by Sayyid Ahmad Khan, scion of the noblest families of the Mughal court. He wished to build bridges both between Islam and Western learning and between Muslims and British rule. His College in the town of Aligarh, and the wide-ranging intellectual movement it came to represent, was his means to this end. Many see its outcome leading to Muslim separatism and the creation of Pakistan.

Hali's *Musaddas* or elegy entitled *The Flow and Ebb of Islam* was inspired by the person and vision of Sayyid Ahmad Khan. The Sayyid reckoned that being its cause was his 'finest deed'. Nor was this mere flattery because poetry was the most powerful of all the Indo-Muslim arts and this poem the most powerful advocate of his mission. It epitomized the Aligarh movement in its consciousness of the glories of the Islamic past, its awareness of the decay of the present, and its certainty that to progress Western knowledge must be embraced. It epitomized the Aligarh movement, too, by abandoning the artificial intricacies of contemporary Persianate Urdu poetry (the poetry of the Courts) in favour of a new virile straightforward style, better suited to the ear of an emerging 'middle class'. Sayyid Ahmad Khan hailed it rightly as the first modern Urdu poem. Its reception, moreover, was without parallel. It went through at least six editions between its official first edition (1879) and second (1886). It became the stuff of dramatic presentations, was adopted by government for schools and inspired much imitation. Not surprisingly it was the anthem of the Aligarh movement; recitations at conferences and public meetings could be relied upon to leave the audience in tears.

Hali, meaning 'the man of the present' was the pen-name of Altaf Husayn of the Ansaris of Panipat, whose association with Muslim power went back to the sultans of Delhi. Born in 1837 he ran away to the imperial city in his teens and so experienced 'this last sparkle of Delhi the picture of which,' he declared, 'steals upon my heart'. He felt most keenly the decline of Islam which was burned into the consciousness of his class and his generation. In the 1870s he worked in the government book depository in Lahore where his job was to correct Urdu translations from English; he also took part in the poetic assemblies on serious Victorian themes organized by the Director of Public Instruction. Dying in 1914 he was the leading poet of the era between Ghalib and Iqbal.

The *Musaddas* is Hali's masterwork. Epic in scale, in its first edition it consisted of 297 six-line stanzas with an introduction and substantial footnotes. The opening rubai sets the tone:

If anyone sees the way our downfall passes all bounds,
the way that Islam, once fallen, does not rise again.
He will never believe that the tide flows after every ebb
once he sees the way our sea has gone out.

He examines the depths to which contemporary Islam has sunk, describes the evils of pre-Islamic Arabia, trumpets the reforms which the Prophet Muhammad brings, and celebrates the achievements of the caliphate in all fields of human endeavour, deploying Gibbon and other Western scholars in his footnotes to support his case. Then, he draws the contrast with the condition of Muslims in British India. Nearly half the poem is devoted to attacking the decadence and failure of his Muslim contemporaries—the rich, aristocrats, mystics, scholars, doctors, poets, fanatics and bigots.

There is meanness in everything we do
Our ways are worse than those of the most base.
Our forefathers' reputation has been eaten away by us.
Our step makes our countrymen ashamed.
We have thrown away our ancestors' credit,
and sunk the nobility of the Arabs.

He finishes lauding British achievements but also warning them that their time, like that of the Muslims, will pass.

Shackle and Majeed have produced the first readily available translation in English of this important work. Unfortunately it lacks the punch of an earlier part-translation published by Shackle along with D.J. Matthews and Shahrukh Husain in 1985. Compare their version of the opening rubai:

Behold the gloomy depths of our disgrace!
Islam has lost its former glorious place.
By rule, each ebb is followed by a flood:
Can this low tide of ours its course retrace?

This said, in preparing the edition they have had to steer a course through Hali's various second thoughts. They print his introductions to both the first and second editions. For the poem itself they provide the standard Urdu text of the second edition (294 stanzas) with their translation on the facing page. They omit the supplement to the second edition of 162 stanzas, in which Hali strove to put his criticism of his contemporaries in a more positive light. The work begins with an excellent introduction of eighty pages.

Important themes emerge. There is the manipulation of the image of the Prophet which is so much a feature of modern Muslim movements, as different groups have sought to fashion the exemplar of the perfect Muslim life to their particular agendas. Here we are offered an image which 'owes just as much to Victorian values as to any putative Islamic ones'. The virtues of frugality, cleanliness, sobriety, self-discipline, and self-improvement are stressed. The Prophet 'made them realize the value and worth of time, and imparted to them the keen desire and urge to work'. The poor were to lift themselves by their efforts; the rich to show charity to the poor. Farewell idle aristocrats! Farewell simple dependence on God's mercy! Hail dutiful bourgeois citizens of capitalist society!

There is the role of empire in forming Muslim self-image. Throughout the poem Hali assumes a homogeneous Indian Muslim community thus appearing to reflect British categorization of society by religion as manifest in the census. Equally this Indo-Muslim community is seen to be part of a worldwide Muslim community whose centre lies in the Arab lands. This new pan-Islamic consciousness was growing alongside the spread of European empire in the Islamic world, as it has been sustained by Western dominance ever since.

These Muslim self-images, moreover, were continually reinforced by the impact of print and, in particular, by the growth of the vernacular press. For the British print was a tool of imperial management. Indian Muslims, on the other hand, adopted print in the nineteenth century as a weapon in their cultural resistance to empire. Side by side with the adoption of print came a shift, amongst the elite at least, from orality to literacy. The evanescent world of oral transmission became less potent. More and more Muslims came to see their image reflected in the printed word, a word which often their rulers had done much to shape. Hali, himself, who seems to have seen his poem as one to be read rather than recited aloud, refers to it as a 'house of mirrors', in which Indian Muslims 'may enter to study their features and realize who they were and what they have become.'

The *Musaddas* strikes a poignant note for contemporary Indian Muslims. Hali wrote in the context of the early stirrings of Hindu revivalism and the realization of Muslim loss of power. There is a sense of the fragility of Islam's position in the subcontinent. The roots were shallow. It was an exotic presence. Its traces were in danger of being wiped out. Not surprisingly the Musaddas played a substantial role in creating the mindset in which Muslim separatism emerged and the movement for Pakistan flourished. But how much more poignantly must the poet speak now, in the aftermath of the demolition of Babur's mosque by Hindus and the emergence of a Hindu revivalist party which tells Muslims that they must become Hindus in public life.

Shackle and Majeed explore other themes, too, to excellent effect. Taken together this late-nineteenth-century poem with its late-twentieth-century introduction form a work of much value for understanding modern Muslim societies: the agony at loss of power; the anger and self-hate derived from weakness; the need to act on earth to achieve salvation; and their physical and mental shaping by interaction with the West.

*A Greater Raj**

The establishment of the Delhi Sultanate, which led to Muslim rule in much of India, is arguably as important in the history of the Muslim world as the conquest of the Americas has been in that of the Western Christian world. It prepared the way for millions of new Muslims to be recruited to Islam to the extent that now one-third of the world's Muslims live in South Asia. It brought to the Islamic world an area of great wealth, which, in the early modern period, was able to support a major flowering of Islamic culture. It laid the foundations, moreover, of the Muslim society which, from the eighteenth to the twentieth century, was to generate many leading ideas in the Islamic world in the spheres of modernism, reformism, 'fundamentalism' (better known as Islamism), as well as some of its leading organizations—such as the most widely followed Muslim movement in the world today, or so we are led to believe, the Tablighi Jama'at or 'Preaching Society'. The Delhi Sultanate shifted the centre of gravity in the Muslim world towards the East.

The Sultanate also transformed the world of Hindu India. For the following eight centuries Hindu political power was to be much circumscribed. A Muslim ruling class was established which, however assimilated it became, and however much it needed the alliance of the powerful in Hindu society, always looked, in part at least, to the wider Muslim world for inspiration, and was refreshed by new blood from the central Islamic lands. Thus Muslim strands were added to the food, the dress, the music, the languages, and the art and architecture of India. Indians from all levels of society, but in particular from the agricultural and artisan castes, converted to Islam. The basis was established from which a separate Islamic civilizational principle could be asserted against that of the Hindu. However we rate the role

* Peter Jackson, *The Delhi Sultanate: A Political and Military History*, Cambridge University Press, extent 367pp.

of British rule in enabling the politicization of religion on the subcontinent, or that of the Cold War in helping to entrench the political division which accompanied independence in 1947, the fact remains that the Delhi Sultanate began a process which sees South Asia divided between a Muslim Pakistan and Bangladesh on the one hand, and on the other a secular India, the latter in recent years having acquired a distinctive saffron tinge. Now that there are 'Muslim' and 'Hindu' bombs of nuclear capacity we are confronted with the possibility of devastation such as even the Mongols could not have achieved.

The platform for the establishment of the Sultanate began to be established from the 1170s by Afghan invasions of northern India which were led by chieftains from the minor principality of Ghur. By the beginning of the thirteenth century much of northern India was under Ghurid control. The year 1206, when the Turkish slave, Qutb al-Din Aybak was, according to one chronicler, given the title 'Sultan' by the Ghurid family, is usually regarded as the point at which a separate kingdom began to be established out of Ghurid territory. Aybak's descendants continued to rule northern India from Delhi until in 1290 they were overthrown by another Turkish family—the Khiljis from Afghanistan. These sultans dealt effectively with Mongol invasions from the northwest and expanded the authority of the Sultanate far into the south of the subcontinent. In 1320 the Khiljis were replaced by the Turkish Tughluq dynasty who took the Sultanate to its highest peak. In their early years they ruled much of India, dealt ruthlessly with rebellion, saw off Mongol raids, planned an invasion of Central Asia, and thought nothing of moving the capital from Delhi to central India and back. The Moroccan traveller, Ibn Battuta, stayed for some years at the court of Muhammad bin Tughluq (r. 1325–51) and has left a full account of the Sultan's learning, devotion to Islam, generosity, gallantry, the grandeur of his court, and the ease with which he shed blood. A whiff of danger pervades Battuta's account of his time in the hands of a man clearly intoxicated by power. Understandably, he was keen to accept the Sultan's offer to lead an embassy to China.

Muhammad bin Tughluq's reign saw the beginnings of the break-up of the Sultanate; in the south the Hindu kingdom of Vijayanagar began to emerge as well as independent sultanates in Bengal and the Deccan. In 1398 the invasion of Timur (Tamerlaine) saw the end of the Sultanate as a serious power. From 1450 there was a slight recovery under the Lodi Afghans, who succeeded in reasserting the authority of Delhi across the Indo-Gangetic plain from east Punjab to Bihar. But they were no match for yet another invasion from Central Asia. This time it was not the purely destructive raid of a Timur but a series of expeditions led by a descendant of Timur, Zahir al-Din Muhammad Babur, who was determined in the family tradition to create an empire of his own. From 1526 he and his descendants built the Mughal Empire on the wreckage of the Delhi Sultanate and its successor states.

Jackson provides a much needed new overview of this important but too-little-known period of Indo-Muslim history. He focuses on political and military matters and leaves almost entirely to one side the world of saints and scholars which the late K.A. Nizami made so conspicuously his own. His research is rooted in deep knowledge of the Persian language sources, in large part the work of choniclers which he has consulted in libraries in Britain, Europe, Turkey, and South Asia. The historical value of these sources is subject to rigorous appraisal and, where possible, differing versions of the same text have been compared. This comprehensive and careful study of the documentary sources is supported by epigraphical and numismatical evidence and accompanied by a careful review and synthesis of existing research in the field. There is no doubt that this is a work of considerable scholarship and judiciously held opinion.

So judicious, indeed, is Jackson's approach that on occasion he is unable to come to a final opinion. He is, for instance, not sure why the Ghurids were able to establish the Sultanate. As we might expect, he dismisses the explanation of the Muslim chroniclers that the sultan was bound to win because he had God on his side! He dismisses, too, the argument which found favour with Indo-Muslim historians of the 'progressive' era, when socialist brotherhood was thought to have much in common with Muslim brotherhood, that Muslim armies prevailed because caste limited the capacity of Hindus to exploit the full military potential of their society and because the urban masses of early-thirteenth-century India were attracted to the egalitarian values of Islam. His alternative explanations involve aspects of military technology: the numbers of horse deployed, skilful cavalry tactics, vigorous use of the crossbow—which contemporary Crusaders were also putting to good use in West Asia—and the sheer size of the armies that the Ghurids were able to bring to bear. But as to the weight which should be given to any element in the argument, or any combination of them, we are given no clue.

Jackson is no more sure of why the Sultanate was able to successfully to expand in India. He notes the Muslim rhetoric; the way in which Amir Khusraw, the poet and Sufi of late thirteenth century Delhi, likened the Turk to the lion and the Hindu to the gazelle. He refers to the way in which Muslim chroniclers refer to small Muslim forces being the equal of much larger Hindu ones, which is a view that has had an enduring resonance in Indo-Muslim culture; I vividly remember in the 1960s a distinguished Muslim professor of History, with the very best of secular and non-communal credentials, declaring in an unguarded and emotional moment 'one Muslim is worth four Hindus'.

Such rhetoric aside, Jackson also draws attention to the administrative reforms of 'Ala al-Din Khilji, which enabled larger bodies of troops to be raised for lower pay; the importance of divisions amongst Hindu states; the effectiveness of Muslim archers; the capacity of the Sultanate to mobilize larger numbers of horses, and the superiority of the Khilji and Tughluq sultans in siege warfare—the campaigns to annex the central and southern areas of India were almost invariably siege campaigns. Again, however, we are given no guidance as to which elements in the argument, or combination of them, might be given precedence.

There are other areas, fortunately, about which Jackson is more certain. Developing successful relationships with Hindu subjects was the key both to Mughal and British dominion in India, and so it was for the Delhi sultans. Once again the rhetoric of the Sultanate does not make it seem so. The sultan was the; 'Sovereign of Islam' or the 'Emperor of the Peoples of Islam'; he was definitely not sultan of the Hindus. Indeed, as Peter Hardy, the scholar of Sultanate historiography once wrote, for the Muslim chroniclers the Hindus 'were never interesting in themselves, but only as converts, capitation tax payers, or as corpses'. But the fact was that the Sultanate was utterly dependent on Hindu support: Hindus manned the bureaucracy; Hindu infantry fought in the army, and at times dictated the succession to the throne; Hindu labourers made the mighty building projects of the sultans possible; Hindu bankers and brokers financed the extravagance of the Muslim nobility; and the odd Hindu minister kept the Sultanate's finances in order. Sultans, moreover, were as likely to repair Hindu temples as to knock them down; the poll tax on non-Muslims was not consistently applied, indeed, it is difficult to see how it could have been enforced outside the main centres of Muslim power. Jackson quite rightly lifts his assessment out of the arena of Hindu–Muslim jockeying for position, which in the twentieth century has bedevilled judgement, and places it firmly in that of pragmatic calculations of power:

> For the Sultan the paramount distinction was not that between Muslim and Hindu (important as that may have been) but between peaceful subject and agent of government on the one hand and troublemaker and rebel on the other.

The Mongols were the great fact of Eurasian existence in the thirteenth and fourteenth centuries and Jackson, as a Mongol expert, is particularly effective in dealing with the continuing, at times almost annual, threat they presented the Sultanate. The Mongols invaded India for slaves, gold, and silver; they were not particularly keen to stay as the climate, amongst other things, did not agree with them. At times they had a powerful position around Lahore and in the Indus valley. In 1302–3 they penetrated the suburbs of Delhi as far as Haus Khas. But for the most part the sultans seemed to have no great difficulty in dealing with the menace. Indeed, ‘Ala al-Din Khilji was confident enough to give them a distinctive taste of their own medicine. In 1305, for instance, he built a tower of the heads of slain Mongols, a typically Mongol practice, and had large numbers of Mongol captives crushed beneath the feet of elephants for the entertainment of the people of Delhi.

Jacksons's deep knowledge of Central Asia makes him equally sure-footed in explaining one of the more curious episodes in the Sultanate's history—the reign of a woman, Raziyya. The sultana was brought to power in 1236 as a figurehead, but came to clash with her supporters as she became increasingly self-assertive, wearing men's dress and riding in public on an elephant. In 1240 she was overthrown and killed. Raziyya, the chronicler tells us, had all the attributes of a successful ruler. Her rule as a woman, however, was unprecedented at this stage in Muslim history. What is interesting is that her supporters should have thought that she could rule a Muslim state at all. Jackson places this episode very firmly in the context of the greater freedom women of the steppes enjoyed and of the relatively recent conversion of the Turks to Islam. He suggests that the Turkish slaves of Iltutmish

(r. 1210–36), in making their master's daughter sovereign, were reflecting their steppe and pagan background.

Materialists will be pleased to know that there is a clear association between the entrenchment of this Muslim regime and the growth of a flourishing and more complex economy. The overall impact, for instance, of the taxation and pricing policies of Ala al-Din Khilji (r. 1296–1316) was to transfer significant quantities of agricultural surplus from Hindu chiefs to the Muslim ruling class, from the countryside to the towns. Indeed:

> the Delhi Sultanate accelerated the process of urbanisation over much of northern India, as well as fostering the development of a money economy and an expansion in craft production....

At the same time the long-distance trade grew vigorously in what K.N. Chaudhuri has demonstrated was on land and sea a Muslim-dominated 'trading world of Asia'. Indian trade reached from Egypt through to China. In the 1360s the great trading region of Gujarat was able to sustain a revenue demand two and a half times the size of that generated by the fertile Gangetic plain.

The question remains why Timur's invasion should have given the Sultanate its deathblow. His victory came because he had greater resources of men and money than earlier invaders. Moreover, he had welded his forces into a formidable war-making machine. More important, however, was the sharp decline in the military establishment of the Sultanate under Firuz Shah Tughluq (r. 1351–88) and his successors. Agrarian decline does not appear to have been a cause; the period is marked by investment in irrigation and agricultural expansion. Nevertheless, there was a reduction in government revenues available to support the military; more resources were being spent on building works and charity; there was inflation and the Sultans found themselves forced to pay their troops not in cash but in land. This led to military identification with the land and military resistance to royal power. After Timur's invasion the sultans were no more than one amongst several small regional rulers in northern India.

This work of original scholarship and synthesis, despite Jackson's unwillingness at times to reach firm conclusions, explains as no other has done before the many factors, in particular, the nature of military power and government, which contributed to the establishment of an Islamic presence in South Asia. By the same token it explains how vast new resources of people, wealth and human achievement were added to the Muslim world and at the same time a new civilizational strand was added to South Asia which has been, ever since, a source both of strength and of tension.

I have only one complaint which is that Jackson has restricted himself to written sources on paper, stone, or metal. The imposing legacy of Sultanate architecture is ignored. Yet surely there is no better way of grasping the pride and sense of achievement of the early sultans of Delhi than noting the Qutb Minar, Qutb al-Din Aybak's great tower of victory which reaches over seventy-two metres in height, the neighbouring Quwwat ul-Islam (Might of Islam) Mosque, or the nearby Alai Minar, the base of a second great tower which Ala al-Din Khilji intended should be twice the height of the Qutb Minar. Surely, too, the power of the Tughluqs, as the rulers of the greater part of South Asia, is expressed in the massive ruins of Tughluqabad, the vast fortfied city and palace complex built by Ghiyas al-Din Tughluq between 1321 and 1325 no less than their military ethos is expressed in Ghiyas al-Din's magnificent tent-shaped mausoleum surrounded by a great battlemented wall, which adjoins it. To these should we not add the Firuz Shah Kotla, the citadel of the city of Furuzabad founded by Firuz Shah Tughluq in 1354, and the ruined mosque close by with room for 10,000 people and so impressive, so it is said, that Timur after worshipping there made it the model for his own mosque in Samarqand. Nowadays, Firuz Shah Kotla is better known as one of the arenas in which the might of Indian cricket is displayed. But for those who succeeded the Delhi sultans as rulers of India, these and many other imposing remains stood as reminders of the grandeur and magnificent aspiration that had gone before them. Over the past two centuries, they have been powerful reminders to the Muslims of South Asia of what they have lost and to the Hindus of what they think they endured.

*Glimpses of a Lost World**

Once the Shah said to Enayat, 'My heart lusts for a nice virgin boy.' Enayat went out and returned with a little woman. 'You wretch,' the Shah said, 'I asked for a tender youth but you bring me a tiny woman.' Enayat said, 'She has "both".' The Shah said, 'But I wanted to play with the boy's balls.' 'Do the doing with this woman,' Enayat rejoined. 'And as for the "playing", grab my balls.'

This is among the fifty-five jokes with which the poet Mir Taqi Mir concludes his autobiography. The Shah in question is Abbas II of Iran (d. 1660); Enayat is his sidekick Enayat Gul. They were frequent interlocutors in the jokes of northern India in whose courts, in the eighteenth century, large numbers of Persians sought their fortune. Such jokes were part of the armoury of poets, whose task was to be good company for their patrons as well as the crafters of words into 'strings of pearls'. Telling and enjoying jokes was a important feature of Muslim society and is well supported by the traditions of the Prophet. Indian editors of printed editions of Mir's autobiography, so we are told, left the jokes out; they did not coincide either with 'Victorian values' or with the image of poetic genius. Mir, however, clearly wanted to share them with his leaders. 'Now the pen has on its tongue some witty tales,' he wrote 'which it lays out for the friends' sake.' We, moreover, must be thankful to C.M. Naim for including them. They are among the several ways in which his translation of Mir's autobiography, and the rich scholarly support which he appends to it, enables us to savour what it was to be human in the cultivated Muslim world of eighteenth-century northern India.

Mir was the greatest poet of his age. His work was known throughout the Deccan as well as in the north. He was the only poet whose verses travellers would take to offer as gifts to their hosts. His

* Zikr-i Mir, *The Autobiography of the Eighteenth-Century Mughal Poet*, Mir Muhammad Taqi 'Mir' (1723–1810), C.M. Naim, ed. and trans., Oxford University Press, extent 214pp.

fame rests in particular on his ghazals, or love poetry, which make him one of the leading love poets of world literature. 'His Urdu ghazals,' writes Naim, 'are noted for an immediately recognizable voice almost luminous in its intensity, an intriguing mix of self-mockery and self-assertion, a beguiling simplicity of expression that soon reveals its layered quality, and an economy and preciseness of language that reflects Mir's dazzlingly confident use of the different registers of a vernacular.'

Mir lived at a time when the court poets of India wrote in both Persian and the vernacular. He spoke most powerfully, as he put it, in the language that he heard 'on the steps of the Jama Masjid', Delhi's Friday mosque. Through his art he was helping to forge that language into the great literary vehicle it has become today.

Mir's life spanned the effective destruction of the Mughal Empire. He was born in 1723 at Agra, during the reign of Muhammad Shah, the 'voluptuary'; it was a time when the Mughals could still imagine that their authority reached over the greater part of the subcontinent. Born into a family which claimed descent from the Prophet, his grandfather had been a high-ranking official of the Mughal court. After his father's death, when Mir was seventeen, he went to Delhi where he found service with prominent nobles. He witnessed the great calamity which befell the imperial capital in the mid-eighteenth century: its sack by Ahmad Shah Abdali of Afghanistan in 1760. For much of the following ten years or more, Mir was supported by Shah Alam's finance minister, Nagar Mal. From 1771 he lived a life of great privation, until he was able in 1782 to get himself established at the court of the Mughal successor state of Awadh. For a time, under Nawab Asaf al-Dawlah he received a handsome pension. Nothing, however, was forthcoming from the Nawab's close-fisted successor, Saadat 'Ali Khan, and in 1810, Mir died poverty-stricken in Lucknow.

As compared with biography and, in particular, with collective biography in which are recorded the contributions of the learned and holy, or the poetically gifted, in sustaining and transmitting the core values and skills of Muslim civilization, autobiography is a poorly developed genre in Islamic literature. Indulgence in autobiography suggests a too highly developed sense of individual worth as against the deference which the individual owes to wider community purpose. Notable exceptions are the autobiography of that great intellectual and spiritual figure, al-Ghazzali (d. 1111), and the memoirs of those remarkable Mughal emperors, Babur (d. 1526) and Jahangir (d. 1628). Indeed, autobiography as a genre does not begin to be practised at all widely in the Muslim world until the twentieth century when it came to be powered both by a growing sense of individualism and by Western influence. Mir's autobiography, therefore, has a special interest as a rare example from the eighteenth century. Naim most helpfully places it in the context of two other autobiographical works written by leading poets whom Mir knew, Anand Ram Mukhlis (d. 1751) and Shaykh Muhammad 'Ali Hazin (d. 1766). He shows how similar to the latter Mir's work is, not least in the substantial narrative of political events.

This said, Mir wittingly and unwittingly tells us much else. Nearly a third of his book is devoted to establishing his father as a leading Sufi; the centrality of spiritual devotion in his life is set out and the impact of his spiritual presence on others is made clear. Naim comments that we have no record of Mir's father as a leading Sufi, and suggests that Mir is burnishing the reputation of his father, so that he is at least the equal in background of leading rival poets such as Khwaja Mir Dard.

Whatever Mir's reasons, it does cause him to place in his father's mouth a fine set-piece statement on the power of love. It is what any Sufi might have said, but it loses none of its force for that:

> My son, practise love, for it is love that holds sway over everything.
>
> But for love, nothing would have taken shape. Without love, life is a burden. To give one's heart to love, that is perfection. Love creates and love consumes. Whatever exists in the world is a manifestation of love. Fire is love's ardour; wind is love's agitation.
>
> Water is the flow of love; earth is the repose of love. Death is love's inebriated state; life is love's sober state.... The state of love is above the states of worship, gnostic knowing, asceticism, companionship, sincerity, desirefulness, friendship, or being loved.
>
> All agree that the movement of the heavens is raised by love—they keep going round in circles and never reach their desired ones.

Something of the life of the poet emerges. In Delhi Mir would hold his *mushaira*—the assemblies at which poets would show off their paces, trump their rivals, and seek patrons—on the fifteenth of the lunar month. This would have been full moon, which suggests that they were held outside and attendance was probably large. 'Suddenly I found myself in the neighbourhood where I had lived,' Mir writes on returning to Delhi after devastation of the Afghan invasion, 'where I gathered my friends and recited verses, where I lived the life of love and cried many a night; where I fell in love with slim and tall [beloveds] and sang high their praises ....' Throughout his autobiography, there is the constant search for patrons. Poets needed patrons to keep body and soul together; patrons needed poets to project their reputations in the most powerful medium of the day. Turbulent times, unfortunately, meant that the political and physical mortality of patrons was high.

Mir's account of his life enables us to glimpse intimacy between people such as can otherwise be sensed only in paintings. 'When I was a little child,' he writes, 'my nanny, as she would wash my face [and doubtless to make him look up] would say to me, "Moon! Moon!" and I would took up in the sky ....' His father seems to have been the very model of a 'new man', hearing all the young Mir's needs, eating with him, sleeping next to him. '"Live happily, keep smiling you should know that I am always ready to fulfil your every desire .... Do not clench your brow like a bud; smile, open up like a flower" ... That is how he talked to me every day and nurtured me with great care, says Mir of his father.' Furthermore, Naim brings to his scholarly commentary insights from Mir's poem, *Incidents of Love*, a record, perhaps, of intimacy with the mistress of a patron.

Verbal flirtation becomes physical flirtation:

> She places her feet on his chest. She crushes his fingers with her foot and then rubs them better.
>
> At this bidding, but only after coquettish delay, she transfers a wad of pan from her red-stained lips to his.

It is a rare treat to be given access to such examples of human tenderness in eighteenth-century Muslim India.

Mir loved Delhi: 'The seven climes are in its every lane,' goes one of his couplets; 'Does Delhi have its equal anywhere?' A good chunk of his account is given over to the sack of Delhi in 1760 and its aftermath:

> In the morning—which was like the morning of Doomsday—the armies of the Shah and the Rohilla [Najib al-Dawlah] poured in and set about looting and killing. They knocked down the doors of the houses and tired up the owners, and some they burned while others they beheaded. A world was destroyed. They did not let up for three days and nights ... I, who was already a beggar, became poorer still. I was left destitute and penniless, and my humble abode, which was on the main road, was leveled to the ground.

Returning to Delhi the following year, he noted: 'at every step I shed tears and learned the lesson of mortality. And the further I went the more bewildered I become. I could not recognize my neighbourhood or house. There were no buildings to be seen, nor any residents to speak to.' So much attention is devoted to the destruction of Delhi, because, one suspects it meant the destruction of the world in which he had matured and which had sustained him. The power of the Mughals was at an end, and he must seek his fortune at the courts of their successors. The tone of his writing and the nature of his descriptions bear excellent comparison with the accounts by the leading Urdu poet of the nineteenth century, Ghalib, of the pillage and destruction of Delhi by British troops in 1957, as they suppressed the Mutiny uprising. This was, of course, another defining moment for north Indian Muslims, who, on this occasion were forced to face up to the reality of British power.

The British make their first appearance in Mir's account as 'Christian traders', who had been settled in Bengal for some time. As they move into the affairs of Upper India, they are made to appear just as players in the game of politics who; by Mir's account, play the game rather well; they receive none of the opprobrium, for instance, that he reserves for the Sikhs. In other fine set-piece, Mir describes the festivities during the visit by the governor-general, Warren Hastings, to Nawab Asaf al-Dawlah Lucknow in 1784. He goes to town describing the food, the fireworks, the flowers, the lavish entertainments; 'a firangi dance was held, a lovely scene—a house of joy, filled with joy'. He concludes:

> What a splendid guest! What an exemplary host! ... The guest, a man of perfect sagacity; the host, an embodiment of hospitality. Their likes had never been seen by the eyes of ages, nor heard by the ears of sages. In that manner they continued to meet for six months, day and night, and conversed and exchanged thoughts.

It is probably a good thing that Mir did not realize that the 'splendid guest' had a different view of the occasion. Hastings wrote to his wife of the debts of the Nawab and of the horrors which three years of famine had brought to the streets of Lucknow.

There is some grim prescience in the juxtaposition of these two very different understandings of the same event. As the British asserted their power over India, the courtly world which sustained Mir's poetry of love was in large part to be destroyed. As Muslims sought to succeed under the British dispensation, his high-flown Urdu was to be modified in a more workmanlike direction. We are deeply grateful to C.M. Naim for enabling us to savour something of the human world of Muslim northern India, before all became enveloped by the British and their utilitarian purposes.

*A Pit Full of Honey**

The Urdu language is one of the most powerful symbols of the cultural identity of nearly a quarter billion Pakistanis and Indian Muslims. It is also the second most-widely spoken language in Britain. Urdu has one of the richest literatures of all South Asian languages to which Hindus as well as Muslims have contributed. It deserves the attention equally of those interested in forms of literary sensibility, in the cultural heritage of South Asia, and in what it is to be human in another world.

The word Urdu is derived from the Turkish 'ordu' meaning camp, from which comes the English word 'horde' as applied to Mongol hordes or camps. The language grew out of the interaction from the thirteenth century between the Turkish- and Persian-speaking rulers of India and the local population; it was the language of the camp, the Muslim rulers of India spending as much time in camp, imposing their will on their subject peoples, as in settled mode.

From the fifteenth century Urdu became established in the Muslim kingdoms of the Deccan as a medium of poetry and some prose. From the eighteenth century it gained major force as a language as it came to be widely used in northern India, and most particularly in the great political capitals of Delhi, Lucknow, and Lahore. From the nineteenth century the language gained from the patronage of the British, who called it Hindustani and used it instead of Persian in government offices. In the late-nineteenth century it developed as a symbol of Muslim identity in northern India as opposed to the Hindi of the Hindus. There was irony in this. Urdu and Hindi are at bottom the same language, sharing the same grammar and syntax. The differences are that Urdu has many Persian and Arabic words while Hindi has increasingly embraced Sanskrit ones; Urdu is written in the Persian script, Hindi in Devanagari.

* Ralph Russell, *An Anthology of Urdu Literature*, Carcanet Press, extent 312pp.

For more than fifty years Ralph Russell has been teaching Urdu language and communicating his understanding of its literature with a rare passion; in South Asia and amongst cognoscenti across the world his name is synonymous with love of the language and the scholarly study of its literature. Russell's first encounter with Urdu came with war service while attached to the Indian army. From 1951 he taught it at the School of Oriental and African Studies, pioneering the modern teaching of the subject and producing major scholarly works such as his treatment of Ghalib, greatest of all Urdu poets, with his friend and collaborator, Khurshidul Islam. From the 1970s he took the lead in pressing for the needs of Urdu-speaking communities in Britain to be more adequately met, and particularly for the language to be taught in schools. He also initiated the teaching of Urdu to English-speakers who worked with Urdu-speakers. In 1981 he took early retirement to devote himself to this community work.

Russell's anthology, therefore, is the outcome of a lifetime's intense engagement with Urdu, its speakers, and its literature. The work was first published in 1995 under the poetic title, *Hidden in the Lute*, which effectively hid its existence from this writer. Now, republished under a prosaic but more helpful title, it merits review. No one in the West today speaks with such authority about Urdu or is better able to communicate its pleasures to those who do not read the language than Russell.

Because communication is at the heart of Russell's concerns, he has no space at all for the greatest Urdu poet of the twentieth century, Iqbal; he 'is above all a Muslim poet, and makes his most powerful appeal to his fellow Muslims.' In fact he begins his anthology with a selection of twentieth-century short stories, as these were much influenced by Western literature and should be readily accessible to the English-speaking reader. Amongst his choices are three stories by women writers, Ismat Chughtai and Rashid Jahan, both of whom caused a stir by testing the boundaries of the permissible. In 1941 Chughtai was tried for obscenity.

No less accessible are Russell's selections from the popular literature which can be bought at railway and bus stations all over northern India and Pakistan in cheap booklets printed on newsprint: stories of Akbar, the Mughal emperor, and his Hindu minister, Birbal, Mullah Dopiaza ('Two Onions'), the prophets, and so on. Their flavour, and particularly their dependence on ready wit, is evident:

One morning Akbar said to Birbal, 'Birbal, last night I dreamt that I had fallen into a pit filled with honey, and you into one filled with refuse'. Birbal at once replied, 'Lord of the World, I too had just such a dream, but in my dream I was licking you and you were licking me'.

Poetry is the greatest literary expression of Urdu; it is certainly the one on which Urdu-speakers place most value. The poetic genre both most highly prized and most popular is that of the ghazal, or love poem. Major monographs on Urdu's love poets have been at the heart of Russell's scholarly work and their essence is distilled in this book. He explains the central importance of understanding the context from which the ghazal emerges; it is a society in which all romantic love is illicit, and doomed to end in tears. The lover is fated to be consumed by love and to lose the beloved.

When once our hearts catch fire no power avails to save us from our fate
Like lamps that burn throughout the night we are steadily consumed.

My eyes still see you; *you* live in my heart
Though years have passed since you would come and go.

Russell explains the interplay, as in much European medieval poetry, between earthly and spiritual love. 'The ghazal poet,' he declares, 'is clear that true love for God is as compelling and all-embracing as human lovers' love for each other.' This leads, on the one hand, to a religious understanding which is profoundly humanistic and, on the other to a contempt for those who are religiously orthodox and self-righteously observe the requirements of their faith:

If pilgrimage could make a man a man
Then all the world might make the pilgrimage.
But shaikhji is just back, and look at him—
An ass he went: an ass he has returned.

Russell also explains elements of wordplay, multiple connotation and contrast, which are largely lost in translation:

Your long tresses come to mind and glistening teardrops dim my sight.
And all is dark; the rains have come; the fireflies glimmer in the night.

We learn that in the rainy season the clouds are really dark and that it is the romantic time of year, and also discover the interplay between long black tresses and dark night, tears and rains, glistening teardrops and glimmering fireflies.

And then we are told how to listen to a ghazal. It is bound by a very strict unity of form, with a well-defined single metre throughout and the requirement that the poet introduce his pen name into the final couplet. On the other hand, each couplet is separate and there will not normally be a unity of theme throughout the poem. It is poetry designed to be heard, not read. Its pleasures lie in 'the shape and sound' of each couplet. It is meaningful music made with words.

In just under sixty pages Russell supplies us with an outstanding introduction to this complex and sophisticated art form. The quotations above are all from Mir (c. 1723–1810), though many, too, are used from his favourite Ghalib (1797–1869). The book is well worth buying for these pages alone.

This said, the anthology also introduces us to the work and thought of Sir Sayyid Ahmad Khan (1817–98) and his followers of the Aligarh movement, who tried in all aspects of life to build a bridge between Indian Muslims and their British rulers. In Urdu literature it meant a revolution. In prose the emergence of a much more straightforward style and new forms of every kind: essays, literary criticism, biography, the novel, the short story. Russell cannot resist quoting from the satirist, Akbar Ilahabadi, who launched many a verse attack on Sir Sayyid's efforts:

Akbar does not deny the need for moving with the times
But understand that loyalty has its importance too.

Why feel so proud because the times have changed you?
True men are those whose efforts change the times.

The anthology also offers a taste of the novel, Rusva's *Umrao Jan Ada*; the wonderful letters of Ghalib, including the magical one in which he recalls his love for a long-lost mistress; Farhat Allah Beg's recreation of the last mushaira, or poetic symposium, held in Mughal Delhi before the catastrophe of 1857; and the maxims of poets on poetry: 'Poetry', according to Ghalib, 'is the creation of meaning, not the matching of rhymes'; for Mir 'poetry is a task for men whose hearts have been seared by the fire of love and pierced by the wounds of grief.'

This anthology is a most accessible gateway to the world of sensibility, metaphor, and imagination of the mother culture of Britain's largest linguistic minority. Its literary forms were in part crushed by British rule but gained new shape and power as they responded to it. From the headwaters of South Asian Urdu runs one of the many streams which inform and enrich British literary culture today.

*The Music of the Sufis**

Over the past fifty years, and especially as anthropologists have made their contribution, we have come to have a much fuller understanding of the roles played in Islamic history by Muslim mystics, or Sufis as they are usually called. We understand more clearly the role of Sufi orders in transmitting ideas across the Muslim world, as for instance since the seventeenth century key revivalist ideas have been carried by some lines of the Naqshbandiyya. We have come to appreciate through analysis of the social roles of Sufis how they have contributed to the Islamization of societies. Time and time again we have been reminded of how they have been used to legitimize power. The two books under review advance our understanding of these and other aspects of Sufism.

Simon Digby brings to life the world of a group of Sufis based in Awrangabad, which is well-described as a 'colonial town' of the Mughal empire in India's Deccan. His *Sufis and Soldiers in Awrangzeb's Deccan* is the first translation into English of the *Malfuzat-i Naqshbandiyya*, anecdotes about the lives of two Sufi saints, Baba Palangposh and Baba Musafir. Both had come to India in the mid 1670s from Ghijduwan near Bukhara. Like many of their contemporaries from Central Asia, Afghanistan, and Iran, they came to seek their fortune under Mughal rule.

Baba Palangposh was a military Sufi who, until his death in 1699 guarded the army of Ghazi al-Din Khan, the Mughal general whose son was to found the Hyderabad state. Indeed, the author of the *malfuzat* regarded the rise of Ghazi al-Din as the result of Baba Palangposh's spiritual aid:

* Simon Digby, ed. and trans., *Sufis and Soldiers in Awrangzeb's Deccan*, Oxford University Press, 2001, extent xxvii, 275pp; Richard M. Eaton, *Essays on Islam and Indian History*, Oxford University Press, 2000, extent 275pp.

> From the arrival of Baba Palangposh the star of his felicity was brought to the apex of fortune. In whatever direction he turned to confront the armies of the enemy, he was victorious over them with a small body of men, even though they were thousands. He was continually fortunate in his increases in rank; until, after the passage of time, he reached the limit of 7000, which is the highest rank of amir.

Baba Palangposh's role was to bring help in battle through the force of his tawajjuh (attention). He was thought to go ahead of Ghazi al-Din's army firing arrows; during battle soldiers would sense that he was fighting alongside them.

The progress of the Baba's retinue while the Mughal army was on the march was an amazing sight:

> before the cavalcade there were carried up on the backs of porters seventy or eighty or up to a hundred clay tubs of flowering trees ... Wherever he encamped, he found instantly laid out the 'rosegarden of Iram' ... From 150 to 200 men, faqirs of Wilayat [Central Asia], bearing quivers, went beside his bridle. Another band, bareheaded and barefoot, who had nothing but a single loincloth on their bodies, acquired felicity by looking after the horses and camels and other tasks.

Baba Musafir's style and life, on the other hand, could not have been more different. His regime was a constant cycle of study, meditation, and prayer. He never strayed far from the khanqah or convent which he founded. One the one occasion when he got a sniff of action, courtesy of some marauding Marathas, his performance was more Dad's Army than Mughal army:

> He himself, wearing a green cloak with a headband of a dove-gray colour around his hair, and with a lungi firmly tied around his waist in which was stuck a dagger, with rags on his feet and a lance in his hand, set out for the 'Idgah. He was accompanied by a band of faqirs, men of learning and grantholders.

Baba Musafir served the Central Asian community settled in Awrangabad. He and his successor, Baba Mahmud, the writer of the malfuzat, were clearly successful in their time as they were able to build what Digby declares to be 'one of the most architecturally distinguished and beautiful examples of a khanqah or takya extant in South Asia'. Moreover, it enjoyed the patronage of the first Nizam of Hyderabad. In part, perhaps, as a consequence of this support the successors of Baba Mahmud never succeeded in building a constituency for their spiritual tradition in Deccani Muslim society. In time, as so often happens in South Asia, all became the personal property of Mahmud's descendants and the spiritual tradition withered away.

The malfuzat is, of course, a hagiography. Thus a large number of the anecdotes are designed to illustrate the supernatural powers of Palangposh and Musafir: their capacity to read the minds of visitors or to have foreknowledge of events, their ability to remove obstacles or bring retribution on those who failed to show them respect, and their gifts of healing whether it be in the purely physical sense or in the spiritual sense of those who have come up against barriers in their path towards knowledge of God.

As is usual in the case of this genre of literature there is much information of historical value. We learn about the ordering of the community of the khanqah, its building programme, its gardens, measures for protecting widows, provision for the care of families of disciples, and routine tasks such as cleaning and sweeping. Discipline was rigorously enforced. If a drunkard was foolish enough to pass by the khanqah, Baba Musafir would sally out himself to whip him.

It is clear, as Digby is at pains to point out, that these Sufis had nothing to do with the so-called Naqshbandi revival led by Shaykh Ahmad Sirhindi (d. 1625). Indeed, one of the anecdotes confirms Baba Musafir's support for the doctrine of the 'unity of being' which was anathema to Sirhindi. The extent and apparent ease of travel is also striking. Baba Musafir is said to have performed the pilgrimage travelling overland from Gujarat to Mecca. While there seems to have been a ready system of convents and caravanserais which would enable a traveller to move from the Deccan through northern India to Afghanistan and Central Asia.

What is remarkable, given that Muslims in the Deccan were only a small group in the midst of an overwhelmingly Hindu population, is that Hindus form only a marginal part of the worldview revealed. They are not the subject of proselytization. Marathas are referred to as *ghanim*, or rebels, a term which might equally be applied to Muslims. There are three mentions of the Maratha leader, Raja Sahu, and one of a Hindu revenue official terrorised by a disciple of Baba Musafir. These are conquering people who hold themselves apart from the Hindu world. Such a view was to persist into the nineteenth century and underpin the development of Muslim separatism.

Simon Digby is one of the most learned scholars of Muslim South Asia alive today. Twenty-two years ago he brought the house down in a seminar at Berkeley with an intervention of thirty minutes or so on musical dogs in Islamic art. He has a taste for knowledge which subverts the commonplace view. Baba Musafir was a skilled musician and one of his disciples befriended the dogs of Awrangabad. Amongst the illustrations to the text is a painting attributed to the school of Golconda, though Digby asserts from internal evidence that it is more likely to have been executed in Awrangabad, of a dog enjoying the music of Sufis. Deep and wide-ranging learning of this kind informs the excellent introduction which supports the malfuzat. It is particularly good to know that this is just first elucidation of the text. A whole volume of commentary is promised.

Much of the scholarly life of Richard Eaton has been devoted to exploring the broader significance of Sufi activities in South Asia. His *Sufis of Bijapur 1300–1700: Social Roles of Sufis in Medieval India* (1978) demonstrates how by performing a range of social roles Sufis were gradually able to draw the local population into an Islamic milieu. His work on the shrine of Baba Farid Ganj-i Shakar at Pakpattan has shown how, as from the thirteenth to the nineteenth centuries the peoples of West Punjab abandoned nomadism for settled agriculture, they came to take on an Islamic identity for which the shrine of Baba Farid formed an iconic focus. His *Rise of Islam and the Bengal Frontier 1204–1760* (1993) set out the close relationship between the cutting down of the jungle, the expansion of rice cultivation and the establishment of Islam in the area now known as Bangladesh. Here again Sufis played a leading role in working with the indigenous population to build bridges between the cult of Allah and local religious figures. This is a body of work which has made a major step forward in explaining how South Asia has come to have c. 350 million Muslims. Indeed, in explaining how more Muslims nowadays live east of the Hindu Kush than west, a fact of major geopolitical significance.

Indeed, in explaining how more Muslims nowadays live east of the Hindu Kush than west, a fact of major geopolitical significance, Eaton's *Essays on Islam and Indian History* contains key articles in which his pathbreaking arguments about the Islamization of South Asia are summarized. But the volume also contains an important set of historiographical essays of which three in particular demand attention. One masterly overview places Islam in the context of world history and then explores the changing ways in which Western historians have from the eighteenth century onwards thought about it. As a number of historians of the Muslim world now like to do, he adumbrates a vision of an Islamic world system—'history's first bridge connecting the agrarian belt stretching from Gibraltar to China'—which preceded the emergence of a Western world system. He also indicates how, as his own research has done so much to explain, South Asia has moved in recent times from being part of the periphery of the Muslim world to being its 'cultural and demographic epicentre'.

A second major essay moves away from Islam to consider the impact of the Subaltern Studies project on Indian historiography and the transformations it has endured as it has encountered literary theory, post-modernism, and cultural studies. As a historian who has always preferred a good day in the archives to doses of literary theory he enjoys the irony that the Subaltern Studies Collective, which was launched to recover India's history from 'Colonial, Nationalist and Marxist metanarratives', has ultimately been taken over by an intellectual movement which has 'ended up *reaffirming* the overwhelming centrality of the British intrusion in India'.

With the final major essay Eaton returns to Islam and the faultlines which the Muslim presence has opened up in South Asia. 'Temple Desecration and Indo-Muslim States' is both an outstanding piece of historical detective work and a howl of rage at the abuse of history by India's Hindu fundamentalists. His starting point was the destruction in 1992 of the mosque built by the Mughal emperor, Babur, in Ayodhya by a Hindu fundamentalist mob, an action which has been justified by accusations of wholesale temple destruction during the period of Muslim dominance, and one which sent a shudder through all those who cared for India. Eaton examines the incidence of temple desecration from the twelfth century onwards and notes that it has nothing to do with a theology of iconoclasm but was entirely part of a rational process of state-building and state-maintenance. Temples were desecrated on the annexation of newly conquered territory or when Hindu patrons of temples were disloyal to the Muslim states they served. Otherwise, if they lay within Indo-Muslim domains they were left alone. This is a historian's answer to propaganda.

Richard Eaton's essays take delight in both the fluidity of ideas in changing historical circumstances and in the way they can be made to serve the needs of the powerful of the day. Both his work, and that of Digby, substantially advance our understanding of Sufism.

*When India Ruled the Waves**

'He who amused himself in playing with the ball that was the head of Prithvivashara' was the Telegu title bestowed on a warrior by a Kakatiya king of Andhra Pradesh in south India. The authors of all four books under review play ball with the heads of writers who have gone before them, and do so with varying degrees of respect. In the progress, all four given south India the unusual, but not underserved, accolade of being centre stage in historical discourse. Three in various ways contribute to a re-envisioning of Indian history that find processes of change from the thirteenth to the eighteenth century which might bear the title 'early modern'.

Cynthia Talbot's targets are those who have found medieval India to be either static or in decline. James Mill gets a hefty boot for asserting in his *History of India* (1826) that the Hindus did not change from the time of Alexander's invasion to their discovery by modern Europe. 'The annals ... from that [Greek] era till the period of the Mahomedan conquests are a blank.' Karl Marx, whose view was no more flattering, is given similar treatment. But these are just the biggest names among the many who, over nearly two centuries, contributed to visions of a 'traditional India' which was either unchanging or in decline from some golden age. Talbot has a different view, her medieval India is dynamic with expanding commerce, increasing numbers of religious institutions, and several evolving political systems.

* Cynthia Talbot, *Precolonial India in Practice: Society, Religion and Identity in Medieval Andhra*, Oxford University Press, extent 305pp; Uma Das Gupta, ed., *The World of the Indian Ocean Merchant, 1500–1800, Collected essays of Ashin Das Gupta*, Oxford University Press, extent 511pp; Sanjay Subrahmanyam, *Penumbral Visions, Making Polities in early Modern South India*, University of Michigan Press; distributed in the UK by Plymbridge, extent 295pp; Joan-Pau Rubiés, *Travel and Ethnology in the Renaissance, South India Through European Eyes*, 1250–1625, Cambridge University Press, extent 468pp.

James Mill never took the precaution of visiting India to check the truth of his assertion. Talbot's study is based on the records in Telegu of the thousands of donations to temples in Andhra carved on stone pillars, rock slabs, and temple walls between 1000 CE and 1650. Her particular focus is the years 1175–1324, when the Kakatiya dynasty flourished and the largest quantity of inscriptions was produced. She reveals what extraordinary rich historical resources these inscriptions are and relishes the opportunities they offer to deal with the realities of Andhra—hence the 'in practice' of the title—as compared with the normative ideal which would be expressed in religious or courtly literature.

The following excerpt from one inscription gives a sense of the kind of material Talbot has been dealing with:

> May all fare well and prosper. In the 1,222 years of the Shaka era [1300 CE] on the 1st (day of the) bright (fortnight) of the lunar month) Yeshtha, a Friday:
>
> The doctor of horses Vasudeva Pandey, son of Ananta Pandita, of the Atreya *gotra*, in order to endow the illustrious great lord Kshirameshvara with a perpetual lamp for the benefit of his mother and the long life of his son Ananta Peddi: gave 50 milch cows and 2 *Kha(ndugas)* of our land south of Jiyani tank in Penamchchili (village) as lampland.... He who steals (endowed land), whether given by himself or another, will be reborn as a maggot in excrement for (the next) 60,000 years.

Talbot analyses the incidence of inscriptions through space and time. This enables her to demonstrate the gradual shift of population into the interior, the consequent shift of political power from the wet coastal region to the dry hinterland, and the increasing importance of a Telegu cultural identity embracing both regions. Indeed, what she reveals is the expansion of an agrarian frontier, 'a dynamic process of migration and agricultural settlement', with an accompanying cultural identity, which has continued from this period right down to the present. It bears excellent comparison with the expanding agrarian frontier explored in the context of Bengal and the spread of Islam in Richard Eaton's *Rise of Islam and the Bengal Frontier* (1993).

Not surprisingly, Andhra society of this period was socially mobile and very different from the static caste society of *varna*s and *jati*s which the early British scholars of Indian society, heavily influenced by their Brahmin advisers, picked up from classical Sanskrit texts. Men in the inscriptions are described not by varna or jati but by titles. Sons did not necessarily assume the title of their fathers, leading Talbot to conclude that these represented earned status rather than ascribed rank, and that the evidence of her inscriptions undermines the 'reputed centrality of caste in precolonial India'.

Patronage of temples, we are told, was one of the ways in which new communities and identities were formed. In the early part of the period, the great pilgrimage temples of the coastal region had helped to incorporate diverse social communities. The development of temple patronage inland during the Kakatiya era marked a similar process. At the same time it indicated economic growth, as agriculture spread into previously uncultivated areas, as new irrigation facilities boosted production, and as commerce expanded—all developments with which 'the temple as an institution was intimately intertwined'. The spread of temples was central to the formation of Andhra as a regional society.

Kakatiya polity, as Talbot characterizes it, was a world of heroic values built on militaristic foundations. The ideal individual was the warrior such as Ambadeva who, an inscription of 1290 tell us, defeated King Ganpati in battle, robbing him of the title 'Champion over a Thousand Kings', who put King Keshava to flight, seizing all his horses, and whose prowess toppled King Eruva Mallideva from:

> a moving horse in battle with this pride and the host of his allied troops. Having cut off Mallideva's head, Ambadeva then cast down his own weapon and through repeatedly knocking his head around the ground with his feet, as if kicking a playing ball, he who was never tried finally grew weary.

For Talbot, the military hero represents significant developments, beyond their imaginatively brutal uses for defeated enemies' body parts. The late Kakatiya world was one of growing militarism, of the disappearance of ancient lineages of chiefs, of a new emphasis on personal ties between lord and subordinate, of revenue assignments, and of growing central power. These are all developments which the secondary literature associates with the successor regime of Vijayanagara and the region's response to the new Muslim threat from the north. Talbot's placing of these changes further back in time adds further weight to her identification of the thirteenth century as the crucial formative period in the development of Andhra.

Talbot goes through the interesting exercise of comparing her analysis of the significance of the Kakatiya period with accounts handed down by Telegu warrior culture and popular tradition. She finds strong support for her argument that it was in the thirteenth century that the contours of the linguistic state of Andhra Pradesh, which Nehru created in the mid-1950s, took decisive shape.

Talbot concludes calling for a reassessment of Indian medieval history. She has made a case for early modern history beginning in Andhra in the thirteenth century and argues, quite rightly, that 'medieval' India should be seen not unlike Europe as a collection of diverse regions and cultures, in which a multiplicity of historical processes are at work.

The comparison with Europe is just. My first instinct after reading this book was to share it with my European historian colleagues. Quite remarkably for a first monograph, it is a real pageturner. Epigraphical research, requiring no little skill, has been combined with a flair for exposition and constant attention to arguments, great and small, in the field to produce a gripping work of scholarship. Oxford University Press have added to its value by permitting the inclusion of forty-two pages listing Andhra inscriptions from 1000 to 1649. Some may find the arguments too pat, the doubts too few. It is, however, an excellent candidate to help build that much-needed bridge between the 'early modern histories' of Europe and South Asia.

The Calcutta historian, Ashin Das Gupta, who died in 1998, was the founder of Indian Ocean Studies for the period 1500–1800. He, like Talbot, plays ball with the heads of historians, though his style is more to give an ironic tap than a hefty boot. The focus of Das Gupta's lifelong study was the Indian maritime merchant. His pleasure was evoking their world—which reached across the ocean from East Africa and the Hadramawt to Java—explaining their achievements, and, wherever possible, discovering them as individuals. While always most comfortable with work rooted in the archives and following the sinuous paths of micro-history, he remained alert to the bigger picture.

The World of the Indian Ocean Merchant, 1500–1800 represents his collected essays. Many of the themes of his major monographs—*Malabar in Asian Trade, 1600–1800* (1967) and *Indian Merchants and the Decline of Surat* (1979)—were first tried out in this form. The volume is divided into general essays covering broad themes such as 'The Maritime Merchant in Indian History' and 'Trade and Politics in Eighteenth-century India', and more pointed topics such as 'The Broker in Mughal Surat' or 'Gujarati Merchants and the Red Sea Trade, 1700–1725'. This last essay, for instance, gives a lively picture of the problems the Dutch experienced in riding shotgun to the Gujarati fleet and the real difficulties the Europeans had in offering any real commercial competition to the Gujaratis. All is felicitously introduced by Sanjay Subrahmanyam, who draws attention to the sheer quality of Das Gupta's understated but authoritative writing.

Das Gupta's central achievement was to illustrate the dominant role of the Indian maritime trade in the Indian Ocean up to the end of the eighteenth century. In consequence, he had little time for those who argued, and still argue, that the Indian Ocean world was transformed after Vasco da Gama arrived in 1498. The Indian trader remained the dominant force; in the early eighteenth century, over 80 per cent of the Red Sea trade of Surat was carried in Gujarati ships. Much more significant in affecting the position of the Indian trader was the decline of the two great inland centres of consumption, the empires of the Safavids and the Mughals. Similarly, the dominance of the Indian trader also made him sceptical of the masterwork of K.N. Chaudhuri, currently Vasco da Gama Professor of History at the European University Institute—*The Trading World of Asia and the English East India Company, 1600–1760.* What was the value of measuring the growth rate of quantities and the rates of change of prices in the Company record when the bulk of the action was elsewhere? What, in fact, was the real significance of the Company in trading terms when, as Holden Furber pointed out many years ago, much key commercial activity was the private trade carried out by its officials within the shell of the Company? Das Gupta was able to rescue Indian agency in the Indian Ocean from the grip of an imperialist historiography and, by that token, give south India a more prominent place in events.

In speaking for the vitality of south India in the early modern period and in seeking to reshape understanding of Indian history, Sanjay Subrahmanyam both inherits the mantle of Das Gupta and would appear to stride as one with Talbot. In doing so, however, he plays ball with the heads of many historians and social scientists and, when Eurocentric tendencies are displayed, can be savage in his performance.

Subrahmanyam, Director of Studies at the École des Hautes Études en Sciences Sociales, is a historian of unusual powers and wide command of languages. In *Penumbral Visions: Making Politics in Early Modern South India*, he uses these to demonstrate the dynamism and resilience of the region before 1800. He explores the vigour and effectiveness of the Wodeyar state of Mysore on which the famed regimes of Haidar Ali and Tipu Sultan were to be built; he demonstrates how the Carnatic polity of Arcot showed all the signs of becoming a working Mughal successor state until brought low by European control of the ports; and in much the same way he shows how the successful Maratha state of Tanjavur was also crippled by being cut off from the ports, until it surrendered sovereignty in 1799. Other essays reflect on the great pilgrimage centre of Tirupati as an image of El-Dorado in Western eyes, the relationships between state-making and history-making in early modern south India and the nature of the 'public sphere' in the region.

One passionate concern shines through much of what Subrahmanyam writes. He wishes to demonstrate that historical modernity did not flow from Europe but is a global and conjunctional phenomenon. Ottoman historians have benefited from stopping considering the period from the fifteenth to the nineteenth century as one of golden age followed by decline, and thinking of it instead as an early modern period in which real and significant change too place. Similar arguments can be applied to South Asia in the same period. As Subrahmanyam argues:

> While it is evident that changes in terms of institutional arrangements, socio-economic activity, and cultural production in South Asia, do not show a marked convergence with, say, those in England or Germany, it is equally of importance to note that there were changes, which have to be understood in their own terms, and not in terms of some model of blockage, or stasis.

Subrahmanyam's point is that if historians can show the real nature of South Asia in the early modern period, they might 'shake historians of western Europe out of their long complacency, rather than comfort them in their slumbers'.

Travel and Ethnology in the Renaissance: South India through European Eyes, 1250–1625 by Joan-Pau Rubiés offers unwitting support for Subrahmanyam. European historians may not rate the early modern history of the region to be important now, but at the time it was a significant destination for the traveller, particularly from southern Europe. Rubiés analyses the accounts of many, including Marco Polo, Nicolò Conti, Duarte Barbosa, and Pietro della Valle, and throws in an interesting Muslim comparison for good measure. His concern, however, is not to see what we can learn about south India from their accounts, but what these writings can tell us about changing understandings and perspectives in early modern Europe. In this case, the ball game has a different nature; it is about getting inside the heads of early modern Europeans, as they tried to make some sense of great cities like Vijayanagara and a society of apparent idolaters.

Central to his argument is that contact with non-Europeans was intrinsically important to the growth of European culture. Confronting human diversity, and religious diversity, was a profoundly important development in the Renaissance. 'The fundamental breakthrough,' Rubiés declares, 'was not simply to record, but also to interpret difference.' In this work of subtle scholarship and great learning, he demonstrates that the accounts of travellers, ranging from missionaries and traders to curious humanists, influenced the debates that created the Enlightenment. Indeed, they were central to the rationalist transformation of European culture in the early modern period. This leads me to a final reflection. If world travel was key to the reassessment of the centrality of a Christian world view in the early modern period, might not a similar historiographical journey by historians of the West lead to a humbler assessment of the role of Europe in the venture of modernity? We can but live in hope.

*Mixed Fortunes**

In February 1799 the women of the household of Baqar 'Ali Khan, first cousin of the prime minister of Hyderabad and of distinguished Iranian descent, took the extraordinary action for Muslim women of staying two nights in the house of James Kirkpatrick, recently appointed the East India Company's Resident. The women had quarrelled with Baqar 'Ali over the marriage he had arranged for his granddaughter Khayr un-Nisa (Best of Women) aged fourteen. They were taking advantage of the absence of their menfolk at war to put facts on the ground. Khayr, it seems, had fallen passionately in love with Kirkpatrick, whom she had glimpsed at her sister's wedding. The women enabled Kirkpatrick to see Khayr sleeping, and then permitted her to meet him. 'She declared to me again and again', Kirkpatrick explained to his brother, 'that her affections had been irrevocably fixed on me... that her fate was linked to mine...' 'I contrived to command myself so far as to abstain from the tempting feast I was manifestly invited to....' But he did not abstain for long.

The moving story which follows forms the central thread which runs through Dalrymple's wide-ranging and richly-textured narrative. Kirkpatrick fell in love with Khayr; the relationship developed. The risks were great: for the women there was the danger of violent death at the hands of their menfolk, whose honour had been sullied; for Kirkpatrick there was the danger of dismissal for the stupidity of an intrigue with a noblewoman, whose family was centrally placed at the Nizam's court, and for concealing key political intelligence, which the relationship represented, from his masters.

In 1800 Khayr fell pregnant which brought matters to a head. Once more the women showed their mettle. Sharaf un-Nisa, Khayr's mother, so managed the politics of the household and the city that

* William Dalrymple, *White Mughals: Love and Betrayal in Eighteenth-Century India*, HarperCollins.

her father was willing to permit his granddaughter to break her engagement and be handed over to the Resident. Kirkpatrick for his part became a Muslim and secretly married Khayr with the Nizam, himself, standing in for his father.

Of course, such matters are rarely concealed, and certainly not in the highly politicized environment of the Hyderabad court. Kirkpatrick's conduct was subject to a Company enquiry. He was exonerated of charges of rape and of putting improper pressure on Khayr's family. But he was only rescued from the charge of concealing political intelligence by a selfless act on the part of his half-brother, William, who explained to Governor-General Wellesley that Kirkpatrick had told him all—which he had not—and that it was his fault not to have passed on the information.

For three years Khayr and Kirkpatrick lived openly at the Residency with their two children, whose English names came to be William and Kitty. Then tragedy befell them. The beginning was the great sadness which afflicted all Anglo-Indian families. In 1805 Kirkpatrick decided that his children must go to England to be educated. 'My mother has never had any rival in my affections,' declared Kitty forty years later. 'I can well recollect her cries when we left her and I can now see the place in w[hich] she sat when we parted—her tearing her long hair....' Just one thing was left behind to soften the blow, a portrait of the children commissioned from James Chinnery.

At the same time Kirkpatrick was summoned to Calcutta to brief the incoming governor-general. Already ill when he set out, he died there aged forty-one. His will spoke of his 'unbounded love' for Khayr. The following year Khayr and her mother went to Calcutta to mourn at his grave. In Calcutta, Henry Russell, who had been Kirkpatrick's chief assistant in Hyderabad, along with his brother, Charles, played a major part in looking after Khayr. We are given the picture of 'a beautiful, charismatic Mughal noblewoman behaving according to her rank, with a pair of senior British officials running around to do her bidding'. Then Russell became Khayr's lover. The authorities both in Calcutta and in Hyderabad made it clear that, when Russell returned to take up his post in the Residency, Khayr would have to live outside the state. Russell was not prepared to take the risks for love taken by Kirkpatrick. After a dawdling journey in which he enjoyed Khayr to the full, he dumped her and her mother in the decaying seaport of

Masulipatam. Here, they heard through Charles Russell, for Henry was too much of a coward to tell them himself, that he had married. Eventually the women made their way back to Hyderabad where aged twenty-seven Khayr died of a broke heart. Despite desperate letters to England, there is no evidence that she had a word about her two children while she was alive, although six weeks after she died two portraits came.

The story does not quite end there. Khayr's son died a young man in England. Her daughter Kitty, however, both made her mark and made the connection back to Hyderabad. A striking redhead, she made a major impression on Thomas Carlyle who fashioned her into the figure, Blumine, in *Sartor Resartus*, and whose enthusiasm for the 'Hindoo Princess' brought acid comment from Jane who he was wooing. Kitty married an army captain, had four children, and delighted in a loving marriage. One day, she was taken by a friend to tea in a great country house in Surrey, whose owner she did not know. On entering the house she burst into tears; on the stairs was the portrait of her and her brother by Chinnery. The owner of the house was Henry Russell. Through Russell she was able to make contact with Sharaf un-Nisa in Hyderabad. Six years of joyful correspondence ensued, until in July 1847 her grandmother died.

Other strands are woven through the central story. There are the doings of the family of General Palmer, whose family portrait by Francesco Renaldi, suffused with love and affection, forms the jacket of the book. Palmer's wife was Princess Fayz Bakhsh of the Mughal royal family. Her husband, the Company's Resident at Poona, was a close political ally of Kirkpatrick. Her son, William, made and lost his fortune in business in Hyderabad. She was a close friend of Khayr in the happy days in Hyderabad, in mourning in Calcutta, and in the last days in Hyderabad. She was left distraught by Khayr's death, saying she had lost the only real friend she had ever had.

Colourful characters make their appearance. Ochterlony, the Company's Resident in Delhi, whose thirteen wives every evening would process round the city behind their husband, each on the back of their own elephant. General Hindoo Stuart, who converted to Hinduism, although that is not strictly possible, who would take a week off to bathe at the Kumbh Mela, and who campaigned in the press for European women to adopt the sari.

We are given a well-drawn picture of the politics of the Hyderabad court and the ways in which they interacted with the Resident's love affair and the struggle for power in central India between the British, Tipu Sultan and the Marathas. Kirkpatrick was a successful Resident because he lived as Hyderabadis did, and was popular both in the city and with the Nizam, whom he referred to affectionately as 'Old Nizzy', humoured in thoughtful ways, and joined in fishing for tame carp in the palace ponds.

Dalrymple celebrates Kirkpatrick, Ochterlony *et al.* with the title *White Mughals.* Their era was the time when Europeans lived like Indians, spoke Indian languages, wore Indian dress, and loved Indian women. It was a time when civilizations fused rather than clashed. Another strand in the story is Kirkpatrick's opposition to Governor-General Wellesley's newly arrogant attitude to Indian states. It was followed by arrogance towards Indian civilization, the practice of living separately from Indians, and the arrival of growing numbers of European women, all of which in the early nineteenth century brought an end to the era of the White Mughals.

In his introduction Dalrymple berates historians for concealing, what he reveals, for imperialist or nationalist reasons. This may be true, but he fails to do justice to those who, from Percival Spear to Christopher Bayly have been concerned to show the extent to which there was an Indo-British partnership in eighteenth-century India.

Through massive research blessed with serendipity and through imagination and empathy Dalrymple has evoked the world of the British in late-eighteenth century India, as no one has before. Yes, he is self indulgent sometimes, when he cannot bring himself to prune facts he has compiled on a religious ceremony or an abortion. But this does not mar a wonderful book, its story of love, and its celebration of common humanity. 'The Begum and I,' wrote William Gardner who had married the daughter of the Nawab of Cambay,

> from 22 years of constant contact, have smoothed off each other's asperities and roll on peaceably and contentedly ... The house is filled with Brats and the very thinking of them, from blue eyes and fair hair, to ebony and wool make me quite anxious to get back to them again.

*Between Two Worlds**

From early on in its development Islam embraced both a this-worldly and an other-worldly orientation. The guidance which was given to man through the Prophet Muhammad indicated that the way to heaven lay in a full and proper attendance to worldly affairs along the lines that He had indicated. But, as Muslims encountered Christian mysticism, Buddhism and other Asian spiritual traditions, they came to explore the mystical dimensions of the Prophet's message, and to develop what has come to be known as Sufism. By the time of al-Ghazzali (d. 1111), for some the greatest Muslim after Muhammad, the tensions were evident; this most learned man both lived in the world and withdrew from it, and in his writings saw the force of both the this-worldly and the other-worldly positions. From the thirteenth century with the expansion of Islam through Asia and Africa, and with the growing dominance of the thought of Ibn 'Arabi in Sufism, other-worldly piety came to have a strong hold upon many Muslims. This situation persisted down to the nineteenth century when the increasing influence of the great movement of Islamic revival and reform, and the dominance of European power in Muslims lands, led to a massive assault on the other-worldly dimensions of Islam. Muslim revivalists sought to draw on the this-worldly potential of their tradition in order to find ways of sustaining their communities at a time of weakness. It is this concern which energizes Islamist movements throughout the world today.

Riazul Islam belongs to the senatorial generation of Pakistani historians. Taught before independence by Muhammad Habib, who founded India's famous Aligarh school of historians, he is well aware of a duty to tell the truth as he sees it, however uncomfortable it may be. In this book, which is the fruit of many years of reflection on the writings of Sufis of the medieval Indo-Iranian world, he focuses on

* Riazul Islam, *Sufism in South Asia: Impact on Fourteenth Century Muslim Society*, Oxford University Press, extent 489pp.

the fourteenth century, a time when several great Sufis were at work in Indian society. He is concerned in particular to assess their impact on the world in which they moved. But what he achieves is a major exploration of how these Sufis navigated their way between the this-worldly and the other-worldly demands of their faith.

One major area of tension was whether Sufis should place their trust in God for their livelihood, or they should go out into the world to earn their keep, thus exposing their vocations to earthly pressures and temptations. Riazul Islam explores this issue in the context of Sufi approaches to the concepts of futuh (unasked for charity) and *kasb* (earning one's livelihood). He notes the powerful strand of the glorification of poverty in Islam and the enduring presence of *tawakkul*, or complete trust in God. This became expressed in dependence on charity amongst Sufis in Baghdad and Khorasan and came to be institutionalized in India, especially amongst the influential Chishti Sufis. In fourteenth-century Delhi, for instance, the sultan, leading courtiers, disciples, and merchants would make regular donations to the leading Sufi, Nizam al-Din Awliya. The Shaykh would keep a small proportion for his needs and then observe the following practices: of distributing the donations as soon as possible, of doing so to as many people as possible, and of ensuring that all his storerooms had been emptied of donations by Friday. Those who lived thus on charity had to be ready to endure privation, and the anecdotes relating to such saints are full of how they did so.

Kasb was, of course, the obverse of the futuh coin. There was a strong tradition amongst South Asian Sufis of denigrating the earning of one's living, of being subject to the world. This was particularly so amongst the Chishtis. There were others, however—for instance, Sayyid Ashraf Jahangir Simnani, of the less influential Firdawsi order—who was actively in favour of kasb and stressed that earning one's living was following the very example of the Prophet and His companions. Nevertheless, as Riazul Islam concludes, South Asian piety 'retained its strong other-worldly tilt'.

The problems of this-worldliness were illustrated again for Sufis when they came to consider marriage and family life. 'When a Sufi gets married,' declared one major work, 'it is as if he has boarded a boat; when a child is born to him, it means he has drowned.' Anecdotes relating to Sufis are full of their neglect of wives and family. Celibacy, as in other spiritual traditions, was valued above marriage; it was axiomatic that a Sufi could not love God and his children at the same time. Such neglect of family if married, or of Quranic preference for marriage if unmarried, did not attract criticism from their biographers, indeed, it was seen as a sign of sainthood. Such behaviour was in direct opposition to the example of the Prophet, who cherished family life and was renowned for his affection towards children.

Relationships with earthly power was another area in which the other-worldly vocations of Sufis were likely to be tested. Attitudes towards kings differed from order to order amongst South Asian Sufis. Some felt a religious obligation to keep in touch with kings, others would accept such contact as a necessary evil in working for the good of the people, and yet others felt that all such contact should be avoided as one might avoid sin. Amongst the South Asian Sufis it was the popular Chishtis who developed the most distinctive tradition of standing apart from earthly power, a position summed up in the apocryphal statement attributed to Nizam al-din Awliya: 'If the Sultan comes through one door, I will go out of the other'. The embarrassment of a princely visit to a Sufi is made clear in an anecdote of Shaykh Nasir al-din Chiragh's treatment of the Delhi sultan. Once Sultan Firuz came to pay his respects to Shaikh Nasir al-Din:

> The Shaikh was taking a siesta ... As the Sultan waited in the courtyard of the khanqah, it began to drizzle. By the time the Shaikh came out after ablutions and prayers, the Sultan had become drenched in the rain.
>
> The Sultan remarked resentfully to a noble who was present, 'We are not the *badshah* here, they (the saints) are the (real) badshahs.' When he finally came down from the house, the Shaikh, rather than taking the Sultan to the house, sat down with him in the courtyard. After a very brief meeting the Sultan left thoroughly unhappy.

For many South Asian Sufis it remained important to demonstrate to their followers that they were the 'real badshahs'. It was a need which only came to be exacerbated when the power in the land was no longer a Muslim, but a Christian and colonial one.

The one point at which the Sufis might become more this-worldly than the po-faced mulla was in their concern to pursue their spiritually inspired love of their fellow men above a literal obeisance to the holy law, or indeed the externalities of their own calling. The famous verse of the thirteenth-century Shaykh Sa'di of Shiraz was their guide:

> Worship of God is nothing but service of the people; Worship is not tied up with the rosary, the prayer carpet and the patched frock.

This position was echoed by many of the greatest Sufis of South Asia. 'An important task of the disciple is rendering service,' declared Sharaf al-din Maneri in one of his letters:

> In service one acquires many benefits and special favours that are not found in any form of devotion or submission. One is that a person's selfish soul perishes. Pride and haughtiness are removed from his countenance and, in their place, humility and submission appear.

The shortest route to God, declared Nizam al-Din Awliya, 'is to provide comfort to the hearts (of the people)'. Sufi willingness to serve popular need rather than insisting on the formalities of the holy law was to render them suspect in the age of Islamic revival.

Riazul Islam concludes by weighing the impact of the Sufis in South Asia. On the one hand, he admits their great triumphs of humanity and of the human spirit; he also concedes their significant role in sustaining music and poetry. On the other hand, he declares the downside of their impact was considerable: they were not able to spread their high-flown ethnical approach to life widely through society; their cults became centres of popular credulity; their shrines became family businesses; and they smothered the Muslim genius in mathematics and sciences. This last conclusion is questionable; the explanation for the flagging of Muslim science is rather more complex. This said, what Riazul Islam has done is to set out for us the deep-seated tensions in South Asian Sufism, although it could be Sufism in general, between other-worldly and this-worldly orientations, and the preference for the other-worldly, which established itself in the fourteenth century and persisted down to the nineteenth century. This is the Islamic understanding which, for the past two centuries, the Islamic movement of revival and reform has been concerned to obliterate.

*Thoroughly Modern Muslims**

Since it was published in January 2002, *What Went Wrong? The Clash between Islam and Modernity in the Middle East* has been a best seller in the USA. This is unfortunate. It may not have been the intention of the author, Bernard Lewis, one of the best-known scholars of the region, but it reads like a historian's manifesto for regime change. I refer to the plans for war on Iraq which were set out in a report 'A Clean Break: A New Strategy for Securing the Realm', which was written in 1996 for the incoming Likud government by a group headed by Richard Perle. Perle, and other pro-Israeli lobbyists such as Paul Wolfowitz, are, of course, among those who are in the forefront of the campaign by the Bush White House against Iraq.

Just listen to the very last paragraph of the book:

> If the peoples of the Middle East continue on their present path, the suicide bomber may become a metaphor for the whole region, and there will be no escape from a downward spiral of hate and spite, rage and self-pity, poverty and oppression, culminating sooner or later in yet another alien domination; perhaps from a new Europe reverting to old ways, perhaps from a resurgent Russia, perhaps from some new expanding superpower in the East. If they can abandon grievance and victimhood, settle their differences, and join their talents, energies, and resources in a common creative endeavor, then they can once again make the Middle East, in modern times as it was in antiquity and in the Middle Ages, a major center of civilization. For the time being, the choice is their own.

But, as we know, that 'time being', in which Middle Easterners could choose, has turned out to be short. The US is poised to impose its will on Iraq. President Bush in his 'axis of evil' speech has indicated that Iran is also on his list. Strange, is it not, that the one power which

* Bernard Lewis, *What Went Wrong? The Clash between Islam and Modernity in the Middle East*, Weidenfield & Nicolson, 2002; John L. Esposito, *What Everyone Needs to Know about Islam*, Oxford University Press, 2002.

Lewis does not mention as imposing 'alien domination' is the one most capable, and which, with its ally Israel, has most reasons to do so—the USA.

Lewis's argument goes thus. For nearly a thousand years from the seventh century Islamic civilization was the leading civilization on earth. True, the achievement of China could be regarded as comparable, but it was limited largely to one region. Islam, on the other hand, 'created a world civilization, polyethnic, multiracial, international, one might even say intercontinental'. It was rich, commanding great long-distance trades across land and sea. Its achievements in the arts and sciences were the greatest yet, bringing together the knowledge and skills of the ancient Middle East, Greece, and Iran in a most fertile mix with innovations from China and India. Muslims produced time and time again great literature, great art, great architecture, and major advances in science. 'Medieval Europe was,' as Lewis says, 'a pupil'.

With the Renaissance, however, the relationship began to change and Europe set out on a path of scientific and technological change which would enable it to leave the Islamic world far behind. The lessons of change were learned first upon the battlefield. After the last great advance of the Ottomans to the heart of Europe was halted on 12 September 1683, when they were forced to lift their siege of Vienna, a contemporary Ottoman chronicler declared: 'this was a calamitous defeat, so great that there has never been its like since the first appearance of the Ottoman state'. During the eighteenth century Muslim power was forced to become increasingly accustomed to defeat at European hands. The symbolic moment, when it was clear that the order of power in the world had changed, was Napoleon's invasion of Egypt in 1798, an invasion which could only be brought to an end by another European power—Britain.

Lewis then runs through the responses of Muslim Middle Easterners to European power. They were slow to seek to discover the sources of Europe's strength because they had little interest in the place, were unwilling to travel there, and did not wish to learn its languages. Eventually they did understand that the European economy was an important source of its wealth and therefore its military strength. But they never got to the heart of how wealth was made. Matters were exacerbated, too, by the way in which autocratic governments with a high level of involvement in the economy came to command the modernizing projects of middle Eastern states. Differing economic approaches are symbolized in differing forms of corruption. 'In the West,' Lewis states, 'one makes money in the market, and uses it to buy or influence power. In the East, one seizes power, and uses it to make money.'

Muslim societies have failed to modernize, Lewis continues, because they have failed to surmount social and cultural barriers. The key barrier has been the emancipation of women. After a discussion of the advances in women's rights achieved in Muslim societies in the nineteenth and twentieth centuries, we are left with the impression that these cannot amount to a great deal because some Muslim women have chosen not to wear Western dress and others are required, or choose, to cover their Western dress with some form of veil. A key cultural barrier has been modern science. Muslims, for instance, once led the world in astronomy. From the sixteenth century they steadily slipped behind Europeans in this field. By telling us how Taqi al-din's state-of-the-art observatory in Istanbul was demolished in 1577 at the order of the sultan on the advice of the Grand Mufti, Lewis suggests that Islam may have been the problem. Muslims were in general willing to accept scientific advances in warfare and in medicine, when knowledge was a matter of life and death, but unwilling to accept 'the underlying philosophy and socio-political context' of Western scientific achievement. In consequence virtually no cutting-edge science is produced by scientists working in the laboratories of the Muslim Middle East.

Muslim societies, Lewis tells us quite rightly, have had difficulty in creating a secular space. The first Muslim society at the oasis of Medina was created through revelation and then spread through power; there was never any division, as in Christianity, between the realm of Caesar and that of God. In facing the challenge of Europe some Muslim societies, most notably Turkey, did create significant secular spaces, but nowadays Islamist forces are increasingly re-occupying the territories carved out for the secular.

In a similar way, civil society, defined as the forms of human association that lie between the family and the state, is on the retreat. In pre-modern Muslim societies there was a substantial growth of such society in the form of craft guilds, Sufi orders, and many charitable endowments supporting institutions from orphanages to colleges. But the emergence of the modern state, usually in autocratic form, has reduced this healthy growth. This said, Lewis acknowledges the potential for the electronic media to open up significant new space for civil society.

Muslims, we are reminded, have been laggardly in adopting human rights along Western lines, despite the egalitarian ethos of Islam and its early recognition of rights for women, slaves, and non-believers. They have accepted Western concepts of time, the 24-hour day, and the many instruments for planning and monitoring the passing of time, but not—it is hinted—the timely keeping of appointments. They have accepted Western painting, architecture, and literary forms but have not, for the most part, and we are frequently reminded of this, embraced Western classical music.

Lewis concludes that in the twentieth century 'it became abundantly clear in the Middle East and indeed all over the lands of Islam that things had indeed gone badly wrong'. The political outcome has been 'a string of shabby tyrannies'. Muslims have blamed a range of agents for their predicament: the Mongols and the massive destruction they wrought, the imperialism of the British and French, and the impact of US power and its Israeli ally. Some Muslims say the real problem is that interpretation of Islam has come to be dominated by the 'ulama, others that Muslims have not been good enough Muslims. Lewis identifies two solutions which have significant support in the region: Islamism (Muslim fundamentalism) and secular democracy. His preference is clear.

Great scholarship went into the making of this book, but it is scholarship misused. It will, I fear, become a *locus classicus* of the orientalism thesis of Edward Said. All the states of the Middle East are lumped together as being in the same boat despite their different traditions and trajectories—Shia Iran with Sunni Egypt, secular Turkey with Wahhabi Sa'udi Arabia. Then, as an afterthought, he extends his argument, built up on evidence from the Middle East, to cover all the lands of Islam from Morocco and Nigeria to Malaysia and Indonesia. They all have the same problem in Lewis's eyes—their Islam which prevents their effective engagement with modernity in Western form. This is Saidian 'essentialism' writ large, and of course endorsement for Huntington's 'clash of civilizations'.

Lewis is wrong to be so dismissive of the impact of European imperialism and subsequent cold-war rivalries, on Middle Eastern societies. Muslim societies of the region are doing no worse than most states that have emerged from their imperial and cold war experiences in Latin America, Africa, Central Asia, and South and Southeast Asia. Arguably, they are doing better than a good many.

Continued meddling in Muslim societies has only made things worse. Saddam Hussain's unruly career stems in no small part from Western support in the 1980s when the policy priority was restraining the influence of the Iranian revolution. The prominence of Algerians in terrorist activity in Europe stems in large part from the circumstances following the suppression of an Islamist victory through the ballot box in 1991 by the Algerian army with the support, so we are credibly informed, of the French and the US. It is well-known that the rise of the Taliban was in part the outcome of Western measures in Pakistan and Afghanistan to resist the Russian invader, no less than the existence of Hamas, which currently gives Israel such grief, was the outcome of Israeli attempts to produce an Islamist counterweight to Arafat's secular nationalism.

Then, there is the civilizational arrogance which assumes that all modernity must come in Western form. Lewis is astute enough to state that every civilization has its day, but for the moment, he says, all must follow the Western path which 'defines modernity'. The implication is that to be 'modern' political forms must be modelled precisely on those of the West, that Muslim women must move in public in Western dress, or undress, and that Muslims really must get to like Western classical music.

Lewis makes no mention of the considerable scholarship which demonstrates how Islamic forces at work in Muslim societies have been producing modernizing outcomes. Consider the overthrow in 1998 of the dictatorship of Soeharto in the world's most populous Muslim society of Indonesia, which led to the election of a Muslim leader, Abdurrahman Wahid, as president of a reforming civilian government. This was the work of an Islamic democracy movement. In the process, as Robert Hefner has shown in *Civil Islam: Muslims and Democratization in Indonesia* (Princeton, 2000), Muslims renounced the goal of an Islamic state, finding a place for Islam as public religion supported by civil society, as opposed to the solutions of a privatized religion or of a state-imposed faith. The leaders of the movement promoted a pluralist Islam and women's rights.

Nor does Lewis consider the ways in which Islamist (Muslim fundamentalist) forces can have a modernizing impact. Islamist leaders, themselves, tend to be highly educated in 'modern' knowledge, being typically economists, doctors, and engineers. They are particularly concerned with economic development and with bringing their societies up to the technological level of leading industrial societies. Their beliefs, as with the whole reformist movement in Islam reaching back into the nineteenth century, support the development of individualization—the individual is personally responsible for actively advancing Islamic purposes on earth, and should regularly reflect on his or her success in doing so. High levels of personal responsibility fashion increasingly strong senses of the self.

Islamists tend to support bureaucratization and rationalization, promotion by merit, the use of the ballot box, the rule of law, and the codification of that law—shari'a law—into forms which may be applied by modern judiciaries. Their institutions, their schools, clinics, hospitals, meeting places, which have often grown up because the state has failed to provide the infrastructure to support the tens of millions who have moved in recent times from the countryside to the cities, contributes substantially to the structure of civil society. In general, they have created much of the framework, both in organization and in ideas, which has enabled middle and lower-middle class Muslims to enter the workings of the modern economy and state. And here we have a pointer as to why the growth of Islamism has been associated with the widespread reappearance of the veil in Muslim towns and cities. It is in part about cultural authenticity and drawing a distinction against the 'immodest' practices of the West. But it is also about a massive movement of women into public space—into universities, where there tend to be more women than men, and into the modern world of work.

Lewis has no time at all for the greatest Islamist experiment, the Iranian revolution. Nevertheless, as Fariba Adelkhah has recently shown in her brilliant book, *Being Modern in Iran* (Hurst, 1999), it embraces most of the modernizing aspects of Islamism set out above. And, while Iran is certainly not a democracy as we would understand it, there is much greater trust placed in the ballot box than ever there was in the Shah's Iran. Iranians did, moreover, elect their current president, Khatami, in a massive voter turnout during 1997 on a platform of civil society, the rule of law and democratization. When he was re-elected in June 2001, I was in Tehran and vividly remember how many complete strangers, with joy in their faces, just had to come up to tell me what a good result it was.

After Lewis' partisan work, with all the dangers it brings to understanding between civilizations, and therefore to peace, it is a relief to turn to Esposito's *What Everyone Needs to Know about Islam*. Esposito, who is a professor of religion and international affairs at Georgetown University, and a leading scholar of Islam in the generation which succeeds that of Lewis, adopts a simple question and answer format to address the most frequently asked questions about Islam. He covers faith and practice, Islam and other religions, customs and culture, violence and terrorism, society, politics and economics, and Muslims and the West. If you want to know the significance of Mecca or whether Muslims believe in angels or not, he will tell you. If you want to know if women are second-class citizens in Islam or why Muslim men wear turbans and caps, he has the answer. He reveals Muslim attitudes to homosexuality, abortion, and birth control. And he does not dodge the difficult issues relating to jihad, terrorism, and suicide bombers. To every question he provides a dispassionate answer, conveying most importantly the range of Muslim views on particular subjects and the sense that Islam, like Christianity and Judaism, offers guidance from tradition which Muslims are continually interpreting and reinterpreting in order to make that guidance live in the present. This is a highly accessible, well-informed, and wise book, which everyone with a degree of curiosity about the world in which they live should have at their side.

*Heroes in the Harem**

It is extraordinary that no one in recent times has attempted to write an accessible narrative of the lives, power struggles, and achievements of the great Mughals, who ruled India from 1526 to 1707. The men concerned—Babur, Humayun, Akbar, Jahangir, Shah Jahan, and Awrangzeb—were all larger-than-life personalities. Their deeds as warriors, rulers, builders, patrons of the arts, and lovers of women are the stuff of legend. The materials in which to study them are plentiful: there are several biographies written by the family, their reigns attracted chroniclers both favourable and hostile, some had fine pictorial records made, most had Europeans at court noting their doings for audiences at home, and some wrote excellent letters which survive. One would have thought that with such subjects and such materials historians would be clamouring to bring the fabulous story of the Mughals to a wide public. But, Bamber Gascoigne's excellent mini-treatment of 1971 apart, they have not risen to the challenge.

That is, until Abraham Eraly saw the opportunity. From Kerala, and the editor of a fortnightly magazine who has taught history both in India and in the USA, Eraly, aims to rescue the subject from the sterile obsessions of the professional historians and, following Simon Schama, 'bring a world to life'. One suspects, too, that he may have a mission to resist some of the gross distortions of India's past that have been put about in recent decades for political purposes, by helping to build up a solid bulwark of understanding in his domestic reading public. He plans a massive four-volume treatment of his country's history, *India Retold*, of which *The Mughal Throne*, first published by Penguin India in 1997, forms volume three, and is the first to appear.

Eraly certainly succeeds in bringing his Mughal emperors to life. He communicates, for instance, a tremendous affection for Babur,

* Abraham Eraly, *The Mughal Throne: The Saga of India's Great Emperors*, Weidenfeld & Nicolson 2003.

the founder of the dynasty, whose remarkable autobiography, still not well-enough known, expresses his 'intelligence, compassion, energy, ambition, steadfastness' and his great joy in life. This direct contemporary of Lorenzo de Medici comes across as a truly renaissance man: scholar, poet, composer, calligrapher, gardener, and connoisseur of painting, who was also a warrior and a leader of men.

Babur's son, Humayun, is brought to us as a richly talented man. 'In battle he was steady and brave', wrote one chronicler 'in conversation ingenious and lively; and at the social board, full of wit. He was kind-hearted and generous...' He was also an able mathematician. Unfortunately, he became addicted to opium and kept poor company, which contributed to the loss of his empire to the Afghan Suris in 1540, though he did succeed in regaining it in 1555. A few months later, having gone up onto the roof of his library at night to make some astronomical observations, he was killed, falling down the stone stairs. He 'stumbled out of life', as one historian put it, 'as he stumbled through it.'

As the writers of soap operas know, relationships, and particularly those in dysfunctional families, can grip an audience. Eraly makes sure that we get plenty to grip us. Being the sone of a great man has never been an easy thing to be, and Akbar's sons were no exception. Murad and Daniyal died of drink well before their father, and the third, Salim (later Jahangir), a great abuser of substances himself, spent the last fifteen years of his father's reign in rebellion, among other things murdering Akbar's friend and confidant Abul Fazl. In fact, Mughal father–son relationships were rarely happy. Take the bitter recriminations exchanged by letter between Awrangzeb and his father, Shah Jahan, whom, after a bloody succession struggle in which he wiped out his brothers, Awrangzeb had imprisoned in Agra Fort. After complaining that his father had always favoured his elder brother, Dara Shikoh, Awrangzeb goes to the psychological heart of the fratricidal mess: 'You never loved me'.

Mughals were unusually attached to their women. Hearing that his mother, Hamida, was on her deathbed, Akbar immediately abandoned the military campaign on which he was engaged to be at her side. So close was Shah Jahan to his beloved Mumtaz Mahal, who whom he built the Taj Mahal, that in all their years of marriage he was not separated from her. When she died, while giving birth to their fourteenth child, he was devastated; through constant weeping he was forced to wear spectacles and his beard became in a few days one-third white. No less remarkable was the relationship between Jahangir and Mumtaz Mahal's aunt, Nur Jahan, the able and beautiful daughter of his chief minister. His empress from 1611, Nur Jahan had exceptional political and administrative skills, making Jahangir's reign the success it was, as well as sharing in his pleasures in the arts, hunting, drink, and personally intervening when necessary in the war to succeed him. The nature of their relationship, as partners as well as lovers, is nicely encapsulated in a vignette from the Englishman, Thomas Roe, who saw them returning to the camp one night from a romantic bullock cart ride all by themselves, Jahangir holding the reigns.

Eraly makes a point of ensuring that we know about Mughal sex lives. We move from Babur's teenage crush, just after his first marriage, on a boy in a camp bazaar to Akbar's enormous sexual energies, which led to him having nearly three hundred women as wives and concubines in his harem. Like the family of Saddam Hussein, he had procurers—eunuchs in this case—to go into the harems of his officers to select women for him. He even tried his luck, whilst staying at the the saint's shrine, amongst the women of the Sufi master, Salim Chishti. Shah Jahan, after the death of Mumtaz Mahal, gave himself over to a life of sexual adventure which, according to court gossip, included an incestuous relationship with his daughter, Jahanara. 'Her father loved [her],' declared Manucci, the Italian physician, 'to an extraordinary degree, as most lovely, discreet, loving, generous, open-minded, and charitable.' Even the austere Awrangzeb, who restricted himself to four wives, succumbed to sheer sexual attraction. In his forties he was smitten by a Hindu dancing girl, and for a year, until she died, was completely at her mercy, drinking wine and listening to music.

Pleasing in this book are the lengths to which Eraly goes to give each emperor a voice. Listen to Babur, the literary connoisseur, giving Humayun Orwellesque advice on good prose: 'Thy remissness in writing seems to be due to the thing which makes thee obscure, that is to say, to elaboration. In future write unaffectedly, clearly, with plain words, which saves trouble to both writer and reader'. Listen to Awrangzeb on the subject of governance: 'I wish you to recollect', he wrote to his father, 'that the greatest conquerors are not always the greatest Kings ... It is the truly great King who makes it the chief business of his life to govern with equity'.

Eraly does not, of course, restrict his treatment to the family lives and thoughts of the Mughals, fascinating as they are. Full coverage is given to the expansion of the empire and to some of its workings. Two key battles are studied in detail: that of Panipat in 1526 when Babur defeated the Lodi king of Delhi, and that of Samogarh in 1658 in which Awrangzeb defeated Dara Shikoh. There is an interesting discussion of Akbar's Din-i Ilahi, the Sufi-like fraternity which he created focussed upon his person, though Eraly goes rather too far in suggesting that in its secular orientation and faith in reason it held within it promise for the 'modernization of India'. There is a great set-piece treatment of the succession struggle to succeed Shah Jahan, which deserves to become the basis for a film script. And particularly important, given the hate-figure that Awrangzeb has become for many in India, there is a judicious discussion of his policies. Yes, he did knock down temples. Yes, he did impose the poll tax on Hindus. But all he was doing was imposing Islamic law, and in doing so he was almost as harsh on Muslims as he was on Hindus. His actions, we are told, did not contribute to the growing number of risings against the regime which featured in his reign.

In concluding, Eraly gives the Mughals a big plus for setting standards of excellence across the whole field of culture, but an equally big minus for failing to lead India into 'modernity', though why they should be able to achieve what the Ottomans, the Safavids, the Ming emperors, and the Tokugawa shoguns did not, he does not say. It is, surely, clutching at straws to imagine that such an achievement was at the disposal of a dynasty.

This said, Eraly has written an engaging and accessible book. It is not completely up-to-speed with modern scholarship, but that does not matter. What does matter is that it does not contain a single map, which means that most of the action will be a mystery to those who do not already known their Indian topography. With the addition of some maps he deserves to succeed in his ambition to bring to life the Mughal world for a wide public.

*Stories from the Cradle**

Baghdad was occupied by the British before I had finished the sixth grade. I was only fourteen years old then. The fall of Baghdad into the hands of the British was a great catastrophe for me, for I thought the world of Islam was overcome and that at least we had fallen as victims into the hands of a non-Muslim power. I used to watch the march of the British troops into Kadhimain with tears flowing down my cheeks.

Such was the memory of Muhammad Jamali of the British capture of Baghdad in 1917. As the Ottoman Empire finally crumbled, and as almost all the Muslim world fell into Western hands, his feelings were widely shared by his fellow Muslims. Muhammad Jamali went on to lead the development of a modern system of education in Iraq and ultimately in the 1950s to become prime minister. Condemned to death after the revolution of 1958, he lived the remainder of his life in exile until his death in 1917.

His account of his childhood is one of thirty-six collected by the distinguished American anthropologist, Elizabeth Fernea. They span the twentieth century, from the childhood of Jamali, who was born in 1902, to that of the Egyptian, Randa Abou Bakr, teacher of English at Cairo University, born in 1966. The authors are Berber, Persian, Arab, Turk, Circassian, Jews, Muslims, and Christians. Their backgrounds are rich and poor, although a good number hail from the old 'notable' families of the region. As most are written in English, and some by people with considerable experience of the West, they are composed for a Western public, which one author claims 'helped me produce a more honest and critical text'. Overall, as adult reconstructions of childhood, the accounts reveal a rich diversity of Middle Eastern experiences set against the backdrop of the decline of the Ottoman

* Elizabeth Fernea, *Remembering Childhood in the Middle East: Memoirs from a Century of Change*, University of Texas Press 2003.

empire, colonial rule, the rise of nationalist movements, the establishment of Israel, the Arab–Israeli wars, and the rise of oil-rich countries.

Family—as opposed to one's peers—is everywhere the key point of reference. 'Growing up and leaving home,' declares Robert Fernea, husband of the editor, in his thoughtful introduction:

> does not mean the end of playing an active part in a network of family and kin. Families of origin remain a point of reference, a part of each person's past which continues into the present and remains included in the way these people think about themselves.

Thus, these accounts eloquently portray extended families at work, the needs and responsibilities they represent, and the ways in which, modern Middle Easterners never 'leave home'.

Writ large in the child's-eye view is the strength and significance of the role played by women. 'Next to oil,' writes Saif Dehrab, now a senior academic at the University of Kuwait, 'probably the best thing God gave Kuwait was its women. When Kuwait's men were out at sea, it was the women who had to manage the family affairs, make sure that intruders would not come to the neighbourhood, and even keep up the house renovations.' Saif also offers an unexpected titbit. In his Quran school, which was mixed, because the girls were so much better than the boys in memorising and reciting the Holy Book, the mullah would get them to teach the boys while he watched.

The Jordanian writer Janset Shami, offers a striking picture of the willpower of her Circassian mother who was married to one of Ataturk's army officers. Refusing to follow him round from posting to posting, she set up house with her young family in Istanbul. When her husband was promoted to general, she immediately led the family on an expedition into the wilds of Central Anatolia so that all could congratulate him in person. No thought of danger or failure was allowed.

Similar will, and also pride, is recorded by Akile Gursoy, the Turkish anthropologist, as she gives a gripping account of her family's experience under house arrest after the military coup of 1960. With both her grandfather, President Bayar, and her father under arrest, and with the memory of how but two years earlier the leader of a military coup in Iraq had wiped out the royal family there, she tells of how her mother, aunt, and her grandmother, kept up everyone's spirits, won concessions from the soldiers who were guarding them, and gained access to the trials of the Democrat Party leaders at Yassiada.

Births, marriages, circumcision, the appearance of additional wives, and significant deaths are all recounted. One family event, of less importance, but clearly memorable, was the weekly trip to the Hammam. The Moroccan author and translator, Abdelaziz Abbasi, tells of how as a young boy he would he taken along with the women to experience:

> the horrors of the scalding water, the rigours of the scrubbing, the cold water with an orange to suck while cooling off, and the lying on a mound of clothes in the changing room as a crowd of women 'sat around, or hovered over you, bare-breasted as usual and wearing only a mizzar which hung from the waist down' and gossiped about who was marrying, who was ill with the measles, and what the Senegalese soldiers were up to in town.

Common to almost all the accounts, is the enormous emphasis placed in the Middle East on education and educational performance, for women as well as men. To be sure, there is an element of self-selection: most would not have achieved the level of success which brought them to the attention of Elizabeth Fernea had they not benefited from education. There is, however, one group in the Middle East for whom education has acquired a special significance: the Palestinians, for many of whom their human resource is all that remains to them. One Palestinian, currently working as an engineer in the USA, tells of the distinctive attitude of his teachers in the refugee camps of Ain Hilweh:

> Most were very nice and very dedicated. Some were more strict than others but we felt they cared about us .... There was a sense of not only giving you an education but giving you a sense of mission, that part of one's duty as a refugee Palestinian was to make your life worth something .... Dedication to teaching became a part of those teachers; they saw teaching as a national duty.

There is a strong sense in the earlier accounts of the elite world of the last decades of the Ottoman Empire, which lingered on under colonial rule—of how people moved easily between Baghdad, Damascus, Cairo, Beirut, and Istanbul, of how a girl from a notable family might be sent to a convent school in Cairo or Istanbul, of how the boys might be sent to Victoria College, Alexandria, founded by the British to help resist French influence, and then to the American University in Beirut. It was a world in which people of different races and religions mixed with apparent ease.

There are memories of resentment at the colonial presence. Basima Bezirgan, who now works at the University of Chicago, recalls with sadness how the British expropriated, from 1940 to 1947, the childhood home she loved in Baghdad. The distinguished historian, Afaf Lutfi al-Sayyid Marsot, resented the attitude of the English missionaries who taught her: 'As an Egyptian I did not relish the underlying theme, hammered into us daily, of the inferiority of my nation, my religion, my culture.' Lilie Labidi, now a professor of anthropology and psychology in Tunis, remembers how the French soldiers would hand out sweets to children, and how her mother said:

> again and again 'Don't take anything from the French soldiers,' reminding me in this way that we were under French occupation, and that we were not to have any contact with the occupier.

Throughout much of the Middle East, such feelings are now transferred to the Americans.

Arabs brought up in the post-colonial era give a strong sense of the impact of Nasser, of how his defiance inspired their Arab nationalism, and how the wars of 1956 and 1967 deepened their sense of Arab identity. For Shafeeq Ghabra, a Palestinian, who is now a professor of political science at Kuwait University, the 1967 war changed the course of his life. He became an activist, joined Fatah, and visited the refugee camps in South Lebanon. He Made a 'commitment to transform myself into a fighting Arab rather than a passive, defeated Arab like those I knew as a boy in 1967'.

Books of this kind, which reveal the great variety of Middle Eastern experiences, which bring a human dimension to what otherwise might seem a set of abstractions, and which enable the reader to engage in life events that most of us share, have an important role to play in the university classroom They are a key weapon in the university teacher's struggle against prejudice and ignorance. In this light, it is unfortunate that *Remembering Childhood in the Middle East* contains few overt references to the Islamic revival, which was a feature of growing significance in Middle Eastern societies as the twentieth century progressed. For the contemporary student, a major part of the story is left out, and one which needs to be given a human face.

*No Fun, No Bread, No Chance**

The Iranian revolution of 1978–9 was one of the great revolutions of the twentieth century. As in all such mighty upheavals, designed in theory to bring justice, there was much injustice, many died, more were hurt, families were broken, fanaticism took hold on all sides, the claims of humanity were downgraded, the revolution began to consume its own, and many came to live in exile determined to overthrow the new regime.

Masoud Banisadr's *Memoirs* are primarily the story of his exile and of his contributions to trying to overthrow the revolutionary regime. It is a powerful and illuminating record, but also a distressing one. From a well-connected background—his father was a highly educated official of the Shah's regime and a cousin, Abol Hasan Banisadr, was the first president of the Islamic Republic—Masoud tells us what it was like to grow up in Tehran between the late 1950s and the early 1970s to the point when he marries Anna, 'the most beautiful girl I ever had seen and ever would see'. Through the eyes of the young couple we are given a vivid picture of the corruption and inequalities of the Shah's regime, and of the impact of the great inflation of the mid-1970s. Then, after studying at the National University of Iran, now Shahid Behishti, Masoud, like so many of his generation, went to do postgraduate work in the Britain, first at Reading and then at Newcastle.

The revolution drew Masoud and Anna back to Iran; he wanted to be part of the great changes in his society. After being beaten up by supporters of the mullahs as he took part in a demonstration run by the Mujahidin (described by the Shah's regime as Muslim Marxists, but, perhaps, better described as Muslim Leftists), he decided to join the organization, and was told that he could best serve it abroad.

* Masoud Banisadr, *Masoud: Memoirs of an Iranian Rebel*, Saqi Books, extent 473pp.

Recalling his departure, he cries, as so many exiles have done, 'How could I know that this was the last time I would see my beautiful country and have its warm air in my lungs? If I had known, would I ever have been able to tear myself away? Never!' From 1979 Masoud, Anna, and eventually their two children, find their lives increasingly dominated by the requirements of the Mujahidin. In the United Kingdom Masoud raised money for the organization, attended demonstrations, propaganda, and was a regular presence at Labour Party conferences. Subsequently, he was given a diplomatic role, operating both in Europe and the USA, where a regular achievement was putting together the coalition of countries which would support a resolution condemning human-rights abuses in Iran. He did military service, being part of the Mujahidin force which in 1988 invaded Iran from Iraq. During the early 1990s he was the organization's chief representative in the USA. Throughout, by his own account, which there is no reason to disbelieve, he was an enterprising, efficient, and honest servant of the organization. When money was needed in the Britain, he established a successful kebab business to generate it. When the Mujahidin wanted to establish a radio station in the USA, he knew how it should be done, and how funds should be raised.

Sadly, the demands of the Mujahidin were to drive Masoud apart from his family. By the mid-1980s Anna, who had endured much for the cause, amongst other things fearing for its impact on her children, withdrew from active support. Then, the organization itself, aiming to focus the energies of its supporters increasingly on its purposes, began to target any alternative allegiances they might have. The organization knew that Masoud loved Anna deeply, though he saw her but rarely. Several times he was instructed to write her letters of divorce, which (as it turned out) the organization did not deliver. Eventually, in 1995, Anna asked Masoud for a divorce, which, although it hurt him much, he gave. A year later, depressed by this and by the many failings of the Mujahidin, which were increasingly clear, he resigned. Although 'I had indeed lost everything: parents and children, sisters and brothers, relative and old friends, my youth and health ... I have no regrets because I kept my dignity and honour and because I sincerely did what I could in the service of liberty and justice, those pillars of morality that make us human.'

Masoud's story tells us a great deal about the Mujahidin, and not all of it very savoury. The organization had been founded in 1965 by followers of Engineer Bazargan, who was to become the first Prime Minister of the Islamic Republic. Taking note of the bloody way in which the Shah had put down the 1963 uprising, the Mujahidin decided that the old ways of opposing the regime, strike and street protests, were useless and should be replaced by guerilla warfare. In 1971 they conducted their first operation, which was to disrupt the overblown celebration of 2,500 years of Iranian monarchy. Despite close attention from SAVAK, the Iranian secret police force, they were able to make a significant contribution to the eventual overthrow of the Shah, only to lose the subsequent struggle with the mullahs. Now, an exile group, they came to depend on the several million Iranians who had fled the revolution to settle in Europe and the USA.

Saddam Hussein's Iraq became a particular friend, permitting them to build a political headquarters in Baghdad and a military base on the Iranian frontier in Khuzestan. While the world feared the export of the Islamic revolution and welcomed Saddam's willingness to help neutralise the threat, the Mujahidin found many political doors open to them. But, after the dictator's invasion of Kuwait, and the mild rehabilitation of Iran, in European eyes at least, the Mujahidin found their popularity waning in diplomatic circles. 'Look', one Mujahidin joke went, 'in the whole world we have one friend and he is a madman.'

The fantasies and military incompetence of the Mujahidin are made only too clear. In 1988, it would appear, Saddam Hussein delayed accepting Resolution 598, which would bring the Iran–Iraq war to and end, in order to give the Mujahidin an opportunity to invade Iran. Masoud's description of the Mujahidin forces and their performance is worthy of Evelyn Waugh. Many of the soldiers had no training. Masoud commanded a battalion without ever having fired a gun. His men had tanks but did not know how to work them, so, as soon as they came under fire, they leapt out of them to engage the enemy with small arms. As soon as his battalion had advanced over the Iranian border, he realized that he had not brought any bread for his men, so had to send back for it. The Mujahidin imagined, as Vice-President Cheney did in the case of the invasion of Iraq, that as soon as they got over the border, they would be welcomed by a cheering population. Quite the reverse; they were slaughtered. As Masoud admits, 'we were disastrously, fatally, taken in by our own propaganda.'

Masoud's descriptions of the workings of the Mujahidin reveal the extraordinary activities and mumbo-jumbo to which the intelligent, when ideologically driven, are prepared to submit. Every day Masoud's London unit would perform 'matins', gathering in ranks before pictures of their leaders, doing some drill, singing a Mujahidin song, and hailing the Mujahidin. The rules of the group give a sense of things: 'no sex before marriage'; 'total commitment to the organization'; 'no relationships outside the organization'; 'no fun'; 'no private time'; 'no outside work'; 'no private ownership'; even 'no reading of material from outside the organization'. Every full member had a *masoul*, or supervisor, whose word was law. Many supervisors were women, and Masoud makes clear the powerful psychological hold they gained over their supervisees. The organization, moreover, was in a state of constant ideological revolution handed down from above. At one point an 'anti-bourgeois' phase was proclaimed, which was directed particularly at those from outside Iran who had become Mujahidin. Members had to surrender all possessions deemed 'luxurious'. At the same time Masoud came under particular pressure for his 'bourgeois' characteristics: 'I had to examine myself and recognise my behaviour including my "kindness", "understanding", "caring" and "helpfulness" as "bourgeois tricks" to "fool people and keep them in my trap". I had to try very hard not to show any affection towards anybody, even to make others dislike or hate me.'

A later ideological revolution focussed on sex. The leadership commanded all members to divorce their spouses, and hand over their rings. They were told that they were not yet full believers in the Mujahidin ideology because, like everyone else in the world, they were mired in the 'ideology of sexuality': 'The cure was to distance ourselves from our sexuality. The first step was to forget sex for the rest of our lives. Hence we had not only to divorce but to learn to hate our spouses, as love was based on sex and delivered us up to the ideology of sexuality at the same time holding us back from embracing the Mujahidin ideology.' Ideological revolutions such as these were accompanied by interminable sessions of self-criticism and mutual accusation. All were required to lay themselves bare, and if they did not have anything to confess, as was often Masoud's case, the wiser path was to invent confessions. All was very intense; the atmosphere was that of a revivalist sect. 'Every now and then, we were startled by a loud cry as somebody arrived at her or his revolution, following which the leaders would talk with the person amid sobs and tears.'

Not surprisingly the Mujahidin fostered a personality cult focussed on its leadership. Rather more surprisingly the focus of the cult shifted from Masoud Rajavi, who was the major force in the organization in the 1970s and 1980s, to his wife. To many outside the organization Rajavi's marriage to Maryam in 1985 was a scandal. She was the wife of a fellow Mujahidin leader, with whom she was still in love, when, it was said, the politburo instructed the two to divorce so that Maryam and Rajavi could work together as leaders. There was, of course, a specific purpose in a revolutionary organization, which was challenging Khomeini's regime, having a woman at the helm. In his wedding address Rajavi instructed his supporters 'to die and be reborn not from their mother's wombs, but from Maryam'. Soon Maryam was announcing the 'ideology of Maryam'; she was the 'ideological mother' of the Mujahidin. By 1993 she had become 'president-designate' of their intended regime in Iran. Such was the success of the cult of Maryam, and such too was her charisma, that Masoud came to worship her, treasuring any small favour she sent his way. For this reason, when he resigned he had to cut himself off from all contact with her for fear of being dissuaded.

The Mujahidin were always notable for the substantial role which women played in the organization. Under Maryam's rule, however, there was a steady feminization of its concerns and its leadership. The language of her campaigns against male sexuality was worthy of the radical feminist movement of the last quarter of the twentieth century. Soon women were declared to have greater revolutionary potential than men, and therefore to be ideologically superior. All men were given female supervisors. The Leadership Council came to consist entirely of women. The presidential role of Maryam put the final piece in place. All came to learn that 'we must forget our feet and walk with Maryam's feet. Then instead of walking we can fly'. There are elements of Masoud's description of the workings of the Mujahidin which recall, in part at least, those of some Sufi orders. The Mujahidin were required to extinguish their 'sense of self and replace it with love for "God" through the leadership. One was to receive all confidence and esteem from the leader, depend on only him, love only him'. In this case the 'Sufi' master became increasingly a mistress—Maryam.

There are two final observations to be made about this remarkable book. First, it should be read as a warning to all those who, driven by ideals, ignore the claims of humanity. Masoud cleverly indicates to us how small acts of humanity on the part of others help him recover from his obsession with Mujahidin ideology. He also admits that he has had to go through his extraordinary experiences to learn again the lesson he was taught at his grandmother's knee: 'that life is a rainbow, and black and white is another world where people only deal in the extremes ... it is a world to be repudiated and despised'. Second, the book may be read as a confession of enduring love. In the way that Irfan Orga's *Portrait of a Turkish Family* can be read, against the backdrop of the Turkish revolution, as an elegy for a lost mother, so Masoud's *Masoud* reads as a long letter of love, and of explanation, to the wife he has for ever lost.

Islamic Contestations[*]

Barbara Metcalf's work as an historian has brought major new understandings not just to the history of India since 1800 but also to that of the Muslim world in general. Her main achievement has been to chart the development of a 'protestant Islam' in South Asia and to explore its manifestations with sympathy and sensitivity. It is possible to discern three stages in the development of this work. The first led to the publication of her *Islamic Revival in British India: Deoband 1860–1900* (Princeton, 1982), in which she sets out the great creativity of Muslim responses to the challenge of fashioning a Muslim society in India under British rule. Here, she gave particular prominence to the 'ulama of the Deoband school who, by making Islamic knowledge as accessible as possible and by moulding Muslims whose consciences would impel them to make that knowledge work in society, created a 'protestant' temper amongst their followers, Muslims who knew that they must act on earth to achieve salvation. As Barbara Metcalf would be the first to point out, this development of a socially active religious piety was not restricted just to Muslim reformers, but was also manifest amongst contemporary Hindus, Buddhists, and Sikhs.

The second stage lay in her editing and partial translation of Mawlana Ashraf 'Ali Thanawi's *Bihishti Zewar* (Jewels of Paradise) under the title: *Perfecting Women: Maulana Ashraf 'Ali Thanawi's Bihishti Zewar* (Berkeley, 1990). Published at the beginning of the twentieth century this was the archetypal text in the Deobandi reforming tradition. Designed as a *vade mecum* for women, it has been one of the most widely published books in the subcontinent, and often given to a bride at her wedding. Essentially it is a guide as to how to live the life of a 'protestant' Muslim, what one should know,

* Barbara D. Metcalf, *Islamic Contestations: Essays on Muslims in India and Pakistan*, Oxford University Press, Delhi, 2004, extent 365pp.

what one should do, and how one must examine oneself daily to see how far one has kept up to the mark. Fearful descriptions of the Day of Judgement are included to remind one of the dangers of falling below the mark. As a guide to 'protestant' behaviour, its admonitions applied to men no less than women.

The third stage has been her work on the Tablighi Jama'at or 'Preaching Society', begun in the 1990s and yet, so I believe, to be fully published. The Tabligh, which was founded in the 1920s by Mawlana Muhammad Ilyas, an 'alim from the heart of the Deobandi reforming tradition, has become, according to some, the most widely followed Muslim movement in the world today. It takes literally the 'protestant' ethic of 'knowing, meaning, doing'. Followers devote a part of their time each year to going out into the community in small groups and setting an example of right conduct for their fellow Muslims by what they preach and how they behave. The Tabligh has no political interest whatsoever, but that does not prevent it from having an impact on politics.

Through her work on these manifestations of 'protestant' Islam, Barbara Metcalf has done as much as any scholar to explain the activism which animates the Muslim world today. This is as true for the connections, which she had demonstrated lie between the Deobandi presence in Afghanistan and Pakistan's Frontier Province and the rise of the Taliban, as it is for the sense of individual responsibility for putting God's word into action on earch which is felt by reformers and Islamists from Cairo to Jakarta.

Barbara Metcalf's achievement, however is much broader than this; she has been an intellectual leader in her field. First, as a member of the Joint Committee on South Asia between the Social Science Research Council and the American Council of Learned Societies, she became responsible for a project on *adab* in Muslim South Asia, which reflected her strong interest in the process of person formation in Muslim societies developed through her work on Deoband. And then, as the founding chair of a second joint committee devoted to the comparative study of Muslim societies, she was responsible for a series of projects designed to study the networks, shared historical discourses, and shared historical experiences of Muslim societies throughout the world. This resulted in a series of important publications: W.R. Roff (ed.), *Islam and the Political Economy of Meaning* (Berkeley, 1987); D.F. Eickelmann and J. Piscatori (eds), *Muslim Travellers: Pilgrimage,*

Imagination and Religious Imagination (Berkeley, 1990); B.D. Metcalf, *Making Muslim Space in North America and Europe* (Berkeley, 1996); M.K. Masud, B. Messick, and D.S. Powers (eds), *Islamic Legal Interpretations: Muftis and their Fatwas* (Cambridge Massachusetts, 1996); and M.K. Masud (ed.), *Travellers in Faith: Studies of the Tablighi Jama'at as a* Transnational *Islamic Movement for Faith Renewal* (Leiden, 2000). Through this work, as well as through her editorship of the California University Press series 'Comparative Studies on Muslim Societies', she has played a key role in de-orientalizing the study of the Islamic world and in encouraging scholars to consider a new concept—the study of Muslim societies.

It was a tribute to her intellectual leadership that in 1995, and at a relatively young age, Barbara Metcalf was made president of the American Association of Asian Studies. In her presidential address, which has to be set in the context of the destruction of Babur's mosque in 1992 and the damage caused by the politicization of history in South Asia and elsewhere, she sets out her vision of the new approaches to history that are required:

> In the nineteenth century it was useful for colonialists, and later, nationalists, with their own emphases to write a history of difference, a pragmatic benefit which continues for religious nationalists today. On the verge of the twenty-first century, in a world of increasing interdependence, others of us need a history of connection amongst disparate settings, of mobility across space, of analogous institutions that are not 'Western' or 'Eastern', of engagement with other geographic areas in our disciplines that belies Orientalist specificity.

Barbara Metcalf's *Islamic Contestations* draws together a series of essays she has written and lectures she has given, while pursuing the path set out above. All have been published before but, as is the case with scholarly publication, they have been scattered across many publications, not all of them easy to obtain. They reflect the development of her scholarly interests over thirty years as well as her continuing concern to challenge preconceptions and to show respect for the lives and the values of others. She uses the word 'contestation' in the title:

> to point to the extent to which Muslims, like their Hindu counterparts, have been engaged in recent times in renewing and rethinking the historical traditions of their faiths. 'Contestation' points both to actual debates amongst Muslims and to the multiple dialogues with Islamic texts and symbols undertaken by individuals and groups.

Barbara Metcalf begins her collection, as all historians should, with an autobiographical introduction which provides an excellent context for her intellectual development. She acknowledges, as all scholars must, the teachers who particularly influenced her: Jean Kopytoff, who taught an honours seminar at Swarthmore on the British Empire; Philip Curtin, who encouraged her to find other dynamics than Western influence in the non-Western world; Ralph Russell, who impressed on her the importance of speaking as well as reading Urdu; Hamid Algar, the remarkable Naqshbandi Sufi of Berkeley, who guided her in understanding the writings of Muslim scholars; and Ira Lapidus, also of Berkeley, who has embodied throughout his own work the importance of studying not Islamic but Muslim societies.

To the question, why did she opt to do her first research on Deoband, Barbara Metcalf says she does not really know. Nevertheless, she admits to being struck by her sense of discomfort with the description of Deoband—which had been founded only in 1867 and clearly broke with traditional patterns of education—as 'traditional'. Moreover, she saw in it the possibility of developing a critique of modernization theory, the idea 'that all peoples everywhere were moving towards a form of society, politics, and culture whose script had already been written in the West, and that "progress" was stimulated only by contact with the West on the part of societies that had, heretofore, been largely stagnant and unchanging'.

Barbara Metcalf, like the author of this review, has certainly had her share of criticism for her subject of study. In India there has been criticism for the focus on 'non-progressive' elements—'not very helpful in current political contexts'. Amongst some in the West there has been incredulity that one should study a subject so apparently obscure. The Iranian revolution began to shut the mouths of these critics. The Islamic activism of recent years has shut them altogether, as it has become clear that scholars such as Barbara Metcalf have knowledge that is central to understanding key issues of our time. It demonstrates the enormous importance of each new generation of scholars being permitted to pursue those subjects they feel are important, regardless of the prejudices and preconceptions of their elders, and providing that they can provide satisfactory intellectual justification for their choices.

Barbara Metcalf divides her collection into four sections. The first entitled 'New Roles, New Contestations for the 'Ulama' offers three articles about the Deobandi ‘ulama. One demonstrates how these ‘ulama in the nineteenth century created popularly supported seminaries based on British institutional models, and in doing so fashioned something entirely new in the colonial period—‘the existence of the ‘ulama as a distinct social group with characteristic training and roles’. Another examines some of these ‘ulama at work as muftis, demonstrating how, through their fatawa; they were concerned with individual ritual practice and behaviour in everyday life; they did not follow blindly the practice of the past but argued their cases afresh from scripture; and they worked hard to differentiate their positions from those of rival reforming groups such as the Ahl-i Hadith. The third piece analyses the way in which Mawlana Muhammad Zakariyya Kandhlawi, who wrote many of the key texts used by the Tablighi Jama‘at, presented himself in his five-volume autobiography. This article is a marvellous evocation of the nature and the quality of the life lived by a leading reforming scholar in the twentieth century. Zakariyya, as Barbara Metcalf tells us, ‘richly conveys the moral principles, the cherished stories of the elders taken as templates for himself and now offered to others, and many of the specific experiences of his long years as a teacher in a major Deobandi madrasa at Saharanpur’.

A second section contains four essays grouped under the heading, ‘The Variety of “Islamic” Cultural and Political Life to 1947’. One takes up the topic of women, illustrating three different strands of Muslim thought relating to them, emanating from the ‘ulama, from the westernizing Muslims of Aligarh, and from the emerging Islamist ideas of Mawlana Mawdudi. In this, as in many other essays, Barbara Metcalf illustrates the importance of the vernacular print-media for entering the main arenas of expression and debate in Muslim South Asia. A second essay is devoted to the Tablighi Jama‘at in the 1920s and 1930s with the aim of demonstrating the emergence of ‘lay’ leadership in the period, a feature common to all Indian religions. The argument is that the conditions which led to the emergence of the Tabligh and similar religious organizations were similar to those which led to the emergence of nationalism. Barbara Metcalf raises the question of whether ‘religion’ or ‘communalism’ are actually the opposites of modernity and nationalism. Yet another of her nails hammered into the coffin of modernization theory! And then there are two articles on the great Delhi leader, Hakim Ajmal Khan, for whom Barbara Metcalf has the greatest respect. One sets him in the context of the nationalist Muslims but is concerned that it is understood that his interests were much greater than purely those of politics: he was much engaged in his family's hereditary profession of Unani Tibb, but in his case to think and rethink its traditions; he had deep personal bonds with both Muslims and non-Muslims; he lived a rich spiritual life; and was recognized on all sides as a natural leader of the citizens of Delhi. A second piece emphasizes the Hakim's everwidening circles beyond Delhi and asks why in all religious communities indigenous traditions in medicine, art, and music have flourished in India, but not in many other areas of European empire.

A third set of essays addresses 'Islam and Politics since 1947'. This includes Barbara Metcalf's presidential address to the American Association of Asian Studies, which all historians of South Asia should read. Two essays deal with Islamic ideologies and arguments in Pakistan. One of these traces Pakistan's transition from a secular state built on British constitutional models to one which by the mid-1970s was developing a distinctive Islamic ideology. The second examines the Islamizing political ideology of General Zia ul-Haq and his supporters in the Jama'ati Islami, paying particular attention to the regulations he made regarding women and the responses they evoked. The essay illustrates how an Islamic language became dominant in the life of Pakistan. In the last essay in this section Barbara Metcalf draws connections between the rise of the Taliban and the Deobandi presence in Afghanistan and Pakistan. Quite rightly she indicates that this development cannot be seen apart from the Soviet invasion of Afghanistan and the Sa'udi/Gulf money and government encouragement which led to the massive growth of madrasas in Pakistan. But, in the context of the events of 11 September 2001, she is also concerned to argue that, while there is real anger at US policy and action in the world, the 'protestant' organizations of Islam, Deoband, and the Tabligh, are much more concerned with their social, moral, and spiritual agendas. What she does not explain, and what many wish to know, is how in Taliban hands the Deobandi ethic came to be so extreme, so harsh.

The last set of essays goes under the title, 'Islam, Society and the Imagination of the Self'. Here Barbara Metcalf discusses the works of Muslims who have written about their own life experiences. In an excellent essay she reflects on the meaning of Iqbal's great poem on the mosque at Cordoba. She notes the strong tendency amongst nineteenth- and twentieth-century Muslims to identify with symbols of lost worldly glory. She notes, too, how Muslim attachment to symbols outside the subcontinent has led to accusations of disloyalty. But the central theme is Iqbal's emphasis on the role of the individual creative self which once awakened will recover 'a past glory of superiority over Europeans in morality as well as in the arts and sciences of civilization'. From this essay we can draw the connection which runs through many aspects of the Islamic revival from the activist Muslim self of the 'protestant' trend to the creative passionate self of Iqbal's modernism. It was Iqbal, after all, who made the all-important transition, which was to be followed by many major Muslim thinkers of the twentieth century, of replacing the idea of the Islamic caliphate with that of the caliphate of man, that is, of each individual Muslim, an idea whose full potential has by no means been realized.

Two final essays of note draw on Barbara Metcalf's study of accounts of pilgrimages to Mecca. In one she notes the changing nature of these records and how they can be used as windows onto major changes taking place in Muslim societies. They should 'be read as part of an enduring yet shifting constellation of three poles: changes in society generally, changes in concepts of individuality, and changes in the interpretation of central religious symbols of which two—the hajj and the Prophet—are relevant here'. The second hajj piece focuses on just one pilgrimage narrative, that of the well-known writer, Mumtaz Mufti. Written by Barbara Metcalf as a contribution to the debate over Rushdie's *The Satanic Verses*, she demonstrates how Muslims themselves 'have a rich tradition of writing ironically, even phantasmagorically, about Islamic symbols'. This said, she does admit that Mufti's irony, which has the Black Stone speaking to him with the face of a Hindu/Punjabi idol and Allah leaving the Meccan sanctuary in a party of African pilgrims, was not acceptable to all in Pakistan.

Few have done as much as Barbara Metcalf to make the many different voices of Muslim South Asia heard. In doing so, most importantly, she listens to all these voices with respect, and encourages us to do so too. These are essays which all who are interested in the history of India should read, not just for their content but also for their approach. They are particularly to be recommended to young historians setting out on a course of research. It is an irony that the USA, which over the years has fostered the scholarship of Barbara

Metcalf, and many like her, seems unable to draw on her knowledge and understanding of the Muslim world. If only it could adopt more of her courtesy and respect for other ways of being human, the world might just be a better place.

Index